CALCUTTA
The Living City

CALCUTTA
OXFORD UNIVERSITY PRESS
DELHI BOMBAY MADRAS

CALCUTTA

The Living City

Volume I: The Past

Edited by

Sukanta Chaudhuri

Oxford University Press, Walton Street, Oxford OX2 6DP
OXFORD NEW YORK
ATHENS AUCKLAND BANGKOK BOMBAY
CALCUTTA CAPE TOWN DAR ES SALAAM DELHI
FLORENCE HONG KONG ISTANBUL KARACHI
KUALA LUMPUR MADRAS MADRID MELBOURNE
MEXICO CITY NAIROBI PARIS SINGAPORE
TAIPEI TOKYO TORONTO
and associated companies in
BERLIN IBADAN

Oxford is a trade mark of Oxford University Press

© Oxford University Press 1990

First published 1990
First paperback edition 1995

Design: Jayanta Ghosh

Picture Research: Arup Sengupta
                           Tapati Guha Thakurta

Printed in India
at Graphitech India Limited, Bidhannagar, Calcutta 700 091
and published by Neil O'Brien, Oxford University Press
5 Lala Lajpat Rai Sarani, Calcutta 700 020

CONTENTS

THE CONTRIBUTORS

POROMESH ACHARYA
carries out research on education at the Indian Institute of Management, Calcutta. He is a well-known authority on the history of education in Bengal

AMIYA KUMAR BAGCHI
is Director of the Centre for Studies in Social Sciences, Calcutta

SUMANTA BANERJI
is a journalist living in Delhi.

SABYASACHI BHATTACHARYA
is Professor of History and Dean of the School of Social Sciences, Jawaharlal Nehru University, New Delhi

PRABODH BISWAS
is a Librarian at Presidency College, Calcutta

HIREN CHAKRABARTI
is Curator of the Victoria Memorial, Calcutta. He has previously been Professor of History at Presidency College, Calcutta and Director of the West Bengal State Archives

JAYA CHALIHA
is a well-known free-lance writer on the life and antiquities of Calcutta

JOYOTI CHALIHA
works in a Calcutta advertising firm and is also a free-lance writer

MONIDIP CHATTERJEE
is Professor of Architecture at Jadavpur University, Calcutta

SUKANTA CHAUDHURI
is Professor of English at Presidency College, Calcutta

PRITHA CHOWDHURY
is a teacher in a Calcutta school and a free-lance writer

RABINDRA KUMAR DASGUPTA
retired as Director of the National Library, Calcutta. He has also been Tagore Professor of Bengali at Delhi University

SIVAPRASAD DASGUPTA
has been Professor of Geography at Presidency College, Calcutta and Director of the National Atlas Organization of India. He is now attached to the Centre for Man and Environment, Presidency College, Calcutta

KALYANI DATTA
retired as Senior Lecturer in Sanskrit from Basanti Debi College, Calcutta

CHITRA DEB
is a writer on social and historical subjects. She is attached to the Ananda Bazar Patrika newspaper group, Calcutta

PARTHA GHOSE
is Academic Programme Co-ordinator at the Satyendranath Bose National Centre for Basic Sciences, Bidhan Nagar, Calcutta

SIDDHARTHA GHOSH
is an engineer at the Glass and Ceramic Research Institute, Calcutta, and a pioneer in the study of industrial archaeology in the city

TAPATI GUHA THAKURTA
is a Fellow at the Centre for Studies in Social Sciences, Calcutta

BUNNY GUPTA
is a well-known free-lance writer on the life and antiquities of Calcutta

RADHA PRASAD GUPTA
retired after a career in Calcutta's commercial world. He is one of the leading experts on the art, life and culture of old Calcutta

SIDNEY KITSON
is a member of the Indian Police
Service, currently posted as
Director-General of the
West Bengal Home Guards

**DHRITI KANTA LAHIRI
CHOUDHURI**
is Professor and Head of the
Department of English, Rabindra
Bharati University, Calcutta. He
is also an enthusiast in architecture
and an international authority on
wildlife, especially the Indian
elephant

SWAPAN MAJUMDAR
is Reader in Comparative
Literature at Jadavpur University,
Calcutta. He is currently serving
as Director of the Indian Cultural
Centre, Suva, Fiji

RAJYESWAR MITRA
is one of Calcutta's foremost
musicologists as well as a classical
singer

RUDRANGSHU MUKHERJI
is Reader in History at Calcutta
University

KIRANMAY RAHA
is a retired civil servant and a
writer of long standing on the
theatre and cinema

SUBIR RAY CHAUDHURI
is Reader in Comparative
Literature at Jadavpur University,
Calcutta

NIKHIL SARKAR
is Assistant Editor of the Ananda
Bazar Patrika, Calcutta, and a
well-known authority on Bengali
printing and bibliography

SUMIT SARKAR
is Professor of History at Delhi
University

PRADIP SINHA
is Professor of History at
Rabindra Bharati University,
Calcutta

P. THANKAPPAN NAIR
came to work in Calcutta from his
native Kerala many years ago. He
is now a full-time urban historian
and a Fellow of the Asiatic Society
of Bengal

NOTES AND CONVENTIONS

Ascriptions :

All unsigned matter is editorial. This includes the unascribed short features and boxed items accompanying larger articles, whose authors are not responsible for these adjuncts.

The signed articles all conform to a common spirit of civic pride and involvement; but their particular views may be the authors' alone.

The Spelling of Bengali Names:

This book introduces a new system for uniform transliteration of Bengali names (except those of contributors, where personal preferences have been retained). This necessarily means departing from customary spellings and individual practices, but the gain in uniformity and authenticity may be thought to compensate.

Simplicity has been a major consideration. We have avoided diacritical marks, and retained some customary English shortenings: Mukherji or Ganguli, for instance, rather than Mukhopadhyay or Gangopadhyay. But in most cases, Bengali forms have been adopted (Thakur not Tagore, Basu not Bose), in Bengali rather than Sanskrit pronunciation. Sanskrit forms have, however, been retained in titles which are Sanskritic in origin and context (Vidyasagar, Vachaspati); where, moreover, the Sanskritic form might be so common that departure would cause confusion (Vivekananda, Vidyasagar). As a rule, Sanskrit compound letters have also been represented by their modified Bengali pronunciation; but the *ksh* compound has been retained in full in words like *Lakshmi,* which have an all-India circulation.

All-India currency has also suggested the use of *-bazar* rather than *-bajar* as a place-name ending. Old British forms of a few names have been retained in the case of institutions of that period or ambience (Cossipore Club, Tollygunge Club).

Indian celebrities have usually been referred to by their first names as in common Indian practice. They have, however, been indexed under their surnames.

Following Indian practice, adjuncts to first names such as 'kumar', 'chandra' or 'nath' have been affixed to the first names.

As regards Bengali letters, অ and আ have both perforce been rendered by *a;* ঔ by *ou. Sh* has been used for শ and ষ and *s* for স. The final *-a* often used in English transliteration of Indian names (*Rama, Ashoka*) has been omitted, as it is never sounded in Bengali.

Because of the system adopted, the names of some well-known organizations may be found to differ somewhat from the current forms (*Ramkrishna* not *Ramakrishna* Mission, *Bahurupee* not *Bohurupee*).

As this account indicates, the system is not without inconsistencies. Total consistency seems impossible without the use of special notation; even then, the result might seem unacceptable in terms of impression or impact. We have aimed rather at a reasonable and practicable compromise.

Citation of Dates:

Dates of birth and, where applicable, death have been cited wherever possible – often by editorial insertion – after the names of famous persons, to enhance the book's value as a work of reference. Such dates are often hard to find, especially in English-language publications. Though checked with every possible care, they may be inaccurate in a few cases, as nearly all of them have necessarily been taken from secondary sources. We hope this will not impair their general usefulness.

Figures, especially in statistics, have often been cited by the lakh (hundred thousand) rather than the million: thus 1,00,000 not 100,000; 10,00,000 not 1,000,000.

PREFACE TO THE 1995 EDITION

Calcutta turned three hundred in the year 1990. The occasion seemed to call for a book that would adequately bring out the complex, compelling quality of the city. Calcutta has engaged observers of urban growth and of general humanity to an unusual degree. The attention is not justified by the city's current political or economic role, nor by its vaunted cultural life, substantial though all these are. Nor can it be due only to the deprivation and misery identified with the city : the world has far worse to show.

The crucial word is 'identified'. There is a representative, symbolic dimension to Calcutta that grips the imagination, makes the city an epitome of the post-colonial urban myth. Going a little further, it gives the myth a rare imaginative currency. Calcutta has too much significance to warrant dismissal, yet so much (or more) to retard easy acceptance. Perhaps it is this paradox, sharpened to acuteness, that provides the compelling force.

To bring out the elements of this unique compound, over eighty committed citizens and expatriates contributed their expertise to this book. The product, one hopes has captured something of Calcutta's lasting, underlying being.

Externally Calcutta has not changed much since then. There is a great new bridge on the skyline, a few other public works of note. The urban sprawl has spread and thickened, to the east and south-west in particular. Satyajit Ray is dead; side by side with iconic veneration, there is a new popular music and new currents in the other arts.

But there are other changes too. The greatest, of symbolic as well as material import, is the virtual disappearance of power cuts. This was the first sign of a distinct change of spirit, otherwise unremarkable even six months ago. The city and state are now wooing prosperity with the same zeal with which they had once spurned it. Political equations are being reworked. Maybe Calcutta will redefine its relation to the rest of India.

These are very recent, very uncertain factors. Formal changes of ideology can be gauged; not so readily the transformation of a community, still less the first glimmerings of transformation. Perhaps the citizenry will grow harder, more competitive, more prone to see visions than to dream dreams. This might cancel or merely modify the more feckless, importunate spirit of the tribe. We cannot tell. Even as Calcutta alters she remains individual, enigmatic.

The changes are so telling yet so uncrystallized that *Calcutta : The Living City* could not be revised. That would be to set about a new book; but the moment for such an effort has not yet arrived.

We have left the collection as it is, testament to three hundred years of living urban growth. It is the same city, though it grows and changes as living things will. Even in change there is continuity. Will the reader of 2090 — if there be any — recognize in these papges the contours of his own city? Will he recognize them all too closely, as nothing will have changed in a hundred years? That seems increasingly unlikely. We might rather fear total difference, total estrangement. This book, put together by people from Calcutta, should at least ensure that whenever the city views herself in the mirror, whatever her state at the time, she will see fired in the glass the face she wore after three centuries of life.

INTRODUCTION

This volume of *Calcutta: The Living City* deals with the past: firstly because old Calcutta was intensely alive, but also because the 'living city' of today owes much of its life to earlier times. Calcutta's past has been studied extensively in the last few decades: largely by local scholars and enthusiasts, but also internationally as part of the Raj Revival. Without disparaging these valuable studies for a moment, one can fairly say that they are often impelled by a search for the nostalgic and the exotic. It is time the fruits of this research were applied to a fuller understanding of the city as it was, is and will be. We hope that this collection will help such an understanding – particularly in conjunction with Volume II, but indeed even by itself.

Certain conclusions suggest themselves at once. The occasion of this book, as of innumerable other publications and celebrations, is the city's tercentenary; but we may ask whether Calcutta really 'began' three hundred years ago. Certainly the British settlement which became the official nucleus of today's Calcutta was set up in 1690, after abortive starts made earlier. But the region had seen flourishing settlements from some time before: Sutanuti and Gobindapur, Kalighat where the pilgrims came, the textile centres of Chitpur and Baranagar. There is more to the issue than mere quibbling over dates: it concerns the question of Calcutta's social origins and composition. The formal, and dominant, note of the city's history was undoubtedly colonial; but as these earlier settlements remind us, colonial forces operated here in a terrain rich in competing systems and traditions. These were sometimes supplanted, sometimes transformed by fusion with the colonial experience; at times the latter acted only as a catalyst; at times it left the 'native' discourse untouched and even unsuspected.

This leads to other conclusions. There is a strong element of compradorship and subservience in the new city culture that evolved in old Calcutta, an unusually active local participation in the colonial process. There is also a deeper absorption of new concepts and values inculcated by that process, leading to a phase of intense intellectual activity and social awareness – including some radical reforms – often called the Bengal Renaissance. As our article on the subject explains, the validity of the term has been questioned, as also, more deeply, the achievement of the age. But however we designate it, it was by any reckoning a period of exhilarating thought and change, a notable chapter in the world's cultural history, as the entire range of relevant articles will demonstrate.

This is not merely a matter of patriotic pride but of historic significance. Britain as well as other colonial powers set up a number of major ports and urban centres in south–east Asia. Some of these are now far ahead of Calcutta in civic and economic growth, while others have declined. But perhaps excepting two other Indian centres, Bombay and Madras, there is no city where the colonial impact has given birth to a new society and culture so complex, so creative, so stably indigenized. Ultimately, that culture passed beyond colonial confines to acquire an independent life that the colonial ethos would emphatically disown. The extent of this achievement, and its intrinsic value in absolute terms, has perhaps not been generally recognized.

The strivings of the 'Bengal Renaissance' passed imperceptibly into the first stirrings of nationalist thought. This suggests another aspect of Calcutta as a colonial city and indeed the colonial capital: as a place of encounter between the British and the Indians on the material plane. The articles on the city's early economy bring out the exploitation and deliberate suppression of Indian enterprise, diverting the energies of the local youth to a mean search for employment. This could not, of course, have occurred without the self-seeking acquiescence of the local community: for as these articles also describe, other traditional forms of Indian entrepreneurship adapted creatively to the colonial order and lived to trounce it. Hence taken all in all, Calcutta saw a marked separation between ideas and resource, between an enlightened civic spirit and the means to realize its goals. Only in recent decades has the trend been countered to some extent.

If local capital was not sunk into Calcutta's development, still less was the British; and as our contributors point out, such funds as were gathered were unblushingly concentrated on the 'White Town'. Not only were civic amenities wretched in the Indian quarters; there was no planned infrastructure, and the 'Black Town' grew in such a way as to frustrate future planning. An unkempt, neglected, even insanitary air was always part of the milieu of 'native' Calcutta. All that was valuable in its life and culture grew in tandem with this working anarchy, and in various causal relations with it.

This lays bare the riddle of the city's life: from the outset, Calcutta has defined its special strengths and excellences against a background of disorder, deprivation and cynicism exceeding that of most other cities and questioning the very rationale of urban culture. This was partly concealed up to the mid-twentieth century by the attention lavished on the White Town, and on an admittedly laudable rigour in maintaining basic civic functions even outside it. Again, Calcutta has long been the city of opportunity to the whole population of eastern India, and their inflow has frustrated all exercises in planning. The city's economic attractions have operated in good part at the unorganized subsistence level; hence its very growth has paradoxically fostered a decline of the civic infrastructure.

Hence too, finally, the remarkable curve in Calcutta's history. The city grew in collaboration with colonial rule or, more broadly and humbly, by a necessary reliance on the colonial system. But this symbiosis bred resentment and disillusion, creating a classic tradition of protest politics and economic discontent, even while the collaborative role persisted. And in all these developments, Calcutta only focussed, sharply and disturbingly, the basic spirit of colonial and post-colonial India. Calcutta and Bengal are now often placed in counterpoise to the rest of India; but the nation still finds itself ensnared by this reviled and fascinating city, which has taken upon itself so much of the burden of India's bitter inheritance.

The history of 'Calcutta culture' is valuable in itself; much more so as illustrating the process of colonial urbanization to a unique degree with unique consequences. The present volume traces the earlier stages of the movement. The full process, in both civic and cultural terms, will emerge in detail from the next volume.

ACKNOWLEDGEMENTS

A book like this incurs innumerable debts in its making. Only the chief ones can be acknowledged here. I must ask forgiveness of all those who have offered help, advice or information, but whom it is not possible to mention here by name.

Thanks, first of all, to our contributors who gave so unstintingly of their time and expertise, as of their patience with the importunities of an editor who knew so much less than they did. Many of them also offered help and guidance far beyond the confines of their own articles. This has made the book a truly collective effort.

For some of the short entries and boxed items in this volume, I am indebted to Professor Monidip Chatterji, Mr Siddhartha Ghosh and Ms Maitrayee Sinha. Ms Abhaya Dasgupta, Mr Sujoy Gupta, Mr Amlan Dasgupta and Dr Prabodh Biswas have provided unfailing support in my seemingly endless task. Mr Chittaranjan Banerji gave valuable guidance in the early stages.

Of the many Calcutta libraries used in the course of editorial work, my greatest debt is to the National Library, the Presidency College library, and the library of the Ramkrishna Mission Institute of Culture.

Professor D.K. Lahiri Choudhuri and Mr D. M. Alney gave generous help with the illustrations. The institutions which supplied illustrations, often under special arrangements for which we are most grateful, include the Asiatic Society of Bengal, the Victoria Memorial, and the National Library in Calcutta, and the India Office Library and the Victoria and Albert Museum in London. Mr Ramkrishna Datta gave valuable assistance with the maps and diagrams and Ms Supriya Guha with the desk-editing and proof-reading.

It is no doubt superfluous to thank the staff of the Oxford University Press.

CALCUTTA: THE NAME

Calcutta (Bengali *Kalikata* and colloquially *Kolkata*) hides mysteries even in its name. It may have been desperation as much as folk humour that invented fanciful derivations like *kal kata* (cut yesterday) – a grass-cutter's supposed reply to a misunderstood question from an Englishman. More designedly fanciful is the adaptation of *Golgotha*, the Biblical 'land of skulls', from the high mortality rate among the colonists.

The name may derive from *Kilkila* – an ancient province 21 *yojans* (160 square miles) in extent, 'with the Saraswati on the West and the Jamuna on the East, and containing the towns and villages of Hooghly, Basberia, Bhatpara, Khardaha, Sialdaha, Govindapur, etc.' (A.K. Ray, *A Short History of Calcutta*). In the *Ain-i-Akbari* (*c*.1590), the form *Kalkata* itself occurs as one variant of a place-name on Raja Todar Mal's rent-roll; but there are other variants, and in any case the name refers to a *mahal* (region or district), not a village or town. Going back to remote antiquity, the name has been derived from *Kol-ka-hata* – the territory or settlement of the Kols, certain pre-Dravidian tribes. But there is no record of the Kols ever having inhabited lower Bengal, and the very name *Kol* seems to be of late origin.

A favoured explanation at one time was that the place had been marked by a *kata*, warehouse and kiln, for *kali* or unslaked lime made by burning crustacean shells. But others have doubted the extent, antiquity or indeed existence of such a trade here, and the explanation is now seldom advanced.

It has also been suggested that. in order to compete with the cloth exported by the Portuguese from Calicut (hence *calico*), the English stamped 'Kalikat' on their own exports from Bengal, giving rise to the name.

Khal, in Bengali as in other North Indian languages, is a canal or ditch; *kata* means cut or excavated. This etymology has sometimes been advanced with respect to the Maratha Ditch; but that was dug long after the city's foundation. More convincingly, the *khal* has been taken as the Beliaghata canal or creek, which once ran west from the Salt Lakes through present-day Creek Row and Lenin Sarani (Dharmatala). It has even been suggested that *Khal-kata* is the source of the English form *Calcutta*, while the Bengali *Kalikata* has a different origin.

The latter. is most commonly derived from the name of the goddess Kali of Kalighat. It would be simplistic to derive it directly from *Kalighat,* as the two names occur side by side in early texts. But many variants have been suggested, such as *Kali-kota* (the home or abode of Kali); *Kalighatta,* a North Indian distortion of *Kalighat;* and the most Sanskritic, *Kalikshetra,* the field or terrain of Kali.

Goddess Kali of Kalighat

Ironically, Kalikata or Calcutta was much less important than Sutanuti or Gobindapur, the two other villages which formed the nucleus of today's city. Its very unimportance, and consequent emptiness, afforded the British room to settle there. The subsequent rise of this obscure village is the subject of this book.

1.1
Kali of Kalighat

THE SITE OF CALCUTTA GEOLOGY AND PHYSIOGRAPHY

Siva Prasad Das Gupta

The physiographic setting of Calcutta (22° 34' N, 88° 22' E), both at the time of its foundation in 1690 and in the present day, is dominated by the meandering river Hugli (Ganga). Hugging the east or left bank of the river there stretches a narrow belt of comparatively high natural embankment (known as a *levée),* some 2 to 5 kilometres wide. This gradually slopes down to flat low-lying alluvial plains on the east.

The Hugli now forms the westernmost limit of the Gangetic delta – the largest delta in the world, built up by the slow deposition of river silts into the sea. Hence Calcutta is a typical riverine city surrounded by marshes, tidal creeks, mangrove swamps and wetlands. At the head of the delta near Farakka, the Ganga bifurcates into two major distributaries, the Padma and the Bhagirathi-Ganga. It is the lower (tidal) reaches of the Bhagirathi-Ganga which are known in official parlance as the Hugli. This is the very lifeline of the city, with a large conurbation (more than a hundred urban centres) stretching about 70 kilometres on either side of the river.

The Bhagirathi-Ganga course used to carry the main flow of the Ganga till the end of the sixteenth century, when the main stream was suddenly diverted along the course of the Padma. That is why the river at Calcutta, particularly upstream of Khidirpur, is regarded as the original Ganga in common parlance even though on maps and documents it is invariably labelled the Hugli (earlier spelt Hooghly) after the town of the same name, a major trading centre before Calcutta came into existence. From Khidirpur, the former course of the Ganga turned south-eastwards along the now feeble channel known as the *Adi* (original) Ganga or Tolly's Nulla. The present channel of the Hugli below Khidirpur represents the lower section of an older distributary, the Saraswati, which used to take off from the Hugli near Tribeni (50 kilometres north of Calcutta) and run almost parallel to the Hugli on its west.

Surface Configuration

In August 1690, when Job Charnock was looking for a good landing-place on the Hugli to set up an outpost of the East India Company, the present site of Calcutta was possibly the best available. It provided not only the space for strong fortifications and a growing trade centre, but also – being 130 kilometres from the sea – a safe and commodious harbour for the large sea-going vessels of those days. Though Charnock was severely criticized by many of his countrymen for having chosen an extremely unhealthy site, close to the steamy marshes of the Salt Water Lakes, the location was actually ideal from the navigational point of view, as also for defence, being protected by the mighty Hugli river on one side and a vast expanse of salt marshes and wetlands on the other.

Later, when steam replaced sail, the draught of the river (especially during high tides) was sufficient even for the largest steamers, given a little bit of piloting. Towards the interior too, Calcutta was connected by numerous rivers, navigable canals and trunk roads with the rich hinterland of all upper India.

The long though rather narrow *levée* along the left bank was fairly firm, high (above normal flood levels) and wide enough to lay out a good strand road and other roads parallel to it. The three original villages of Sutanuti, Gobindapur and Kalikata afforded not only the high land needed for Fort William and its five-square-kilometre parade ground (the Maidan), but also enough space for the massive business houses, residential quarters, villas (sometimes truly palatial) and other establishments needed for the administrative and commercial activities of the East India Company and the growing British Raj. The city proper (i.e. the core area under the Calcutta Municipal Corporation) covers no less than a hundred square kilometres, with a population of 3.3 million (1981). With the addition of three erstwhile municipal areas in 1984, the total area of the Corporation is now 187.33 square kilometres.

Needless to say, the landscape of 1690 has changed radically over three hundred years of growth. The natural vegetation of lush green tropical jungle has disappeared to make room for the great Maidan and the Fort. The abundant mangrove swamps have been drained off by excavating drainage channels round the city. There were numerous depressions, low-lying waterlogged areas, ponds, ditches, *nullas* and tidal creeks even within city limits in the early days. Two tidal creeks were particularly prominent: the Beliaghata Creek, now largely filled up but commemorated in the name of Creek Row; and Chitpur Creek, later deepened in part to form a segment of the so-called Maratha Ditch. Most of the depressions have been filled up by continuous dumping of all the rubbish that a growing city generates. We may not unaptly describe Calcutta as a city built on its own garbage.

Such anthropogenic changes have transformed the original topography of Calcutta beyond recognition; but the lie of the land remains more or less as before. The riverside *levée* is still the highest part of the city, sloping gradually away from the river towards the Salt Lake area, the original and natural backyard of

2.1 *Lower Bengal with the principal rivers and early and recent settlements*

the city. At Garden Reach, the *levée* is nearly 7 metres above mean sea-level. Eastward at Tiljala, this is reduced to less than 3 metres. Calcutta's entire drainage and sewerage network, as well as the disposal of its waste water, depends on this natural eastward slope of the ground. The recurrent problem of waterlogging during the rains is also largely due to the fact that the Hugli often flows at a level higher than many parts of eastern Calcutta, especially during the spring tides.

There has been much modernization and techno-scientific innovation in the past; there promises to be much more in the years to come. But it must be realized that the problems and prospects of Calcutta continue to depend chiefly on the state of the Hugli river. If it dries or gets silted up, Calcutta will be doomed, as has happened with many a river-dependent alluvial city in history. That is why the Hugli is now being revitalized by diverting more water into it by means of a barrage across the main Ganga at Farakka, above the point where it separates into the Padma and the Hugli.

Geological Foundation

Calcutta rests on a clay bed deposited by rivers forming the lower plain of the Gangetic delta. The clay overlies a thick pile of alluvial sediments deposited in the recent geological era. The upper 300 metres of this alluvial pile clearly

2.2 *View from the Eastern'Bypass today. Much of the Calcutta region must have looked like this once*

belong to the Quaternary age (commencing about 1.5 million years ago). It consists of successive layers of clay, silt, sand and sometimes coarser sediments or even pebbles. These subsurface layers have not yet been clearly divided or classified; but a tentative division can be made as follows:

System	Series	Lithology
Quaternary	Holocene (15,000 before present)	Clay, silt, sand (occurring in stream channels and shallow depressions)
	Pleistocene (1,500,000 before present)	Clay, sand, pebble, *kankar,* etc.

Data relating to these subsurface sediments is obtained by drilling boreholes from time to time. These indicate the existence of a thick clay layer at a depth varying from 254 metres in the north of the city to 414 metres at Garia in the south. South of Garia, the clay bed slowly rises. Its thickness is not definitely known, as the deepest borehole drilled so far has failed to reach its bottom.

The entire sedimentary pile is capped by an extensive clay bed, 30 to 60 metres or even more in thickness within the city proper. On the southern periphery, especially at Tollyganj, this thins off and is hardly 9 metres thick. Sometimes the clay cap is overlain by thin disjointed strips of silts and fine sands, especially in depressions and along old abandoned river beds. Elsewhere, peaty matter occurs at many places within the clay cap, at depths of 3 metres or thereabouts.

Both the bottom clay and the top clay are sticky and plastic to semiplastic in character, impervious to water and dark grey in colour. Between them lie thick layers of sand of varying grain sizes: fine, medium, coarse, or even somewhat gravelly. Small isolated patches of clay are often set among them, or sometimes a pebble zone of varying thickness (from 4 metres at Dhakuria to 25 metres at Khidirpur). Even deeper pebble zones have been found: one at Taratala in south-west Calcutta is at a depth of some 130 metres.

These subsurface sandy layers of great thickness can hold a lot of water in the pore space between the grains of sand: the quantity of water depends on the size of the grains. Being trapped between impervious clay layers at the top and bottom, the thick sand beds serve as an immense water reservoir.

Calcutta is, as it were, balanced upon a huge natural raft of clay, literally floating on an enormous reservoir of water stored within the sand grains underneath. This ground water is held under great pressure exerted by the alluvial sediments above them. The pressure falls or rises as water is pumped up in large quantities for human use, or brought back into the sandy aquifers (water-bearing layers) through underground seepage of rainwater. At the same time, the clay is being tunnelled through and through to provide for sewerage, water-supply pipes, power cables, telephone cables, gas lines and now the Metro Railway. If in one sense Calcutta's life is reliant on the river, in another it is floating on a frail clay raft on a vast underground sea.

BEFORE CALCUTTA

Monidip Chatterji

Before Calcutta, there were at least five other capitals or urban centres in Bengal at different times: Gour, Rajmahal, Dhaka, Nadia and, of course, Murshidabad, the seat of the last Nawabs of Bengal. Calcutta can thus be considered as the sixth capital of the province of Bengal.

In the sixteenth century, when Portuguese traders commenced operations in Bengal, the two great centres of maritime trade there were Chattagram or Chittagong (Porto Grande or the 'Great Harbour') and Saptagram or Satgaon (Porto Piqueno or the 'Little Harbour'), the latter now an insignificant village north-west of Chunchura. To reach Satgaon, sea-going vessels could come up the river (which then flowed through the now depleted channel of the Adi Ganga or Tolly's Nulla) as far upstream as Betore on the west bank and the site of today's Garden Reach on the east bank. From there the cargo was transferred to country boats. Betore thus became a seasonal colony of thatched huts, erected every year when the ships arrived from Goa and dismantled when the last one had returned.

In the late sixteenth century, the merchant-princes of Saptagram began to seek fresh markets as their original seat declined owing to the caprices of the river. The great majority settled at Hugli: a Portuguese settlement since the late fifteenth century, dominated from the 1630s by the Dutch, the leading European traders in Bengal at the time. However, four families of Basaks and one of Sheths came further downstream to found the village of Gobindapur on the east bank, named after the Sheths' deity Gobindaji. Northward of this, they proceeded to set up the Sutanuti Hat or cotton and yarn market. In between Sutanuti and Gobindapur was the lesser settlement of Kalikata. These three villages became the site of the original British holdings that grew into the city of Calcutta; but as C. R. Wilson points out, at least four other settlements must be considered part of the original constituents of the city: Chitpur and Kalighat east of the river, and Salkia and Betore on the west bank.

It is therefore obvious that while the British foundation of Calcutta may be traced back to Job Charnock's landing on 24 August 1690, there were flourishing settlements on the site of the city at a much earlier date. Indeed, in the early seventeenth century the English were conducting their Bengal trade from Baleshwar (Balasore) and Hariharpur in Orissa. It was only in 1651 that they were permitted to set up a factory at Hugli. Other factories came up in Dhaka, Kashimbazar and Patna. But they also developed a trading connection, exceeding that of the other Europeans, with the Sheths and Basaks of Sutanuti. Job Charnock was struck by the commercial and tactical advantages of the site; but there were to be several false starts and inconclusive landings, and unconcerted British attempts to settle at Hijli, Uluberia and even Chattagram, before he had his way.

JOB CHARNOCK

Prabodh Biswas

There is little reliable information about the birth and early life of Calcutta's founder. Even his career in India is enshrined as much in legend as in sober fact.

We do, however, possess Job Charnock's will as well as that of his father Richard of the parish of St Mary Woolchurch in London. Job was born around 1630-31, the younger of two sons, during his father's earlier residence in the parish of St Catherine Cree Church. He came to India about 1655-56.

We first find Charnock's name in the East India Company's records in 1658, as a Junior Member of the Council of Kashimbazar with a salary of £20. From there he was sent to Patna; and, on the expiry of his original covenant in 1664, agreed to stay on if he were placed in charge of the Patna factory. The Company, clearly valuing his services highly, acceded.

Charnock stayed in Patna till 1680. Here, it seems, he first acquired the Indian ways that constitute the stuff of the Charnock myth. He is said to have adopted many local manners and customs, even superstitions and beliefs, including worship of the *panch peer* or 'five saints' in the manner of poor Muslims, especially in Bihar. Patna is also one of the conjectured places where Charnock is reported to have won a Hindu wife whom he snatched from the *sati*'s pyre. In 1680, Charnock took charge of the Kashimbazar factory. In 1686 he became the Company's Agent in Bengal, and was plunged into the turmoil that led up to the founding of Calcutta.

Long-standing hostilities between the English and the silk weavers and traders of Murshidabad resulted in the closure of the outlying English factories in Bengal and Charnock's withdrawal to Hugli. Threatened even there by Shaista Khan, the Nawab of Bengal, Charnock beat a fighting retreat to the trading village of Sutanuti. This was his first stay at the site of the future city of Calcutta.

Over the next few years, Charnock was driven from place to place. He abandoned Sutanuti for Hijli, farther south at the rivermouth; returned to Sutanuti after making peace with the Nawab; but was hustled out from there by his compatriot Captain William Heath. Heath had been sent by the authorities in Madras to set up the Company's new Bengal headquarters at Chattagram (Chittagong). All Charnock's efforts failed to persuade Heath of the superior advantages of Sutanuti. After an abortive Chattagram campaign, the English returned to Madras in 1689, where Charnock spent a frustrating year and a half.

Finally in 1690 Madras allowed him, not without misgivings, to sail once more for 'Chuttanuttee'. It was a final and permanent return. The exact place of Charnock's landing is not known: it may have been near today's Mohantuni's Ghat, between Beniatola and

Shobhabazar Ghats. The date was Sunday 24 August 1690.

Charnock died on 10 January 1693. (His tombstone reads 1692 according to the old practice of ending the year in March). His 'Mausoleum' in St John's Churchyard was erected by his eldest son-in-law Charles Eyre (himself the Company's Agent in Calcutta) in 1697; but we are not sure whether it is the original grave, a transferred site or a cenotaph. Eyre's wife Mary (d. 1697) is commemorated on the same gravestone, and her youngest sister Catherine (d.1701) on another stone in the Mausoleum. The middle daughter, Elizabeth Bowridge, survived in Calcutta till 1753.

Beyond this, virtually all we hear of Charnock is report and controversy. His supposed Hindu wife, for instance, may have been a concubine. There could have been no formal marriage between a Hindu and a Christian, and we have no evidence of conversion. Again, was she Hindu or Muslim? Charnock, says Alexander Hamilton, used to sacrifice a cock on her tomb every year 'after the pagan manner'. This would be anathema to the memory of a Hindu lady, but was part of the accustomed worship of the *panch peer,* whom Charnock is said to have revered.

Where indeed was the lady's tomb? Tradition would place it at the eventual site of Charnock's own; but even that site is uncertain, and there is no evidence that his wife was buried there before him. So hazy indeed is the figure of Mrs Charnock that she has become virtually a character of pure legend.

Another enduring Charnock myth relates to the huge tree under which he is said to have sat, smoking his hookah, observing and talking to the locals while conducting his business. This has sometimes been identified with a huge pipal at Baithakkhana near Shealdah; sometimes with the famous banyan of Bat-tala or Bartala; sometimes with the equally venerable neem of Nimtala, by which Charnock is said to have steered his ship to shore in 1690. This last is perhaps most likely.

In the two and a half years that he lived after August 1690, Charnock made no vigorous attempt at planning or organizing the nascent city. He left behind a reputation for indolence and indecision in his old age, sapped by the climate and the rigours of his earlier life. He is said to have developed a savage temper, flogging his servants for little or no cause. His

colleagues and successors like Sir John Goldsborough, Sir William Hedges and Colonel Yule have also charged him with mismanagement, theft, brutality and questionable morals. He was indicted for corruption, though generally he enjoyed the trust and confidence of the Company. Through his long career, he undoubtedly put the Company's interests before his own, unlike so many of his venal and temporizing colleagues. He was not a military genius, but the charge of pusillanimity in his battles with the Nawab seems ill-founded.

Above all, to him and him alone goes the credit for founding the city of Calcutta in a planned and determined way. He insisted on the locational advantages of Sutanuti, both military and commercial, though hardly one of his colleagues and superiors shared his optimism. Moreover, he obviously viewed the new settlement as a full-fledged community and not merely a trading post. Above all, and most unusually, he appreciated the role of local culture and tradition in forming such a community.

This catholicity came from a paradox not uncommon in founders of great cities: they are really sojourners to whom all states and cultures are relative values, all settlements nothing but inns of passage. He was, says his epitaph, '*Qui postquam in solo non suo peregrinatus esset diu, reversus est domum suae aeternitatis*' ('a wanderer, who after sojourning for a long time in a land not his own, returned to his Eternal Home').

4.1 *Facing page: Job Charnock*

4.2 *Above: Job Charnock's Mausoleum*

SIRAJ'S CALCUTTA
1756–57

Pradip Sinha

'You are merchants, what need have you of a fortress? Being under my protection, you have no enemies to fear.' This was the assurance held out by Alivardi Khan, Nawab of Bengal from 1740 to 1756, to the English and the French. The legal status of the English in Calcutta till 1756 was that of a zamindar. Alivardi's successor Siraj-ud-daula might have been 'wicked and way-ward', but he was quite sensible in feeling that his own authority as *de facto* sovereign of the Subah of Bengal and Bihar would be adversely affected if he allowed the English to build strong fortifications within his dominion.

In addition to their reinforcing the defences of Fort William, the English were charged with abusing the privilege of *dastak* (permit for duty-free trade) to benefit their officials' private transactions, and with extending shelter in Calcutta to the Nawab's disaffected subjects. The Nawab finally decided to attack Calcutta when a messenger he had sent there was summarily expelled.

On 16 June 1756 the Nawab reached the outskirts of Calcutta with more than 30,000 combatants, supported by heavy artillery led by a detachment of twenty-five Europeans and Indo-Portuguese. He took up his quarters in the merchant Umichand or Amir Chand's villa in Shimulia (Simla) just outside the Maratha Ditch. Many of his troops and camp followers crossed the Ditch and started sporadic pillage in various parts of the Indian town.

The major part of Siraj's troops and artillery crossed the Ditch near Shealdah, and on 18 June the 'Battle of Laldighi' was fought. The English battery to the east of Tank Square (today's BBD Bag) was finally overrun by the Nāwab's army, driving the British to an inner line of defence around the old Fort William – in present-day terms, from Fairlie Place to the southern limit of the GPO and from the river to BBD Bag West. On the morning of 19 June, Governor Drake held an informal council which decided to abandon the Fort. How and when to retreat, however, remained undecided.

As the day advanced, the English came under increasing pressure. The European women and children were evacuated by boat. Many of the men also left, and, amazingly, Governor Drake himself escaped on one of the last boats.

There remained 170 white men led by J. Z. Holwell, the magistrate-collector. Confusion and panic mounted among this residue: de-moralization led to their raiding the supplies of liquor left in abandoned European houses. On the afternoon of 20 June, Holwell decided to surrender.

What followed was the confused course of events associated in European chronicles with the infamous Black Hole tragedy. The officially accepted European version was that 146 prison-ers were forced on the night of 20 June into the Fort prison, a room measuring 18 feet by 14 feet 10 inches, with only two small grated windows. No more than twenty-three emerged alive next morning, according to Holwell, who claimed to have been one of the survivors.

Holwell's veracity has been widely questioned. It has been pointed out that a room of that size could in no way accommodate 146 European adults. Bholanath Chandra, a nineteenth-century writer, tried without success to cram 146 lean Bengali villagers into a fenced area 18 feet by 15 feet. It is also pointed out that there could not have been 146 Europeans left in Calcutta that evening. After his triumph, Siraj allowed many Europeans to escape: even Holwell, as he himself admitted, was offered a chance.

It seems the number was about sixty, of which forty-odd lost their lives. It was certainly an unfortunate event, but the reports appear to have been grossly exaggerated. It also seems certain that Siraj had no direct responsibility in the matter.

'After the siege', writes A.K. Ray in his *Short History of Calcutta,* 'the name of Calcutta disappeared from history for a time.' The Nawab renamed the town Alinagar after his grandfather Alivardi Khan. (This has been suggested as the source of 'Alipur' as well.) The name of 'Calcutta' was restored in January 1758, after the British regained control of Bengal.

Though the name of Alinagar did not stick, Siraj's invasion left a permanent impact on Calcutta's history and cityscape, if only by the damage it caused and the rebuilding carried out subsequently. But the extent of this damage also seems to have been greatly exaggerated in English accounts. To the English indeed, the Sack of Calcutta must have appeared little short of a devastation. But in fact, of the four contiguous villages of Gobindapur, Kalikata, Sutanuti and Chitpur, only Kalikata or 'White' Calcutta suffered extensively. Even here, the southern portion escaped much damage, while the tombs (including Charnock's) in the old churchyard, so close to the scene of fighting, were left standing. The Black Town escaped major damage, barring the burning down of Barabazar during the first onslaught. (Gobindapur had been fired earlier by the English themselves.)

Governor Drake and the English evacuees set up temporary quarters at Phalta, some 40 miles downstream from Calcutta, until the arrival of Major Kilpatrick from Madras, followed by Robert Clive and Admiral Watson in December. They set out northwards with their forces by both land and river, capturing the fort at Bajbaj through a soldier's drunken valour on 29 December; then the earthworks at Metiabruz and the old fort of Makwa across the river; and finally, on 2 January 1757, Fort William itself after virtually no fight. Manikchand, Siraj's Governor in Calcutta, fled to Hugli.

Clive moved out to encamp in Baranagar. Meanwhile on 3 January, the British declared war on the Nawab. Hugli Fort was captured on 9 January, and the town devastated over the next ten days. Siraj was aroused at last: he advanced against the British and reached Calcutta again on 3 February 1757, once more putting up at Umichand's house. Clive launched a raid upon it but withdrew after a fierce skirmish. However, circumstances forced the Nawab to a peace with the British.

Taking advantage of this pact, the British under Clive's leadership carried out a devastating sack of Chandannagar and gradually recommenced hostilities with the Nawab. The stage was thus set for the Battle of Palashi (Plassey) on 23 June 1757, which gave the British effective control over Bengal for the time to come.

(Author assisted by Maitreyi Sinha)

5.1 *Facing page: The Holwell Monument or 'Black Hole Monument'*

THE GROWTH AND DEVELOPMENT OF OLD CALCUTTA

P. Thankappan Nair

The Early Years

In the late seventeenth century, the British in Bengal lit upon three villages on the left bank of what they called the Hugli river, which was really the west branch of the Ganga. Sutanuti, Dhee (or Dihi) Calcutta (or Kalikata) and Gobindapur were close to the point (in line with Betore and modern Garden Reach) where contemporary European traders moored their ships for want of the draught needed to proceed further. Some 25 miles upstream lay the town of Hugli, where the Portuguese had set up a factory or trading lodge in 1535, and the Dutch had followed suit in 1636. The British also acquired a foothold there in 1651. Hugli was the rising commercial centre of the time, while Ṣatgaon or Saptagram, the ancient trade capital of western Bengal, went into decline.

Sutanuti was the centre of a flourishing textile trade. During the shipping season (September to Marçh) it had a *hat,* or temporary market, for cotton yarn (*suta*). This was to meet the demand of the chintz weavers of nearby Chitpur village. The whole trade was controlled by the Sheths and Basaks of Gobindapur, who had migrated there after the decline of Satgaon. To the north lay Baranagar, first a Portuguese but by this time a Dutch settlement, famous for its *rumals* or handkerchiefs.

Job Charnock, the East India Company's agent in Bengal, was convinced of the potential importance of the area. He had even occupied Sutanuti for two short spells between 1686 and 1688. (The article on Charnock gives details of this.) On 22 June 1688, Charles Eyre and Roger Braddyll wrote to Charnock from Dhaka that Nawab Ibrahim Khan of Bengal 'will grant us his *parwanna* also for building at Calcutta with ground sufficient for a town or two as you desire'.

Charnock's enthusiasm was not generally shared. Elihu Yale, his superior in Madras, had expressly advised him against such a settlement. But by 1690, Charnock wanted nothing less than to locate the Company's Bengal headquarters there. With this aim, and at the Nawab's invitation, he landed again at Sutanuti from Madras on 24 August 1690 with his councillors Francis Ellis and Jeremiah Peachie.

They had an unpropitious start, being forced by incessant rain to spend three days and nights on board their vessels. On 28 August they ordered the erection of a mud-walled, thatch-roofed settlement: a 'drawing room', a cook-room with due ancillaries, and an apartment for the Company's servants, as well as a guard-house, a warehouse and a cloth-sorting room. The Secretary's office was in disrepair, Charnock's and Peachie's earlier houses 'past standing', and Ellis without a house at all: all this had to be attended to.

In Kalikata the British found a convenient site for settlement. Sutanuti, to its north, was bounded by the river on the west, the Chitpur Creek to the north, and the rough line of the present Central Avenue and Lalbazar to the east and south respectively. Gobindapur, further south, is now occupied by Fort William and the Maidan. These two villages feature on old maps, like Thomas Bowrey's of 1687 and George Herron's of 1690, but Kalikata, situated between the two, finds no mention there. As it had no settled native population, it was easy for the British to occupy the site, where, in 1696, they began construction of the original Fort William even without legal title to the land. (The present-day Fort was built further south in 1757.)

The three villages were part of a *khas mahal* or imperial *jagir* (i.e. an estate belonging to the Mughal Emperor himself) whose zamindari rights were held by the Sabarna Raychoudhuri family of Barisha-Behala, in the southern suburbs of modern Calcutta. It was only on 10 November 1698, nearly six years after Charnock's death, that his son-in-law and successor Charles Eyre acquired the zamindari rights from the Sabarna Raychoudhuris for Rs 1,300. The extent of the land is not stated on the transfer deed, but a survey of 1707 mentions a total of 5,076 bighas and 18.75 cottahs. The Company paid regular rent to the Mughals for these villages till 1757.

Zamindari rights were obviously crucial for any move to improve the land and to weld the region into an ordered metropolis. The British settlement was surrounded by thirty-eight villages held by others, and though in January 1717, the Company was permitted by the Mughal Emperor Farrukhshiyar to rent or acquire zamindari rights in them, it was unable to procure the land from the zamindars. Only some 155 bighas out of the 228 constituting John Nagar – the area between present-day Park Street and Dharmatala Street (now Lenin Sarani) – were rented in 1746 and amalgamated with Kalikata.

On the rest of the land, independent zamindars survived till 1757, remaining outside the authority of the Company and Fort William. They even obtained concessions from the British on the latter's land: the Sheths, who owned 110 bighas in Jorabagan within Sutanuti, had their rents abated in 1707 as 'being possessed of this ground ··· before we [the British] had possession of the towns, and being the Company's merchants and inhabitants of the place'. There were many such holdings in the hands of prominent families in Gobindapur. When the

area was cleared to build the new Fort William after 1757, they had to be given alternative land elsewhere: the Debs in Shobhabazar, the Thakurs in Pathuriaghata and Jorasanko, the Ghoshals in Bhukailas (Khidirpur). Many other inhabitants were moved to Shimulia or Simla.

The English portion of Calcutta was confined to the old Fort William area (today's B.B.D. Bag). The area south of Dharmatala was a jungle, while the 'native quarters' to the north consisted of a number of straggling villages. With the return of security provided by the Fort, the Europeans developed a craze for villas far out in what were then the suburbs, among sleepy villages like Chourangi, Baliganj, Rasa Pagla (Tollyganj), Garden Reach and Chitpur.

6.1 *Above: Chourangi. T. & W. Daniell*

6.2 *Below: 'Street scene in Native Town'. Balthazar Solvyns*

11

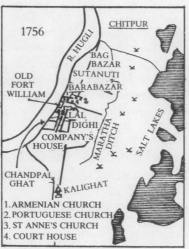

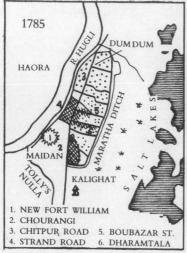

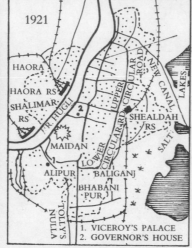

6.3 *Four stages in the growth of Calcutta*

6.4 *Clive receiving the Diwani of Bengal. Benjamin West*

Most of the land was private property, and attempts at state acquisition led to endless legal wrangles. There was thus no attempt at concerted civic development till 1911. 'Improvement' was effected chiefly by laying arterial roads through the least inhabited parts of the native town and digging tanks to drain the marshy terrain. After 1804, the funds came chiefly from the Improvement Committee set up by Lord Wellesley. For thirty years, it held lotteries (hence the common appellation 'Lottery Committee') and reserved 15 per cent of the net proceeds for civic development. This helped to finance major roads, such as Amherst Street (now Raja Rammohan Sarani), and the axis of Cornwallis (Bidhan Sarani), College, Wellesley (Rafi Ahmed Kidwai Road) and Wood Streets, with a series of tanks along it to provide drinking water.

The Maratha Ditch, dug in 1742, was a historical as well as a geographical landmark (which moreover earned Calcuttans the sobri-

quet 'Ditchers'). Maratha raiders or *bargis* were strafing the west bank of the Hugli. Indians and Europeans co-operated in excavating a ditch, starting from a point where the Chitpur Creek met the river, about three miles north of the old Fort, and meant to extend in a three-quarter-circle back to the river at a similar distance below the Fort. However, the Ditch was never completed, and was partly filled up in 1799 to create the Circular Road. The area contained within its arc was the original town of Calcutta. (The last vestiges of the Ditch were filled up in 1892-93, with earth and rubble from the construction of Harrison – now Mahatma Gandhi Road.).

In 1756, Nawab Siraj-ud-Daula invaded Calcutta. The following year, he was defeated by Robert Clive at Palashi (Plassey). The new

puppet Nawab, Mir Jafar, rid the British of all the independent zamindars inside the Maratha Ditch, granted them '600 yards without the Ditch', and rented to them 'all the land lying to the south of Calcutta as far as Kulpi' for Rs 225,000 annually. The acquisition of the zamindari of the 24-Parganas District was confirmed by having the land presented to Clive in 1759 as his personal *jagir*. In 1765, this curious *ad hominem* arrangement was ended by making the district (10,82,543 bighas, 15 cottahs) a perpetual gift to the zamindari of the company after ten years – in effect, after Clive's death in 1774. A small part of the district was amalgamated with Calcutta and the rest farmed out.

By 1762 the English owned 6,057 bighas, 13 cottahs in Calcutta and collected Rs 17,744 and 12 annas as ground rent. Their net revenue from the Calcutta lands fluctuated widely in this decade, the highest being Rs 11,16,395 in 1767-68. It did not fall below Rs 10,00,000 thereafter. This was further assured when, on

12 August 1765, Shah Alam I, the Mughal Emperor, granted the British the Diwani of the Province of Bengal (including present-day Bihar and Orissa) – i.e. the right to collect land revenue and administer justice, to the exclusion of 'our royal descendants, future as well as present'. The Diwani left the Province of Bengal 'in possession of the said Company, from generation to generation, for ever and ever.' Thus the British became masters of Bengal, though the Mughals retained nominal sovereignty.

Boundaries and Divisions

Calcutta had no legally defined boundaries before 1794. In popular parlance, the name was confined to the Fort William region, old or new, the rest being European 'suburbs' or 'native town'. The first attempt at definition came from Alexander Hamilton, an inhabitant and house-owner, in 1708: 'The Company's Colony is limited by a land-mark at Governapore [Gobindapur] and another near Barnagul [Baranagar], about six miles distant; and the Salt-Water Lake bounds it on the land side.' The earliest official description dates from 1754:

The Company's Settlement of Calcutta is situated upon a bow of the River Ganges the Points of which are Salmons Garden to the Southward and Perrin's Garden to the Northward. Our bounds extend inland in a kind of Curve too, the greatest distance of which from the River is about a Mile and a Quarter.

The account then laments the incomplete state of the Maratha Ditch, not only as a defence but also as thwarting an 'excellent means of levying with great exactness the customs on all inland Importations'.

In 1774, Warren Hastings proposed the boundaries of Calcutta for policing purposes as 'South – Carry Jurie [Khari Juri, a village under Mathurapur thana]; North – Palta, a village in Calcutta Pergunna; East – Baddadherry [Bidyadhari] river; West – Ganges'. The Charter of the Supreme Court of Judicature at Fort William, set up in the same year, does not spell out the Court's area of jurisdiction. A 1779 judgment, however, cites the 'Kidderpore Nullah' as the southern boundary, completing the circuit of the Hugli and the Maratha Ditch or Circular Road. H.T. Colebrook's account in 1793 is roughly the same.

At last in 1794, the Governor-General Lord Cornwallis fixed the boundaries of Calcutta for municipal and judicial purposes practically as they were to remain till 1867. A proclamation of 11 September 1794 gives a detailed account, which is adequately summarized in an Act of 1840:

north, Marhatta Ditch; *east,* Circular Road [which was constructed along the eastern portion of the Ditch]; *west,* the Hooghly; and *south,* Lower Circular Road to Kidderpore Bridge and Tolly's Nullah to the river, including the Fort and Cooly Bazar [Hastings].

6.5 *Warren Hastings*

The municipal limits have gone on expanding ever since, but the old demarcation survives in the 'Original Jurisdiction' of the Calcutta High Court.

Meanwhile, the suburbs of Calcutta were defined by an 1857 'Act · · · for the order and good government of the suburbs of Calcutta'. Modernizing the spellings wherever possible, the list comprises Garden Reach (Muchikhola), 'Singeratee', 'Indree', 'Sonai', Barberia, Rajarampur, Bhukailas, Dakshin Sherpur, Khidirpur, Baikunthapur, Adi Ganga Char, Ramchandrapur, Ekbalpur, Mominpur, Balarampur, Alipur, Zirat, Radhanagar, Gopalnagar, Durgapur, Chetla, Jarul, Daulatpur, Sonadanga, Majherhat, Moyerpur and Shahpur. A few of these villages were excluded from the suburbs by a Government notification of 1877, but several villages from 24-Parganas were added instead. A separate Suburban Municipality had been set up the previous year.

Finally, in 1889, the suburbs were divided among four municipalities: North Suburban (Chitpur and Kashipur), East Suburban (Maniktala), Suburban (Garden Reach) and South Suburban (Tollyganj). Some parts of the 24-Parganas were freshly added to the last two, while some inner-lying thanas (police sections) of the old Suburban Municipality become part of Calcutta proper. Thus Entali, Beniapukur, Baliganj, Bhabanipur, Northern Tollyganj, Alipur, Ekbalpur and Watganj all became 'added area wards' under Calcutta Corporation. To the east, Corporation limits crossed the Maratha Ditch for the first time to include the 'fringe area wards' of Ultadanga, Maniktala and Beliaghata.

These municipal limits correspond roughly to what is felt even today to constitute 'Calcutta proper' or the core of the metropolis. Inclusion within the common limits, however, did not rob the original villages of their names or even something of their character. Let us examine in order their names, locations and features of interest. *(See map on page 22.)*

The Thirty-Eight Villages

As said before, the English obtained from Emperor Farrukhshiyar in 1717 the right to rent thirty-eight villages surrounding their settlement in Calcutta, but had little success in doing so. Of these, five lay across the river in present-day Haora District: Salkia, Haora, Kasundia, Ramkrishnapur and Betore. The remaining thirty-three have merged into Calcutta. A few are impossible to locate, but the majority are remembered in street names. They ringed British Calcutta on the north, east, south and south-west. Spellings have been modernized wherever possible in the following account.

Dakshin Paikpara was the quarter of the *paiks* or native watchmen, who acted as policemen and were also employed privately by wealthy Indians to guard their persons and property. The area flourished under the care of Radhagobinda Sinha, who helped the Company in obtaining the Diwani of Bengal. His family was elevated to the Kandi Raj or Paikpara Rajas from the days of Gangagobinda Sinha (1749-93), the Diwan of Warren Hastings. The adjacent village of **Belgachhia** was famous for the private houses of the nineteenth-century babus: we find Prince Dwarakanath Thakur inviting Europeans to his villa in this quarter. Nearby too lay **Dakshin Dari,** but **Bahir Dakshin Dari** is difficult to locate. The venerable village of **Chitpur** also lay to the north.

Hogalkundi or **Hogalkuria,** near modern Maniktala, derived its name from *hogla* leaves or elephant grass, used as thatch: it may have grown there round a *kunda* or tank, or been sold there, or simply provided the roofing for its *kureys* or huts. John Zephaniah Holwell, the Zamindar or Collector of Calcutta in 1752, specifically noted this 250-bigha village as lying outside his jurisdiction; its proprietor was Krishnachandra Ray, the Raja of Nadia.

Ultadanga lay outside (*ulta,* across or on the opposite bank) the Maratha Ditch, beyond Halsibagan, the garden of the Sikh millionaire Umichand or Amir Chand (d. 1758). The form *ulta-dingi,* an upturned boat, may truly refer to an accident, or to boats upturned for repair.

Shimulia or **Simla,** so called from its *shimul* or silk-cotton trees, was a 1,000-bigha area also owned by the Raja of Nadia. Holwell rented it for the Company in 1754 for Rs 2,281 per annum. It extended to Dihi Bahir Simla, shown by Upjohn in his 1794 map as lying outside the Maratha Ditch. A dependency of Simla was **Macond,** rented in 1754 as well, but antiquarians have failed to locate it. They have also lost track, after an 1840 mention by Dr Ronald Martin, of **Kamarpara,** adjacent to Bahir Sura (see below); perhaps it has become modern Kamardanga.

Kankurs, a species of melon, grew well in **Kankurgachhi,** an early reclamation from the Salt Lakes. More dramatically picturesque is the name **Bagmari,** no doubt owing to a *bagh* (tiger) once having been killed here. (The Rev. James Long records a famous instance of such a kill, armed only with a knife, by the Highlander officer 'Tiger' Duff; but that was at Dumdum.)

The eastern fringe of Calcutta continued through the villages of **Shura** and **Bahir Shura** (Shura East), perhaps the resort of *shunris* or liquor-sellers, **Dolland, Shrirampur, Choubaga, Tapsia, Shiltala** (now Tiljala), **Sangassey** (perhaps modern Sapgachhi, at Tiljala), **Gobra, Kulia** and **Tangra** – the last no doubt named from the *tangra* fish, being the prize catch of the area before it was reclaimed. The original marshes and tidal lakes are also recalled as we move inward to **Hintalee** or **Entali**: the *hintal* is a type of date-palm that grows only on tidal land. (Creek Row to the west is another tell-tale name.) **Colimba** and **Jala Colimba** (the latter identified with Dingabhanga) take their name from the *colimba* or musk-melon that grew on such soil. This was corrupted to *Kalinga* and hence to *Collin,* in the modern Collin Street!

Jackals howled around **Shealdah,** identified by antiquarians as Shrigaladwipa (Jackal Island). It was, says Long, a narrow causeway, raised several feet above the surrounding terrain with a ditch on each side, leading from the east. There was hard fighting here in 1757, with thirty-nine English soldiers and eighteen Indian sepoys killed on the spot as the English dragged their guns through the rice fields. Nearby Beliaghata was an inland port and mart of the Salt Lakes. The name probably indicates a sand-packed (*beley* or *belia*) jetty rather than a paved one; but it may derive from the *bhauliya* or *baulea,* a type of boat that no doubt once resorted there in large numbers. **Mirzapur** too may have been Mritaja-pur, land reclaimed from *mrit* or marsh, but is no doubt more readily explained as the abode of the Mirzas. Spread over 1,000 bighas, it was in the hands of an independent zamindar in 1752. **Arcooley** (corrupted to Arpuli) lay to its south-west in the present Medical College area.

Today's Calcuttan will be amazed above all by the idea of **Birjee** and **Chourangi** as villages. Birjee occupied the south-eastern end of today's Maidan, the Victoria Memorial and Rabindra Sadan area; there is still a Birjee *talao* (tank) in the grounds of the Nehru Children's Museum. Chourangi, once jungle, grew rapidly after Gobindapur was cleared in 1757 for the new Fort William; the Europeans took up their quarters here. Chourangi is a name that has defied etymologists. There is however the tradition of a yogi, Chourangi Giri, who according to legend discovered an image of the goddess Kali's face and founded the original Kalighat temple.

Finally, we must remember **Shehparra** and **Garedalparra,** the sites of which, like that of 'Bahir Dakshin Dari', have not been identified.

Grams and Dihis

These thirty-eight villages gradually reconstituted themselves as fifty-five *mauzas* or *grams* (whence the name 'Panchannagram', fifty-five villages, applied to the region). These were grouped under fifteen *dihis*. Many of the original names recur, as we might expect, at either the *gram* or the *dihi* level; modern street names often help to locate them. Spellings have again been modernized in the following list:

Dihi Sinthee: Sinthee, Kashipur, Paikpara
Dihi Chitpur: Chitpur, Tala, Birpara, Kalidaha
Dihi Bagjola: Dakshin Dari, Kankuria, Noabad
Dihi Dakshin Paikpara: Belgachhia
Dihi Ultadanga: Ultadanga (part), Bagmari, Gouribari
Dihi Simla: Bahir Simla, Narkeldanga
Dihi Shura: Shura, Kankurgachhi, Kuchnan, Dattabad
Dihi Kulia: Mallikabad, Kulia
Dihi Shealdah: Shealdah, Beliaghata
Dihi Entali: Entali, Pagladanga, Nimakposta, Kamardanga, Gobra, Tangra
Dihi Tapsia: Tapsia, Tiljala, Beniapukur (in-
cluding Karaya)
Dihi Shrirampur: Choubaga, Dhulanda, Sapgachhi, Antobad, Nonadanga, Bondel Uluberia, Bedeadanga, Kustia, Puranagar, Ghughudanga, Shrirampur
Dihi Chakraberia: Baliganj, Gudshah or Garcha, Chakraberia
Dihi Bhabanipur: Bhabanipur, Neejgram
Dihi Manoharpur: Beltala, Kalighat, Manoharpur (now Manoharpukur), Mudiali, Sahanagar, Kaikhali

The Thanas: A Survey of Old Calcutta

At a somewhat later stage in the growth of old Calcutta, when it truly became an integrated colonial urban settlement after Palashi, another basis of division affords an important guide to the spread of the city and the major centres of growth: the areas of jurisdiction of the various *thanas* or police stations. Police stations provided the crucial depositories for urban statistics relating to old Calcutta. They also looked after the civic needs of the people, as the Police Commissioner doubled as Municipal Chairman till 1888.

The earliest list of thanas, for both police and municipal administration, was prepared in 1785. Its thirty-one names (modernized below) coincide in part with those of the *dihis* and *mauzas:*

Armenian Church, Old Fort, Chandpal Ghat, 'South of the Great Tank' [Laldighi or B.B.D. Bag tank], Dharmatala, Old Court House, Domtola, Amragali and Panchanantala, China Bazar, Chandni Chowk, 'Trul Bazar', Jhamapukur, Charakdanga, Simla Bazar, 'Lullunch' [Raja Ramlochan's] Bazar, Malanga and Pataldanga, Kabardanga, Baithakkhana, Shyampukur, Shyambazar, Padmapukur, Kumartuli, Jorasanko, Mechhuabazar, Janbazar, Dingabhanga, Sutanuti Hatkhola, Dayehata, Hanspukur, Colimba, Jorabagan.

These were reordered in 1888 under twenty-five Police Section Houses. The twenty-five wards created under the Calcutta Municipal Act of 1899 corresponded precisely to these divisions, which mark the final picture of urban settlement in old Calcutta.

Let us move from north to south, thana by thana, locating the focal points of settlement.

Shyampukur has long been overtaken in importance by the adjacent settlements of Bagbazar and Shyambazar. This area was the citadel of the Bengali aristocracy. Bagbazar

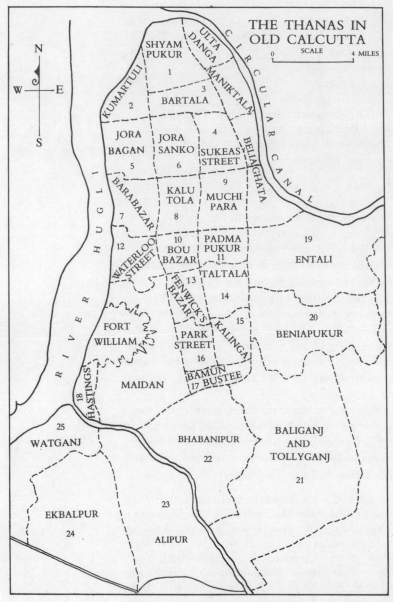

THE THANAS IN
OLD CALCUTTA

SCALE

0   4 MILES

SHYAM PUKUR

1

KUMARTULI

2

3

BARTALA

ULTA DANGA

MANIKTALA

CIRCULAR CANAL

JORA BAGAN

5

JORA SANKO

6

4

SUKEAS STREET

BELIAGHATA

BARABAZAR

KALU TOLA

8

9

MUCHI PARA

7

RIVER HUGLI

10

WATERLOO STREET

12

BOU BAZAR

PADMA PUKUR

11

19

ENTALI

13

TALTALA

FENWICK'S BAZAR

14

FORT WILLIAM

15

KALINGA

20

BENIAPUKUR

PARK STREET

16

MAIDAN

BAMUN BUSTEE

17

HASTINGS

18

25

WATGANJ

BHABANIPUR

22

BALIGANJ AND TOLLYGANJ

21

EKBALPUR

24

23

ALIPUR

6.6 *The thana divisions*

may be a corruption of *bank-bazar*, the bazaar on a *bank* or bend of the canal; but it is commonly related to the riverside garden (*bag*) owned by Captain Charles Perrin in the early eighteenth century. The bazaar was set up nearby on the property of Purnachandra Dey. The garden was sold by Perrin to the Company, which resold it in 1752 to J.Z. Holwell, the celebrated Zamindar or Collector, for Rs 2,500. Following a breach in the river bank near Perrin's garden in 1714, the Company ordered preventive earthworks. 'Perrin's redoubt' was completed in 1755, a year after Colonel C.F. Scott began manufacturing gunpowder at the garden.

Bosepara nearby was set up by Basus and Pals migrating from Hugli District. Nidhuram Basu is believed to have arrived before the British came to Sutanuti.

Shyambazar existed in 1757, if not earlier, though in 1743 it had been designated 'Cow Cross'. The bazaar or mart was called 'Charles Bazar' by Holwell. It was founded by Shobharam Basak but named after Shyam Ray or Gobinda (Vishnu), associated with the goddess Kali now at Kalighat.

Kumartuli, named after the potters (*kumars* or *kumbhakars*) who settled here, still retains its early fame for clay images of gods and goddesses. Some of the most famous Bengalis of the eighteenth century lived here: Nandaram Sen and Gobindaram Mitra, 'Black Zamindars' or Deputies to the English Collectors, and Banamali Sarkar, whose grand house or *bari* was celebrated in a Bengali rhyming proverb along with Gobindaram Mitra's *chhari* (stick), the Sikh merchant Umichand's *dari* (beard) and the other Sikh merchant Huzoorimal's *kari* (money). Before 1911, Kumartuli was the thana with the city's highest concentration of Hindus (95 per cent).

Bartala was named after the twin banyan (*bar* or *bat*) trees that stood as late as 1897 to the north of Beadon Square (now Rabindra Kanan). The Rajas of Shobhabazar, on whose land they grew, had ordered that a man who plucked their leaves would have his fingers chopped off; if he broke off a branch, his hand; and he would lose his head if he laid an axe at their root. These Rajas were the most orthodox Hindus of Calcutta, and Shobhabazar came to symbolize the values of the old leaders of urban society. Today, the only witness of its departed glory is the Nabaratna Temple of Siddheswari Kali.

Sukeas (corrupted to Sukea) **Street** was named after the Armenian merchant Peter Sukeas. He lived in a palatial mansion, from whose tank he used to let the public fetch drinking water – one of his many charities. This area was the home of Raja Rammohan Ray, Pandit Ishwarchandra Vidyasagar, Dinabandhu Mitra and other nineteenth-century celebrities. The Law (Laha) family, which produced a galaxy of scholars, also lived here.

At **Jorabagan**, the 'Zora [Jora] Bari Bag' or 'two-house garden' is marked near the present Rabindra Kanan (Beadon Square) on Forresti and Olifres's map of 1742. Its other name was Sheth Bagan, from a 110-bigha garden owned by the Sheth family. It was here that Captain Commandant William Holcomb proposed to build one of the batteries to defend Calcutta against the Marathas.

Next to Kumartuli, Jorabagan had the highest proportion of Hindus (93.5 per cent), among whom were such established families as the Thakurs of Pathuriaghata, the Singhabahini Malliks, and the descendants of Diwan Ramlochan Ghosh, Diwan Baidyanath Mukherji, Diwan Radhamadhab Banerji and Raja Sukhamay Ray of Posta.

Jorasanko is so called from the two (*jora*) wooden or bamboo bridges (*sanko*) that spanned a small stream at this point; but the present writer would like to derive the name from the two temples here devoted to *Shankar* or Lord Shiva. The celebrated seat of the Thakur family, Jorasanko was also the home of the Sinhas (including Kaliprasanna Sinha), the Pals (including Krishnadas Pal), and the families of Diwan Baranasi Ghosh and Chandramohan Chatterji. The area thus became the cradle of the Bengal Renaissance, as attested by institutions like the Adi Brahmo Samaj, the Jorasanko Bharati Natya Samaj, the Kalikata Haribhakti Pradayini Sabha, the Minerva Library and the Oriental Seminary.

Barabazar was also first named after Shiva, popularly called 'Buro'. The upcountry merchants who ousted the Sheths changed the name to 'Bara Bazar', the big market. This grew out of the old Sutanuti *hat* or market.

Modern Barabazar is a creation of the Marwaris. Their phenomenal success came in the second half of the nineteenth century, but the market has been traced back to 1738 by Orme. In the siege of 1756, the Nawab's troops set fire to the bazaar and took possession of the quarters where the principal merchants lived, farther north in Jorabagan and Kumartuli.

In 1752, under orders of the East India Company's directors, collector Holwell settled the Company's workmen of diverse trades in separate quarters. **Kalutola** was the home of the Company's *kaluas* (*kalus*) or oil-pressers, who may have supplied mustard and other oils to the Barabazar merchants as well. The area harks back to the beginning of the eighteenth century.

To Kalutola migrated two illustrious families, the Sens and the Dattas. The best-known member of the former is Keshabchandra Sen. Tarachand Datta and Harihar Datta were pioneer Urdu journalists in India, while Sagar Datta's charities were celebrated.

Since there was no **Muchipara** thana in the 1785 division, its rise must be assigned to the early nineteenth century. It is clearly named after the *muchis* (cobblers and leather-workers) who were the most numerous residents of the area.

Boubazar is commonly explained as the *bahu* or bride's bazaar, as Bishwanath Matilal is said to have gifted the market at premises No 84A (near the crossing with Nirmal Chandra Street) to his daughter-in-law. However, the bazaar (and street name) have been traced back to 1749, long before Matilal's birth. An 'Avenue leading to the Eastward' was marked at the spot in a map of 1742. There were several (*bahu*) markets along its course; among them is the Baithakkhana Bazar (premises Nos. 155-58) where many (*bahu*) articles were sold.

Adjacent to Boubazar was **Padmapukur** thana. There were so many tanks (*pukurs*) here that it is difficult to locate the one with lotuses (*padma*). The Byaparitola Tank in Dingabhanga became Wellington Square (now Subodh Mallik Square). The area is marked as Shankharitola (the quarters of the *shankharis* or conchworkers) in Mark Wood's map of 1784.

The **Waterloo Street** Police Section, though small, had been split among three thanas in 1785: Old Fort, 'South of the Great Tank', and Old Court House. Waterloo Street itself was built by the Lottery Committee around 1828, but no doubt the settlement, so close to the old Fort, goes back to the early days of the British in Calcutta.

Fenwick's Bazar stood east of the present New Market. Edward Fenwick (fl. 1764-1812) held important offices under the Company, although they dismissed him more than once. His father, Captain Thomas Fenwick, who served the Company for thirty-four years without home leave, received land at John Nagar in compensation for a house near the old Fort. On this land, the son built his market.

Taltala was, of course, named after its *tal* or palmyra trees, supposed to have originated in Bengal. A predominantly Muslim area housing the Calcutta Madrassa, its early Hindu settlers included Durgacharan Banerji, father of Surendranath Banerji.

The etymology of **Kalinga** or Colimba has already been described. The area, one of the original 'thirty-eight villages', grew along with the garden-houses of Chourangi. Its celebrated early inhabitants included Justice Stephen Caesar le Maistre and James Augustus Hicky the journalist.

Known first as Badamtala, then as Burial Ground Road (from the cemetery near its southern end), **Park Street** received its present name in the 1840s; the deer park it commemorates belonged to Sir Elijah Impey (1732-1809), Chief Justice of the Supreme Court in the 1780s. His villa had been built in 1749 by William Frankland, later Zamindar and Collector of Calcutta. The Company attempted to buy the property for its Governors, but the Directors demurred, and the house became the private property first of Henry Vansittart, Governor from 1760 to 1764, and later of Impey. It stood on the present site of Loreto House on Middleton Row (earlier Vansittart Street).

After the digging of the Maratha Ditch, Park Street was developed as a European residential quarter. Its fashionable identity today derives from that beginning; but the next thana, **Bamun Bustee,** reminds us of the complementing reality. Doubtless named after *bamuns* or Brahmins, this was actually a *bustee* or cluster of hutments surrounding a large tank, occupied by the servants of the Park Street sahibs. The thana finds no separate mention in Wood's or Upjohn's maps.

Today, the area has a very different character. This was because in 1859 the owner, a barrister called Peterson, conveyed the central tank to the Municipal Commissioners free of cost in perpetuity. In return, the Commissioners were to develop the tank (now Victoria Square), build new roads and provide water. This enabled Peterson to oust the slum-dwellers and sell the rest of the property as superior building sites for Europeans. The scheme cost the civic body Rs 20,000. The return in municipal rates may have made the investment worthwhile.

Hastings was the site of a Muslim burial ground predating the erection of the new Fort William. When the new Fort was begun in 1757, the workmen or coolies camped here, giving rise to the name 'Coolie Bazar'. It was renamed 'Hastings' as it grew into a township for the Ordnance and Commissariat Departments, and the Harbour Master's Department of the Port Commissioners.

Entali was once part of the Salt Lakes, beyond the Maratha Ditch. Its marshy and pestilential stretch was the refuge of Oriya palanquin-bearers, poor Christians and Muslims and other depressed communities; caste Hindus shunned the area on account of the municipal slaughter-house and Chinese-owned tanneries and piggeries. In the nineteenth century, the low cost of land attracted many factories, most of which remain to this day.

Beniapukur is mentioned by Holwell in the mid-eighteenth century, but the thana dates from the early nineteenth century. Influential *benias* or merchants, more specifically the *gandhabaniks* or perfume and spice-traders, settled here and dug a tank or *pukur*.

Baliganj and **Tollyganj** formed a combined thana. A *ganj* is a market, and *bali* means sand: the place grew up around a market for the sand in such plentiful supply from the *chars* or riverine islands of Bengal. Baliganj was the seat of the garden-houses of eighteenth-century Europeans like George Mandeville the Zamindar/Collector, and Warren Hastings's friend Colonel Gilbert Ironside. Emily Eden called Baliganj 'our Eltham or Lewisham' in 1840. Writing in 1907, H.E.A. Cotton notes the 'fine maidan' and quarters of the Governor-General's bodyguard, surrounded by 'many very fine European residences standing in extensive grounds'. After the suburban railway opened up the area, Baliganj also became a citadel of the educated Bengali middle class.

Tollyganj, called Rasa Pagla in the eighteenth century, was a jungle sprinkled with European garden-houses. It was renamed after Colonel William Tolly (d. 1784), who in 1774 rendered the Adi Ganga or 'Tolly's Nulla' navigable; it became the chief inland waterway from Dhaka through the Salt Lakes to Calcutta. The Mysore Princes, sons of Tipu Sultan, settled here after the Vellore Mutiny in 1806, and a small Muslim community grew up around their *kothis*. They also extended their patronage to the Tollygunge Club and the Tollygunge Golf Club in the early nineteenth century.

Bhabanipur existed as a *dihi* in 1765; part of Dihi Chakraberia was also subsumed within it. Here is said to have stood the original shrine of Kali (Bhabani), about a mile from the present site of Kalighat, to which the shrine was shifted only in 1809. By the temple flowed the Adi Ganga, described by Holwell as a 'small brook'. The construction of Harish Mukherji Road and Lansdowne (now Sharat Basu) Road, and the

extension of Hazra Road to Kalighat, helped to open up Bhabanipur at the beginning of this century.

Bhabanipur developed along rigid caste and occupational lines. The *kansaris* (braziers), *shankharis* (conch-workers), *telis* (oil-pressers) all had their *paras,* while commodities were sold in *pattis,* like the *chaul-patti* (rice market) identifiable even today. At the same time, Indian lawyers, including the most illustrious ones of old Calcutta, flocked to live in Bhabanipur: the Sadar Diwani Adalat, the Company's highest appellate court, had shifted to the old Military Hospital building there, and the District Judge's Court was in nearby Alipur.

Alipur is possibly a derivative of Alinagar, the name Siraj-ud-Daula gave the city (after his grandfather Nawab Alivardi Khan) on sacking it in 1756. But the name has also been associated with Ali Naqi Khan, who had his house in this area as well as a ghat named after him on the Adi Ganga or Tolly's Nulla.

At first a Muslim locality, Alipur was taken over by the British elite in the latter part of the eighteenth century. Warren Hastings built Hastings House and perhaps Belvedere, Philip Francis his 'lodge' (now the Magistrate's house), and Richard Barwell the house which became the Military Orphan Asylum and then St Thomas's School. Later, Alipur became the headquarters of the 24-Parganas District. and acquired military installations and a meteorological observatory. The bustee lands around adjacent Zirat Bridge were acquired for the Zoo.

The gracious life of the old Calcutta elite is still evoked by the open spaces of Alipur, around Belvedere Estate (once the Lieutenant-Governor's palace, now housing the National Library), Hastings House, the Zoo, and the gardens of the Agri-Horticultural Society.

No one knows why **Ekbalpur** is so called or

6.7 *Coolie Bazar Ghat. Charles D'Oyly*

6.8 *The Belvedere*

how it grew; but as the name hints, it developed as a Muslim area. This happened for a number of reasons, such as the displacement of many Muslims from Zirat, under Alipur thana, to make space for the Zoo, and of still more from the land acquired for King George's (now Netaji Subhash) Docks in Garden Reach: the uprooted took refuge in Ekbalpur. Another factor was the migration of Momins or Muslim weavers from Bihar and UP (who have given their name to Mominpur within this thana) after the 1857 Mutiny. Many of them had to enter the city surreptitiously. In Calcutta, they took up seafaring as an occupation, and were attracted to Ekbalpur by the proximity of the Khidirpur docks (perhaps from the Muslim name Khijir, or perhaps Kedarpur after Kedar or Lord Shiva). One of the oldest Muslim burial grounds in Calcutta, the 'Solah Anna', is located on Ekbalpur Road.

6.9 *A patua or 'Bazaar painter'.* Solvyns

It is worth recalling that Garden Reach, beyond the compass of the thanas, also became a Muslim area when Wajid Ali Shah, the Nawab of Awadh, and his large entourage settled at nearby Metiabruz (*matia buruj* or earth-built fort) after his deposition. This made the Europeans withdraw from their garden-houses there, in favour of Alipur and Baliganj.

Watganj too is closely connected with the Khidirpur Docks, and commemorates their virtual founder Colonel Henry Watson (1737-84). After working for the army and the Company, and becoming Chief Engineer in Bengal for the latter, Watson set up the first dockyards in Bengal. Here were built the frigates *Nonesuch* (thirty-two guns) in 1782 and *Surprise* (thirty-six guns) is 1788. Watson also acted as second to Philip Francis in the latter's historic duel with Warren Hastings.

Other Localities and Landmarks

I have only touched briefly on the most important quarters and localities within each ward or thana. With an old map or street guide and an elementary knowledge of Bengali, one can work out the fascinating growth and distribution of settlements in old Calcutta, and even something of the landscape. Many of these *paras, talas, pukurs, bag(an)s, ghats* and *bazars* have disappeared or acquired new names, but enough survive to convey the flavour of the scene.

Paras (localities) were the primary units of old Calcutta. There would be a natural tendency for particular castes, professions or communities, or migrants from the same village, to live together. Today's street names still recall the *paras* of particular castes (*Bàmun*/Brahmin), families (Banerji, Bishwas, Datta, Ganguli, Naskar, Ray, Santra, Sikdar), professions (*darjis* or tailors, *guris* or molasses-sellers, *jelias* or fishermen, *kansaris* or braziers, *kasais* or butchers, *syakras* or goldsmiths), and migrants from other provinces (Urias or Oriyas). Old Calcutta had many more such names.

Smaller than the *paras* were the *tolas* of professional groups like the *ahirs* (cowherds or milkmen), *byaparis* (merchants), *kalus* (oil-pressers), *kambulias* (blanket-sellers), *patuas* (*pat*-painters), and *shankharis* (conch-workers). *Tuli,* the diminutive of *tola,* marked a still smaller quarter like Kumartuli.

Trade and commerce also created markets,

which in turn lent their names to their localities. *Hats, ganjes* and *bazars* could be named after the products sold there — *garan* or mangrove wood at Garanhata, yoghurt (*dai*) at Dayehata, chicken (*murgi*) at Murgihata, sand (*bali*) at Baliganj. Or they could be named after the founder or owner: European, like Fenwick and the Italian Edward Tiretta, or Indian, like Chhatu Babu (Ashutosh Dey or Sarkar, son of the renowned merchant Ramdulal Dey), Anath Babu (Anathnath Dey, Chhatu Babu's adoptive nephew), and Jadu Babu (Jadunath Choudhuri, Rani Rasmani's grandson). The biggest market of all, Barabazar, was (and is) divided into many specialized *pattis,* named after the products sold there: *khangra* or brooms, *maida* or flour, *sindur* or vermilion.

Many quarters were named after the gods worshipped there: Manasatala, Panchanantala, Shashthitala, Shitalatala, Shibtatala. Others, more picturesquely, recall old groves or avenues – Bakulbagan, Dalimtala, Jhautala, Taltala – or even particular trees, like the twin banyans of Bartala or a famous neem (margosa) tree at Nimtala, destroyed in the fire of 1882. Gardenhouses could also designate a locality, usually by the owner's name: Europeans like Perrin, Surman or Anthony (grandfather of the famous poet-singer Anthony Phiringi), or Indian families like the Basaks, Ghoshes, Haldars, Naths, Sheels, Sheths and Sikdars. The Garden of Garden Reach appears to be the Botanic Garden across the river, founded in 1786.

Even more vital than trees were the ponds or tanks, the main source of water in premunicipal days. The communities who formed *paras* would often dig tanks for their exclusive use. There were thousands of tanks within the Maratha Ditch: 823 in Bhabanipur alone as late as 1888, two decades after piped water was introduced. Many of these *pukurs* are named after the founding communities (*ahirs, benias*) or families (the Basus, Niyogis, Sheths or Tarafdars); others have descriptive names like Chunapukur (full of *chuna* or small fish), Jhamapukur (lined with *jhama* or burnt brick), Jorapukur (twin tanks), or Padmapukur (lotus-tank).

A different set of landmarks grew up along the river bank – the *ghats,* crucial in an age of water transport, as well as in a religion and way of life that laid great stress on access to the river. The numerous ghats built by the Hindus are all upstream from Khidirpur, as below it the river is considered *kata-Ganga* (i.e. man-made). The orthodox alignment of the holy stream continues along the Adi (original) Ganga or Tolly's Nulla, upon which stands Kalighat.

Many of the ghats were named after the founders, who set them up as acts of piety or of philanthropy: Kashi Mitra, Ramratan Dattaray (Ratan Babu), (Ram Mohan) Mallik, Babu Rajchandra Das of Babu Ghat. The first ghat to be paved with stones (*pathar*) was appropriately named Pathuria Ghat. Interspersed with these are ghats recalling the old trading villages (Sutanuti, Chitpur) and the harbour-masters (*mirbahars*) of Mughal times. Others honour the new trade of British Calcutta: Armenian Ghat, Rustomji Ghat (after Rustomji Kawasji Banaji, a Parsi shipping tycoon), Clive Ghat (formerly Blythe's Ghat after a shipbuilder) and Kailaghat (from *killa,* the Fort, corrupted to *kaila,* coal, on account of its chief cargo). Except for Rustomji Ghat, all these abut upon the central business district, as did the Bankshall (probably from Sanskrit *banik shala* or trading house), the first marine yard on the river, built in 1700. The river has its own life, and its growth was a major corollary to the life of the growing city on land.

The fundamental point of this account is that from the earliest times, Calcutta developed in keeping with the continuing spirit of its life and growth – spontaneously, variedly, by the natural economic and social drives of countless groups who flocked there for survival and self-improvement. (The growing area and population are charted in Table 1.) This was the outcome of the English spirit as much as of the Indian. The English at that time were traders, and planning was alien to their motives and outlook. That came two hundred years later in New Delhi, where visible embodiment of imperial power was the chief end in view.

Indians from a continually expanding hinterland headed for Calcutta to earn a living from employment, manufacture and services under the security afforded by the guns of Fort William. Villagers could thus transplant themselves unmolested to the *paras,* pursuing their traditional arts and crafts .

Yet, intellectually or commercially no less than physically, Calcutta was never a walled city. Life in Calcutta increasingly induced a modification of old attitudes through free exchange between castes and communities. The physical checks to growth indeed helped in this

6.10 *Old Calcutta,*
based on Upjohn's
Survey 1792-93

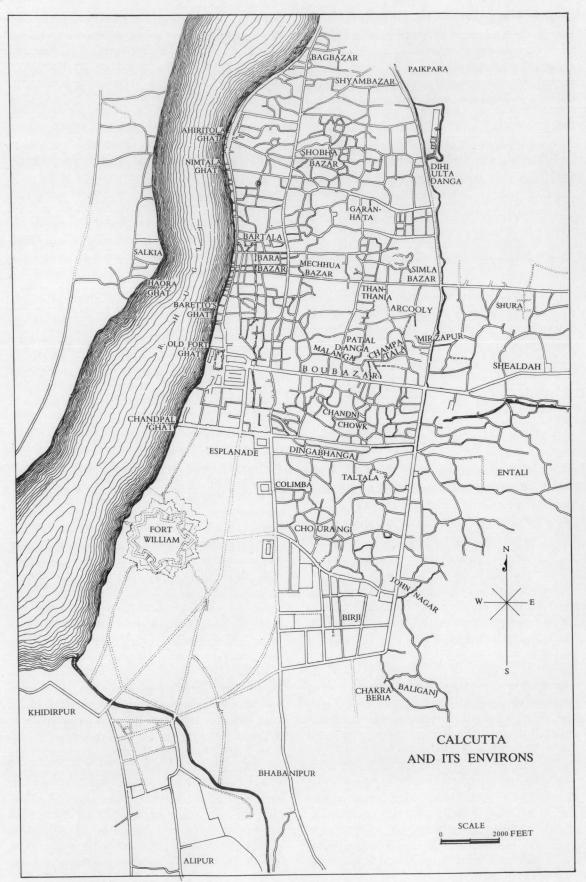

CALCUTTA
AND ITS ENVIRONS

TABLE 1 Area and Population of Calcutta, 1698-1911

Year	Area	Population	Sources and authorities
1698	5,076 bighas & 18 ¾ cottahs (= 1861 acres)	....	Wilson, *Early Annals* I, p.286
1746	5,472 bighas & ½ cottah	....	Holwell, *Tracts,* 3rd edn., p.209
1762	6,057 bighas & 13 cottahs	....	Long, *Selections,* no.581
1794	4,997 acres	....	A.K. Ray, *A Short History of Calcutta,* p.58
1821	–do–	179,917	Assessors' estimate
1831	–do–	187,081	Captain Steel's estimate
1837	–do–	229,714	Captain Birch's estimate
1840	–do–	361,369	Simms's estimate
1850	–do–	413,182	Chief Magistrate's estimate (often considered unreliable)
1866★	–do–	377,921★	Dowleans's Census
1872	–do–	447,601	Chick's Census (often considered unreliable)
1876	5,037 acres	429,535	Beverley's Census
1881	–do–	433,219	Census of 1881
1891	13,133 acres	468,552†	Census of 1891
1901	20,547 acres	847,796††	Census of 1901
1911	–do–	896,067††	Census of 1911

Notes: ★ *Population for Fort and Port area formally included from this year onward.*
 † *Population of the Old Town. The population of the expanded municipal area in this year was 681,560.*
†† *Population of the expanded municipal area.*

respect – the river on the west, the Salt Lakes on the east, and Dutch-occupied Baranagar to the north. Expansion was only possible southwards; but even there, the urge to dwell as close as possible to the seat of power ensured concentration towards the centre.

The six square miles within the Maratha Ditch thus came to have the world's highest density of population in that age. It was a heterogeneous population, sinking differences of caste, creed and colour under the sheer compulsion to interact and survive together. The compulsion has grown stronger ever since, as has the spirit that it fostered. Hence Calcutta did not disintegrate when the capital was shifted to New Delhi in 1912. It has kept growing and living by the ever-renewed confidence and vitality of its inherent human forces.

KALIGHAT

Kalyani Dutta

When the dead body of the goddess Durga or Sati was dismembered by Vishnu's war-discus *(sudarshan chakra)*, the toes of her right foot were said to have fallen beside the old course of the Bhagirathi or Hugli River (the old or *Adi* Ganga). The place became one of the fifty-one (or fifty-two) *pithas* of the goddess: Kalighat, inseparable from the life of Calcutta and, as some think, directly or indirectly the source of the city's name. The manifestation of the goddess here is known as Dakshinakali; her consort Shiva is Nakuleshwar; Vishnu in the form of Krishna, dwells under the appellation of Shyam Ray in an adjacent temple. The association of these three deities makes Kalighat a unique meeting-point for both Shakta and Vaishnav pilgrims, for ascetics as well as householders.

No one knows for certain when the temple was founded. It has been variously traced to the Gupta and the Sena periods. Brahma himself is said to have picked up the goddess's toes and face beside a small pond to the east of the temple, the *hrad* (lake) or *Kalikunda*. Yet it is also said that the temple has shifted its location: that it was earlier at Bhabanipur, and before that perhaps near today's Posta Bazar, much farther north. There is no evidence to support these claims.

Nor is there any reliable reference to the temple in old texts. Authentic records of Kalikshetra go back to the early eighteenth century, by which time, if not a little earlier, the Sabarna Raychoudhuri family had settled in the Barisha-Behala region, to the south-west of today's city, and obtained rights to the temple and its lands. Their property included the villages of Sutanuti, Kalikata and Gobindapur, the rights to which they sold to the British in 1698. Their rights to the temple land were also lost long ago. They had in any case entrusted the actual worship to the Haldar family. The latter's descendants still control worship; the Mishras dress the goddess; yet

7.1 *Kalighat, with the Kalikunda and 'pagoda'. Solvyns*

Facing page

7.2 *Above: Returning from Kalighat with a sacrificed goat. Mrs Belnos*

7.3 *Below: Charak Puja festivities. Mrs Belnos*

others conduct the puja. Over them all presides the Kalighat Temple Committee.

In those days the temple was set in thick forest, infested by robbers and made fearsome by the rites of *tantriks* and *kapaliks*. Puja was held in the small hours of the night, with animal sacrifices. Perhaps the atmosphere enhanced the fame of the goddess and her seat; certainly she attracted munificent devotees.

When Churamani Datta of Hatkhola died, Brahmins boycotted his funeral on account of his son Kaliprasad's irreligious behaviour. Only Santosh Raychoudhuri of the Sabarna family attended with his followers and partook of the funeral feast. The grateful Kaliprasad gave Santosh a large sum of money, which he is said to have employed in rebuilding the temple in its present 90-foot-high form. It cost Rs 30,000 in those days and took seven or eight years to build, finishing in 1809 after Santosh's death. The Sikh Huzoorimal paved the adjoining *ghat* or landing-stage, another Sikh, Tara Singh, set up the temple of Shiva Nakuleshwar, while other benefactors through the nineteenth century added to the temple complex and the nearby Keoratala (Sahanagar) cremation-ground. Yet others gave gold ornaments and gold covers for the goddess's face, tongue and limbs. In 1822, Maharaja Gopimohan Thakur made what was probably the biggest ever gift of gold: policemen were called to keep order at the accompanying feeding of Brahmins and the poor.

The most amazing act of worship was performed by the East India Company itself: in 1765, it offered a thanksgiving *puja*, no doubt as a politic act to appease its Hindu subjects, on obtaining the Diwani of Bengal (including Bihar and Orissa). The sum spent is cited variously as having been between Rs. 5,000 and Rs. 30,000. In 1836, *The Friend of India* estimated that 'Kaleeghaut yields twenty-two lacs of rupees yearly and the endowments belonging to the temple produce not less than six lacs every year'.

This income came less from land than from offerings. Kalighat is both the scene of many festivals, and the object of vows and votive offerings. Apart from the regular pujas on Tuesdays, Saturdays and month-endings and at the dark of the moon, there are special pujas and *bratas* (vows or vigils) for housewives and widows, the dedication of new account-books by shopkeepers at the Bengali New Year, and

7.4 *The Kali temple, today*

encased in silver and at festivals in gold. Even her tongue is sheathed with gold. Her feet cannot be seen. The original face and toes of Sati are said to be preserved in an iron chest in the sanctum sanctorum *(garbhagriha)*. At the goddess's bathing ceremony, the seniormost priest – himself blindfolded – takes the swathed and invisible toe-relic and bathes it in the Kalikunda.

But the probing imagination has sometimes conceived of an unhappy deity behind this sumptuous image. In Durgacharan Ray's satiric fantasy *Debaganer Martyey Agaman* ('The coming of the Gods to the Earth') the goddess laments, 'What can I do but weep? The humans are sucking my blood. With men it's all over when they die, but I have no peace; I am imprisoned at Kalighat.'

The cause of her lament was the sight of animal sacrifice. *Balidan* has called forth repeated protests. In 1915, Anathkrishna Deb of Shobhabazar collected many scriptural passages condemning such sacrifice, held a debate and printed a pamphlet. Twenty years later, Pandit Ramchandra Sharma went on a protest fast in the temple courtyard; Rabindranath Thakur sent him greetings in a four-stanza verse tribute.

But perhaps the goddess laments for humans too. Her pity may be roused by Mother Teresa's nearby Nirmal Hriday, home for dying destitutes, the only significant new addition to the Kalighat scene. Or she may be moved by recalling the old shops, crafts and trades that have now disappeared: the *pat* paintings, the coloured pictures of Kali from the Bowbazar Art School, the woodcuts of Benimadhab Bhattacharya and Nrityalal Datta, the wooden and earthenware toys. But shopkeepers still deal in ironware, brassware, stoneware and conch-ware, framed prints of the goddess in newer styles, and all kinds of ordinary goods. The old red-light area still exists, but so does the inheritance of Sanskrit scholars who lived round the temple: Mahimanath Haldar, Nakuleshwar Bhattacharya, Amareshwar Thakur, Sachchidananda Bhattacharya, Nagendranath Shastri.

All this makes up the pageant the goddess sees. There are far grander and far older temples than Kalighat, but it can match them in its crucial role as the centre of a community, a society, a full vision of life.

the *snanjatra* or ceremonial bathing of the goddess's relics; and, of course, there is Durga Puja and Kali Puja proper. Shivaratri is celebrated at the temple of Shiva Nakuleshwar, and Dolejatra (Holi) at Shyam Ray or Krishna's temple. In earlier times, Nakuleshwar also saw the Charak festivities at the year's end, with the hoisting of devotees on hooks piercing the flesh.

After the Gangasagar Mela in winter, sadhus from all over India end their round of pilgrimage with a trip to Kalighat. The common devotees tie small stones to the tree at Manasatala, to the north of the temple, as they make a wish or vow; when it is fulfilled, they offer puja and sacrifices, especially of goats. Litigants are the most numerous votaries; but there are ministers and MPs, lawyers and administrators, traders and speculators. Once it used to be landlords praying for success in their disputes over property. No less important, all Hindu ceremonies – *annaprashana* (a child's first rice-meal), *upanayana* or the sacred thread ceremony, above all marriage – can be carried out with Kali as a witness. To be married at Kalighat has long been the common man's resort in a love-match or elopement.

The goddess who bears witness to this pageant is not featured like the common image of Kali. She is fully and richly clothed, hung with ornaments, her face and hands commonly

(Translated from Bengali)

CHITPUR

Bunny Gupta and Jaya Chaliha

If Calcutta had her Chaucer, he would have revelled in Chitpur: its sobriety and ribaldry, the pilgrim and the courtesan. Indeed, Chitpur harks back closer to Chaucer's day than the city of Calcutta itself: the temple to the goddess Chitteshwari or Chitreshwari, from which the locality is often held to take its name, was founded by Manohar Ghosh around 1610. (A reference to *Chitrapur*, an alternative source-name, in Bipradas Pipalai's poem *Manasamangal* of 1495 appears to be a later interpolation.) Of course, today's Chitpur is really the area around what is properly no more than the Chitpur Road: the original village of Chitpur, to which it led, lay further to the north.

The home of Chakrapani, Commander-in-Chief of the Nawab of Bengal's army, Chitrapur had a flourishing colony of artists *(chitrakars)* who may have lent the place their name. When the Marathas ceased to pose a threat, members of the disbanded army turned into thugs and robbers. The jungle around Chitrapur was one of their dens, and the artists fled to settle in Kalighat. The most notorious bandit of the region was Chitey Dakat (dacoit), who was said to sanctify his maraudings by first offering human sacrifice at Chitteshwari's temple. He too is sometimes said to have given his name to Chitpur.

Along the pilgrim's path, from the north past Chitteshwari to Kalighat, mushroomed dharamshalas and shops. These grew into habitations, and a network of lanes and by-lanes burgeoned from Chitpur Road itself. A city within a city, Chitpur's divisions were self-descriptive, named after landmarks or occupations. The chicken *(murgi)* market was Murgihata; twin *(jora)* bridges *(sanko)* over a creek distinguished Jorasanko; butchers *(kasais)* slaughtered animals at Kasaitola; and the *kumars* (potters) of Kumartuli fashioned the clay from the river beside their homes into pots to be sold at Sutanuti market. Gradually, they took to making images of gods and goddesses, worshipped in increasing numbers in the mansions all around and later at community pujas in the city. Today Durgas and Kalis board planes to Britain, Canada and the USA. But the *shankharis* (conchshell-workers) have dwindled: only a few families carry on in roadside shops.

Chronicles describe a nine-turretted or *nabaratna* temple of Kali built at Kumartuli by Gobindaram Mitra, the Collector's Deputy or 'Black Zamindar', in 1725. Its 165-foot spire was a navigational aid: sailors called it the Pagoda. But the nearby promenade, Captain Perrin's riverside garden, was a white preserve where only the Company's servants could take moonlight walks. It was, alas, bought by Holwell in 1752 to set up a gunpowder factory.

The city's oldest road (and the first to be so designated), Chitpur brings the history of old Calcutta to life. When the new Fort William was built in the 1750s at Gobindapur, most of

8.1 *The Chitteshwari Temple*

the displaced inhabitants migrated to north Calcutta. With the blessings of the Company, some of the Bengali *nouveaux riches* proceeded to adulterate the Greek orders along Chitpur Road in a notorious riot of 'Bengal Baroque, gaudy stucco and rotten Rococo'. Yet the architecture has a value quite besides the merely nostalgic.

Jorasanko became the seat of a branch of the Thakur (Tagore) family when Nilmani Thakur was obliged to leave the family's palace at Pathuriaghata. Students of Rabindra Bharati University now people the corridors where once walked Dwarakanath, 'Prince' of merchants, the ascetic Debendranath, and Rabindranath himself. Hence Chitpur is also the site of the Adi Brahmo Samaj, and the road has been renamed Rabindra Sarani.

A Cooke and Kelvey clock sits atop the Corinthian columns of the palace of a branch of the Malliks of Pathuriaghata. A one-time owner, Pradyumna Mallik, was master of a fleet of fourteen Rolls Royces and a buggy drawn by two zebras. Another branch of the family struck root at Chorbagan. Raja Rajendra

Mallik's Marble Palace there is an immense private museum, while his menagerie gave the Chitpur area the honour of housing Calcutta's first zoo.

There were less exalted gentry and aristocrats as well. Risque ditties and lewd verses tell of Chitpur as the nineteenth-century Babu's playground. The *phool babu* would emerge in the evening, his parted hair shining with pomade, pleated dhoti-end in one hand and silver-topped ebony cane in the other, chewing a fragrant *khili* of *paan* on his way to his paramour. Sonagachhi continues to be the city's most celebrated red-light district.

On a different key, the *jatra* or rural theatre companies came at the invitation of the urban Rajas during Durga Puja. They found Chitpur a useful *adda* and have since opened permanent offices there. Supporting crafts appeared as well. Sheikh Mahabat Ali, wig-maker, hangs yak-tail whisks on his door advertising costumes for hire. Real-hair wigs and beards are in demand by theatre groups in major cities, while the cheaper jute substitutes are used by the *jatra* players of Bengal. In Chitpur too, the

8.2 *Chitpur Road, 1867. William Simpson*

brass bands once practised Scottish airs and 'For he's a jolly good fellow' to enliven the marriage procession of a Bagbazar Babu.

As the city grew, a cultural centre sprang up at Bartala or Bat-tala. It began as an extension of the arts in the older centres of Nadia and Hugli. Illustrated Bengali religious works, both Hindu and Islamic, were printed at Bat-tala. In 1818, a press started here by Bishwanath Deb took the first step towards popularizing Bengali literature. Sales were promoted by canvassers who also took books to the village fairs and in exchange brought back manuscripts for their employers, which in turn were printed at Bat-tala. The distinctive Bengali *panjika* or almanac also came to be printed here.

Illustrated books appeared from Bat-tala too, and artists arose to provide for them. The city's European artists interacted with those in Bat-tala. In 1808, Monsieur Jean-Jacques Belnos had a studio at Kasaitola where he gave lessons for Rs 20 a month and sold his miniature paintings for Rs 130 each.

Older still is Chitpur's Muslim heritage. The upper and middle-class Muslims of old Calcutta

lived at the two extremities of the town. The exiled descendants of Tipu Sultan were banished to Tollyganj in the south. In his magnificent palace to the north, Reza Khan, Deputy Nawab of Bengal, lavishly entertained those very Englishmen who had once prosecuted him. The Dutch and the French too arrived in pleasure-barges at the nearby ghat to spend a pleasant day with the Nawab. Today Biren Mandal sits making violins on the ground floor and points up to the room where Michael Madhusudan Datta lived while writing most of his best-known works including the *Meghnad-badh Kabya*. The Mandals make and repair violins and sitars for the greats. Their treasure-chest holds a certificate from Yehudi Menuhin, whose violin they repaired in 1952.

The lone tobacco shop selling aromatic mixtures of *amburi* and *badshah pasand,* or the crochet-capped henna-haired men sitting among cut-glass bottles of *attar* and tiny phials of *surma* (kohl) might possibly direct us to where hookah pipes may be re-twined with silver wire. They are the last vestiges of the *nawabi* style once cultivated in these quarters. In

8.3 *View of Chitpur with the Nakhoda Mosque. Desmond Doig*

the middle of the last century, the towering minarets of the present Nakhoda Mosque (built in 1926) had not yet appeared; but that part of Lower Chitpur Road rivalled the Chandni Chowk of Delhi. Its display of hookah bases – crystal, silver, or damascene-worked in the style of Bidar – have disappeared. The Kabuliwalas have taken their chappal trade to Mominpur. Yet, as Id approaches, Holy Qurans in decorated jackets and boxes, with carved wooden rests, appear in greater numbers on shop counters. *Lucknowi kurtas, burkhas, zari*-worked red-and-blue velvet caps and waistcoats are laid out for the festive day. Piles of dates and vermicelli line the road to prayer. At Muharram again, Chitpur Road resounds to breast-beating and cries of *Hasan Husain*.

Elaborately crafted paper-and-foil *tazias* emerge from Golkuthi Imambara, which also houses a little school run by a Mrs Aaron.

Chitpur does not exhaust its treasures. Marble shops that once supplied Italian tiles and statuary to the mansions and baroque gardens of the grandees, now exhibit stone angels from old cemeteries. In one of the few surviving shops, the white lions of the Ashoka Pillar are supported by the black headstone from the grave of William Makepeace Thackeray's sister.

Kalutola's fruit stalls, patronized by the Jewish community, still offer the pick of the orchards of Kulu and Kashmir, Malda and Muzaffarpur. A narrow entrance on Lower Chitpur Road leads into Tiretta Bazar, the colonnaded arcade where Armenians and Portuguese shopped for birds and beasts. This was the market for selective shoppers: it stocked the choicest foodstuffs, cigars and shoes. Edward Tiretta, a Venetian exile who became Calcutta's Superintendent of Streets and Bazaars, built this market. It fetched him an income of Rs 3,500 in 1783. However, bankruptcy drove him to offer this valuable property as first prize in a lottery. Charles Weston, who lived opposite, won it – only to auction it for Rs 3 lakh to Maharaja Tej Chandra of Bardhaman, whose heirs still own the market. The leopard cubs and columns are gone; instead, electrical fittings and TV trolleys are set out for sale among high-rise buildings.

Though Calcutta's Chinatown around Chhatawala Gali has migrated eastwards, the Wanley and Foley shoe-shops and Mao's Dental Clinic have resisted the move. And true connoisseurs of Chinese food find fresh bean curd, Chinese sausage and authentic spices in the tiny shops behind Poddar Court. Chitpur is Calcutta's museum: all the city's communities, its social classes, men and women of all periods of its history, find their nook or monument here. Which means, in effect, that the street belongs to all India.

CALCUTTA AND THE CURRENTS OF HISTORY
1690–1912

Pradip Sinha

Imperial Durbar. Tuesday, 12th December 1911. The correspondent of *Capital,* the organ of Calcutta's European business community, expressed shock and surprise at the announcement of the transfer of the capital from Calcutta to Delhi. 'This was a bolt from the blue,' he wrote, 'and the Durbaris were so taken by surprise that they forgot to demonstrate... . There was a large consensus of opinion at Delhi that the strongest motive underlying the change was the desire of the Simla clique to be removed as far as possible from the influence of public opinion as expressed by the organs of the independent press.'

The nature of the penalty was obvious: Calcutta would suffer financially and commercially. It would remain a great seaport and centre of trade in jute, coal and tea, but a vast diversion of import traffic might follow as a result of the railway war that had been going on for some years. The *Englishman* deplored the 'thoughtless infliction of loss on a progressive community'. A British commentator called it an 'administrative earthquake'.

A letter from the Secretary of the Bengal Chamber of Commerce to the Home Secretary of the Goverment of India was more moderately worded, but expressed a hope that Delhi would be merely a ceremonial capital while the Department of Commerce and Industry remained in Calcutta. Calcutta was perceived as the foremost commercial centre of India, the Queen of the East. The Master of the Calcutta Trades Association referred movingly to this image at their annual dinner following the transfer of the capital: 'We have heard much lately of the history of Calcutta being the history of India.... Calcutta has been made by her trade.' As a punning correspondent of *The Statesman,* very likely a European 'burgess' in Calcutta, observed: 'the CAPITAL is, and always will be, in CALCUTTA.' Such confidence was far from untypical; but it was mixed with apprehension that the city might now lose its pre-eminence unless its citizens made extraordinary efforts to prevent it.

The transfer of the capital left the Bengalis of Calcutta relatively calm. *The Bengalee,* edited by the veteran nationalist leader Surendranath Banerji, published a manifesto welcoming the move. It was signed by some of the foremost leaders of Bengali public opinion. They admitted the controversy, but argued that the transfer might actually serve local interests and aspirations by leading to provincial autonomy for Bengal. At the same time, the restoration of Delhi to its former glory, they continued, 'must appeal to the patriotic and loyal sentiments of all true-hearted Indians'.

The manifesto signals the evolution of an important segment of the urban community in Calcutta: the upper middle class of professionals and publicists that acquired prominence in the late nineteenth century. In the early twentieth century they formed a cohesive social unit, central to the development of so-called New

India, with an outlook operating concentrically at regional, pan-Indian and worldwide range. Regionally it stood for a united Bengal of Hindus and Muslims: it therefore welcomed the creation of a new Bengal Presidency out of what was called Bengal Proper. This is no way conflicted with a pan-Indian outlook of which Delhi was conceived as a symbol. Its world outlook embodied liberalism, involving social and religious reform, freedom of opinion, racial equality and constitutionalism.

Insofar as this social stratum represented a class, it was a transmuted form of the traditional literati-cum-gentry. Its links with mercantile interests had almost been severed through a century of development. A British merchant, an important member of the Bengal Chamber of Commerce, noted in 1912 'the process whereby Bengalis have been almost entirely ousted from their natural share in the internal distributing and banking trade'. Their resulting state provided a fertile seed-bed for ideologues and liberal cosmopolitans, but it was somewhat removed from the world of reality. To these people, the economic consequences of the transfer of capital could appear mundane indeed. The British business interests might look for an ally in this 'progressive community', but that expectation went against the spirit of the situation.

The Beginnings

Calcutta was basically a commercial city, a port town where both Europeans and Bengalis had made fortunes in the late eighteenth and early nineteenth centuries. The foundation of the British settlement in 1690 was a natural consequence of the shifting centre of gravity of India's external trade from western to southern to eastern India. Bengal was to emerge as the premier trading region of the East India Company in the eighteenth century. When Charnock established a trading settlement on the site of Calcutta in 1690, after two abortive attempts and a brief war with the Mughals (1688-89), his aim was to set up a fortified centre that, along with Bombay and Madras, would complete a triangle of British power. It was a lucky accident that in 1696 a local rebellion by Sobha Singh, a feudal lord of southern Bengal, provided a threat to security that enabled the British to obtain the Mughal Governor or Nawab's permission to erect Fort William. In 1698 the British position was

further strengthened by the purchase of zamindari rights to the villages of Sutanuti, Gobindapur and Kalikata.

With the expansion of the textile trade, the East India Company began to view Bengal as the rising investment area in India. The Company had long been aware of the productive potential of Bengal and its contribution to international trade. Bengal was India's granary; it supplied India and the world with muslin and silk yarn; it had abundant stock of saltpetre. These last three products gave it paramount importance for the European trading companies. Adam Smith noted how the economic capability of Bengal derived from an extensive home market based upon inland navigation.

Apart from this key role in commerce, Bengal from the mid-eighteenth century supplied the wherewithal with which the growing colonial state could be sustained, especially after the Permanent Settlement of Bengal revenue in 1798. By 1856-57 Bengal contributed 44 per cent of the total British Indian revenue, this being 260 per cent more than Bombay. The share had declined by 1884-85, but even then it represented nearly 25 per cent of the total or 160 per cent more than Bombay.

These figures tell a story about Bengal's position in modern India and Calcutta's in modern Bengal. Bengal can be seen as the most exploited region in colonial India with Calcutta as the nodal point of this process of exploitation, which disrupted the internal dynamics of Bengal's decentralized system of production. In spite of its productive capacity, eighteenth-century Bengal did not have the type of urban agglomeration that we find in the Surat manufacturing zone in western India. Manufacture was carried on in smaller clusters, more rural than urban, though there were the two urban centres of Dhaka and Murshidabad. Calcutta made a rude intrusion into this scene, disrupting a harmony of centuries. It grew as a typically colonial city, linking the hinterland of primary production with the plantation and mining enclaves, and exporting the entire product (as well as providing the services involved) in the interests of an externally-oriented imperial economy. Hence it flourished as long as the resources of its hinterland were of paramount importance in the colonial economy; when this ceased to be the case in the

early twentieth century, its development was interrupted at a vital point of growth. Anthropologist Nirmalkumar Basu called Calcutta a 'premature metropolis'; we may perhaps also call it an incomplete one.

The cleavage in Calcutta's urban fabric into a European and an Indian town was a physical manifestation of two processes, sometimes contradictory to each other. At the economic level, the European or White Town tended to specialize in a relatively narrow sector of the total economic life of Calcutta – narrow but highly capital-intensive and part of a global network or system. It was an artifact of planning and high-level real estate development. Warren Hastings, apart from his role as Governor General (1774–85), was an avid real-estate developer and institution-builder. Wellesley, Governor-General from 1798 to 1805, was determined to leave behind the country-house mentality that had governed the growth of the White Town till his day, and build on a grand scale. He transformed the White Town into an almost exemplary artifact of colonial settlement.

The Indian or Black Town, on the other hand, reflected in its physical set-up those principles which distinguished its communities from the European ones. It was a teeming settlement which a European visitor described as the New Babylon, a huge and mixed crowd of people many of whom were only marginally connected with the main channels of economic activity in the zone. Its original nucleus was the Great Bazaar, expanding from a yarn and textile mart into one of the largest wholesale markets in India. By the late nineteenth century the pan-Indian business communities had established their hold over it, while, generally speaking, the regional Bengali business community withdrew to join the expanding group of urban landlords. The Banians and Diwans – intermediaries of the English in trade and administration – began to set up their own clusters of great households surrounded by tenements of servitors and rent payers.

The new middle class accommodated itself within this spatial entity, modifying the latter as it grew, and developed as minor functionaries of an all-India administrative and commercial network. The components of this network introduced new elements in the urban set-up not organically related to the Indian experience. But at a cognitive level, the expanding White Town made little impact on the Native Town as a whole except in institutional-cum-recreational centres such as College Street and Cornwallis Street, which were quietly absorbed in the local life-style.

The Indian and European Towns were in fact the two broad divisions of a spatial entity which also accommodated the nuclei of other towns – Mughal, Jewish, Armenian, Chinese, Anglo-Indian, Marwari, traditional Bengali and so on.

9.1 A 'White' quarter: Old Court House Street. T. & W. Daniell

9.2 *'Native' huts facing grander buildings. View of Clive Street. D'Oyly*

The Reverend James Long, Calcutta's pioneer sociologist, drew attention to this complex constitution of the city in 1872. In the 1860s Bholanath Chandra, a Bengali traveller to Delhi, observed that the real Chandni Chowk was not there but on Chitpur Road in Calcutta. In its historical context Calcutta therefore unfolds a personality associated with colonial, Asian, macro-Indian and regional traditions. To Bhabanicharan Banerji (1787-1848), a Sanskritist serving in the new role of editor of a Bengali newspaper, Calcutta was like the sea: streams of money flowed away from it and rivers of money flowed into it. Yet the Sanskrit scholar felt exhilarated by the presence in the city of not only the Goddess of Wealth but Narayana, the ultimate god of the Hindu pantheon, tranquil and serene.

The mosaic of Calcutta was made up at least in part from pre-colonial tradition. It transformed compradors into Rajas; showered wealth upon Mughals, Armenians, Jews and others; nurtured the *gharanas* of classical music and dance alongside a vital popular culture of impromptu songs, theatricals and mime. The tableaux vivantes of Calcutta painted by Kaliprasanna Sinha in his *Hutom Penchar Naksha* ('The Screech-Owl's Sketches', 1862) could as well have come from Chunchura, Hugli or any other of those mercantile centres where Indians and Europeans met in a non-colonial setting.

The New Urban Class: Endeavours and Aspirations

The colonial context changed the nature of this concourse of cultures. It threw up a class, neither feudal nor bourgeois, that fostered a development of all-India significance: India's earliest modern culture, an expansive force if only up to a point. Yet it lacked some of the basic material and structural elements of modernization. Periodically in the nineteenth and early twentieth centuries, it attempted to build a material base in business, industry or technology; but its aspirations were more striking than its achievements.

By the end of the nineteenth century, the culture of subordination of a subject race was giving way to the assertion of a new state of mind. To describe it as elitist, confined to the literati-cum-gentry or *bhadralok,* would be to limit oneself by a functionalist approach to history. The intensity of the mental processes involved raised it above mere demand for a share of the loaves and fishes by a 'microscopic minority', as the shrewd but somewhat threatened Europeans saw it. What happened to that mentality later in the twentieth century, and whether it got lost in an era of mass politics, is another story.

Within our period, that intensity of mind elevated the tone of public life and left a cultural legacy as well. To a sensitive and relatively dispassionate observer like Henry W. Nevinson, publicist and traveller, it was an experience to observe Calcutta in 1907 during the early phases of nationalism. He heard a public speech by Surendranath Banerji:

Except for Mr. Gladstone, I have heard no speaker use the grand and rhetorical style of English with more assurance and success... . It was oratory such as, I suppose, Cicero loved to practise, and Pitt and Brougham – such oratory as few living Englishmen dare venture on for fear of drowning in the gulfs of bathos. But Surendra Nath loved it as Cicero might.

Nevinson might have noticed that Surendranath's contemporaries, though differing from him in some fundamental respects, shared his urge for elevation and excellence. For them standards had been set: the question was how to disseminate them. Nevinson wrote:

There is a religious tone, a spiritual elevation... characteristic of Arabindo Ghose himself and of all Bengali Nationalists contrasted with the shrewd political judgement of the Poona Extremists. In an age of supernatural religion Arabindo would have become what the irreligious mean by a fanatic... . He was of the stuff that dreamers are made of, but dreamers who will act their dream... .

Nevinson did not meet or write about Rabindranath Thakur (Tagore). Like Arabinda, Rabindranath would have emphasized the need for courage in a subject race – an inner self-generated strength or *atmashakti*. That inner strength sustained the endeavour to be a complete man.

A harmony pitched so high might have proved difficult to sustain, defeated by over-exertion of the self or by the immediate social environment. Swami Vivekananda tried to beat this possibility, at the cost of some suffering to himself. And a certain sadness was associated with Rabindranath Thakur.

By the beginning of the twentieth century, Bengali aspirations sought new outlets through the Swadeshi movement. Its early phase was marked by a breezy optimism, an expectation of new horizons being opened up – Calcutta merging with the rest of Bengal and with India. Yet frustration lurked beneath the surface. Committed to creating a new India, Calcutta was itself threatened by an emerging communal divide, a new type of politics exploiting locality, province and nation.

Despite a hundred and fifty years of urbanization, Calcutta was placed in the least urbanized region of India by the end of the nineteenth century. In 1891, the proportion of urban to total population in the Bengal Presidency was 4.8 per cent, in Madras 9.9 per cent, in the North-West Provinces (U.P.) 11.3 per cent, and in Bombay 19.5 per cent. The overwhelming predominance of Calcutta further reduced urban growth elsewhere in Bengal. The educated Bengalis were probably the largest urbanized community in India; but their links with rural Bengal, except through their kin the landed rural literati, were particularly weak. Having no control over the new productive forces, they could act as an urbanizing force in the city's rural hinterland only to a very limited extent or not at all. But as has been pointed out, they could and must needs move in the opposite direction, upwards, trying to storm the very citadels of imperial rule.

The Rise of Nationalist Sentiment

How is he, who has appreciated the genius of Shakespeare and Bacon ... who has read and discussed so much about the equality of man, to bear the insolence of the civil servant or of the low-born English merchant whom he is obliged to call his master?

9.3 *Arabinda Ghosh*

35

9.4 *Surendranath Banerji*

The situation was favourable for literary activities oriented towards nationalism. Dinabandhu Mitra's *Nildarpan* ('The Mirror of Indigo'), published in 1860, was the first political drama in Bengali literature. In 1873–74 Bankimchandra Chatterji gave the literary renaissance a steady direction through *Bangadarshan,* a literary journal reflecting awareness of a national cultural identity.

This interpretation of culture as a basis for national identity was influenced by symbols and images generally associated with the Hindu tradition. Rajnarayan Basu's *Hindu Dharmer Shreshthata* ('The Superiority of the Hindu Religion') was described as 'the first public assertion of the age-long Nation-spirit against the threatened domination of our thought and life by the aggressive and colour-proud civilization of Europe'. Rajnarayan presented the philosophical monism of the Upanishads as the governing principle of Hindu thought.

At the social level, the new cultural-literary activity stood for a certain degree of conservatism. The social reform movement, including the new marriage law for the Brahmos, came in for criticism as being imitative of Western customs and institutions. It was felt that petitioning a foreign government for reform measures tended to strengthen the hold of an external political authority by adding to it a moral and spiritual force.

The era was, however, politically dominated by Surendranath Banerji (1848–1925), who infused into the youth of Calcutta an admiration for Joseph Mazzini and his Young Italy movement. Surendranath took a leading part in the foundation of the Indian Association in 1876 and conceived it as a kind of Indian Parliament with constituencies spread over the subcontinent. It became an important forum of Indian public opinion on political questions, and was the main organizational force behind the All-India National Conference held in Calcutta in 1883. The Conference later merged with the Indian National Congress at Surendranath's initiative.

The Congress was set up largely at the initiative of the retired English civilian Allan Octavian Hume: his first move had been to address an open letter to the graduates of Calcutta University in 1883. The inaugural session was actually held at Bombay in December 1885, under the chairmanship of a

The words are from Girishchandra Ghosh (1829–69), a leading journalist of mid-nineteenth-century Calcutta. The educated Bengali, he wrote in 1858 (immediately after the suppression of the Revolt of 1857), would not behave 'in the style of an Eastern slave when addressing his Emperor'.

One of the early incidents that triggered off the 1857 Revolt had occurred at Barrackpur, near Calcutta, when the sepoy Mangal Pandey refused to bite on cartridges greased with animal fat. But the Revolt itself left Calcutta and Bengal virtually unscathed in a direct or military sense. The 'educated Bengali' pledged his loyalty to the British Empire in 1857; but he also sought to assert his identity as a member of a self-respecting community. He ridiculed the Europeans in Calcutta for their panic at the Revolt and for exaggerating the atrocities committed by the rebels, calling the Europeans 'atrocity-mongers'. In a forceful article in the *Hindoo Patriot* entitled 'Who are the People of India?', Girishchandra poured scorn on 'the class of European writers who maintain that we have no civilization, no public opinion or national feeling'.

1861 saw the 'Blue Mutiny' in Bengal, when farmers rose against the forcible cultivation of the unremunerative indigo crop. This offered an unprecedented opportunity to the educated community in Calcutta to close its ranks and come out in protest against the tyranny of the European indigo planters.

Calcutta lawyer, Umeshchandra Banerji ('Woomesh Chunder' or W. C. Bonnerjee, 1844-1906). The second session of the National Conference was held at Calcutta at about the same time, and the second session of the Congress followed there in 1886.

The Indian Association, the Indian National Conference and the Indian National Congress in its early phase were concerned with similar issues. In its first session in Calcutta, the National Conference debated over questions of industrial and technical education, larger participation of Indians in the Civil Service, separation of the executive from the judiciary, and more representation of Indians in the governance of the country. Till 1905, the year of the Partition of Bengal, the Indian National Congress passed resolutions almost along the same lines, though perhaps in a broader perspective.

The Partition of Bengal in 1905 gave a rude shock to the 'constitutional method' of agitation. A younger section of Congressmen, led by Balgangadhar Tilak from Maharashtra, Lajpat Rai from Punjab and Arabinda Ghosh and Bipinchandra Pal from Calcutta, wanted an end to mere talk and a recourse to action. At the Congress session held in Calcutta in 1906, Dadabhai Naoroji declared that 'India should have *Swaraj*, like that of the United Kingdom or the Colonies'.

The Partition of Bengal in 1905 might well have been justified in administrative terms. Bengal was indeed a very large and populous province and the outlying regions, especially the eastern districts with a Muslim majority, tended to be neglected. Hence the rationale behind Lord Curzon's order dividing the Bengal Presidency into two parts: Eastern Bengal and Assam with a population of 31 million, and the rest of the area with a population of 54 million comprising 18 million Bengalis and 36 million Biharis and Oriyas. But the political result of such a partition was likely to benefit the ruling power. 'Bengal united is a Power, Bengal divided will pull in different ways .... One of our main objects is to split up and thereby to weaken a solid body of opponents to our rule,' wrote Risley, Home Secretary to the Government of India.

In the Swadeshi Movement that followed the agitation over the Partition of Bengal, Bengal politics started moving in a direction which moderates like Surendranath Banerji found increasingly difficult to control. Apart from the rise of extremism, political Swadeshi carried things to a point where many of the issues of future Indian politics – including boycott and passive resistance, the relations between Hindus and Muslims and those between the elite and the masses – came up as on a tide. After the Swadeshi movement Calcutta, so far the nerve–centre of Indian politics, did not offer a suitable ground for a dispassionate appraisal of its political background. The literary and cultural movement seems to have gained a new momentum and afforded relative security for the majority of the elite, while a more assertive participation in politics could be largely left to the revolutionary movement or terrorism.

Surendranath, the 'uncrowned king of Bengal' till the first phase of the Swadeshi movement, receded into the background with his politics of moderation. Ultimately, he became almost a tragic figure on Calcutta's political scene, believing that the Bengali community in Calcutta would still hold on to nineteenth-century liberal ideals and to the possibility of a steady adjustment with the ruling power and European interests.

The community had meanwhile acquired new and more radical attitudes, though often beneath a veneer of suave culture. To such a people, the British mercantile community might have intermittently held out the olive branch, as the *Englishman* did in 1912. But one fears that more often, the sahibs shook their heads and said that these people were impossible, that they did not play the game. Even Rabindranath Thakur, coming from a family described by the *Hindoo Patriot* in 1879 as 'Europeans among Bengalis', was not amenable to the reasonable compromises expected of his class. He had indeed compared the Government of India to a circus company, 'skilfully directing a dance of strange and wonderful animals of diverse species staged before the civilized world'.

The Bengali memory could hardly be free from old wounds. Subhashchandra Basu, who had come down from Cuttack to Calcutta and imbibed the political spirit of the city, sought to explain the psychological situation in the early twentieth century:

The [revolutionary] movement was born out of a conviction that to a western people physical force alone makes an appeal... . In the street, in the railway, in the tramcars, in public places and in

public functions, in fact everywhere, the Britisher expected the Indian to make way for him, and if he refused to do so, the Indian would be assaulted... . The trouble began with Macaulay... . [He] wrote a scathing denunciation of the Bengalees and called them a race of cowards. That calumny went deep into the hearts of the Bengalee people.

Yet Macaulay's name was associated with a system of education that had given shape to the urban educated Bengali community. The conflicts arising from the situation could partly account for the intensity of personalities like Subhashchandra's. One way of avoiding the conflict was to divide one's world into two compartments: an intellectual life fed by Byron and Shelley, Mill and Huxley, and a domestic life of wry or indulgent compliance with the traditional social order. The majority of educated Bengalis appear to have settled down to this double life, as the Report of the Calcutta University Commission (1917-19) noted.

But an interaction of the two spheres was inevitable. Throughout the nineteenth century, the urban Bengali sought to evolve structures of life ranging from Anglicism through Brahmoism to neo-Hinduism. The quest involved issues of import for Indian society as a whole: inter-caste marriage, for example, or the joint family or attitudes to elders. The innovations had somehow to be wedded to tradition.

Rameshchandra Datta (1848-1909), civilian, Sanskritist, historian and novelist, wrote a letter of great documentary interest to his son-in-law in 1894. He agrees that the young man should not degrade himself by penance for the 'sin' of crossing the ocean to England. He should also use his own discretion in choosing a 'partner for life'. But let that 'partner' conform to Hindu usage in her conduct, and let the son too conciliate his father. 'We depart from them [old Hindu customs] only when we do so on principle', as with inter-caste marriage or widow remarriage, 'so that the greater Hindu society, of which we are only a portion and the advance guard, may take heart and follow.'

That concluding optimism was characteristic of a section of the urban community in Calcutta. The urban Bengali's experiments with structures of life were a continuing process from Rammohan Ray onwards. In his preface to the `Kena Upanishad` (1817), Rammohan expressed his desire to correct 'the

9.5 Rameshchandra Datta

38

exceptionable practices [of caste rituals and discriminations] which not only deprive Hindus, in general, of the common comforts of society but lead them frequently to self-destruction.' In the course of the century, interdining and commensality became usual among educated males. The students' 'messes' in the city served to extend the urban custom among young men from rural areas.

But of course, the adaptation of a traditional society to a new urban environment was a long and complicated process. The urban Bengali in the early nineteenth century might have tried to 'cut his way through beef and ham and wade through bottles of beer', or greeted the goddess Kali with 'Good morning, Madam.' But the situation did not present clear-cut alternatives, rather a dilemma: hence we find all kinds of permutations and combinations.

Caste: Rejections and Transformations

How the institution of caste fared in the new urban situation is difficult to document. An interesting viewpoint is revealed by the sociologist Bhupendranath Datta, Swami Vivekananda's brother and one of the early Indian Marxists, in his *Swami Vivekananda, Patriot and Prophet*, while explaining the contemporary dominant role of his own caste, the Kayasthas. The Kayasthas had backed the Afghans against the Mughals in the sixteenth century. The Afghan defeat ousted the Kayasthas from their proud position of landlords in favour of the Rarhi Brahmins of western Bengal. British rule gave them the chance to hit back and rehabilitate themselves. They now learnt English, as formerly Persian. A liberal force grew up among them, and they took a leading role in socio-religious movements which broke caste rules or at least deviated from caste orthodoxy.

In the late eighteenth century, however, the Kayasthas among the urban rich often took it upon themselves to organize the amorphous urban society along clearly orthodox lines. Raja Nabakrishna Deb, the former Political Banian of the East India Company, sought to organize his own sub-caste in 1781 through a conference of genealogists, men of unsullied caste or *kulins*, and representatives of families belonging to his sub-caste. He was thereby aspiring to acquire the position of *goshthipati* or leader of a sub-caste, which represented *samaj* or society for all practical purposes. In course of time, new aspirants to the position split even the sub-caste into factions. Ostracism was one way by which a social leader could enforce caste orthodoxy. But the attempt to combine the factions under the umbrella of *dharma* or the ideology of social order failed. A regimented caste society came under attack from within as well as from new forces. 'Caste – that is in my cashbox,' the millionaire Ramdulal Dey is reported to have said while opposing the ostracism of his benefactor's son.

Later in the nineteenth century Christianity, Brahmoism, sea-voyages, interdining, widow remarriage, inter-caste marriage and tensions within joint families were causing all kinds of strain within the caste structure. Bhupendranath Datta narrates how Gobindachandra Datta of the Datta family of Rambagan made a sea-voyage to Bombay to take up a lucrative post. Disgusted by the penance he was made to undergo, he turned Christian. Alternatively, such a person could become a 'Hindu revolutionary'.

In the final analysis, caste survived through the institution of marriage as enforced through that other traditional institution, the joint family. Caste ideology operated through what may be called the purity syndrome as represented in the family by the child-wife and the widow. Hence, with some exceptions, the educated middle class of Calcutta voiced strong protest against the Age of Consent Bill of 1891, which sought to raise the minimum age at marriage for girls from ten to twelve. But it must be recognized that the force of the protest was not normal for that time; practices were changing, albeit slowly.

The situation is clearly reflected in an account of Calcutta student life in 1912-13 by the linguist-to-be Sunitikumar Chatterji (1890-1977). That life demonstrated, he says, 'the mind of civilized man in its various stages. The twentieth century jostles with the eighth or twelfth century, mid-Victorian England and eighteenth-century France with sixteenth-century Bengal... .' A major characteristic was 'equality': caste pride, very rarely displayed, was treated with a good-humoured rebuff. Another feature was the 'marriage epidemic', to which Third and Fifth Year students (i.e., between eighteen and twenty-one) were most susceptible. Educated youths were having more and more voice in the choice of their brides; but as etiquette forbade them to see the girl before

9.6 *Above:* 'A *Light Refreshment'* : *Brahmins taking 'forbidden food' in a European restaurant. Gaganendranath Thakur*

9.7 *Below: Sunitikumar Chatterji*

the wedding, their intimate friends would be deputed for the purpose. For the girl to claim a reciprocal liberty was, of course, virtually inconceivable as yet, except among the Brahmos.

A lesser but more direct challenge to tradition was posed by the 'heterodox luncheon' – a Western-style meal in a restaurant in a cosmopolitan part of the town. Orthodox Hindus abhorred such unsanctified eating-places; they grew increasingly popular with students, acquiring with them some of the functions of the continental café.

At the centre of it all, Chatterji observed, stood the Calcutta University Institute. With its library and reading room, its athletic section and rowing club, its social gatherings, dramatics and various other facilities for students of all colleges to meet each other, the Institute was a cultural centre and a nursery of talents of all descriptions. It was, concludes Chatterji, undoubtedly one of the best clubs in India, aiming at the 'moral and intellectual improvement of the students and the educated classes'.

Swadeshi and the Crisis of the Urban Middle Class

Sunitikumar belonged to that early twentieth century milieu of cultivated hilarity which prevailed alongside an atmosphere of high seriousness. Politics, terrorism and mysticism were serious business. The Calcutta Bengali

would not have survived if he did not have another compartment to his mind, filled with fun, music, relaxed conversation and nonsense. Sunitikumar's friend Sukumar Ray, the writer of nonsense verse, formed an informal association called the Monday Club, a weekly get-together of gourmets and raconteurs with no particular purpose. And *adda* itself was virtually institutionalized around this time.

Yet from the turn of the century, the Bengali *bhadralok* could not avert a sense of crisis. In an article entitled 'The Problems of Life in Bengal', the *Hindoo Patriot* referred to several depressing factors: the rising cost of food and curtailed resources of the family bread-winner, turning his remoter dependants adrift; as also new 'artificial' wants, created by English education and contact with Englishmen, often not matched by the means to meet them. 'The number of educated men is annually increasing by thousands, and how are they to live?' The job market was overcrowded, and the victims had neither experience in agriculture nor capital to set up in trade.

As the organ of the British Indian Association, representing a relatively well-to-do section of Bengali urban society, the *Hindoo Patriot* could not fully reflect the intensity of the crisis. It emerges in journals like the *Amrita Bazar Patrika* and *Sadharani*. The thin upper crust of the *bhadralok* could take up law, medicine or uncovenanted civil and judicial

service; a few more could turn into rentiers-cum-printers or similar mutants. The greater and humbler section were consigned to petty employment under the colonial state and the commercial firms. That their bookish education was inadequate for an expanding community, under pressure from below by new upwardly-mobile social groups, was keenly felt and strongly expressed by Praphullachandra Ray (1861-1944), India's pioneer experimental chemist and founder of the chemical and pharmaceutical industry in the country.

In *Bangalir Mastishka o Tar Apabyabahar* ('The Bengali Brain and Its Misuse', 1910), Praphullachandra hit out at conventional college education as the worst constraint on aptitudes for applied science, industrial skills and money-making pursuits. In his own life he succeeded as an experimental chemist, pioneer industrialist and businessman. He had a touching faith in the Swadeshi spirit and considered the Partition of Bengal to be a godsend: 'Curzon indirectly acted as the awakener of Bengal,' he wrote in his *Life and Experiences of a Bengali Chemist*.

Praphullachandra was not a political man, but politics was only one band in the complex Swadeshi spectrum. It constituted a whole set of beliefs and actions aimed at lifting Bengal out of the rut into which she was perceived as having fallen. Despite its emotionalism and

9.8
Praphullachandra Ray

9.9 *'Indian Ink : The ink cannot be washed out.' Cartoon on Praphullachandra Ray's Swadeshi endeavours. Gaganendranath Thakur*

quixotic aspects, it induced serious thinking and action in an entire generation, extending from Calcutta to interior towns and remote villages. The phenomenon was broadly identified with what was called 'nation-building activity'.

Swadeshi can also be viewed as the attempt by a metropolitan community to broaden its base. In its initial stage the movement generated great hope. A leading journal, *Dawn,* edited by the Swadeshi ideologue Satishchandra Mukherji (1865-1948), commented in 1908 that Bengal had led the rest of India in the development of an Indian Swadeshi ideology permeating all classes, transcending caste and creed. It was expected to signal the dawn of a new India with an industrial and commercial future.

This optimism persisted till the thirties. In his *The Economic Expansion of the Bengali People* (1934), the sociologist Binaykumar Sarkar (1887-1949) referred to the structural changes in Bengali society. There were institutions which did not exist in urban Bengal a generation ago: chambers of commerce and other trade associations as well as trade unions. The lower orders were getting involved in organized movements. The Bengali people had acquired new qualifications, attitudes, activities and professions, creating new social groups like company promoters and directors, bank managers, insurance agents, manufacturers, exporters and importers. In Bombay, Punjab and the Central Provinces, Bengali coal merchants were as prominent as Bengali chemists and engineers.

Binaykumar also highlighted the progress made by Bengalis as manufacturers and merchants over the two previous decades. Their enterprises were small in size but large in number, thereby differing from the scenario in Bombay. Binaykumar realized that Bengali capital was still at the 'kindergarten stage' of modern capitalism. He suggested collaboration with Marwari and British capital. Bengalis were still a poor people, he observed, and the progress of Bengal was to be viewed as the amelioration of poverty.

The awareness of poverty was quite real, and co-existed with optimism of Binaykumar's variety. Two significant documents of the early twentieth century bear testimony to the Bengali predicament: the Report of the Calcutta University Commission (1917-19) under Sir

Michael Sadler, and the Minutes of Evidence before the Indian Industrial Commission (1916-17). The Sadler Commission observed that the contrast between Indian and Western cultures was creating painful dilemmas for the thoughtful student in Bengal. Behind the new foreign literature and philosophy, with the invisible influences operating through them, there stood the image of colossal power, mainfested through political achievements, stupendous industrialism, the triumph of applied science and immeasurable resources of wealth.

There was a strong feeling among educated Bengalis that the swelling stream of wealth had somehow passed them by to benefit the European merchant or the non-Bengali Indian trader. They expected a skilled working class to grow in the industrial belt to relieve the distress of the poorer section of the middle class and divert them from ill-paid sedentary jobs. Even a philosopher like Brajendranath Sheel (1864-1938) remarked: 'We Bengalis are backward in mechanical and manipulative dexterity... . A writ of *mandamus* is necessary to overcome the *non possumus* of our "pure culture man".'

In the Minutes of Evidence before the Indian Industrial Commission, the number of aspiring entrepreneurs from Calcutta is striking. Their basic problem was lack of capital. They might get credit from suppliers, but if the demand for their product fell, they must needs run to Marwari money-lenders, who charged a ruinously high rate of interest. Hence the would-be entrepreneurs demanded an industrial bank with government support to finance small industries. With collateral improvements in agricultural technique, there would be a definite improvement in the condition of the people. Some of the witnesses before the Commission had returned from Japan or Germany, and urged the Japanese model of industrialization where the state played a major role.

The Secretary of the Indian Mining Federation pointed out another interesting feature of Bengali capital. The few rich families were employing their wealth chiefly in trades like rice and jute, and in money-lending. The new industries derived their capital from middle-class savings, which were necessarily limited. This paradox of the poor middle class representing a major source of capital was also emphasized by other witnesses. A witness

9.10 *Binaykumar Sarkar*

pointed moreover to a sharp division in the middle class itself. Its upper section aspired after judgeships, seats on the Executive Council, lucrative practices at the bar or fame in journalism or politics. They were thus bartering their jewels for broken glass, as the Sanskrit proverb has it.

The most trenchant paradox was that the Swadeshi Movement, which began in Bengal, should finally have benefited the manufactures of other Indian states at Bengal's expense. The point was made by Praphullachandra Ray and some other leading citizens of Calcutta in a memorandum, *Swaraj and Economic Bengal*. It was also the leading theme of S. Wajid Ali (1890-1951), a cultivated Muslim barrister of Calcutta, in his *Bengalees of Tomorrow*, published in 1945 but largely written much earlier. The Bengali middle class, said Ali, had set India on the course of modernization of ideas. Now the Bengalis themselves must accept the logic of the consequent economic gospel.

The new realism in Calcutta society was supposed to have been an antidote to Swadeshi emotionalism. Yet the Swadeshi impulse, in so far as it stood for a newly awakened national self-respect, had achieved significant success in the metropolitan Bengali's traditional fields of activity. Ashutosh Mukherji's (1864-1924) genius for organization attracted all-India and to some extent world attention to scientific research at Calcutta University. The organization of the laboratories was seen as not only an academic programme but a national achievement. One of Ashutosh's foremost collaborators in this respect was Praphullachandra Ray, despite their differences over other issues. As a student at Edinburgh, Praphullachandra had seen the original work being done by Japanese students of science 'while India ... was sleeping the sleep of ages ... It is a matter for sincere congratulation that contributions from our advanced post-graduate students now bulk largely in the pages of the chemical journals [of the world].'

But academic success alone could not satisfy Praphullachandra. The man was essentially kind – a Gandhian before Gandhi, a later convert to the spinning-wheel – but he was ruthless in the pursuit of success, though not for himself. Witnessing the failure of one Swadeshi industrial enterprise after another, he wrote: 'Apprenticeship in business should start

at a very early age. The *Mahajan gadi* is an ideal place for acquiring the skill of a bazaar merchant.'

The Marwaris

What Praphullachandra had in mind was the spectacular transformation of the Rajasthani or, as popularly termed, the Marwari community from traders to industrialists. The Bengali metropolitan community watched with wonder and some disbelief the changes at the apex of the social pyramid. From the labyrinth of Barabazar in central Calcutta was emerging a plutocracy by the side of the Bengali 'barrister-ocracy', 'advocatocracy' and related '-cracies'.

By the end of the nineteenth century quite a number of Marwari firms had operated from Barabazar for decades, and set up connections in the sprawling Bengal hinterland (particularly the jute-producing areas) through agents, branches and representatives. The vital new opening in jute was virtually monopolized by them in the Calcutta market. Almost equally important was their capture of the wholesale market in imported cloth; another sector was trade in pulses and *kirana* (spices, seeds etc.). Besides these, the Marwaris undertook commission agencies, brokerage for British firms and the highly lucrative traditional calling of indigenous bankers of *shroffs*. Thus stage by stage, the Marwaris replaced first the Bengalis and then the North Indian Khatris in the 'great bazaar' of Calcutta.

In the further metamorphosis into industrialists, their growing hold over the Calcutta share market seems to have been particularly significant. They were unsurpassed in getting advance news, as also in spreading false news and confusing the market to their advantage. Even the *Englishman* admitted that in the art of options, the Marwaris were masters.

The speculation markets of Calcutta suffered a setback with the outbreak of the First World War; but the growing defence demand for sandbags revived the sagging jute industry, while new possibilities for profit and speculation opened up in grain, cotton and specie. Fortunes were made and unmade. Thomas Timberg in *The Marwaris* has traced the career of Keshoram Poddar (1883-1945) from broker to prosperous merchant to leading stock market speculator who used his stock holdings to deal directly with large British jute-manufacturing firms. He imported sugar from Japan and Java during the wartime shortage; invested in real estate in Calcutta's European quarter; ran ferries; bought a colliery and a flour mill; took interest in brick kilns and caused rumours of having nearly cornered the brick market. He was worth about Rs 3 crore at his height, though he suffered a temporary crash after World War I.

Other Marwari houses entered industry more securely with their wartime profits. The most important of them was of course the Birlas. They built their first jute mill in Calcutta in 1919. By the 1930s there were four other Marwari jute mills in and near the city.

Till Independence, however, the Marwaris remained basically a community of traders, owing to both their conservatism and British obstructionism. Their evolution as a commercial community led to a degree of capital accumulation which the high-thinking Bengalis could not dream of matching. The sophisticated Bengali engineer R.N. Mukherji could build a spectacular organization on his own, using a European-type set-up, but capitalism can scarcely be an individual effort. The metropolitan Bengali had come to treat merely mercantile people as marginal. Binaykumar Sarkar talked about wedding College Street with Clive Street; but that remained an enticing vision, shaping Bengal's culture and fantasy rather than her economic life.

E. P. Richards, the idealistic architect of the Calcutta Improvement Trust, expressed utter and innocent surprise in his Report for the Trust in 1914. 'The value of jute that entered Calcutta in 1910-11 is put officially at over £ 10,000,000 and the value of the jute of all kinds exported was £ 23,000,000.' Why then was the city not exploiting this 'splendid trade' to best advantage?

Migration and labour

Richards was also concerned about the immense congestion in Calcutta's old native business district. A torrent of migration had started – of porters, carters, and a motley crowd of labourers, mainly from some districts of Bihar and eastern U.P. The Census Reports from 1891 to 1931 indicate the trend; but a systematic study of this vast unorganized sector has not been made. Some preliminary findings regarding the organized sector, especially the

jute inustry, have been presented by Ranajit Dasgupta.

Fifty jute mills had come up by 1911 within a radius of about forty miles from the city, employing 2,00,446 persons. A notable feature of this work-force was the gradual replacement of local by migrant labour. It has been marked that one significant trend of urban migration did not occur in Calcutta. Commonly the rural inhabitants immediately surrounding a growing city pour into it, the gap they leave being filled by migrants from remoter areas. But in Calcutta, The Royal Commission of Labour (1929) observed that the great majority of jute workers came from beyond a radius of 250 miles from the city. This was different not only from the classic models in England but also from other emerging industrial centres in India like Bombay, Ahmedabad or Kanpur. Some villages near Calcutta rapidly grew into jute-mill townships, but they remained islands in a deeply agrarian society.

Local labour was more important in metal-based and engineering industries, constituting a significant component of the skilled work-force. Here the Mahishyas, a Bengali agricultural-artisan caste group, made their presence felt first as skilled workers and later as entrepreneurs in small-scale engineering concerns. The artisan-turned-manufacturer is a classic phenomenon of social transformation. But it was more tantalizing than tangible in the social setting of the Calcutta region. The demand for skilled labour remained extremely limited, though a sociologist of the thirties talked about the 'mistrification' (*mistri*, mechanic) of Bengali society.

The economic expansion of Calcutta had peculiar repercussions on the sprawling Bengal countryside. Increased trade added to the price of agricultural produce, particularly from the 1870s onwards. Jute, the 'golden fibre', made its influence felt. But more interestingly, the metropolis had a 'leapfrogging' effect on the social consciousness of rural and rural-urban Bengal.

Signs of new consciousness among the peasantry were visible not so much in the districts close to the city as in remoter areas, particularly north and east Bengal, where pockets of relative prosperity emerged. The initial impact of British legal notions emanating from the metropolis kept certain sectors of rural society in a state of animation for a period. A new class or subclass of relatively prosperous peasants appeared in certain areas. They spearheaded new agrarian combinations against landlords and moneylenders. But a compromise followed. A growing reliance on agriculture among a mounting population led to meagre subsistence farming on increasingly fragmented holdings. This 'Malthusian agriculture', and the fading romance of jute, led to a depression in the 1920s and 1930s whose implications are still unexplored.

Looking back, it appears as though the watershed in the city's history, as perhaps that of Bengal and India, was the 1930s. For the Bengali metropolitan community, certainly, a cycle of experience ended with the end of the decade. Memoirs, and memories, of that period have yielded a substantial body of Bengali literature. One can even speak of the 'Golden Thirties' with a thriving commercial theatre, a pioneering film industry, Bengal's own traditions of music, the leisurely conversational sessions, football, politics, good scientists and Indologists, the spiritual legacy of the nineteenth century, terrorism, musclemen, the Bengali circus, novels of sentiment, the comparative freedom of women, and, over the entire scene, the presence of Rabindranath Thakur, the ultimate civilized man. But the idyll was less than total, and simple regret or nostalgia would be an inadequate response to its inevitable end. The real time of truth was soon to come, when war, famine, riots and Partition struck the city and the nation.

'FOREVER ENGLAND'
BRITISH LIFE IN
OLD CALCUTTA

Rudrangshu Mukherjee

The social life of the British in Calcutta in the late eighteenth and early nineteenth centuries was obviously moulded by the circumstances in which they found themselves. As these circumstances underwent remarkable and rapid changes over a few decades, their attitudes and ways of life also saw significant change. There were, however, some continuities.

The British came to Calcutta as traders. To back up the trade, they needed military personnel and bureaucrats. According to one calculation, before the Battle of Palashi (Plassey) there were seventy-six civil servants of the East India Company in Calcutta, and 260 British soldiers and officers at Fort William; the number of non-official Britons, i.e. those not in the employ of the Company, was less than a hundred. The Company's servants, writers, factors and merchants drew £10 to £40 as annual salary. Most if not all of them supplemented this income through private trade. Profits from this trade, particularly after Palashi, could be enormous: enough to transform an ordinary Englishman into a 'Nabob' with a large estate 'back home'.

By the beginning of the nineteenth century, however, the situation had changed. The Company's civil and military servants had increased in number. They had been forbidden private trade since 1787, but salaries were now very generous: up to £500 per annum after three years' service, £1,500 after six and £4,000 after twelve. In the army a Lieutenant drew about £250 and a Lieutenant-Colonel £1,500. Though lower than the salaries received by the civilians, the pay in the army was good by English standards.

In the days before Palashi most Britons, especially those in the service of the Company, lived in Fort William. Their quarters were neither attractive nor healthy. Unmarried officers were housed in rooms leading off a single corridor. These small chambers were supposed to combine the functions of parlour, bedroom and bath:

For the latter indispensable accessory to an Indian toilet, provisions had been made, by enclosing a corner of the room with a parapet a foot high, and by piercing the outer wall to let the water off. Naked and comfortless as any quarter in England, the appearance of this one was not rendered more prepossessing by the circumstances of the walls being adorned with sundry deep indentations, stains of suspicious colour, and a profuse sprinkling of ink, all of which told of the choleric temperament of a former occupant, probably some 'jolly cadet', who... impatient of the stupidity of a bearer or *Khidmutgar,* for being ignorant of *his* language, had perchance striven to render himself intelligible by hurling, in rapid succession, at the head of his domestic, an empty brandy bottle, a boot-jack, and an inkstand. [Quoted in Michael Edwardes, *The Sahibs and the Lotus : The British in India*]

We shall return to this passage in another connection, but for the moment let us look at the living conditions described. They are obviously not well suited for any kind of social life. The occupants of these gloomy barracks met for dinner and supper at a common table, taking their seats according to their rank; at the head of the table sat the governor. At night the gates of the Fort were shut.

Immediately after Palashi, things changed very fast. For one thing, and most importantly, new and previously inconceivable avenues of profit-making opened up for both the Company and its servants. Utilizing their political power in a variety of ways, the British established their domination over trade and, further, the production of a number of valuable commodities: textiles, salt, opium. This boom naturally led to changes in living conditions. Men could now afford to live spaciously and

luxuriously. This is Alexander Macrabie's description of his brother-in-law Philip Francis's house:

There is a drawing room on the upper storey about fifty feet long, a dining room below as large – besides two spacious halls, and a suite of three rooms upon each floor to the East and West – that is, fourteen rooms in all, with a principal staircase and two back staircases. The apartments are proportionately high. Twenty-five feet I believe.

One consequence of expansion and grandiose living was an enormous increase in house rent in the European part of Calcutta. Francis paid £1,200 per annum for his house, one of the best in town, and Hicky paid £300 a year for a *kutcha* house on the Esplanade. Away from the European quarter, rents were still low. Mrs Eliza Fay, the wife of a barrister of the Supreme Court, who lived in Calcutta from 1780 till her death in 1817, wrote in a letter:

Our house costs only 200 rupees per month because it is not a part of the town much esteemed: otherwise we must pay 3 or 400 rupees.

The houses in the 'White Town' were emblematic of the British dominance in Calcutta; so were the armies of servants that the more important Britishers employed. The number of servants was indeed indicative of status. Alexander Macrabie, the Sheriff of Calcutta, who lived with Francis, Livins and Collings in Francis's house ('chumming' being a common practice because of the housing shortage), wrote thus to his father in 1775:

My own Establishment consists of a Sircar, a Broker and Interpreter, – a Jemmadar [steward, head servant] who stands at my Door, receives messages, announces Visitors, and also runs by the side of my palanquin to clear the way. I am preceded in all my Peregrinations by two Peons or running Footmen and as many Hircarahs [*harkaras*] or Messengers... . Eight Bearers for my Palanquin complete my Train... . Mr F[rancis] keeps five [horses] and according to the cursed fashion of this idle country, has ten fellows to look after them, besides a coachman to keep the whole in order. He has moreover twelve Palanquin Bearers, for no reason that I can learn except his being a Councillor – four Peons, four Hircarahs, two Chubdars [*chobdars*, staff-bearers] who carry silver staves, two Jemmadars. These are without Doors – Within, a Head Sircar, or Banyan or Broker or Agent... . House keeping comprador and his mate go to market, two

10.1 *A Khansama. Colesworthy Grant*

cooleys bring home what he buys – Consomar [*khansama*] takes charge of it. Cook and two Mates dress it. Baker in the house. Butler and assistant take charge of Liquor, Abdar and his Mate cool them. Two Side Board Men wait at Table. House – two Metrannees [*methranis,* sweeper-women] to clean it, two watchman to guard it, a Durwan to keep the Door. Tailor, Washermen and Ironing Man for each Person. Mashalgees, Torch Bearers F[rancis] 4, M[acrabie] 2, L[ivins] 1, C[ollings] 1.
We make a flaming Funeral appearance. Two Mallies or Gardeners, Cow and poultry feeder and Pork Man...
Let me see

Mr F	62
Mack	20
L & Coll	28
	———
	110
	———

One hundred and ten servants to wait upon a family of four People.

Such lavish living indicated the kind of social life such men could have. An almost daily routine was the evening drive when the sahib, with his memsahib if he had one, went forth to take the air. A carriage was a status symbol, a part of the fashion. William Hicky writes in his *Memoirs*:

It being necessary to keep a carriage for Mrs. Hicky, I purchased a neat London-built chariot, for which I paid three thousand sicca rupees, a phaeton for my own use at eighteen hundred, and three excellent draught horses which cost me seventeen hundred and fifty, then considered a very reasonable price.

Henry Roberdau's account of 1805 paints a vivid picture of this evening ritual:

About a quarter of an hour after sunset the carriages gradually came out till at last all the city may be said to be assembled; high and low, rich and poor, great and small, all mix promiscuously in this varied scene. There are vehicles of all kinds, Coaches, Chariots, Landaus, Sociables, Phaetons, Curricles, Buggies &c. ... Here you may see some fond but awkward equestrian risking his Neck to keep up with the Landau of his beloved; there some lone Priscilla (past her teens) rolling in vain her sparkling orb, to allure some wealthy Nabob.

The evening ride was then an important occasion to socialize and show off. So were the frequent dinner parties at which, if Hicky is to be at all believed, the flicking of bread pills about the table was a major accomplishment.

10.2 *A banquet: 'Our Burra Khanah'. G. F. Atkinson*

One Englishman, indeed, had earned a reputation by his skill at snuffing a candle from a distance of three or four yards with such pills. Another, Captain Morrison, let it be known at one party that if any bread pills were flicked at him he would consider that an insult. No sooner had he spoken than such a missile hit him in the face. He responded by hurling a plate bearing a leg of mutton at the offender, knocking the latter straight out of his chair. This led to a duel in which Morrison seriously wounded his challenger. A life of leisure born of ill-gotten profit could produce strange ways of passing the time.

Boat rides up or down-river were very popular. Here again the size, nature and decoration of the boats were important symbols of power and position. Hicky had a barge that was 48 feet long, with a crew of fourteen. As the author of *Hartly House* fitly observed, the 'budgerows' *(bajras)* or barges that plied the Hugli would have put to shame the handsomest pleasure-barge on the Thames. This was the nub of the paradox: men who in their own country could never have conceived of a life of leisure and luxury found themselves living such a life in Calcutta. And they did so not because they earned it by merit, but merely because the trading body for which they worked had acquired political power in a very rich province of India, and allowed its servants to make fortunes in any way they could.

Other popular sports were hunting and

shooting. Pig-sticking was the greatest draw of all, but shooting with a gun was much practised too. We also find references to cricket matches, tennis, billiards and fencing. Dancing was a prized entertainment hampered only by the lack of suitable English ladies. The late eighteenth-century British community in Calcutta had a singular preponderance of males.

It might appear that this account exaggerates the leisure at the disposal of the Briton in India. I can draw support from a well-known account in James Mackintosh's *Travels in Europe, Asia and Africa* (1771-81) of a day in the life of an Englishman in Calcutta:

About the hour of seven in the morning, his durvan opens the gate and the viranda is free to his circars [*sarkars,* stewards], peons, harcarrahs, chubdars, huccabadars [*hookaburdars* or hookah-bearers] and consumas, writers and solicitors. The head-bearer and jemmadar enter the hall, and his bed-room at eight o'clock. A lady quits his side, and is conducted by a private staircase, either to her own apartments or out of the yard. The moment the master throws his legs out of bed, the whole posse in waiting rush into his room each making three salams, by bending the body and head very low, and touching the forehead with the inside of the fingers, and the floor with the back part. He condescends, perhaps, to nod or cast an eye towards the solicitor of his favour and protection. In about half an hour after undoing and taking off his long drawers, a clean shirt, breeches, stockings and slippers are put upon his body, thighs, legs and feet, without any greater exertion on his own part than if he was a statue. The barber enters, shaves him, cuts his nails, and cleans his ears. The chillumjee [basin] and ewer are brought by a servant whose duty it is, who pours water upon his hands and face, and presents a towel. The superior then walks in state to his breakfasting parlour in his waistcoat; is seated; the consumah makes and pours out his tea, and presents him with a plate of bread or toast. The hairdresser comes behind, and begins his operation while the houccaburdar softly slips the upper end of the snake or tube of the hucca into his hand; while the hairdresser is doing his duty, the gentleman is eating, sipping and smoking by turns. By and by his banian presents himself with humble salams.... If any of the solicitors are of eminence, they are honoured with chairs. These ceremonies are continued perhaps till ten o'clock, when, attended by

10.3 A civilian going out. Mrs Belnos

his cavalcade, he is conducted to his palanquin, and preceded by eight to twelve chubdars, harcarrahs, and peons... . If he has visits to make, his peons lead and direct the bearers; and if business renders his presence only necessary, he shows himself, and pursues his other engagements until two o'clock, when he and his company sit down, perfectly *at ease* in point of dress and address, to a good dinner, each attended by his own servant. As it is expected that they shall return to supper, at four o'clock they begin to withdraw without ceremony, and step into their palanquins: so that in a few minutes, the master is left to go into his bedroom, when he is instantly undressed to his shirt, and his long drawers put on, and he lies down on his bed, where he sleeps till about seven or eight o'clock. Then the former ceremony is repeated, and clean linen of every kind, as in the morning, is administered.... After tea, he puts on a handsome coat, and pays visits of ceremony to the ladies; returns a little before ten o'clock; supper being served at ten. The company keep together till between twelve and one in the morning, preserving great sobriety and decency; and when they depart, our hero is conducted to his bed room, where he finds a female companion to amuse him until the hour of seven or eight next morning. With no greater exertions than these, do the Company's servants amass the most splended fortunes.

An English lady's life was similarly leisure-oriented. Indeed, time hung heavier still upon her. *The Life and Times of Mrs. Sherwood, 1775-1851* (1910) suggests the following account.

Such a lady was normally woken before sunrise by her ayah, to go out for a morning drive in a carriage or open palanquin after having put on a dress 'completely clean, fresh from the dhoby'. After the drive, she returned to bed to sleep for a couple of hours. She was awake again before breakfast, which she attended after an 'elaborate toilet' in which 'she went through every process of bathing, hair-dressing, and so on under the hands of one or two black women.' Breakfast was a meal when 'many gentlemen' dropped in and it continued for some time. After breakfast the lady retired to a room to read, to do a little 'fancy work' or to receive a lady visitor to gossip. 'She knows, a contemporary female observer commented, 'a good deal of the gossip of the Europeans, but little of the ways and habits of the natives.' 'Tiffin' was the major meal, when much wine and pale ale was drunk; guests would be present, so our lady appeared there after a change of dress. She slept again in the after-

noon, rising just before sunset to prepare for the evening drive. The preparations involved 'an entire change of every article of wearing apparel'. On her return she sat down to dinner with her husband, 'after which she most often goes out to a ball or assembly, for which a last and still more magnificent toilet must be made.'

These descriptions highlight an important aspect other than leisure. In the life of the English, the Indians entered chiefly to provide service – the ayah, the barber, the bearer, the waiters, the woman who disappeared through a secret staircase in the morning. This exemplified the Englishman's relationship with the Indian world that he encountered. It was the sign of his dominance, his superiority. And this superiority came to be more marked as the English settled down in the early nineteenth century.

An example will make the change clear. In the eighteenth century, even for a few years after Palashi, there was a certain dependence of the newly-arrived Englishman on his agent, the banian or *dubash*. He was, after all, a complete foreigner to the customs of India. The banian helped him to settle down, found him a house and servants, and if need be even procured a 'sleeping dictionary': a native mistress from whom the sahib picked up the local language.

10.4 *Our Magistrate's wife. G. F. Atkinson*

Often he also advanced money to start the sahib on his private trade. The banian, in return, earned a commission or had a share in his master's profit.

However, it did not take long for the Englishman to realize that it was his position that was bringing in the profits, while the banian merely provided certain services. The question of equality did not arise. Indeed, the rich and famous Indians of Calcutta in the late eighteenth and early nineteenth centuries often owed their fortunes and estates to the special favours they received from important Englishmen. A very notable example was Krishna-

10.5 *Top :*
Europeans watching dancing boys.
Mrs Belnos

10.6 *Below:*
William Osborne with hookahbardar and punkahwalla.
Emily Eden

kanta Nandi (Cantoo Babu), the founder of the Kashimbazar Raj family. He was a successful trader in silk before he became a banian to Warren Hastings, and built up large landed estates in northern and western Bengal through his close personal ties with the Governor-General.

Service was the major but not the only interface between the Englishman and the 'natives'. It became the custom among the sahibs to be honoured guests in the houses of wealthy Bengalis during festivals like the Durga Puja, or to attend a nautch or dance soirée. Indeed, nautches became so popular that soon Englishmen began arranging such entertainments amongst themselves. Similarly, in the second half of the eighteenth century, Englishmen developed a special fondness for the hookah. But these imitations of or borrowings from Indian life and customs tended to be temporary. As the English became more settled, self-confident and conscious of their 'mission' in India, they became increasingly sectarian and insular. To be anglicized was to be civilized.

The insularity only exacerbated the Englishman's racism, for be it remembered that even when he lived in the barracks of Fort William, a 'jolly cadet' chucked all manner of things – 'an empty brandy bottle, a boot-jack and an inkstand' – at his servants. From the beginning of their stay in Calcutta, the conquerors left their imprint on the conquered in the crudest possible way. A diarist in the *India Gazette* of 30 December 1780 confessed, with some glee, that he derived much pleasure from kicking and flogging his servants for trifles.

This racial arrogance, passing into the sadistic or the impersonally inhuman, was the bond that linked the young writer of the Company, smoking a hookah and watching nautches in the second half of the eighteenth century, to the suave competitionwallah of the nineteenth century who wanted to 'civilize the natives'. Frank Brown, who had spent a long time in India, wrote home to his father in 1857:

...if a man who left this country thirty years ago were now to visit it he would scarcely credit the changes he would universally witness in the treatment of the Natives, high and low. The English were not then absolute masters everywhere. Now they are, restraint is cast away ...and [they display] a supercilious arrogance and contempt of the people

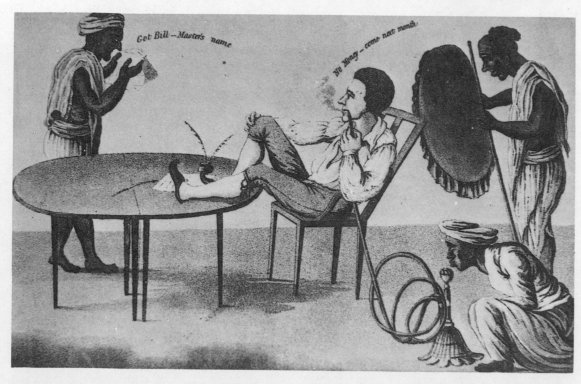

Got Bill - Master's name

No Money - come next month

10.7 'A scene in Writers' Buildings'. James Moffat

William Howard Russell, the perspicacious correspondent of *The Times,* concluded:

The fact is, I fear, that the favourites of heaven, the civilizers of the world... are naturally the most intolerant in the world... . 'By Jove ! Sir', exclaims the Major, who has by this time got to the walnut stage of the argument, to which he has arrived by gradations of sherry, port, ale, and madeira, 'By Jove: Those niggers are such a confounded lazy sensual set, cramming themselves with ghee and sweetmeats, and smoking their cursed chillums all day and all night, that you might as well think to train pigs.'

Even those charitable souls who considered Indians worthy 'to train' were not quite free from this attitude. Shibnath Shastri records how Ramtanu Lahiri, as a lad from the districts, had to run behind David Hare's palanquin crying 'Me poor boy, me take in your school'. Only after many days of such humiliation did the benevolent Hare turn to speak to the boy. The scene has almost a symbolic poignancy: a Bengali boy running behind a white man's carriage in quest of English education and civilization. The hierarchy of Calcutta social life is perfectly reflected in this single vignette.

It was this sense of superiority, born out of political dominance, that gave English social life its insular and paradoxical character – paradoxical because they were in India but not of India. Their expanding corner of the 'foreign field' remained 'forever England'.

Michael Edwardes cites an itinerant story-teller in a Bihar village who described the strangeness of the situation in a vivid and telling metaphor:

The sahib sits upon the lotus. The lotus sits upon the water. The sahib will get his feet wet and catch a chill and die. But like the ant who aspires to climb to the top of Mount Kailas, it will take a long time.

And indeed the incubation of the cold virus, like the gestation of the Indian elephant, took an inordinately long while.

THE JEWS
OF CALCUTTA

Pritha Chowdhury and Joyoti Chaliha

The night of 4 August 1798 bore silent witness to the arrival in Calcutta of the herald of a new community. His name was Shalom ben Aharon ben Obadiah Ha-Kohen (Shalom Cohen). An ambitious young merchant, he had journeyed from his native Aleppo to Baghdad, and thence via Basra, Bombay and Surat to Calcutta, then the hub of commerce and the centre of British power in India.

Long before Cohen, Jewish traders had kept temporary residence in Calcutta; but the Calcutta community is new compared to the thousand-year-old settlements in western and southern India. Most Calcutta Jews trace their antecedents to the migrants from Baghdad and other parts of the Middle East, and through them back to the Babylonian Jews. They were drawn to India by the prospects of trade, coupled with freedom from the persecution periodically launched against them in the Middle East.

The early Jewish settlers provided links in a chain of trading posts stretching from Shanghai to London, dealing in opium, indigo, cotton yarn, silk and piece-goods, Veniceware, precious stones, gold leaf, ivory and coffee. They were self-reliant men of ultra-conservative outlook, orthodox practitioners of their faith, close-knit by their venerable historical legacy.

The Calcutta community was set up by Shalom Cohen and consolidated by his son-in-law Moses Duek Cohen. Flamboyant and adventurous, Shalom's fortunes went through many ups and downs. Debts forced him to flee to Dutch Chunchura and French Chandannagar. Business took him to Lucknow as jeweller to the Nawab of Awadh and to the court of Ranjit Singh in Punjab. He died in 1836 and was buried in the Jewish Cemetery at Narkeldanga Main Road, the original plot of land for which he had himself gifted to the community.

Moses Duek Cohen, though astute in business, is best remembered for his dedicated service to the community. As *paqid* (official head), he played a leading role in framing the first Constitution of the community (29 August 1825) and in establishing the first formal synagogue, Neveh Shalome (Abode of Peace) in 1826 as well as the first purpose-built synagogue, Bethel, in Pollock Street where it still stands. His death in 1861 saw the end of an era. The leadership now passed to the Baghdadis, who by this time far outnumbered the settlers from Aleppo.

A meagre fifteen in 1799, the community had by 1813 made its presence sufficiently felt to warrant inclusion in the 'Original Calcutta Annual Directory and Calendar'. By 1825 their number had risen to 200. In 1841 Elazar Arakie Cohen established the first Hebrew printing press in the city; and Hebrew presses functioned there (with some interruptions) for the next sixty years. With a population of 600 in

Kumartuli, though Nandaram Sen (fl. 1700) has precedence in time. Both were 'Black Zamindars', Indian deputies to the British Collector of Calcutta. The last Babu was perhaps Bhubanmohan Niyogi of Bagbazar. For the earlier part of the intervening century and a half, the 'Babu Culture' of Calcutta was closely linked with the Great Houses. But it acquired wider ramifications, and the total phenomenon is surveyed elsewhere in this book.

As I remarked before, the Great Houses were not based on hereditary occupations or feudal landed wealth. Under the new dispensation, where wealth flowed from skilful tending of British interests, the advantages lay with the commercial and legal literati, and with those who could act as middlemen and manipulators. Such persons took up posts in British 'factories' under such titles as *diwan, banian, vakil* and *mutsuddi*; but their common function was as intermediaries between Englishmen and Indians, whether in conducting trade, arranging political deals, collecting debts or looking after accounts and documents. The appellation of 'Babu' basically carried such clerical connotations, however exalted its later aura might have been.

Such functionaries were necessarily astute men who imbibed all the pragmatic skills of their English principals to set themselves up as traders and moneylenders on their own account. The British, ignorant of local languages and practices at that stage, had to rely entirely on these *banians*. How the latter exploited their position is seen from the career of Ratan Sarkar (fl. 1679). A washerman (*dhoba*) by trade, he heard that a British ship was looking for a *dobash* (*dobhashi* or interpreter) and erroneously offered himself for the job. But his ingenuity enabled him to carry out the task, and he built upon this advantage to become one of the wealthiest Calcuttans of his time.

However, most founders of great houses were Kayasthas. As hereditary scriveners in medieval times, they found it easy to adapt to commercial and political service under the Company. There were relatively few Brahmin families, among the most celebrated being the Ghoshals of Bhukailas. The Tantubaniks or cloth merchants and Subarnabaniks or gold merchants were already rich, but could not make much further profit from the new colonial situation. Again there were exceptions like Lakshmikanta (Naku) Dhar (fl. 1762-75), a

Subarnabanik, ancestor of the Posta Raj family.

Most founders of Great Houses began humbly; and needless to say, their wealth did not come from the salary that John Company paid its Babus. Gobindaram Mitra was notorious for his violence and extortion: he claimed, plausibly enough, that he could not keep up his position on fifty rupees a month. Again when Mir Jafar, made Nawab after Palashi, paid compensation for the damage done during Siraj-ud-Daula's sack of Calcutta, Gobindaram was one of the 'Native Commissioners' appointed to disburse the money. He appropriated a sizeable part of the sum, as did his colleagues Shukdeb and Nayanchand Mallik, Shobharam Basak and Ratu (Ratan) Sarkar – all founders or members of *banedi* lines. According to Marshman, eight crores of rupees from Siraj-ud-Daula's treasury were appropriated by three persons: Nabakrishna Deb, Ramchandra Ray and Amir Baig Khan. The first founded the Shobhabazar Raj and the second the Andul Raj

family. Their salaries from the Company amounted to sixty rupees; but Ramchandra left property worth a crore and twenty-five lakhs, while Nabakrishna spent nine lakhs at his mother's legendary funeral.

Nabakrishna Deb (1733-97) was the *munshi* (a sort of tutor-cum-secretary) in Persian to Warren Hastings. He owed his rise to his role in the conspiracy to topple Siraj-ud-Daula, and in winning over many zamindars to the English cause. Krishnakanta Nandi (?-1793), founder of the Kashimbazar Raj family, won Hastings's favour by helping him to escape the Nawab's sudden attack and to return to Calcutta. Ramchandra Ray was first Clive's *sarkar* and then

13.1 *Facing page: A Banian. Solvyns*

13.2 *Gobindaram Mitra's nabaratna temple. T. & W. Daniell*

13.3 *Dwarakanath Thakur's Belgachhia Villa*

diwan of the Company's trading centre. All these men connived actively with the British in overthrowing the Nawab. For this loyalty, Krishnakanta's son Loknath, Ramchandra's son Ramlochan and Nabakrishna himself were honoured with the title of Raja Bahadur. This was the basis of their families' claim to be Great Houses. Many other such founders were also devoted to British interests. Gangagobinda Sinha (1749-93), founder of the Paikpara Raj family, was Hastings's ally in many secret machinations. His superior in office, Raja Rajballabh Som (or Sen: 1698-1763) had a long and mutually beneficial family association with the Company.

But most importantly, the Indian servants of the Company, like their British superiors, won wealth and acclaim through private trade and usury on an enormous scale. The Bengalis of the day were certainly not averse to trade as their modern descendants are said to be. The immensely wealthy Lakshmikanta Dhar lent money to the Company and privately to Clive; his descendant Sukhamay Ray (?-1811) acquired the title of Raja. The Sheths, Malliks and Matilals were equally acclaimed for their wealth, as were Ramdulal Dey (Sarkar: 1752-1825) and his sons Ashutosh and Pramathanath (Chhatu Babu and Latu Babu).

Ramdulal's rise to wealth had a celebrated beginning. He was steward to Madanmohan Datta (1710-87) of the famous Datta family of Hatkhola. Hearing of a sunken ship on sale with its cargo, he made a lakh's profit on the transaction with money entrusted to him by his master. When he offered Madanmohan the profit, the latter was so impressed with his honesty that he gave Ramdulal the sum to set

himself up in business. As this incident shows, Madanmohan himself had a reputation for honesty and philanthropy.

From equally humble beginnings came Gauri (perhaps Gaurishankar) Sen. He too is said to have owed his wealth to the generous honesty of his partner Baishnabdas (or Baishnabcharan) Sheth (fl. 1743), perhaps the greatest merchant of his time. When a consignment of zinc bought on Sen's account was found to contain much silver, Sheth insisted on forgoing all share in the profits. Gauri Sen's philanthropy has been immortalized in a Bengali proverb, as also the frequently misguided generosity of Diwan Hari Ghosh (?-1806), whose retinue of idlers and parasites is remembered as Hari Ghosh's *gohal* (cowshed).

Philanthropy was one means of displaying wealth; I shall treat it later in detail. A more notorious means was preposterous luxury, ostentation and waste, usually in a competitive spirit – a *nouveau riche* adaptation of feudal pomp and arrogance. The great families built palatial houses all over north Calcutta. With minor variations, they all follow the same pattern: dwelling-house, women's quarters, *thakur dalan* or gods' sanctum with adjoining *natmandir* or stage for performances, office, parlour, strongroom, servants' quarters, stables and granary. But there was a marked spirit of rivalry in their construction and decoration, as in the grotesque acts of extravagance that shocked and fascinated the common man. The proverb went, *Kayet marey kheyaley, Banik marey deyaley*: Kayasthas are killed by their extravagant whims and the merchant castes by their walled-in parsimony (or, by another explanation, their division of property by raising walls). Another rhyming proverb was handed down the decades, attributing to the tycoons of the moment the crowning excellence in such blessings as *bari* (house), *gari* (carriage), *kari* (money) or *chhari* (stick, hence power).

Gobindaram Mitra has gone down in urban folk-history as the first Bengali to drive a coach and pair, though some give the honour to Nabakrishna Deb. Gobindaram's greater claim to extravagant Babu-dom lies in his lavish celebrations of *Dole* or Holi, Durga Puja and other festivals. It was he who fired the urge for conspicuous consumption in the Bengali society of his times. At Durga Puja, he had the entire image of the goddess wrapt in gold and silver leaf, and spent fifty thousand rupees on the fortnight-long worship. Thirty to fifty maunds of rice were offered to the deity. A thousand Brahmins were fed and given gifts, and there were nautches and banquets. Gobindaram's mansion at Kumartuli stood on fifty bighas of land. He also had a villa, Nandan Bagan, where he housed his three favourite mistresses.

More easy-going Babus carried their extravagance to open folly and absurdity. They deemed it vulgar to take stock of expenses, and knowingly allowed their servants to cheat them. There is truth behind the apocryphal stories of the treasurer who claimed that his master's money had shrunk when put out to dry, or that white ants had eaten up the chandeliers.

The Babus' physical luxury scarcely seems credible today. Ramtanu Datta (Tanu Babu, fl. 1800) of Hatkhola wore no *dhoti* more than once; and though these were of finest Dhaka muslin, he would have the borders torn off lest they chafe his skin. His entire palace was washed down daily with rose-water, and all his utensils were of gold or silver. His rival in madness was Nilmani Haldar, who drove a coach and eight. Once Nilmani bought a superior imported mirror and sent it to Ramtanu for inspection. Ramtanu noticed a

small flaw in a corner, and had the mirror broken as unworthy of its master. He also sent Nilmani the cost of a replacement.

Darpanarayan Thakur (1731-93), Rajkrishna Deb (1781-1824), Sukhamay Ray, Chhatu Babu and Latu Babu – all these were famous for their love of luxury. The Basu family of Shimulia (Simla) produced eight scions (the 'Ashta Basus' or eight Basus) whose addiction to drink has become a legend. The traditions of Babudom were staunchly upheld by the last great exponent, Bhubanmohan Niyogi. He burnt ten-rupee notes to light his cigarettes, and distributed a thousand Benarasi sarees among the prostitutes of Sonagachhi on the last day of Saraswati Puja. He also played a generous role in setting up the public theatre in Calcutta.

Lavish hospitality and the entertainment of sahibs was another aspect of early Babudom. The most usual occasions were festivals – *Dole*, Jhulan or a Puja – or family ceremonies like a child's rice-eating ritual or *annaprashana*, marriages and funerals. The Durga Puja of the Shobhabazar Raj family was commonly granted precedence. No other Puja could begin before theirs: hence its announcement was announced by the firing of cannon. At immersion-time too, the Debs' image led the rest.

The crowning touch of status would be

13.4 *Europeans attending Durga Puja, perhaps at Nabakrishna Deb's house. Alexis Soltykoff*

13.5 *The 'Tagore Castle'*

imparted on such occasions by the presence of Europeans, the more the better. Lord Clive and other dignitaries attended Nabakrishna Deb's first public (*baroari*) Durga Puja – held to celebrate the British victory at Palashi! At the marriage of Ramdulal Dey's two sons, there were separate 'assemblies' for Europeans over two days and for Indians over four.

Although most of these families were emphatically Hindu, their pomp and ostentation derived from the precedent of Muslim Nawabs and Umraos, and after 1856 the direct example of Wajid Ali Shah, the deposed Nawab of Awadh, in his residence-in-exile at Garden Reach. Again, although these houses derived their wealth from the British, they set up a plausible system of urban feudalism on their own account. Binay Ghosh has called Nabakrishna Deb Calcutta's greatest *zamindar* as well as a 'new-style *munshi*'. Like other founding fathers, he bypassed the educational and professional proclivities of the *munshis* in favour of a conservative assertion of

wealth and power. Nor, in the eighteenth century, could the Great Houses transcend the familial pride of rank and wealth for a higher assertion of individual intellect or personality. This required education and taste, which could only grow over several generations.

Binay Ghosh has distinguished four types of culture prevailing in various parts of Calcutta in Nabakrishna's day:

Sutanuti culture (north Calcutta): the new urbanfeudal culture of the city 'Rajas', of which Nabakrishna was the most influential proponent.

Kalikata culture (central Calcutta): a mercantile culture propagated by the Tantubaniks or cloth-merchants like the Sheths and Basaks, as well as the Subarnabaniks. This was a curious amalgam of old and new elements.

Gobindapur culture (south-central Calcutta): the new English culture of the Nabobs or European *nouveaux riches*.

Bhabanipur culture (south Calcutta): middle-class Hindu culture.

Although the four zones interacted, the first element grew increasingly influential through the late eighteenth and early nineteenth centuries. And as the generations passed, it acquired a new sophistication and a new responsible interest in education and social reform.

An interest of sorts had always been there. Nabakrishna maintained a large assembly or *sabha* of scholars and religious men at his 'court', inviting some of the finest intellects from the traditional centres of learning at Shantipur and Nabadwip. But Nabakrishna's extreme conservatism and Hindu revivalist programme reflect a general tendency in the early days of the Great Houses. At that stage, their philanthropy largely consisted in religious works and conventional charity. The lavish spending at festivals, and extravagant or misguided donations, showed how religious and charitable motives could merge with the arrogance of wealth. Such spending consisted chiefly in temple-founding, gifts to Brahmins and feeding or support of the poor.

One-quarter of Ramdulal Dey's fortunes went to fund thirteen temples at Varanasi. He also had his wife weighed in gold and donated the sum to Brahmins. Eight thousand Brahmins and a hundred thousand poor men were fed at his funeral.

We should specially recall two eminent women who were among the chief philanthropists of their time: Rani Rasmani (1793–1861) of Janbazar and Rani Swarnamayee (1829–97) of Kashimbazar. In their works, we see how new motives mingle with the old. Rasmani's greatest achievement was the founding of Dakshineshwar temple; but she carried out many other works of more direct social benefit, and was indeed one of the chief contributors to the city's development. Swarnamayee, although not a permanent resident of Calcutta, spent generously on many noble causes there, the education of women above all.

The mid-nineteenth century saw two allied developments. On the one hand, the extravagant upstart 'Babu Culture' came to be pilloried as never before. 'They are not truly great men', wrote Bhabanicharan Banerji in *Kalikata Kamalalay* (1823). 'They have simply grown rich by canvassing, commissioning, cheating and pimping.' Kaliprasanna Sinha was even more penetrating in *Hutom Penchar Naksha*

Rani Rasmani

Rani Rasmani's life (1793-1861) followed the classic fairy tale of the poor man's beautiful daughter. Born in a humble peasant family, her exceptional beauty brought about her marriage to the immensely wealthy Rajchandra Marh, himself responsible for many public works in the city. Widowed at the age of forty-three, Rasmani continued to use the family wealth for remarkable feats of planned social uplift as well as charity.

Her most considerable benefaction, the Dakshineshwar Temple, was an instance of social reform no less than piety, for she was of low caste and the Brahmins had opposed the foundation. She also won for poor fishermen the right to fish in the Ganga, and spent much money in stopping certain steamer services to this end.

She commanded vast estates in the city, including several prominent markets such as Jan Bazar, Rasmani Bazar in Beliaghata, and Jadu Babu's Bazar gifted to her grandson of that name. But her title of 'Rani' is not derived from her rank or property: it was simply the name by which her mother fondly called her in her childhood.

13.6
Dakshineshwar Temple, built by Rani Rasmani

(1862): as the Nawabs declined and the English rose, he wrote, 'The great bamboo groves were chopped down and little twigs began to fill with pith. Clerks, grocers and oilmen became Rajas, and money grew greater than lineage.' Pyarichand Mitra's *Alaler Gharer Dulal* (1858) also gives a scathing account of decadent Babudom.

The withdrawal of Englishmen from their former familiar mixing with Indians was also no doubt a factor in the decline of the old prodigal upkeep of the Great Houses. But the deepest cause was the decline in Indian trade and commerce as the imperialist economy struck roots: the very source of the Babus' wealth was drying up.

Hence the distaste for the old extravagance was symptomatic of a second and more radical change in outlook. This can usually be traced in three stages. The founder of a Great House is often not himself a great Babu. This role is assumed by his sons and perhaps his grandsons. Hence their fortunes begin to ebb – a Bengali proverb says wealth does not last more than three generations – and their descendants have to absorb a more realistic and enlightened attitude. It is often from the third generation that the scions of the Great Houses are seen to acquire a progressive attitude, genuine social commitment and diverse accomplishments. They become major conduits of the new Western education and culture, as well as a new philanthropy oriented to social change. Theirs is the overhelming contribution to the social and religious reforms of the day, perhaps most significantly in the matter of female emancipation and education.

These new trends find their first classic expression in the public life of Raja Rammohan Ray (1772–1833), though his private life was that of any other Babu of his day. Rammohan influenced innumerable men, but two in particular: Debendranath (1817–1905) of the Jorasanko Thakurs and Keshabchandra (1838–84) of the Kalutola Sens. Both men adopted Brahmoism and, what is more important, attempted to spread a more general enlightenment throughout Bengal. Education and social reform are major concerns of the Great Houses in their latter days. It is significant that Loknath Ghosh's 1881 list of 'aristocracy and gentry' includes several families and individuals of recent middle-class origin and no great wealth, who owe their

eminence entirely to scholarship and social work. Ishwarchandra Vidyasagar (1820–91) is the outstanding example of the type.

The Asiatic Society was set up in 1784 and the Fort William College in 1800 – harbingers of a new interest in Indian learning and culture. There followed, one by one, such academic and social institutions as the Atmiya Sabha (1815), the Hindu College (1817), the Calcutta School Book Society (1817), the Calcutta School Society (1818), the Female Juvenile Society (1819–20), the Gouriya Sabha (1823), the Sanskrit College (1824), the Ladies' Society for Native Female Education (1824) and the Academic Association (1828). Though some of these institutions were founded wholly or partly by Europeans, virtually none could have continued without social and financial support from the Great Houses, and many were established by them directly. The School Book Society had a committee of sixteen Europeans and eight Indians, including Radhakanta Deb of Shobhabazar and Ramkamal Sen of Kalutola. The Gouriya Sabha included Umanandan and Prasannakumar Thakur of Pathuriaghata and Dwarakanath Thakur of Jorasanko, besides Radhakanta and Ramkamal. The Gauriya Sabha was conservative in outlook, vehemently opposed to the iconoclasm of the 'Young Bengal' group; but it was not reactionary or obscurantist. It fostered Western education, and its members took part in fundamental social reforms. We may indeed describe the Sabha as marking a more mature and effective phase of the new reformist mentality.

Ishwarchandra Gupta, poet and journalist, has a telling observation in the *Sambad Prabhakar* of 13 March 1853:

We have seen an end of the old pleasures of kite-flying, chess, draughts and dice, of idle talk, of the tabla and sitar, of card-playing and pigeon-fancying. Young men now discuss virtuous matters like Bacon's Essays, Shakespeare's plays, Kalidasa's poetry, the verse of the Gita, the meaning of the Vedas.

The new Great House culture achieved its perfection among the Thakurs of Jorasanko, who have been treated in a separate article; but it had many other eminent exponents as well. Among them were the other branches of the Thakur family, and another Jorasanko family, the Sinhas. Kaliprasanna Sinha (1840–70) not only ridiculed Babu Culture in his satirical

13.7
Keshabchandra Sen

writings; in conjunction with expert scholars, he made a notable Bengali translation of the *Mahabharata*.

Again, there was a remarkable inflorescence in the Shobhabazar Raj family under Radhakanta Deb (1783-1867). His grandfather Nabakrishna had patronized learning as part of a wider programme to consolidate his status. Radhakanta was himself a scholar and writer, and a genuine patron of learning and the arts. His greatest feat was the publication of the Sanskrit encyclopaedia *Shabdakalpadruma* in eight volumes over half a century at a cost of sixteen lakh rupees, from a press set up in his own house. He published his Bengali textbook *Shikshagrantha* in 1821, and brought out Gourmohan Vidyalankar's book on female education, *Streeshikshabidhayak*, the same year. He also himself composed the book *Vedanta: What It Is*, though the title-page only mentioned Mrityunjay Vidyalankar as the editor.

Ramkamal Sen (1783-1844) founded the Sen family of Kalutola. Beginning life as a humble press worker, he became *diwan* of the Bank of Bengal and was active in innumerable causes. He virtually founded the Agri-Horticultural Society, and helped to set up the Indian Museum and the Calcutta Medical College. He was Principal of Hindu College and Secretary of the Sanskrit College, compiler of the first English-and-Bengali dictionary, and a regular contributor to the Journal of the Asiatic Society.

Ramkamal's grandson Keshabchandra became a leader of the Brahmo Samaj, as did Debendranath Thakur of Jorasanko and his descendants. This was one expression of the new reformist zeal of the Great Houses. In another direction, it made some of their scions turn to Christianity, most notably the three sons of Rasamay Datta (1779-1854) of Rambagan. Rasamay was the first Indian Commissioner of the Court of Requests (Court of Small Causes) and one of the founders of Hindu College. His sons travelled extensively abroad; one of them, Gobindachandra, had as his daughters Taru (1856-77) and Aru Datta (?-1876), well-known for their English verse. Rasamay's great-nephew, the writer Rameshchandra Datta (1848-1909), was one of the earliest Indian members of the Indian Civil

Service. The first member had been Satyendranath Thakur (1842-1923) of Jorasanko.

These details of religious conversion and professional endeavour show how the Great Houses were adapting to the times, while themselves sponsoring enlightened change in a decadent system. This brought about a happy social situation by the late nineteenth century where the social elite of Calcutta were, to a large extent, men of education, taste and social commitment, distinguished by professional or intellectual achievement rather than lineage. Civilians, lawyers and academics could share a common level of distinction with the hereditary elite. Not that the latter abandoned all pride of state. The marriage celebrations of Pramodkumar Thakur of Pathuriaghata in 1880 recalled the old excesses, though the heads of the house at the time, Jatindramohan and Shourindramohan, were both men of learning, taste and enlightenment.

To the end, the life-styles of the Great Houses remained an amalgam of the old and the new. Perhaps that is why their histories remain inseparable from that of a city where so many eras and ethics have existed side by side.

13.8 *A house of the Mallik family*

(Translated from Bengali)

JORASANKO AND THE THAKUR FAMILY

Chitra Deb

If there is one family in Calcutta that, over three hundred years of history, can be designated as the leading family of the city, it can only be the Thakur (Tagore) family, which exercised the greatest influence on the reawakened Bengali spirit. In fact the Thakurs are not one family but several, the Jorasanko branch being the most illustrious by having brought into being one of the brightest stars in the Indian firmament. It is a matter for debate how far Rabindranath Thakur's genius was the product of his family environment; but there can be no question that the environment provided him with an expansive and liberal humanism that no other 'great house' could have afforded.

The fame of the Jorasanko Thakurs stems from the time of Dwarakanath Thakur (1794–1846). In wealth and pomp, Jorasanko fell far short of many other lordly houses and indeed the original seat of the Thakurs themselves at Pathuriaghata. All these families, including the Thakurs, obtained wealth from contacts with the British, and subsequently invested it in land to become zamindars.

The Thakurs were originally surnamed Kushari. The founder of the clan is taken to be Jagannath Kushari of Jessore, degraded in the eyes of his intolerant fellow-Brahmins by marrying into a family of 'Pirali' Brahmins, i.e. those stigmatized by contact with Muslims. About the time when Calcutta was founded,

two of the Kusharis, Panchanan and Shukdeb, came to seek their fortune in Calcutta. They took quarters in Gobindapur and set up in the stevedoring business. Their non-Bengali neighbours would call them, as being Brahmins, *Thakurmashai* or 'holy sir'. The British followed suit, and 'Thakur' became the family name. Panchanan's descendants established themselves in Pathuriaghata, Jorasanko and Kailahata, and Shukdeb's at Chorbagan. To distinguish between themselves, the branches spelt their name in English as 'Taguore', 'Tagore', 'Tagoor' and 'Thakur' respectively.

Panchanan's descendants prospered – especially his grandson Darpanarayan (1731–93), through moneylending. Darpanarayan spent as abundantly as he earned. When he quarrelled with his brother Nilmani over the family property, the latter left the homestead in reduced circumstances – carrying, however, the image of the family deity, Lakshmijanardan – and set up house at Mechhuabazar, which later came to be known as Jorasanko. The foundations of the first house on the Jorasanko site were laid in 1784: of course, this bore no resemblance to the present house.

The special role of the Thakurs in Bengali history and culture was inaugurated by Dwarakanath Thakur, son of Nilmani's second son Rammani, but adopted by the childless first son, Ramlochan. Hence Dwarakanath inherited the Jorasanko property and Ramlochan's vast wealth. Later Dwarakanath bought the adjoining land and extended the house, also erecting a separate *baithakkhana* or outer building.

Dwarakanath was not unaffected by the weaknesses of wealth. He was prodigal and luxury-loving, as evinced by the gargantuan banquets at his villa in Belgachhia. His epicurean ways led his European friends to call him 'Prince'. But the overall course of his life was at the farthest possible remove from idle luxury.

Ramlochan had left his foster-child ample landed wealth. Dwarakanath added to it, first as an agent of Mackintosh & Co. and then as a merchant on his own account. He also grew to be legal adviser to many zamindars and other rich men. Despite these avenues to wealth, he also took up employment in the 24-Parganas Collectorate as *Serestadar* (Superintendent under a judicial officer), then Collector, and finally Diwan of the Nimak Mahal, i.e., of the salt trade.

We next see him as founder of the Union Bank with a capital of Rs 16 lakh. Again, as partner in Carr, Tagore & Co. he expanded the company's trade in many fields including shipping. He is said to have voyaged to England on his own ship.

But Dwarakanath's true achievement lies in his unique concern for national and social uplift. Raja Rammohan Ray was his friend and associate. Together they joined the venture of ensuring English education for Indians by the foundation of Hindu College; and Dwarakanath played an active and generous role in the early days of the Calcutta Medical College. He was also involved in the movements for suppressing *sati,* ensuring freedom of the press, setting up juries in civil courts and reforming the police force. In a word, he won respect and acclamation for the Thakurs at home and abroad, and created the family's future predilection for accepting and reconciling the finest legacies of both Indian and Western civilization.

After Dwarakanath, the leadership of the Jorasanko line passed to his two elder sons, Debendranath and Girindranath. Debendranath (1817-1905) steeped himself in the philosophy of the Upanishads, so that posterity has called him *Maharshi,* the great sage. His religious zeal kept him apart from the wealthy society of his day: so in truth did the family's economic decline owing to commercial reverses in Dwarakanath's last days.

Debendranath joined the Brahmo Samaj in 1843 and later took charge of running it as well as its journal, the *Tattwabodhini Patrika.* Girindranath (1820-54) too joined the Samaj along with his brother, but his descendants did not. Hence his sons Ganendra and Gunendra, and Gunendra's sons Gaganendra, Samarendra and Abanindra, became an independent unit within the Jorasanko establishment, living in the *baithakkhana* building which has now disappeared. But their relations with Debendranath's descendants were always most cordial, as with the Thakurs of Pathuriaghata, Kailahata and Chorbagan. Debendranath's family, however, was ostracized by these latter for being Brahmos. In the same way, Gnanendramohan Thakur of Pathuriaghata was disowned by his father and deprived of his inheritance when he turned Christian. The old social order clearly held sway in full strength in the new city.

Or almost in full strength: for the ostracized, like the Thakurs, were thereby spurred to establish and distinguish themselves in other ways. Their pathfinding role in so many spheres was in good measure to overcome the stigma of being 'first Piralis and then Brahmos'. And ultimately, the rest of Bengal society had to follow.

Among Debendranath's children Dwijendranath, Satyendranath, Hemendranath, Jyotirindranath and Swarnakumari stand out – apart, of course, from Rabindranath himself. More than from any other single source, it was from this group (and their cousins Ganendranath and Gunendranath) that the rising new currents of Bengali literature and culture drew their strength.

Dwijendranath (1840-1926), the Maharshi's eldest son, was a true philospher. He consorted with the learned men of the National Society and the 'Bidvajjan-Samagam', both of which he helped to found. But his mind was immersed in the lonely depths of the doctrine of the Gita and the composition of his philosophical works. Yet he also found time to devise a system of Bengali shorthand.

Satyendranath and Ganendranath were among the first students to pass the Entrance Examination of Calcutta University, and Satyendranath (1842-1923) became the first Indian member of the Indian Civil Service. But his true identity was as a pioneer of women's uplift in India. He first rescued the women of his own family from the *purdah* system. His wife Gnanadanandini (1851-1941) went to Eng-

Facing page
14.1 *Above:*
Dwarakanath
Thakur

14.2 *Below:*
Debendranath
Thakur

This page
14.3 *Above:*
Swarnakumari Debi

14.4 *Below:*
Gnanadanandini
Debi

land; she attended gatherings at the Viceroy's palace; she even visited her husband's place of work. Not surprisingly, she became a liberationist in her own right. Other Thakur women followed suit. Bengali society could never be quite the same after Kadambari Debi (?-1884) went riding on the Maidan with her husband Jyotirindranath.

The Maharshi's third son Hemendranath (1844-84) was an enthusiast in education, especially in varied subjects for the young. It was largely thanks to his efforts that Rabindranath could write in his memoirs, 'We learnt much more at home than we had to at school'. This included various branches of science and mathematics – and the girls were taught in step with the boys. It was no wonder that in later life, so, many men and women of the family distinguished themselves in so many ways.

Swarnakumari Debi has recalled how in her early days, their governess would write something on a slate which the girls then had to copy. When Debendranath discovered this, he at once stopped such a mindless and mechanical method and brought in a better teacher, Ajodhyanath Pakrashi – a male outsider in the women's quarters. He would himself teach his daughters many things verbally, and then ask them to write them in their own words.

All eight daughters of Hemendranath justified such an upbringing. Pratibha practised Western music and Abhigna Rabindrasangeet; Manisha played the piano; Pragna ran a journal, *Punya;* Shobhana wrote stories in English. Sushama delivered thirty-eight lectures on Indian philosophy and other subjects in America between 1927 and 1929. Their three brothers Hitendra, Kshitindra and Ritendra also wrote books on literature, art and music. And brothers and sisters alike left proof of their artistic skills.

The name of Jyotirindranath (1849-1925) is most closely linked with Rabindranath, as he fashioned within their own dwelling a seedbed for the latter's growing mind. The magazine *Bharati* was published from Jorasanko with Swarnakumari as editor: Rabindranath had this family paper as a vehicle for his youthful efforts. He also helped Jyotirindranath in writing plays and setting them to music. Every afternoon there would be a literary discussion on their rooftop, attended not only by all the Thakurs but by their cultured friends. The moving spirits behind this too were Jyotirin-

dranath and his wife Kadambari. Nowhere else in late nineteenth-century Calcutta could we have found such a circle: so vigorous, so easy-flowing in its intellectual fare. Though Shilaidaha and Shantiniketan were to exercise a profound power on Rabindranath later on, there can be no doubt that the most seminal influence was the home of his youth.

Debendranath shut out from his home the somewhat decadent aristocratic entertainments of the time. To compensate, some sons of the house like Ganendra, Gunendra and Jyotirindra set up their own private theatre. At first men played women's roles; but gradually the women too would act before an audience of friends and relatives – as three of them, nieces of Rabindranath, were to do later even at a public performance of his *Balmiki Pratibha*.

After Rabindranath, the most illustrious of the Jorasanko Thakurs were three of Gunendranath's children – Gaganendranath (1867-1938), Abanindranath (1871-1951) and Sunayani (1875-1962). They made an immense contribution to Indian art. Needless to say, they too were fundamentally influenced by the cultural ambience of Jorasanko while retaining closer links with tradition in this branch of the family. The work of the two brothers has been discussed in detail elsewhere in these volumes.

Facing page

Left
14.5 Top:
Jyotirindranath
Thakur

14.6 Middle:
Gaganendranath
Thakur

14.7 Bottom:
Abanindranath
Thakur

Right
14.8 Rabindranath
Thakur, aged 35 by
Abanindranath
Thakur

14.9 Thakur family
dramatics:
Samarendranath,
Gaganendranath
and Abanindranath
in a scene from
Rabindranath's
'Phalguni'

But we must not forget that many other Thakurs, of these and later generations, have also distinguished themselves by any reckoning. Dwijendranath's second son Sudhindranath (1869-1929) edited the monthly *Sadhana* and wrote two volumes of verse, popular in their day. His short stories initiated a new theme in Bengali literature, the love of animals. His son Soumyendranath (1901-74) was also a poet and essayist; but his chief claim to remembrance is political, as a prominent Marxist and founder of the Revolutionary Communist Party of India.

Satyendranath's son Surendranath (1872-1940) too had political links in his day, with terrorist organizations. He later became a founder of the Hindusthan Co-operative Insurance Company, and one of the pioneers of banking, insurance and the co-operative movement in India. This is also the place to mention the leading role of Rabindranath's son Rathindranath (1888-1961) in introducing scientific agriculture in this country. His greatest if more predictable achievement was, however, to ensure the preservation of his father's manuscripts, and related documents and archives, at Shantiniketan.

In the cultural sphere again, Birendranath's son Balendranath (1870-99) was a writer of great potential: Bengali letters lost by his untimely death. Hemendranath's three sons Hitendra (1867-1908), Kshitindra (1869-1937) and Ritendra (1870-1936) all had many gifts. Hitendranath was a fine artist and a pioneer of chromolithography as well as editor of the magazine *Punya*. Kshitindranath wrote a valuable biography of his great-grandfather Dwarakanath. Ritendra was a serious student of scripts and alphabets. His two sons Subhagendra (Subho, 1912-85) and Basabendra (1916-) became well-known painters, and Subho Thakur wrote poetry as well. Yet other illustrious men were linked to the family by marriage, like the writer Pramatha Choudhuri. His wife, Satyendranath's daughter Indira (1873-1960), was distinguished alike in the fields of literature, music and women's movements.

Though the cultural role of the Thakurs has received the greatest attention by far, their importance on final assessment is a composite one: commercial and political as well as literary and musical. They played a collective role in every patriotic movement of their times: Nabagopal Mitra's Hindu Mela, the Congress and the National Conference, the Rakhi Festival of 1905, and the Nationalist Movement generally. The story of the Thakurs is inseparable from the story of Calcutta, Bengal and India.

(Translated from Bengali)

THE LOST WORLD OF
THE BABUS

Subir Raychoudhuri

English civilization has pulled down the three hundred and thirty million deities of Hinduism, and set up, in the total space once occupied by them, its own tutelary deities, Comfort and his brother Respectability.

Bankimchandra Chatterji,
The Confessions of a 'Young Bengal'

Babu Culture was a product of Bengal's encounter with the West. The response to an alien culture can be studied in two different aspects – tension and change within the society, and confrontation and interaction with the external force. Babu Culture was essentially Hindu-dominated and Calcutta-based. In its familiar use, the term refers to the lavish and extravagant life-style of the city's *nouveaux riches* in olden times. This group consisted of absentee landlords, the new mercantile class, *banians* or agents of the British and other such. But the full implications of the term are much wider. I must therefore start with a definition of the term 'Babu'.

Even to the Bengali, 'Babu' has no fixed meaning. Attached to a name, it is a polite form of address like 'Mr' in English. But *babugiri, babuana* are derogatory words suggesting foppishness, dandyism and the display of wealth. Abantikumar Sanyal in his monograph *Babu* (1987) cites Gnanendramohan Das's derivation of the word from Persian *ba*, with, and *bu*, scent or fragrance: apparently lawyers from Bengal would anoint themselves with costly perfumes when attending the Mughal

courts. But such an explanation does not agree with the specifically Hindu identity of the Babu. The more usual explanation is from Persian or Turkish *baba,* father or master – or, as some prefer, the Sanskrit *bapta,* one who sows the seed, i.e., father.

Whatever the origin, the attributes of Babudom are more complex. Babus are the people whom the Portuguese called *gentoos,* from *gentio,* a gentile or heathen (i.e., Hindu) as distinguished from a *Moro* or 'Moor' (Mohammedan). This is the explanation in Yule and Burnell's dictionary of Anglo-Indiana, *Hobson-Jobson* (1886). The word was also used by the British, as in Halhed's *A Code of Gentoo Laws* (1776).

When did 'Babu' begin to be used as a form of address? Mahendranath Datta (1869-1956), Swami Vivekananda's brother, states in his book *Kalikatar Puratan Kahini o Pratha* ('Old Stories and Customs of Calcutta') that it was not in vogue in his childhood. People would then use familial terms like *dada* (elder brother), *kaka* or *mama* (uncle), or more formally, *mashai* or *mahashay. Babu,* says Mahendranath, is the gift of 'our English education'. It gradually replaced other forms of address. We also find the compound *Babumashai,* but this is usually sarcastic.

Western-educated Bengalis despised the word 'Babu' because the sahibs applied it to Indians in a derogatory fashion. Indeed, the word reflects all the contempt of the ruler for the ruled. The disparaging references to Babus in Kipling and other British Indian writers are well-known. In the English writings of nineteenth-century Bengalis too, the 'Young Bengal' model is preferred, though that again was a special version of Babu Culture. The term 'Young Bengal' was first applied to Henry Derozio and his followers. Later, it was extended to all Western-educated Calcutta-based Babus: 'with a smattering of English which he fails not to dignify with the name of solid learning,' as an article in *The Citizen* of 8 July 1871 put it. This special mutation of the Babu was also called the *ejuraj* or 'educated raja', i.e., the Western-educated elite.

In the days of the Nawabs, 'Babu' was a title of honour. Siraj-ud-Daula conferred it on Diwan Shyamram Som. 'Babu Bahadur' was a title of honour even in the early years of British rule: the *Sulabh Samachar* records the existence of one as late as 1871.

I do not know when 'Babu Bahadurs' were created or abolished, but 'Babu' has never been a term of respect with the British. When Rabindranath Thakur (Tagore) renounced his knighthood in 1919 after the Jalianwala Bag massacre, *The Englishman* expressed relief that it could henceforth allude to the poet by the more appropriate title of Babu. The poet Sudhindranath Datta, in his autobiography *The World of Twilight* (1970), comments:

Every paleface appeared to take perverse pleasure in calling them [educated Indians] Babu in deliberate disregard of their present achievement and latent dissociation.

15.1 *A Babu.*
Kalighat pat

15.2 *Radhakanta Deb*

Sudhindranath also cites two delectable anecdotes. Accosted as 'Babu' at a garden party, the young Rabindranath Thakur suavely replied, 'The assurance of your manner suggests a long stay in this country, and yet, sir, you remain ignorant of the fact that only our servants address us as "Babu".' And Sudhindranath's uncle Manmatha Mallik answered an official letter to 'Babu M. C. Mallik' by addressing his reply to 'Babu X. Y. Smith, Secretary to the Government of India'.

Bankimchandra's satirical essay *Babu* beautifully illuminates the relation between Babu and Brown Sahib on the one hand, and black Babu and white 'Nabob' on the other:

The word 'Babu' will have various meanings. To those who will be installed as the rulers of India, known by the name of Englishmen, 'Babu' will mean clerk or shop-keeper. To the poor, the word 'Babu' will mean a richer man. To servants, 'Babu' will mean master. Different from all these, some few men will be born who will be desirous only of living as 'Babus', and it is these whom I am praising. Those who contest this will listen to the *Mahabharata* in vain. Reborn as cows, they will become food for Babus. (Adapted from the translation by S. N. Mukherji and Marian Maddern)

The escapades of the last class, Babus *par excellence,* produced a popular genre of literature in the last century. The trend was set by Bhabanicharan Banerji in his *Kalikata Kamala-*

lay (1823), *Nababubilas* (1825) and *Nababibibilas* (1831). Pyarichand Mitra, the famous Derozian, wrote his novel *Alaler Gharer Dulal* (1858) to show 'the pernicious effects of allowing children to be improperly brought up, with remarks on the existing system of education, self-formation and religious culture, and ... the condition of Hindu society, manners, customs etc.'. There is equally spirited satire of Babudom in Kaliprasanna Sinha's *Hutom Penchar Naksha* (1862). And two plays, Michael Madhusudan Datta's *Ekei ki Baley Sabhyata* ('Is This Civilization?', 1860) and Dinabandhu Mitra's *Sadhabhar Ekadashi* ('The Wife's Widow-Fast', 1866) are staged even today despite the dated nature of their theme.

Mention may also be made of satiric fantasies like Kedarnath Datta's *Sachitra Guljar Nagar* (1871), Haranath Bhanja's *Suraloker Banger Parichay* (Part I 1875, Part II 1877) and Durgacharan Ray's *Debganer Martyey. Agaman* (1880). Rajnarayan Basu's *Sekal ar Ekal* (1874), history of Hindu College (1875) and autobiography (1909), and Shibnath Shastri's *Ramtanu Lahiri o Tatkalin Bangasamaj* (1903) and his autobiography (1918) are full of anecdotes relating to the Western-educated Babus of the nineteenth century.

I remarked at the outset that Babu Culture is a product of Bengal's encounter with the West. A section of historians is inclined to dismiss the whole encounter, and the consequent cultural regeneration in the last century, as 'a glaring instance of the bastard culture that is an offspring of the meeting of the East and the West' (J. C. Ghosh, *Bengali Literature*). This is rather a sweeping generalization. In a pluralistic society like ours, responses and reactions can scarcely be uniform. Babu Culture was initially dominated by zamindars, the Shobhabazar Raj family above all. The lead passed gradually to the Western-educated professional urbanized middle class, who came to be called the *bhadralok*. (Opposite them stood the *chhotalok* or lower orders.) But to regard Radhakanta Deb and Bankimchandra Chatterji – or for that matter, their predecessors Nabakrishna Deb and Rammohan Ray – as all products of the same Babu Culture would be absurdly simplistic. There were a number of diverse components entering into the total phenomenon of Babu life, in addition to the ambivalent absorption of Western life-styles and Western ideas, the two not always in conjunction.

The Babus' fondness for *adda,* for instance, is well-known. But contrary to the popular belief, it was not always a time-wasting pursuit of idle gossip. Many ideas of social reform and cultural regeneration originated from these informal gatherings either in private parlours or in public places. In fact, *adda,* oratory, the publication of periodicals and the founding of organizations for different purposes are integrally associated with Babu culture.

It is difficult to overstress the impact of the periodicals on the new Western-educated class. From Rammohan Ray (1772/4–1833) to Rabindranath Thakur (1861–1941), all the stalwarts of the nineteenth century used periodicals as a vehicle for both polemical and creative writings. Brajendranath Banerji's exhaustive catalogue shows the role of the periodicals in various socio-political, religious and cultural movements.

The lead came from the missionaries of Shrirampur (Serampore). *Digdarshan,* the first Bengali monthly, edited by John Clark Marshman (1794–1877) appeared in April 1818. The first weekly, *Samachar Darpan,* came out the next month, on 23 May 1818. (From 11 July 1829, it became bilingual.) The editor was again John Clark Marshman. The first Bengali weekly edited by a Bengali was also published in 1818: it was Gangakishore Bhattacharya's (?–1831?) *Bangal Gejeti.* Between 1818 and 1867, as many as 219 periodicals were published, mostly in Bengali but some in English or in both languages.

The rich texture of Babu life is also reflected in its associations and societies. Some of them were academic or literary, some socio-religious, some formed to protect the interest of the landholders. Through a number of books, Jogeshchandra Bagal drew our attention long ago to the significance of these institutions, as Rajat Sanyal has done more recently in his *Voluntary Associations and the Urban Public Life in Bengal, 1815-1876* (1980). Sanyal has listed 119 associations formed between 1815 and 1876 under twenty-six heads. Interestingly, twenty-five bodies were formed jointly by Indians and Britishers. These included the Calcutta Public Library (1836), the Bengal Social Science Association (1867), the Landholders' Society (1838) and the Bengal British India Society (1843–46).

II

Although Babu Culture was essentially Hindu-dominated, the Hindu elite was greatly influenced by the Persianized *nawabi* culture. It is important to note that up to the beginning of the nineteenth century, Hindus and Muslims participated in a common elite culture; but they diverged in their response to British rule and Western education. As A. F. Salahuddin Ahmed puts it in his *Social Ideas and Social Change in Bengal: 1818-1835* (1968):

While the Hindus had welcomed English rule with enthusiasm, the Muslims regarded it as a calamity.... The establishment of English rule...brought in its train new ideas from the West which produced a deep stir in Bengali society. The Muslim response was largely negative; it was born of a contempt for those who had snatched away power from their hands. In fact, the Muslims were now rapidly losing the positions of privilege which they had enjoyed for centuries.

In spite of this parting of ways, the early exponents of Babu Culture did not give up their *nawabi* lifestyle. Rajballabh Ray-Rayan, Rammohan Ray, Dwarakanath Thakur were all ardent practitioners of *nawabi* culture. Nabakrishna Deb, a 'native collaborator' in founding British rule in India, started his career as Persian tutor or *munshi* to Warren Hastings. He was an orthodox Hindu, deeply involved in caste politics; but his sumptuous worship of the gods smacked heavily of *nawabi* grandeur, and was accompanied by nautches starring *baijis* from the Muslim courts of Murshidabad and Lucknow, while Clive and other British dignitaries graced the ceremonies as well as Jews, Armenians and Muslims. Indeed, Nabakrishna started the public or community worship (*baroari puja*) of Durga to celebrate the British victory at Palashi! Nothing illustrates better the amalgam of motives in the early 'aristocratic' Babu, as well as his ostentatious pride of wealth.

Nabakrishna is said to have spent nearly a million rupees on his mother's funeral. On this occasion, he displayed a collection of holy images worshipped by the great families of Bengal. At the end of the ceremonies, he returned all the images except one of Gopinath belonging to Maharaja Krishnachandra of Nadia. Nabakrishna is said to have seen the god in a dream, expressing a desire to stay in the Deb family. As Nabakrishna's biographer N. N. Ghosh puts it, 'a friendly dispute developed into a regular quarrel', and Krishnachandra

15.3 *A Calcutta dandy. Kalighat pat*

went to court. Nabakrishna, not to be worsted, sent his adversary an exact replica of the image but kept the original.

Nabakrishna hankered after power, both social and political, as well as money. In order to raise his family in the caste hierarchy, he spent an immense sum in order to marry his grandson Radhakanta to a girl of higher caste: their surname was consequently changed from 'Dey' to the Brahmin-sounding 'Deb'. Ramdulal Dey's descendants also changed their patronymic to 'Deb'.

Ramdulal's overnight rise to prosperity through a deal over a sunken ship is a well-known story told elsewhere in this volume. He too sought social power and religious distinction, and looked upon his wealth as a means to obtain it. 'Society is in my iron safe,' he once remarked. 'I'll buy up all the *kulins*' [Brahmins of pure caste]. The occasion of the remark was the so-called Kaliprasadi Scandal, when Kaliprasad Datta was ostracized by the Brahmins at the time of his father Churamani's funeral for having kept a Muslim concubine. Ramdulal came to Kaliprasad's rescue and made good his boast: he did win over the *kulins*.

Animosities between castes and groups were endemic in old Calcutta, and Brahmins were always handicapped by their lack of wealth. When Nabakrishna Deb was offered the *talukdari* of Sutanuti, the local Brahmins sent a deputation to the Governor-General Warren Hastings, protesting against having to become tenants and 'subjects' (*prajas*) of an 'outsider'. (Nabakrishna originally came from Murshidabad.) Hastings offered Nabakrishna an alternative estate, but the latter refused to change on the ground that it had become a matter of prestige.

III

It would be wrong to surmise that caste politics was the concern of only those Babus who lacked formal Western education. Bankimchandra, indeed, pointed out in 1882 in a famous controversy over Hinduism with the missionary William Hastie, Principal of the General Assembly's Institution, that 'Caste...is non-essential. There have been and there still are many Hindu sects who discard caste distinctions.' But religion and caste were a vital reality in everyday life. They played a dominant role in the affairs of both Hindu College and Sanskrit College, though the class characters of

the two institutions were poles apart. About the outlook of the Hindu College students, Bankimchandra's satirical *Confessions of a 'Young Bengal'* gives a clue:

We have cast away caste. We have outlived the absurdity of a social classification based upon the accident of birth. But we are not such ultra-radicals as to adopt for our catchword the impracticable formula of 'Equality and Fraternity'.

Ishwarchandra Vidyasagar got strong support for his social reforms from the alumni of Hindu College. But as Principal of Sanskrit College, he had a more bitter experience of the other institution. Time and again, he had to complain about 'the pupils of the Junior Department of the Hindu College [who] frequently coming into the premises of the Sanskrit College quarrel with its junior pupils and beat them.' On 28 August 1852 he even informed F. J. Mouat, Secretary of the Education Council, that the Hindu College students had hired three European sailors to beat up the Sanskrit College boys.

The reason is not far to seek: it lay in differences of class, background and outlook, a vulgarized reflection of the Anglicist-Orientalist controversy. Both Hindu and Sanskrit Colleges preserved and protected Hindu interests; but whereas Hindu College was open to all castes, Sanskrit College at first admitted Brahmins and Baidyas only. Even Vidyasagar, despite his enlightened social reforms and his insistence on Western learning and English studies in the Sanskrit College curriculum, had to proceed cautiously in this respect. When Mouat proposed opening Sanskrit College to students of all castes, Vidyasagar (in a letter of 28 March 1851) agreed in principle, but suggested 'as a measure of expediency' that only Kayastha students should be allowed for the time being. He cited the precedent of a relative of Radhakanta Deb, a Kayastha, who had been admitted earlier in 1828-29. He also attached a note signed by a number of teachers who were 'averse to this innovation'.

Vidyasagar was handicapped by his milieu. He did not hesitate to criticize publicly his old teacher and colleague, Taranath Tarkavachaspati, when the latter opposed his anti-polygamy movement. But he knew that educational reforms could not be carried through by antagonizing his colleagues.

An anonymous rhyme of the last century bemoaned:

Jat marley tin Seney,
Keshab Seney Wil-seney Isti-seney.

Caste, this declared, has been destroyed by three 'Sens': Keshab Sen the Brahmo leader; 'Wil-sen' or Wilson's Hotel, where Hindus would guzzle 'forbidden food'; and the 'Isti-sen' or station, as the niceties of caste could not be observed on railway journeys.

When Hindu College was opened, orthodox Hindus like Radhakanta Deb thought Western education would not affect the rigid structure of Hindu society. But the contradiction between the College's name and its secular curriculum soon became evident. Many students, such as Maheshchandra Ghosh, Krishnamohan Banerji, Gnanendramohan Thakur and Michael Madhusudan Datta, embraced Christianity. This was taken by the traditionalists to indicate a concerted attempt by the Christian powers to destroy Hinduism. When a teacher of the College, Kailaschandra Basu, turned Christian in 1848, Radhakanta Deb and Prasannakumar Thakur wanted him removed; and we know how Derozio was forced to resign from the College 'without even the mockery of a trial'. The resolution of the College Committee on this last occasion reads:

All those students who are publicly hostile to Hinduism and the established custom of the country and who have proved themselves as such by their conduct, should be turned out.

This was later amended to read: 'the parents…if they have reason to think that the College is the cause of hostility to Hinduism in their children, can at any time withdraw them from it.' The College authorities now clearly disclaim initiative in the matter of such expulsions.

The European members of the Committee declined to vote in the Derozio affair, as being 'a subject affecting the state of native feeling'. But twenty-three years later, in 1853, a new challenge arose when Hira Bulbul, a well-known Muslim prostitute, wanted to enrol her son at the College. This time neither the Government nor the British members of the Committee (who constituted the majority) remained aloof: they accepted the application, refusing to discriminate on the grounds of religion or birth.

15.4 *Left: Prasannakumar Thakur*

15.5 *Right: The Reverend Krishnamohan Banerji*

15.6 *A Babu and his Bibi. Kalighat pat*

should either take full responsibility for running the College or make it over to the Government. The latter course was accepted. In 1855, the Government took over the institution, renamed it Presidency College, and abolished all considerations of religion and social position. But the erstwhile school branch retains its old name of Hindu School to this day, and its admission rules remained unchanged until as late as 1974.

Macaulay believed that Western education would eradicate 'idolatry' from India. He wanted the Babus to act as intermediaries: 'interpreters between us and the millions whom we govern – a class of persons Indian in blood and colour, but English in tastes, in opinions, in morals, and in intellect.' As my account shows, the Babus' response was ambivalent in the extreme. Many of them blindly imitated the English; yet they resisted any attempt to denationalize their culture. This was vividly illustrated in the Jagadananda Mukherji affair. During the Prince of Wales's visit to Calcutta in 1876, Jagadananda, a government lawyer at the Calcutta High Court, agreed to let him view the women's quarters of his house: the Prince had desired to see a typical *zenana*. Even the Governor-General Lord Northbrook was shocked at the idea, as needless to say was the entire Hindu community. Jagadananda was lampooned on the stage. Subsequent developments, detailed in the article on the old Calcutta theatre, led to the enactment of the notorious Dramatic Performances Act.

So long as the Babus were collaborators in founding the British Empire, sometimes acquiring fortunes overnight by such means, they did not realize that the ultimate motives of ruler and ruled could not be identical. The disillusionment came when the Babus – and their mutant species, the Brown Sahibs – started demanding an equal share in power and administration. They grew sadder and wiser after the furious European reaction to the 'Black Acts' of 1836 and 1849, which proposed to abolish the exemption enjoyed by Europeans from the jurisdiction of the Company's criminal courts, and the Ilbert Bill of 1883 empowering Indian magistrates to judge Europeans accused in criminal cases. Moreover, there was a serious move after the 1857 Revolt to shift the capital elsewhere. All these factors gradually alienated the Babus from their rulers.

Hindu society was shocked and alarmed. Many guardians withdrew their wards from the College, and a new institution called the Hindu Metropolitan College was opened with D. L. Richardson, a former teacher of Hindu College, as Principal. The agitation became so intense that the Governor-General Lord Dalhousie had to intervene. He censured the Education Council for violating the admission rules of Hindu College: Hira Bulbul's son had to leave.

But that was not the end of the matter this time. At the beginning of 1854, the Government told the Managing Committee that they

As this sense of alienation increased, the Babus grew more and more interested in forming political organizations to ventilate their own grievances. The Indian League (established on 25 September 1875) was perhaps the first of its kind to overtly declare among its objects: 'To adopt means for the development of the economic resources of the country'. But the spirit of *daladali* (factionalism) was innate in the Babus. The League split within six months. The Indian Association was formed on 26 July 1876 by the dissidents, who included Ananda-mohan Basu (1847-1906), Shibnath Shastri (1847-1919) and Surendranath Banerji (1848-1925).

As the Babus were pushed into the background in both administrative and economic affairs, they gradually grew restive and chose the path of agitation. This was first confined to meetings and petitions, but later they began to contemplate violence. In the Report of the Sedition Committee (1918), S.A.T. Rowlatt made some interesting observations on the spread of revolutionary ideas and the formation of secret societies among the Bengali *bhadralok*. His immediate context was the revolutionary movement attempted by Barindrakumar Ghosh (1880-1959), the brother of Shri Arabinda. Rowlatt's subsequent remarks on the nature of the *bhadralok* are even more penetrating:

The *bhadralok* of Bengal have been for centuries peaceful and unwarlike, but, through the influence of the great central city of Calcutta, were early in appreciating the advantages of Western learning.... In their own province *bhadralok* still almost monopolise the clerical and subordinate administrative services of Government. They are prominent in teaching, and at the Bar. But, in spite of these advantages, they have felt the shrinkage of foreign employment; and as the education which they receive is generally literary and ill-adapted to incline the youthful mind to industrial, commercial or agricultural pursuits, they have not succeeded in finding fresh outlets for their energies. Their hold on land too has weakened owing to increasing pressure of population and excessive sub-infeudation. Altogether their economic prospects have narrowed, and the increasing numbers who draw fixed incomes have felt the pinch of rising prices. On the other hand, the memories and associations of their earlier prosperity, combined with growing contact with Western ideas and standards of comfort, have raised their expectations...[so that] a growing number have become less and less inclined to accept the conditions of life in which they found themselves on reaching manhood. *Bhadralok* have always been prominent among the supporters of Indian political movements; and their leaders have watched with careful attention the events in the world outside India.

Macaulay had envisaged a 'fusion of culture'. The Babus belied that expectation too. Instead of disseminating new ideas among the tradition-bound Indian masses, they widened the gap between the educated class and the common people. They remained as distant from the masses as the sahibs were from them. And while Babus of various types carried into effect a new cultural awakening in Bengal, the 'Babu Culture' specifically so called came to consist chiefly in a vulgar display of wealth.

The only contact with the masses remained through religious festivals and indigenous art forms like the *jatra*. In his book *The Parlour and the Streets* (1989), Sumanta Banerji has elaborately discussed the socio-political factors behind the schism between *bhadralok* and *chhotalok* culture in Calcutta and the marginalization of the latter. He takes the *jatra* as an important example; but in fact, it appears that even in Calcutta, the *jatra* was never threatened by any other art form, imported or indigenous, until the advent of the cinema in the late 1920s. Moreover, all the major exponents of Western-style theatre in Calcutta, from Girishchandra Ghosh (1844-1912) to Bijan Bhattacharya (1917-78), drew largely on the indigenous form. Rabindranath Thakur's views are too well-known to need repeating here. In fact, the *jatra* became a very popular medium of public agitation in the Swadeshi days. Mukunda Das's (1878-1934) *jatra* was equally popular with both *bhadralok* and *chhotalok* audiences.

I may conclude by qualifying my opening remark. Babu Culture was the result of an imperfect encounter with the West. Moreover, with the radical shifts in the economic power structure of Calcutta, the glamour of Babudom faded away: ultimately 'Babu' came to mean nothing but a clerk. Krishnadas Pal observed in his *Young Bengal Vindicated* (1856):

It is indeed a sorry feature in the character of young Bengal that with all his knowledge and enlightenment, with all his boasted love of freedom, he prefers the kennel of a *keranee* [clerk]. Indeed his *pugree* and *chapkan* have been his ruin.

But the sad reality is that his *topee* and *pantaloon* proved equally disastrous.

15.7
Anandamohan Basu

THE WORLD OF RAMJAN OSTAGAR
THE COMMON MAN OF
OLD CALCUTTA

Sumanta Banerjee

The pageantry of the English nabobs and memsahibs and of the Bengali diwans, banians and Babus has engrossed us too long. It is time to remember the anonymous citizen of nineteenth-century Calcutta – the artisan and the hawker, the servant and the coolie, the cobbler and the tailor, the street entertainer and the prostitute. It was his toil that made possible the high life of the 'city of palaces'. He cooked the feasts for the sumptuous parties thrown by the Thakurs and Malliks. He swept the floors of their palatial mansions. He drove them in their broughams for evening outings along the banks of the Hugli. He stitched their *chogas, chapkans* and *pyjamas.*

It is a pity we do not have a Bengali equivalent of Henry Mayhew, author of the massive Victorian study, *London Labour and the London Poor*. In the absence of such documentation, much of the lives of old Calcutta's populace has simply disappeared from the pages of history. From bits and pieces scattered in newspaper reports, memoirs, street names, songs and proverbs, we can at best try to rebuild that twilight world of the shadowy figures who once populated the dark alleys of Calcutta's 'Black Town'.

One such figure whom we can conjure up is Ramjan Ostagar, who may provide us with an entry point for our adventure into the past. It seems odd that so little should be known today

about Ramjan Ostagar's life, for he was apparently well-known in the early nineteenth century: his name was commemorated in 'Ramjan Ostagar's Lane' till the last quarter of that century.

All that we can gather about Ramjan Ostagar today is that he lived in the Nimtala area of north Calcutta, and was a tailor by profession. His name suggests that he was a Muslim: tailoring was almost a Muslim monopoly in old Calcutta, and the Ostagars were the master tailors. It must have been a thriving business, given the variety of sartorial fashions in the Calcutta of the early nineteenth century. The Bengali aristocrats needed Ramjan and his kind for sewing the still fashionable Mughal-style embroidered robes which they sported on formal occasions. The less affluent members of commercial society, the clerks and small employees, the professional 'babus' and traders, flocked to these tailors for their daily attire – the 'banian' (a close-fitting short-sleeved double-breasted tunic, with one side folded over the other and tied with laces), the 'China coat' (an open-breasted coat with bone buttons) and the newly-introduced European shirt with collar and cuffs, popular among the anglicized 'Young Bengal' generation.

However, by the 1830s, Ramjan Ostagar and his fellow-tailors had lost their rich patrons, who were shifting their loyalties to the new English tailoring firms. The plight of Ramjan and his colleagues was vividly described in the *Samachar Darpan* of 9 January 1830:

Ramjan Ostagar and many others like him amassed fortunes by tailoring. But later with the arrival of Mr. Gibson's company and similar firms, the needle-experts [i.e. tailors] have now out of hunger – apart from their inability to buy a piece of land the size of a needle – themselves been reduced to the lean girth of a needle.

Being thus thrust into the sidelines of his profession, Ramjan was soon to be ousted from public memory as well. In 1877, the Municipal Commissioners renamed several streets and lanes, whereby, as the historian A. K. Ray put it, streets formely named after 'lowly individuals' were renamed after 'respectable persons'. Thus by one stroke of the pen, Ramjan Ostagar's Lane became Madanmohan Datta's Lane. The 'respectable' Madanmohan was Diwan to the Collector of Calcutta and Salt Agent of the 24-Parganas.

II

The rise and fall of Ramjan Ostagar epitomizes the changing fortunes of the working class in nineteenth-century Calcutta. Traditionally skilled craftsmen, who had been lured away from the villages of Bengal to the new city in the eighteenth century and had struck it rich, gradually sank into poverty by the middle of the next century, unable to compete with the European tradesmen who began pouring into the growing metropolis, attracted by the rich clientele. The same *Samachar Darpan* lists the occupations and names of indigenous practitioners who were thrown out of work by the arrival of European tradesmen. We hear of Ajuddin Chand Mistri, a master mason; the Pals, well-known carpenters; and Shib Mistri, a famous goldsmith. They were replaced by European retail proprietors like the tailoring company of Ranken, Hamilton's the jewellers, and Monteith's the boot and saddle-makers. The descendants of Ramjan Ostagar and Ajuddin Mistri were employed at low wages by these firms, which won over the city's elite by extending long credit.

By the last quarter of the nineteenth century, the once-prosperous artisans and craftsmen had joined the ranks of the lowliest labourers – the barbers and washermen, the servants and scavengers. The 1876 Census of Calcutta – the first to list the population according to occupation – referred to the 'small number of artisan

16.1 *A Muslim tailor. Colesworthy Grant*

castes (12,864)' in the city compared to the past. 'A Report on Conditions of the Lower Classes' of Bengal observed in 1888: 'as their occupations are hereditary, and are changed with difficulty, they suffer much when any alteration in trade renders their particular handicrafts unremunerative'.

The 1876 Census gives us an interesting list of the variety of occupations among the city's lower orders. There were domestic servants of various categories like *khansamas* or butlers, cooks, gardeners and *punkah*-pullers (those who pulled the elaborate hanging fans); barbers, water-carriers, washermen; transport workers like palanquin-bearers, coachmen, boatmen and porters; flower-sellers and confectioners; artisans like potters, bangle-makers, clay-modellers and braziers; persons manufacturing traditional commodities like oil and salt; and the first generation of the industrial proletariat – the jute and textile-mill workers. Even the popular entertainers were numerous and varied enough to earn the attention of the 1876 Census: street musicians, singers, actors, dancers and jugglers. And of course there were the prostitutes, whose ranks seem to have swelled from year to year.

This motley lived in *kutcha* huts, covered first by thatched roofs and after 1837 by tiles when thatch was prohibited to guard against fire. The number of such huts fell from 53,289 in 1821 to

16.2 *Above: The servants of Lt-Col Gilbert. Anonymous painting*

16.3 *Below: The 'Native Town': D'Oyly*

forced to seek shelter on the outskirts. According to an estimate by Captain Steele in 1831, at least one-fifth of the servants and other workers employed within the town were residing outside its limits. The 1876 Census found that around 10,000 people entered the city every day by the river Hugli from the suburbs.

The *kutcha* huts, cluttered in slums, were chiefly concentrated in the north-central area between Mechhuabazar and Boubazar. But they were thinly dispersed also in the fashionable south, where Beverley discovered 'unsightly collections of native huts' even among 'the palatial mansions of Chowringhee'. According to Beverley: 'The tiled hut or mud *"baree"* that in the mofussil would be occupied by a single family, is in Calcutta the constant home of some eight or ten households…'. Describing these huts, 'the walls of which are of mud, or of matted reed or bamboo', another English observer, J. R. Martin, commented: 'these would not be so bad, but that they are' uniformly placed on the bare ground, or on damp mud, but little raised, which continually emits injurious exhalations.'

50,871 in 1837, and further to 22,860 in 1876, the year of the Census. Explaining the decline, H. Beverley, the officer in charge of the Census, pointed out that 'huts have largely made way for the erection of pucka buildings and the construction of tanks and new roads.' He added: 'Every street that is widened, every new square opened, means so many persons displaced, and as the limits of the Town are fixed, many of them doubtless remove outside it altogether'. Thus, all through the nineteenth century, the poor were being displaced from their original settlements within the city and

We can get an idea of the living standards of the Calcutta poor from an English missionary's account in the 1820s. It seems that the highest-

paid among them was a *khansama* working in some English or rich Bengali household for Rs 8 a month. The lowest-paid was the coolie or day-labourer, at Rs 4 per month. Sweepers, gardeners and water-carriers (the *bhistis* with their leather water-bags) made between Rs 4 **and** Rs 5 a month. About their diet the missionary commented:

The coarsest rice, even in a good harvest season, cannot be purchased for less than one rupee per maund. Wheaten bread is never seen in the houses of the poor, nor any animal food whatever, except a little fish, principally shrimps, which are caught in great numbers in the numerous nullahs and rivers in Bengal.

The plight of the Calcutta poor had not changed in the slightest a decade later, as evident from J. R. Martin's description of the average daily labourer's lifestyle in 1837. With his wife and two children, he eats two maunds of rice in the month.

They eat twice in the 24 hours, at 8 a.m. and at 10 p.m. ... Such a day labourer must have some other resource, otherwise he could not live; if he is a Musselman, he rears a few fowls; or if a Hindoo he has a few fruit trees near his house, and he sells the fruit. If by these or any other means, the labourer can raise half a rupee or a rupee monthly, this procures him salt and a little oil, and one or two other prime necessaries; though vast multitudes of the poor obtain only from day to day boiled rice, green pepper pods, and boiled herbs; the step above this is a little oil with the rice.

The stark poverty which remained confined through the year to the tiled roofs and mud walls, used to converge in a mass of deprivation before the houses of the Bengali rich once or twice a year, whenever there was a *shraddha* or funeral in a stately home. On such occasions the poor were given alms, the custom being known as *kangali-biday*. Reports in contemporary newspapers describe in vivid detail the clamour of the hungry masses. Reporting the funeral of the widow of the multi-millionaire Nilmani Mallik, the *Indian Gazette* of 30 April 1830 described

a great number of poor people, each of whom expected to have had one rupee... The excessive heat, together with the delay that occurred in distributing the money intended for the poor, has caused some mortality among them. Several of

them, alarmed and disappointed, have hurled away home plundering the shops of petty retail dealers of everything upon which they could lay their hands.

III

The bulk of reports in contemporary journals, newspapers and government dispatches may give the impression that the entire city throughout the nineteenth century was obsessed with subtle points of Hindu and Christian scriptures, controversies over 'suttee' and widow remarriage, and meetings in the Town Hall and other places to press the demands of the educated Bengali *bhadralok* for posts in the administrative services.

But the truth is that the vast majority of the city's population dwelt completely outside the world of these reports. The issues that stirred the *bhadralok* were virtually meaningless for them. For instance *kulin* polygamy, one of the objects of reform in nineteenth-century Bengal, affected only the upper castes. *Satipratha* or widow burning was not widely prevalent among the lower-caste Bengali majority. As for widow remarriage, among the lower-caste and lower-class Bengalis the remarriage of a widow, or her cohabitation with a man, was quite often accepted by the socially sanctioned

16.4 *Bhistis or water-carriers. Old engraving*

sanga arrangement. There was a popular saying in those days, 'When the hut collapses, even the goat tramples on it. When one becomes a widow, everyone comes to arrange a *sanga* with her.' In cities like Calcutta, widows from the labouring classes often cohabited with men of their own choice. This was testified by a women textile worker before the Indian Factory Commission in 1890, who said that she was a widow living with an 'adopted husband'.

For the most part, Calcutta's lower orders remained invisible to the *bhadralok* society. They found their way into newspaper columns only when they posed a threat to the economic and social comforts of the *bhadralok*. Thus in 1827, the Oriya palanquin-bearers

16.5 *A maira or sweet-seller. Solvyns*

assembled on the plain of the Fort [William], others at Chand Pal Ghat, in separate bodies. They say these confounded Firingis [Englishmen] have been at their usual tricks of taxing our bodily labour.... They have

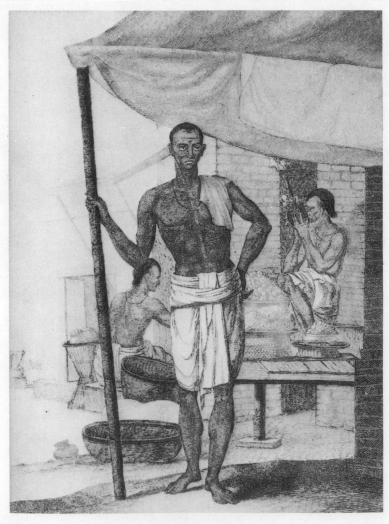

refused, accordingly, to bear palanquins for these few days. (*Calcutta Gazette,* 21 May 1827).

The immediate provocation for the strike was apparently the new rates fixed for the palanquin-bearers by a Government Gazette notification issued on 14 May 1827: 14 annas for a fourteen-hour day according to the 'English clock'. The Bengali *Samachar Darpan* of 2 June 1827 explained the iniquity involved:

Because of the new law fixing rates according to time, the bearers' livelihoods are in jeopardy, since the bearers do not have watches, and the people they carry have them, and since the word of the gentry is more respected than that of the plebeians. There are many among the respected gentry who move around for one and a half hours or more, and pay only for an hour by showing their watches, and the poor bearers cannot say anything in protest.

But such expressions of *bhadralok* sympathy or understanding were few and far-between. In fact, the Bengali gentry was very much a party to the exploitation of the city's poor. In 1834 the salt-workers of Calcutta, known as *khalaris,* staged a demonstration before the Governor-General's house protesting against the custom whereby each of them had to offer a free gift of a vessel-load of salt to the then Salt Diwan, 'Prince' Dwarakanath Thakur.

In 1851, the drivers of bullock-carts (the chief means of carrying freight in those days) went on strike against a proposed tax, and succeeded in getting it repealed. Noting their success, the editor of the *Sambad Prabhakar* grumbled: 'Had I known this before, I would have left the job of an editor and become a bullock-cart driver, and could have become the object of the King's favour!' (17 February 1851). Again in 1859, we find the same paper complaining about a milkmen's strike, whereby *sandesh* – the *bhadralok's* favourite sweet – disappeared from the market.

Since the servant problem was another major concern of the city's 'respectable' classes, we are able to glean from contemporary newspapers a vague idea of the daily chores of those employed in Bengali households. A letter in the *Sambad Bhaskar* of 12 December 1849 complained about the dearth of servants and added:

In the past, servants in this country used to follow the rule of getting up early in the morning, sweeping the sitting-room, filling the hookah with water, shaking out the mat, going to the market, folding the dhoti into pleats, drawing water from the tank or river or well, feeding the cows, cleaning the cow-shed, massaging [the master] with oil, bathing him and wiping him dry and serving him his lunch. All this a servant would do for a monthly wage of one rupee plus food and clothes. Nowadays, no one agrees to do these chores even for Rs 10....

From Rabindranath Thakur's reminiscences (in *Chhelebela*), two servants peer at us out of the dim corridors of the Jorasanko mansion. Brajeshwar was a sort of major-domo. Formerly a village school-teacher, he was probably driven by poverty to take up a servant's job. His penchant for bookish expressions, a relic of his past, was an object of ridicule for his masters, who apparently dismissed him as an upstart. The other servant was Shyam, a simple rustic soul from East Bengal, who entertained the children with hair-raising stories about dacoits.

More graphic thumb-nail sketches of servants have been left by Rabindranath's nephew, the artist Abanindranath. There is the unforgettable Padma Dasi, who looked after the child 'Aban', and disappeared one day after a bloody fight with another maid. The child Abanindranath's last glimpse of her was of a dark face with dishevelled hair and blood flowing down her forehead – 'the figure of a *bhairavi* hewn in black stone with vermilion daubed on her head.' He has left a vivid picture of a typical coachman of those days – Shamsher, the dark-skinned Muslim with his long hair hanging down in curls, his moustaches tinged red with henna and his beard parted in the middle. When taking out his master (Abanindranath's father) for his evening outings, he would change into *churidar* pyjamas, varnished shoes and buckles, a turquoise ring set in silver and a brocaded red cloak, with a brocaded belt round his waist and a head-dress shaped like a huge flat dish. Kaliprasanna Sinha's *Hutom Penchar Naksha* (1862-64) gives us fleeting glimpses of the lower orders of nineteenth-century Calcutta, such as the following:

It is dusk: the milkmen are going to the shops with vessels across their shoulders. The fishwomen have washed their wooden planks, *bantis* [fish-knives] and baskets, and are lighting lamps. Workers with ladders on their shoulders are running fast to put on the gas street-lights.

A host of typical members of the labouring poor pass before our eyes in a rollicking procession. But once the magic of the past has ceased to touch them, they disappear into the smog of Calcutta's past.

IV

The life of the urban poor in nineteenth-century Calcutta, as pictured in these scattered records, is not a pretty one, stained as it is by squalor and misery. Yet theirs was not a world of unmixed gloom. They threw up their own entertainers – singers and dancers, mimes and puppeteers. Waggish humour burst impressively through suffering. The facets of a variegated popular culture suddenly shone out from their dingy slums like a smile on the wan face of a sick child: the songs of Bhola Maira, the sweet seller and *kabial* or extempore singer; the *jatras* of Gopal Urey; the processions of *sangs* (panto-mime jesters); the street dances of the *jhumurwalis*.

Unsurprisingly, the Bengali *bhadralok* and their English patrons could not recognize the importance of these entertainments for the poor, which at times were even invisible to them. Miss Mary Carpenter, an English educationist and social reformer who visited Calcutta in 1868, noticed the poor people in the streets as she drove down Chitpur in north Calcutta. Later, she commented in her travel diary: 'What I saw of the lower orders led me to think their existence a joyless one.' In point of fact, the lower orders' concept of joy was widely different from that propounded by the evangelistic social reformer and her Bengali admirer Keshabchandra Sen who, following her advice, set up a school with the ostensible purpose of educating the city's poorer classes and weaning them away from their 'abominable entertain-ments' (*Sulabh Samachar,* 1 Agrahayan 1277, Bengali Calendar).

These 'abominable entertainments' contributed to a rich popular culture, consisting partly of rural folk forms imported from village homes and partly of innovations born of the new urban environment. The cultural output was both oral, like the *kabi-gan* (extempore poetic contests), *panchali* (five-part) songs and jingling verses; and visual, like comic street-shows in the form of pantomime (*sang*), *jatra* theatres and dances, and the paintings of the Kalighat *pats*.

The thread running through all these popular cultural forms was humour – primarily at the expense of the rich and the famous, the babus and the dandies, the deceitful Hindu priests and the Christian missionaries, who were viewed by the lower orders with mingled distrust and envy. One of the earliest popular sayings coined in eighteenth-century Calcutta lampoons the norms set by these various types of fortune-hunters who converged on the new city:

> *Jal, juochuri, mithye katha*
> *Ei tin niye Kalikata.*

['Forgery, swindling and falsehood, these three make up Calcutta.']

This expresses pithily and scathingly the popular perception of the happenings in Calcutta in those days: Justice Elijah Impey's success in securing a lucrative government job for his relation; Maharaja Nandakumar's payment of Rs 3 lakh to Warren Hastings to procure a job for his son Gurudas Ray; the death sentence passed on Nandakumar by Impey (a friend of Hastings) when Hastings wanted to get rid of Nandakumar by bringing a charge of forgery against him. Things had not changed much by the mid-nineteenth century, when street singers would sing

> *Ajab sahar Kalketa:*
> *Ranri bari juri gari michhey kathar ki keta!*

A strange city indeed is Calcutta. Whores and houses and carriages abound. And how fashionable it is to lie!

So too, popular proverbs like *Companir latgiri, parer dhaney poddari* ['Usurping the wealth of others, the Company's servants have become aristocrats'] indicate a remarkable understanding of the means by which Company traders and officials became 'nabobs'.

While the authors of these *blasons populaires* were anonymous, those of the *kabi-gans* were quite famous in those days. From the late eighteenth century came Gonjla Guin (from a caste of cowherds) and Keshta Muchi (Keshta the cobbler); a little later, Bhola Maira (Bhola the sweet-maker) and Kukur-mukho Gora (Dog-Faced Gora). As their names and surnames often suggest, they came from the lower castes and humbler professions. They stuck to their original occupations and sang in their spare time. Bhola Maira, for instance, used to

run his shop on Bagbazar Street in north Calcutta. One of his surviving songs gives an excellent description of his profession and beliefs:

I'm Bhola, the sweet-maker and pupil of Haru [Thakur – another famous *kabial*] I live in Bagbazar. Autumn, winter, spring, or summer, Bhola's frying-pot is never empty. I may not be as good as the poet Kalidas, being only a simple cook, frying cakes and sweets during the Pujas. But if I find a *kabial* I never back out [from contending with him], however unworthy the rascal might be.

The *kabi-gans* of the late eighteenth and early nineteenth centuries led to the popularity of the folk-theatrical form of *jatra*. A leading proponent of this in mid-nineteenth-century Calcutta was Gopal Urey (1817-57). He was about eighteen years old when he came to Calcutta from Orissa, probably in 1835. He used to sell bananas in the streets. One evening, when he was hawking his goods, his cries attracted the attention of Radhamohan Sarkar, a rich Bengali music-lover who lived in Boubazar. Detecting great promise in Gopal's voice, he recruited him for his *jatra* troupe. Later Gopal formed his own troupe and popularized a stage version of the eighteenth-century poet Bharatchandra's *Bidyasundar* by innovations like dialogues in short, lilting verses. These were commonly in the vivacious measure of *ar-khemta*.

Gopal also introduced a special type of dance in his *jatras*, the famous *khemta*, a jaunty dance popular among both men and women of the lower orders in nineteenth-century Bengal. Comic relief was provided by songs and dances, the artistes assuming the roles of various types of manual labourers. Often in their songs, they satirized their masters' ways. One such song, put in the mouth of Kalua the sweeper in Gopal's *jatra*, makes fun of the babu's dependence on him for cleaning his rooms, which reverses the patron-client relationship by making the employer almost subservient to the menial:

Babu, I work for ready cash. It's grand: the work is difficult, but the Babu has to depend on others. I order my own work, but the Babu has to wait for me. He keeps asking: 'Where is Kalua the sweeper?'

The *jatras* often incorporated street songs about working-class occupations, sometimes even at the latter's expense. A milkmaid's song runs:

Who'll buy milk – flowing pure right from the cow's udders? Only half of it is water from the tap.

Spectacles or visual entertainments were another major component of the popular culture of nineteenth-century Calcutta. They comprised not only varieties of dance like the *jhumur* and the *khemta,* performed at fairs or marketplaces, and the *kathputli* puppeteers, but the more popular *sang* shows or pantomimes. During the annual Charak festival in April, these became a weapon in the hands of the underdog for lampooning the upper classes. The objects of the lampoon ranged from rich Babus to religious hypocrites. The Bengali journal *Gnananweshan* of 27 April 1833, describing a procession of *sangs* in Calcutta during the Charak festival that year, mentioned one that mocked the bloated rich by depicting an old man covered with flowers, with a foot swollen by elephantiasis. Another *sang* was worshipping his foot with all the piety of a devotee. This was followed by a wooden platform borne by other *sangs*. Upon it sat a *guru* counting his rosary beads and muttering prayers. As the bearers moved him round and round, he kept fixing his lecherous eyes on the women watching from the balconies, gazing upwards the next moment with prayerful gestures to his god.

The visual satire of such religious hypocrisy, the foppish dandyism of the babus, and other trends in contemporary society emerge more forcefully in another form of Calcutta folk art – the *pat* paintings of Kalighat, or what came to be known in European circles as 'bazaar paintings'. These were done on cheap paper in water colour by a community of *patuas,* traditional folk-painters, who had drawn on canvas scrolls in the villages, but switched over to paper after coming to Calcutta.

For the city's poorer classes, such comical expressions remained an essential part of their social life. They grew largely from the need to laugh at things which their creators were unable to face and fight. The lampoons and caricatures afforded a temporary sense of superiority, turning their adversaries into figures of fun, ludicrous in their own eyes. Thus they strove to defeat the gloom of their existence through laughter, transforming the squalor into a gay carnival.

V

Ramjan Ostagar and Ajuddin Mistri, Bhola

16.6 *Above: Charak Puja festivities. Mrs Belnos*

16.7 *Below: The Mendicant Cat: illustrating a proverbial Bengali phrase for a religious hypocrite. Kalighat pat*

Moira and Gopal Urey are like memories cast in wax, to be moulded into fanciful shapes by twentieth-century minds. Shadowy monuments to their work and play survive in the few old street names of north Calcutta which have escaped the Corporation's zeal for new nomenclature. Chhidam Mudi the grocer is remembered by a lane which bears his name, while Panchi Dhobani's Gali evokes memories of the laundress of that name. Gulu Ostagar and Ramhari Mistri have had better luck than Ramjan and Ajuddin, for they still have lanes called after them.

The grander memories of nineteenth-century Calcutta are enshrined in magnificent works of architecture, albeit often crumbling ones. The humbler legacy is devoid of such tangible memorials, deriving as it does from dwellers in shifting slums, the tailors, cobblers, grocers, sweet-sellers, barbers and washermen. Some scattered names, torn shreds of song, tattered memories of a few events are all that we can lay our hands upon.

But perhaps we can still salvage from the fast-changing cityscape a few spots made memorable by the labouring people of old Calcutta. Monuments can be raised at Fort William and Chandpal Ghat to the Oriya palanquin-bearers who organized the first strike in the city's history. A plaque might be placed at the site of Bhola Moira's shop, a now vanished thatched hut on Bagbazar Street between the house of Bhagabaticharan Ganguli, a rich citizen, and the printing press of the Sanskrit scholar Anandaram Barua.

At the very least, today's unpriggish *bhadralok* could venture to put Gopal Urey's *Bidyasundar* on the boards again. We could still respond to the lilting tunes and earthy language of the song of Hirey Malini, a witch and an Iago rolled in one, but mellowed by Gopal's breezy humour:

You don't know me yet, my darling: I steer my pinnace across dry land. I'm no ordinary auntie. I'm dangerous: I can show you Varanasi and Mecca at the snap of my fringers. If I want I can trap the moon. By my charm, I can bring out the chaste woman from her sheltered home. I bring her out, and stagger the world.

EDUCATION
IN OLD CALCUTTA

Poromesh Acharya

In old Calcutta different types of education grew side by side. There were indigenous elementary schools called *pathshalas*, indigenous schools of higher learning called *toles,* and also English schools. We have little evidence about indigenous Islamic schools; there might at least have been the primary schools called *makhtabs*.

We hardly know anything about the system of education in Sutanuti, Gobindapur and Kalikata. The first school on record in the city of Calcutta is an English school. However, indigenous schools were scattered all over the city, though concentrated in central and north Calcutta. The number is variously estimated. In his first report on the state of education in

17.1 A'pathshala'.
Solvyns

Bengal, William Adam cited the Calcutta School Society's count of 211 indigenous elementary schools in 1818-19, with 4,908 children (said to be 'one-third the number of Native children capable of receiving instruction'). In the same year, Gourmohan Vidyalankar found 166 *pathshalas* with 3,487 students; Stephen la Primaudaye 200 with 4,200 students, and the *Samachar Darpan* 232 *pathshalas*.

In Calcutta as elsewhere, *pathshalas* were established through individual initiative and were usually single-teacher schools. They generally confined themselves to teaching the three R's by the method of rote. With the growth of the city, the job market for *pathshala* teachers naturally increased; but the incumbents were often those who failed to secure any other *bhadralok* job. The slender fees paid according to each student's means were the only source of funds. The more enterprising *gurus* sometimes ran a grocery shop at the same time.

In the absence of any government policy on education, the elite of Calcutta tried to organize and reform the *pathshalas*. They set up the Calcutta School Book Society and Calcutta School Society in 1817 and 1818 respectively, no doubt inspired by the movement for popular education in early nineteenth-century England. They tried to bring the schools under their supervision, and introduced printed text books. They also introduced new subjects like geography, arranged for training of the *gurus,* and set up five model *pathshalas*.

At first the *gurus* resisted, fearing the invasion of Christianity. In 1819, according to Raja Radhakanta Deb, only eighty-five *pathshalas* agreed to come under the Society's supervision. Here students were enrolled systematically at the beginning of the academic year. Quarterly and yearly examinations were held, and the boys arranged in four classes by 'ability or proficiency'. The first yearly examination of *pathshala* students under the Society's supervision was held in the house of Radhakanta Deb on 25 May 1819.

In the early years, the societies aimed chiefly at improving the quality of education without changing its indigenous character. Of the 78,500 books printed by the School Book Society between 1817 and 1821, 48,750 were in Bengali and only 3,500 in English. (The rest were in Hindustani, Persian, Sanskrit etc.) Bengali was the medium of instruction and

usually the only language taught. Muslims as well as Hindus of all castes were admitted without any discrimination. But there were comparatively few Muslims; and girls generally found no place whatsoever.

The model *pathshalas* of the School Society had hardly any beneficial spread effect. On the contrary, they became model primary schools – a component of the uniform English system set up later by the Government. Other *pathshalas* too either turned into Departmental Primary Schools or withered away.

It would be an unpardonable omission if we did not mention the role of missionaries in spreading elementary Bengali education in Calcutta, among girls as well as boys. Charles Lushington informs us in 1824 that in the early nineteenth century, the Calcutta Committee of the Church Missionary Society set up eight schools in Khidirpur and one at Mirzapur, instructing 800 children in both English and Bengali. The Calcutta Diocesan Committee marked out 'circles', a few miles in extent, each containing five Bengali schools and one central school where English was taught. According to William Adam, their schools in Calcutta taught 697 children reading, writing, ciphering, grammar and geography, as well as religion. 'The Native mode of writing on sand, palm-leaves, and plantain leaves is adopted ·in these schools.' The Calcutta Church Missionary Association had thirteen elementary schools, some in the town and some in the villages, with a total enrolment of about 600. The girls' schools will be described in the next section.

Like other indigenous elementary schools, the vernacular missionary schools either turned into English schools or died away. The Bengal Auxiliary Missionary Society gave the reason when it discontinued every vernacular school except one at Krishnapur: 'the desire to obtain a knowledge of the English language has been so great that a school in which this was not taught, was sure to dwindle away.'

Elementary Schools for Girls

In the second half of the eighteenth century, Calcutta had a number of schools for young European ladies – as much boarding-houses as places of instruction, and also centres for matrimonial alliances. However, the first elementary school for Indian girls was perhaps founded by Mrs Gogerly in 1820, under the auspices of the London Missionary Society. She persuaded a few indigent girls to join her school, provided them with clothes and paid them a pice a day. Even so, the school was closed down after some time.

The Calcutta Female Juvenile Society, organized by the Calcutta Baptist Mission Society in 1819, was more successful. According to Jogeshchandra Bagal, they opened a school at Gouribari even before Mrs Gogerly, in 1819. There were only eight students the first year, but thirty-two in the next: all from the lower orders of Hindu society, and some quite adult. By 1823 the Society had eight schools spread over Calcutta; by 1829 there were twenty. It is reported that in one examination organized by the Society 140 girls, Muslim as well as Hindu, appeared. In addition to reading and writing in Bengali, the girls were instructed in geography, needlework and of course the Bible.

In 1824 the Ladies' Society for Native Female Education in Calcutta and Its Vicinity came into being under the patronage of the Church Missionary Society and the leadership of Miss Mary Ann Cooke. In fact, even before the formation of the Society, Miss Cooke had opened fifteen schools with 200 children, to whom she paid money and other incentives.

According to one report, in 1824 there were fifty charitable schools for Indian girls in Calcutta. The 'Despatch of 1854' found 288 girls' schools in Bengal with 6,869 pupils. In 1862, however, under the grant-in-aid system, only thirty-five were counted, with 1,183 pupils. In early years, school-going girls came from the underprivileged orders of society. The native elite or *bhadralok* were not yet ready to send their girls to school. John Drinkwater Bethune (1801-51) first achieved success in this regard, with the help of Ramgopal Ghosh (1815-68), Dakshinaranjan Mukherji (1814-78) and Madanmohan Tarkalankar (1817-58). The Hindu Balika Vidyalaya or Calcutta Female School came into being in 1849. The Government took it over in 1856, renaming it Bethune School in 1862-63.

However, the School went through a rough time till it was amalgamated in 1878 with the Banga Mahila Vidyalaya, founded by Miss Annette Akroyd (1842-1929) in 1873 at Beniapukur. This was an attempt at a higher English boarding school for girls, managed mainly by some eminent Brahmo Bengali *bhadraloks*. Among the students were

17.2 *A Muslim Maulavi teaching women students. 1829 lithograph*

Kadambini Basu, Sarala Das, Abala Das and Subarnaprabha Basu. Kadambini (1861-1923) became the first woman to pass the Entrance Examination, in 1878.

Bethune School served as an eye-opener. The Bengali *bhadralok* grew eager to educate their daughters, and a number of girls' schools were opened in the second half of the century. Bengali was the medium of instruction and also the chief subject taught, the others being history, geography, hygiene and a little arithmetic. English was generally excluded, as the *bhadralok* still feared that English would prove a bad influence on their womenfolk.

Bethune School became the model for all such schools. The first modern Bengali primer, *Shishu Shiksha,* was actually written for this school by Madanmohan Tarkalankar, poet and Sanskrit scholar, whose two daughters were among the first students.

Remarkably, as the *bhadralok* girls started going to school, the earlier schools for indigent girls gradually disappeared. According to Prasannakumar Thakur, this earlier class of pupils were expected to provide tutors or governesses for *bhadralok* girls whose families would not send them to school. But such 'respectable' families would not admit women of lower class, however educated, in their midst. The Christian instruction they had received also made them suspect among the *bhadralok.*

Indigenous Higher Learning

From a very early period, there existed in Bengal a system of higher Sanskrit learning at institutions called *toles*. These were generally established by individual pandits on rent-free land provided by a zamindar. No doubt the zamindar had a vested interest in preserving the Brahminical social system; but at least the learned pandits found an arena for their creative genius, which bore fruit in those distinctively Bengali systems, the *Navya Nyaya* and *Navya Smriti*.

It is likely that there were *toles* in Sutanuti, Gobindapur and Kalikata, but we have little evidence to show for it. However, there is ample evidence that with the growth of Calcutta there also grew up a number of *toles*. In 1818, William Ward enumerated twenty-eight of them, with a total of 173 scholars. They received generous material and moral support from rich Calcuttans, who wanted to surround themselves with the familiar Brahminical atmosphere of their native villages.

Most of the *toles* were situated in north Calcutta. Hatibagan had six and Shimulia (Simla) three. The largest *toles* were run by Mrityunjay Vidyalankar and Anantaram Vidyavagish, with fifteen scholars each.

Mrityunjay Vidyalankar (1762?-1819) was First Pandit at the Fort William College. He wrote a number of text-books for the students of that College, and is considered the first 'conscious artist' of Bengali prose. In his *Prabodh Chandrika* he discussed the different types of Bengali prose with examples. Two of his eminent contemporaries were Kamalakanta Vidyalankar (?-1843) and Jaygopal Tarkalankar (1775-1846). Kamalakanta, a distinguished paleographer, was Professor of Rhetoric, Ancient Literature and History at the Sanskrit College and Pandit at the Asiatic Society. Jaygopal, also of the Sanskrit College, authored among other works a Bengali textbook called *Shikshasar,* a book on letter-writing called *Patrer Dhara,* and a Bengali dictionary. These Sanskritists made signal contributions to the development of Bengali prose.

In Calcutta, as elsewhere, Sanskrit learning used to be pursued in the traditionally long-drawn and exacting manner. The establishment of Sanskrit College, effectively in 1824, gradually introduced a more modern and attractive system. Its chief architect was Ishwarchandra Vidyasagar (1820-91). He appreciated the advent of English education and culture and the growth of a multi-caste urban

society, rendering the old system more and more irrelevant. Accordingly, during his tenure as Principal of Sanskrit College (1851-58), he introduced a condensed course in Sanskrit along with some exposure to English language and literature. Unfortunately, this has meant that ever since, students of Sanskrit College have divided their loyalties between Sanskrit learning and English education. Their major role in the later nineteenth century was as teachers in Anglo-vernacular schools.

The Calcutta Madrassa or Mahomedan College was established in 1781 to provide Islamic higher education: that is, Arabic, Persian, and Islamic Law. The chief aim seems to have been to produce qualified judicial officers. English was also taught at one stage.

The Madrassa was founded by the Governor-General, Warren Hastings, at the request of eminent Muslims of Calcutta. Hastings provided the building – initially at his own expense, but afterwards charged to the Company.

English Education

In an article published in *Prabasi* in 1930, Purnachandra Dey Udbhatsagar cites sixty-two

English schools in Calcutta before 1850. The first one was established by public subscription as early as 1727 (or possibly 1734) for 'educating poor European children in the Protestant religion'. It was amalgamated in 1800 with the Calcutta Free School. Among the likely founders and benefactors in 1727 was the Sikh merchant Umichand: already we see a collaboration between the foreign power and the native elite. This was to be the central spirit of English education in India: it was essentially a two-way process. Both Indian and Anglo-Indian children attended the first missionary English school, set up for indigent Christians by the Reverend John Zachary Kiernander, the first Protestant missionary in Bengal.

Not until 1835 did the British decide on a definite education policy for India. Thomas Babington Macaulay formulated the policy; the Governor-General, William Bentinck, put the official seal upon it. But its passage was made easy by strong support from the native elite like Rammohan Ray and others.

The policy had its origin in an observation made in 1792 by Charles Grant, a member of the Clapham Sect led by William Wilberforce and adviser to Lord Cornwallis, then Governor-General. Grant had advocated spreading 'the light of European knowledge' through the medium of the English language. Cornwallis initiated a 'great tide of anglicization', as Eric Stokes puts it; his Permanent Settlement was 'a frank attempt to apply the English Whig philosophy of government'. Macaulay belonged to the same school of thought, and was much influenced by Charles Grant.

It was in the late eighteenth century that British colonial policy was being shaped. It is no wonder that English 'mushroom schools' proliferated in Calcutta at this time. The *Calcutta Review* of 1850 portrays a typical scene. The setting is Coolie Bazar (now Hastings), among the bungalows of pensioned and invalided soldiers: of them 'One more learned perchance than the rest, opened a school':

Let us contemplate him seated in an old-fashioned chair, with his legs resting on a cane *morah*. A long pipe, his most constant companion, projects from his mouth.... A rattan – his sceptre – is in his hand; and the boys are seated on stools, or little *morahs,* before his pedagogic majesty. They have already read three chapters of the Bible, and have got over the proper names without much spelling; they have repeated a

Facing page
17.3 Sanskrit College

17.4 The Mohammedan College or Calcutta Madrassa. D'Oyly

The Sanskrit College in Jeopardy

When Macaulay's proposals seemed to threaten the future of Sanskrit studies, Pandit Premchand Tarkavagish (1806–67) composed a Sanskrit *shloka* which he sent to Horace H. Wilson, the eminent orientalist and early patron of Sanskrit College. Translated, it goes:

On the bank of the fair round pond
  [Gol Dighi or College Square],
lined with trees, in the city of Calcutta,
there dwells a lean and lonely deer
named the House of Sanskrit Study
  [Sanskrit College].
Macaulay the king of hunters has taken up
  sharp arrows
to kill this frightened creature.
It cries with tears in its eyes,
'O great Wilson, protect me, protect me.'

column of Entick's Dictionary with only two mistakes; and are now employed in working compound division, and soon expect to arrive at the Rule of Three. Some of the lads' eyes are red with weeping, and others expect to have a taste of the ferula. The partner of the Pensioner's days is seated on a low Dinapore matronly chair, picking vegetables...

These early English *pathshalas,* if we may call them so, grew to satisfy the educational needs of the indigent English-speaking people.

In course of time, particularly after the establishment of the Supreme Court in 1774, Bengalis also felt attracted to English education. However, the first Bengali-run English school was probably set up before 1774. Ramram Mishra, a Bengali, knew a few English words. One of his students, Ramnarayan Mishra, opened an English *pathshala* at Shobhabazar. The students were taught from Thomas Dice's Spelling Book, and charged four to sixteen rupees according to their means. This was followed by Ramjay Dutta's English school in 1791 at Kalutola. Rammohan Napit, Krishnamohan Basu, Bhushanmohan Datta, Shibu Datta and others also opened English schools. Murray's Grammar and Murray's Spelling Book were the two texts generally followed.

More and more schools came up, for Indians as well as Anglo-Indians, sometimes introduc-

ing new subjects and new methods of teaching. A few of them became elite institutions. One such was Sherborne's School, established in 1784, where Dwarakanath Thakur (Tagore), Prasannakumar Thakur and Ramgopal Ghosh had their schooling. The most famous was perhaps the Durrumtollah Academy established by David Drummond in 1810. He claimed to have inaugurated the study of grammar, the use of the globe and the system of annual examinations. He also introduced English literature and Latin classes. Among his students was Henry Derozio.

It is said that by 1820 nearly 10,000 Bengalis knew some sort of English. The Hindu College or Anglo-Indian College had been established in 1817 by the combined efforts of a number of Europeans as well as Indians like Rammohan Ray and Baidyanath Mukherji. It was a great event in the history of English education in Bengal.

Other English schools were set up by Calcutta Bengalis. One of the earliest was the Union School established in 1793 at Bhabanipur, which taught Harishchandra Mukherji, the founder-editor of the *Hindoo Patriot.* But the most successful school was Gourmohan Adhya's (1802–46) Oriental Seminary, founded in 1823 and justly considered second only to the Hindu College. There were also many free schools run by Calcutta *bhadraloks.* Gobindachandra Basak and Pyarichand Mitra (1814–83), former students of Hindu College, established two such schools at Chitpur and Nimtala respectively. The Hindu Free School at Arpuly had 150 scholars. Another such school was the Hindu Benevolent Institution. These schools satisfied the craze for English education among the indigent *bhadralok* who could not afford to pay fees.

As remarked earlier, these Anglo-vernacular schools gradually absorbed the indigenous *pathshalas,* which were undergoing reform under the Calcutta School Book Society and Calcutta School Society. David Hare (1775–1842) was responsible for the School Society's model schools, particularly the Arpuly School, and did much to influence their later growth. To meet the growing demand for English education, parallel English classes were begun; but to guard against neglect of vernacular studies, only students proficient in Bengali were granted the 'privilege' of joining the English classes and later of receiving higher

English education, at the Society's expense, in its own Pataldanga School (later renamed Hare School) or at Hindu College. Thus a balance was sought between the claims of English and vernacular education.

The Hindu College Pathshala established in 1839 and the Tattwabodhini Pathshala of Debendranath Thakur, established in 1840, were influenced by the example of the Arpuly School. The Tattwabodhini Pathshala was later shifted to Banshberia: Debendranath Thakur and Akshaykumar Datta (1820-86) wanted to develop it as a model 'national school'. Unfortunately, it did not survive. It was abolished in 1848; in its place, Alexander Duff (1805-78) set up an English school which still continues. In 1830, Duff had already opened his General Assembly's Institution with five pupils recommended by Rammohan Ray. Its swift success was a victory for Duff's zealous support of English education, and paved the way for Macaulay.

Up to this time, there was no uniform system of education in Calcutta. The General Committee of Public Instruction was formed in 1823; but in the absence of a definite government policy on education, its function was confined mainly to funding and supervising government institutions. Nor was there a central body for holding examinations. The General Committee was sharply divided into two groups, the 'Orientalists' and the 'Anglicists'. But neither showed any concern for vernacular education; the Orientalists chiefly favoured Sanskrit, Arabic and Persian.

The 1822 Report of the Proceedings of the Parliamentary Committee shows that the British Government was anxious to resolve this crisis of education policy, and not unnaturally leant in favour of English education. Most of the members, like James Sullivan, Holt Mackenzie, Charles Lushington and James Sutherland, laid great stress on the spread of the English language in India. James Mill alone thought it impracticable on any scale, recommending instead the translation of European books into Indian languages. The majority opinion prevailed, and Macaulay was made President of the General Committee in 1834. He scored a victory over the Orientalists and also won the hearts of the Bengali *bhadralok*. His historic Minute was issued on 2 February 1835.

The Despatch of 1854, known as Wood's Despatch after Sir Charles Wood, President of the Board of Control, marks another landmark in Indian educational history. It recognized the educational responsibility of the state and suggested a comprehensive educational structure and process. Oriental literature, it proposed, should not be neglected, but European learning should be cultivated. English should be the medium of higher studies for the few, and the vernacular at a lower level for the many. A system of grants-in-aid was also proposed to encourage vernacular education; ironically, it actually proved to benefit English education.

The Despatch also envisaged a complete and integrated system comprising primary, secondary and collegiate education. Provisions were

17.5 *David Hare: statue on College Street*

91

made for a Department of Public Instruction, the establishment of universities on the model of London University – not teaching but examining and degree-conferring bodies – and also for affiliated colleges of different kinds.

The Department of Public Instruction was constituted in 1855-56. Universities were opened in Calcutta and Bombay in 1857. (A proposal for a university at Calcutta had been mooted in 1845 but turned down by the Directors of the East India Company.) Calcutta University held its first Entrance Examination in 1857. A two-year course then led to the First Arts Examination, and another two years to the Bachelor's degree:

The Entrance Examination and college teaching were conducted in English. The vernacular was excluded from the F.A. and B.A. courses in 1864. A process of 'downward filtration' extended this English bias to school education as well, in spite of Wood's Despatch. The Government now began to pursue, almost with a vengeance, a policy of complete and uniform English education.

Hindu College set the pattern in this respect. English not only had pride of place in its curricula but overshadowed all other subjects, including Mathematics. The College's two most eminent early teachers, Henry Derozio (1809-31) and David Lester Richardson (1801-65), both taught English Literature. Even the appointment of Robert Tytler in 1828 to improve the teaching of Mathematics did not

redress the balance. The standard of Bengali was notoriously poor. To check this deterioration, the Hindu College Pathshala was established in 1839. David Hare's *pathshala* at Arpuly had the same purpose: to ensure a good command over the mother tongue before starting English education.

The Hindu College Pathshala was transferred to the charge of the Sanskrit College during Ishwarchandra Vidyasagar's principalship of the latter. Later still, it was attached to the Normal School after this was set up in 1855. But even here, English was introduced by popular demand, and ultimately it became another Anglo–vernacular school. Many more such schools were set up at the initiative of educationists like Vidyasagar and Bhudeb Mukherji.

In 1855 Hindu College was converted into Presidency College and placed directly under the Government. The school section came to be known as Hindu School. For the first time in India, a complete model of an education system covering the primary, secondary and collegiate stages came into existence. In 1856, students of the College were examined for the first time by an external body of examiners.

In 1857 the College was placed under the

17.6 *Left: John Zachary Kiernander*

17.7 *Right: Madoo Rao, a South Indian pundit of Hindu College. Colesworthy Grant*

newly-founded Calcutta University. At its first B.A. Examination in 1858, two students of the College, Bankimchandra Chatterji and Jadunath Basu, became the first graduates of the University. The M.A. degree was first conferred on 1863 on six students from Presidency College. But till 1881–82, only 356 students had passed the F.A. Examination of the University, 105 the B.A. and 32 the M.A.

There were fourteen colleges in Bengal before 1857, nine of them in Calcutta: the Calcutta Madrassa, Presidency College, the General Assembly's Institution, the Free Church Institution, the Calcutta Sanskrit College, Doveton College, La Martiniere, St Paul's and Bhabanipur College. Only eight of the fourteen were affiliated to the University in 1857; in Calcutta, Presidency College, the General Assembly and the Free Church Institution, as well as the Calcutta Medical College, set up in 1835. The first examination of the Medical College was held in 1838; its first hospital, with twenty beds, opened the same year. It also set a world precedent by teaching basic sciences such as Physics, Chemistry and Botany along with the medical courses.

Of the 'general' colleges, the General Assembly's Institution was the most prominent after Presidency College. As said before, it was established by Duff in 1830 'under the direction of the General Assembly of the Church of Scotland'. In 1843 the Church of Scotland split. Duff and other separatists formed a new 'Free Church Institution', renamed Duff College after his death. In 1909 the two colleges were reunited as the Scottish Churches College; in 1929, after the Churches themselves merged, this became simply the Scottish Church College.

The eminence of the General Assembly was challenged by the first affiliated private college set up by Indians, the Metropolitan Institution. This grew out of the Metropolitan Training School (renamed Calcutta Training School) set up by Thakurdas Chakrabarti and others at 1 Arpuly Lane in 1859. Ishwarchandra Vidyasagar became the President of the Managing Committee in 1860, and was directly entrusted with the administration in 1864. He renamed it the Metropolitan Institution and, for the first time, sought collegiate affiliation – though this was granted only in 1872, and at the F.A. level at that.

Of the Institution's twenty-one candidates

Iswarchandra Vidyasagar

If Bengal had a Renaissance in the nineteenth century, Vidyasagar (1820–91) was its Erasmus. Born Ishwarchandra Banerji in a poor Brahmin family of Medinipur, he came on foot to study in Calcutta, learning the English numerals from the milestones along the way. Ten years at the Sanskrit College qualified him for the supreme title of 'Vidyasagar', 'ocean of learning'. He held various academic and administrative posts, in the course of which he laid the foundation for a simpler approach to Sanskrit studies and a union of oriental with Western learning. He reformed Sanskrit College along modern lines. Simultaneously, he laid the foundations of modern Bengali prose through a variety of works from alphabet books to retold Sanskrit and English classics.

Vidyasagar's scholarship was also placed at the service of bold social reform. In spite of fierce opposition, he carried through a campaign for the remarriage of widows and ran up huge debts for the cause. He also campaigned unsuccessfully to end polygamy among upper-caste Hindus, and was a leading organizer of female education. Exceeding his official duties as a school inspector extraordinary, he ran a number of model village schools out of his own purse, and virtually built up the Calcutta college that now bears his name.

It seems that social reform, with lavish and almost sentimental philanthropy, increasingly took the place of conventional religion for Vidyasagar. He spent much of his last years in Karmatar among Santhal tribals, aloof equally from his social peers and the English rulers. But his career epitomizes the finest spirit of enlightened nineteenth-century Bengali society.

17.8 *Ishwarchandra Vidyasagar*

17.9 Thomas Babington Macaulay

for the F.A. in 1874, eight passed – a higher proportion than from Presidency College. Jogendranath Basu of the Institution stood second. 'The Pundit [i.e., Vidyasagar] has done wonders,' remarked the Registrar of the University. In 1879, the Metropolitan Institution became a first-grade college with B.A. affiliation. Among the first batch of B.A. candidates in 1881, 42.1 per cent passed, against 43.5 per cent from Presidency and 40 per cent from the General Assembly.

The Metropolitan Institution served as the model for other private colleges like the City College (established 1881), Ripon (now Surendranath) College (1884) and Bangabasi College (1887). In 1917, the Board of Trustees recognized the seminal role of 'the Pundit' by renaming the Metropolitan Institution as Vidyasagar College.

In 1879 a collegiate section was attached to Bethune School, so that Kadambini Basu, who had passed the Entrance Examination from there in 1878, could continue her studies. In 1881, she passed the F.A., as did Chandramukhi Basu (1860-1944) from the Free Church Normal School. They graduated in 1883; Chandramukhi went on to an M.A. while Kadambini joined the Medical College. Other women had already begun collegiate studies at Bethune School; but Bethune College became a fully separate entity only in 1888.

It is interesting that English and Law were the two most popular subjects at collegiate level. One may discern a hidden design in the system of English education: not merely to produce cheap clerks but, in Macaulay's words, 'to form a class who may be interpreters between us and the millions whom we govern – a class of persons Indian in blood and colour, but English in tastes, in opinions, in morals, and in intellect'. In other words, the English system of education was visualized as a process of socialization.

Clive conquered the country; but Macaulay won a greater battle, and Calcutta became the citadel of English education..

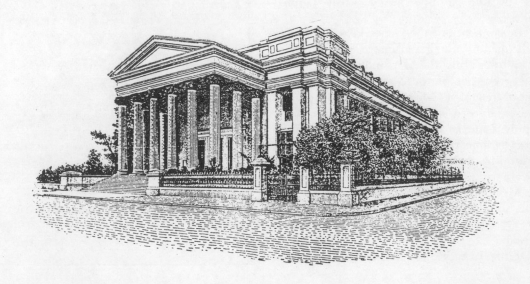

CALCUTTA AND THE 'BENGAL RENAISSANCE'

Sumit Sarkar

The nineteenth century survives as a galaxy of illustrious names for the average educated Bengali of today. Religious and social reformers, scholars, literary giants, journalists and patriotic orators, may be a couple of scientists – all merge to form an image of 'renaissance', *nabajagaran* (awakening) or *naba-jug* (new age), assumed to mark the transition from 'medieval' to 'modern'. Calcutta somehow enters centrally into this image – even though many of the most distinguished figures (Bankimchandra Chatterji or Rabindranath Thakur, for instance) spent the bulk of their working lives outside it. And, twentieth-century nationalism and Left politics apart, the renaissance probably provides today the major justification for recalling the history of our city with some degree of pride on the occasion of its tercentenary: for Calcutta has been otherwise a quintessentially colonial foundation.

This standard middle-class view of the city's cultural history has received some hard knocks in recent years, and most intellectuals who would like to consider themselves radical and sophisticated no longer share it. One has to begin, therefore, with another look at the 'renaissance' debate. I intend, however, to suggest tentatively some ways of going beyond what is by now a rather stale controversy. It is important, for instance, to try to bridge an implicit dichotomy in our historiography: between, on the one hand, 'intellectual' or

'cultural' studies, where the 'renaissance' is normally the central assumption or debating-point, floating more or less in a social vacuum; and, on the other, 'social' or 'urban' history, where the 'renaissance' is often marginalized or all but omitted.

'Middle-class' culture needs to be linked up with the topography and distinctive patterns of everyday life in the premier colonial metropolis. The historiographical rift is related to an implicit assumption that 'intellectual' studies have to concentrate on outstanding figures alone, while 'social history' deals with aggregates and 'objective' tendencies which must remain more or less mindless, because 'popular' mentalities are difficult to reconstruct in a predominantly illiterate environment. But printing – an innovation more far-reaching, perhaps, than even the Western education usually taken to be crucial – quickly started producing large numbers of minor plays and farces, tracts and household manuals and other ephemera, a still largely unexplored 'low life' of literature. These did not constitute 'popular culture' in any unqualified sense: the authors were overwhelmingly upper-caste, often Brahmin. But many such plays and farces were acted as *jatras*. A smattering of literate culture would tend to enter into precisely this intermediate world, the lower-middle-class life typified in colonial Calcutta by the clerk working in British government and mercantile offices. For along with Western education and the printing-press, the office, distinguished by a novel discipline of clock-time, largely made our 'renaissance' what it was.

The Rise and Fall of the 'Renaissance Model'

We may begin with a paradox. The 'renaissance in Calcutta' is a fairly recent construct, for few nineteenth-century intellectuals thought of themselves as participants in a movement characterized by such a term, or even as living

in a city worth being proud about. The sense of a break was there, though quite as often for the worse as for the better (for instance, in Rajnarayan Basu's *Sekal ar Ekal* of 1874), as well as a frequent search for European analogues. Rammohan Ray seems to have modelled his reforming role on Luther's, and Alexander Duff's memoirs record earnest Christian missionary efforts to persuade the Anglicized 'Young Bengal' or Derozians to accept the Reformation prototype in place of their early enthusiasm for the Enlightenment and the French Revolution. Bankimchandra Chatterji in 1880 drew a parallel between the European Renaissance and the religious and cultural achievements of fifteenth- and sixteenth-century Bengal: about the *bhadralok* culture of his own times he tended to be deeply ironic and critical.

Calcutta, interestingly enough, often had a negative image, as a city somehow basically alien, where the gentleman would have his *basa* (residence or lodgings) as against the proper *bari* (home) in the village or small town of his birth or retirement. In contrast to the situation today, there was little sign in the nineteenth century of middle-class pride, antiquarian interest or sentiment about the city: nothing recalling the sense of identification noticeable in Indian cities of long indigenous history like Varanasi, Lucknow or old Delhi: Calcutta certainly did not produce a 'civic humanism' in any way akin to what many historians feel characterized the Florentine Renaissance.

Much of the cultural activity later to be termed a 'renaissance' was in fact located outside Calcutta, around *bhadralok* clusters in district towns or even among the educated Bengali diaspora in other provinces. (One could think, for instance, of Bankim's *Bangadarshan* group, or Ramananda Chatterji's *Prabasi,* originally published from Allahabad.) Again, Bengali high literature in the nineteenth century did not develop any distinctive ways of imaginatively visualizing the new experience of life in a great metropolis, as Dickens did with London or Baudelaire with Paris. Calcutta is never particularly important in Bankim's novels. And as for the semi-popular literature of farces and tracts, or the Kalighat paintings, there Calcutta often became the city of *Kali,* the epitome of the degenerate present or *Kali-yuga.* The present time marked the nadir of this decline *(ghor-kali),* of the breakdown of norms

of caste and gender behaviour, and not, in 'renaissance' fashion, any hopeful new beginning or revival of lost classical glory. Such moods sometimes crept into high-*bhadralok* culture, too.

The 'renaissance in Calcutta', then, is basically the result of an early and mid-twentieth century retrospect, with occasional anticipations as in Kishorichand Mitra's much quoted 1861 Hare Memorial speech about Hindu College students being the first to 'catch the dawn', and a first major systematization in Shibnath Shastri's *Ramtanu Lahiri o Tatkalin Bangasamaj* (1904). Another early presentation was in Bipinchandra Pal's *Banglar Nabajuger Katha* ('The Story of the New Age in Bengal', 1921-24). Calcutta in the nineteenth century was 'the second city of the British Empire', the unquestioned political and economic heart of British India; but *bhadralok* culture, though in a sense largely a product of its colleges, printing-presses and offices, seldom felt at home in the city. Retrospective pride developed only in the succeeding era, when ascendant nationalism accompanied a steady decline in the relative importance of Calcutta and Bengal in the subcontinemt. The 'renaissance' analogue now eclipsed other possible role-models – for unlike the Reformation, Enlightenment or Victorian reform, it could anchor a qualified sense of progress in the postulation of an indigenous, supposedly 'classical' past.

Nostalgia reached its climax in a Bengal which seemed on the point of being shattered by famine and Partition. *Notes on the Bengal Renaissance* (1946), by the Marxist Sushobhan Sarkar, was explicitly written at time when 'disintegration threaten[ed] every aspect of our life', while between 1939 and 1952 Brajendranath Banerji and Sajanikanta Das, two scholars with a totally different, indeed socially conservative perspective, produced a multi-volume collection of lives of nineteenth-century worthies, the *Sahitya-Sadhak-Charitmala*.

Certain rough edges and internal tensions, however, lurked beneath the surface of this mid-twentieth-century consensus. A myth evolved by a basically nationalist discourse glorified our intelligentsia which till the 1870s at least had often accepted British rule as providential. It was difficult, though not impossible, for radical historians to combine admiration of the Bengal Renaissance with enthusiasm for peasant revolts or the 1857 uprising. Few serious scholars could deny that nineteenth-century Bengal had fallen considerably short of the alleged Italian prototype: achievements in the visual arts, for instance, had been conspicuously absent. And if, as had come to be generally accepted, nineteenth-century *bhadralok* culture somehow lay at the roots of Bengal's present fate, that could provide occasion to the intelligentsia for self-flagellation as much as pride or nostalgia.

It is not surprising, therefore, that a trenchant academic critique of the 'Renaissance model' developed in Bengal in the early 1970s, in the context of a Left upsurge which had been followed by considerable disillusionment. Today, this alternative approach seems set to become a counter-orthodoxy. The central, and I think valid, thrust here has been towards a firmer contextualization of the achievements and limitations of the intelligenstia within an overall framework of deepening colonial domination. Unilinear assumptions and analogies consequently need to be abandoned.

The Bengali middle class was bound to be utterly different from the bourgeoisie of early modern Europe, because the forces of 'modernity' and 'development' in metropolitan countries normally produce under development in the colonial periphery. The qualifications made in an undertone by historians like Sushobhan Sarkar – illusions about foreign rule, distance from peasants, an overwhelmingly Hindu orientation in a region where at least half the population were Muslims – were moved to centre-stage, and shown to follow from the 'Renaissance model' itself. It was shown, for instance, how a tripartite periodization of Indian history into ancient, medieval and modern, along with the further equation of 'modern' with colonial, would tend towards denigration of the 'medieval' centuries, often identified (following James Mill) as 'Muslim'. Relatively positive judgements on British rule were also difficult to avoid, though few shared Jadunath Sarkar's enthusiasm for the battle of Palashi (Plassey) as 'the beginning... of a glorious dawn'. And the sharp distinctions between 'reform' and 'revival', so often made in the older 'renaissance' historiography, were shown to be irrelevant within the new framework, for the underlying characteristics and limitations appeared more or less common to all nineteenth-century groups. The assumption of a period of 'Muslim tyranny', for instance, appears alike in Rammohan, Derozian writings and Bankimchandra.

In recent years, this 'revisionist' exercise has received added impetus from the very fashionable 'post-modernist' Western critique of 'Enlightenment rationalism' and 'colonial discourse', for one is assured now of an international audience. It had been argued in the 1970s that colonial conditions had severely limited the degree of rationalism and modernity achievable by our nineteenth-century intellectuals. The further step being advocated by some today is towards a critique of what is termed 'Western rationalism' itself, as a peculiarly – maybe even uniquely – aggressive form of 'power-knowledge'. Michel Foucault and Edward Said have obviously been major influences here.

At this point I must confess to a certain sense of disquiet about where the critique of the 'Renaissance model' seems to be taking some of us today. A simplistic equation of rationalism, science and economic development with human liberation certainly needs to be rejected. Such questioning has become urgent for developed capitalism and socialist societies, and to some extent also for the Third World, in the context of the proliferation of bureaucratic power, mindless consumerism, and prospects of nuclear or ecological doom. But I still feel uncomfortable with the use of an omnibus term like 'Enlightenment (or post-Enlightenment) rationalism', which blurs so many distinctions.

Heuristic devices no doubt always have to abstract from particulars and variations; but is there not some danger here of slipping into 'homogenization', the besetting sin, we are told, of rationalistic power-knowledge? Critiques not dissimilar to those being voiced today had risen from the heart of the Enlightenment itself (Rousseau being an obvious example), and it is dangerously unhistorical to imply that the West of the past two centuries provides in any sense a unique example of power-knowledge, despite the obvious advantages flowing from modern technologies. Ancient Hindu texts prescribed that Shudras and women daring to learn the Vedas should have their tongues cut out, and near-monopoly of Latin high-culture had given the medieval Catholic clergy enormous power for a thousand years.

More directly relevant for our present theme is the way judgements can be inverted without changing underlying assumptions, and old values revived beneath new terminology. The more 'modernist' admirers of the Bengal Renaissance had assumed that English education and Western liberal rationalist ideas had 'inspired' Indian intellectuals, while social conservatives and many militant nationalists had condemned such dependence as unpatriotic. Today there is much talk of a more or less complete surrender to 'hegemonic' colonial discourse (by virtually everyone except Gandhi, according to one recent account). I intend to argue that the possibilities of autonomous appropriations are underestimated in all these approaches. Quite conventional Third-World nationalistic positions seem to peep through the new language, while the frequent counterposing of vague notions of 'community-consciousness' to bureaucratic state power can come perilously close to becoming a 'radical' variant of neo-traditionalism.

Calcutta in the 'Renaissance'

I have argued the need for a closer look at the ways in which Calcutta was, or became, crucial to the 'renaissance'. 'Which Calcutta?' could be a useful opening question here: not to elicit banal statements about the 'renaissance' being a minority or elite affair – which high-culture tends to be in all class-divided societies – but because there were specific spatial, social and temporal limits to the appeal of cultural

Ramkrishna, Vivekananda and the Ramkrishna Mission

When Rani Rasmani built the Dakshineshwar temple in 1855, she installed Ramkumar Chatterji as the priest. Ramkumar was succeeded by his brother Gadadhar (1836-86), who became famous as Shri Ramkrishna Paramhansa and was renowned for his piety, unforced asceticism and lucid and witty exposition of spiritual matters. In an age when the decadent Hindu orthodoxy was provoking censure and even revolt, Ramkrishna afforded a new valid ideal of quintessential Hindu devotion.

Ramkrishna attracted a section of Calcutta's elite, but his most brilliant disciple was Swami Vivekananda (1863-1902), born Narendranath Datta, whose enshrinement of spiritual principles in practical life and social organization almost marked an antithesis to Ramkrishna's contemplative piety. He joined the monastic order founded at Ramkrishna's death and spent the next few years travelling through India. In 1893 he left for Chicago to speak at the Congress of Religions being held there; and, on his return home after a long and triumphant tour of America and Europe, founded the Ramkrishna Mission Association on 1 May 1897. In 1898, Belur Math was set up as the headquarters of the Mission.

Through his voluminous works in Bengali and English, Vivekananda spread – and continues to spread – a general message not only of religious devotion but of patriotism, social reform and good works. But needless to say, it is through the Ramkrishna Mission that his influence has been most clearly channelized. The Mission is legally and functionally separate from the Math or monastic order. The latter is chiefly religious in its activities, while the Mission runs schools, hospitals, orphanages, libraries, work centres, etc. and undertakes relief work and social uplift. By the latest count, the Mission had 53 centres and the Math 50 throughout the world, while another 23 were run by the two in combination.

In the Calcutta region, the most prominent centres – apart from Belur Math itself – are the Seba Pratishthan Hospital, the Institute of Culture at Gole Park, the educational complex at Narendrapur, and other educational institutions at Sarisha, Baranagar, Rahara, Belgharia and Belur. The Hindu identity of the Mission has always been a matter of debate. Parallel orders and breakaway groups have also appeared. But there is no doubt that the Ramkrishna Mission provides a major source of enlightened spiritualism as well as social service. It marks the most remarkable infusion of the western monastic ideal – also perhaps the ancient Buddhist – into the fabric of modern Indian life.

18.3 *The Belur Math*

18.4 *Swami Vivekananda*

patterns later grouped under the 'renaissance' label within the elite groups of nineteenth-century Calcutta. Urban historians divide the Calcutta of the last century into three zones along a rough north-south axis. (I am following Pradip Sinha's *Calcutta in Urban History*, 1978.) A predominatly Hindu 'Indian town' stretched north and north-eastwards from the fringes of Barabazar. To its south lay an 'intermediate zone' with a NW-SE alignment (the pan-Indian traditional commercial centre of Barabazar, increasingly dominated by Marwaris; the quarters of Anglo-Indians and the poorer whites, Muslim service groups etc.). Finally came the 'European town': the British official-cum-business headquarters of Dalhousie Square and the *sahib-para* or Chourangi and the area 'south of Park Street'. The 'renaissance' of the Bengali Hindu *bhadralok* was limited to the first of these three zones, with a somewhat later extension south and south-east of the European town to Bhabanipur, and, some decades later, the new suburb of Baliganj. It left virtually untouched the most influential and prosperous among Calcutta's elite groups: the British, of course (barring individual Indophile well-wishers or patrons), but also Marwari business magnates and even the old-style opulent Bengali-Hindu Babu world of 'comprador-rajas', the *banias* and *diwans* who by the mid-nineteenth century had shifted their interests to urban real estate and rural zamindari. (We tend to forget how exceptional the Jorasanko Thakurs or Tagores were).

A temporal dimension must next be introduced. Eurasians constituted the bulk of clerks in government and mercantile offices till the 1840s, and the professional-cum-clerical white-collar Bengali middle class was still, in Pradip Sinha's words, 'a comparatively new force ... not so markedly visible in the mid-nineteenth century'. The real base of the new 'renaissance' culture was provided by the subsequent rapid spread of English education among upper-caste *bhadralok* groups. The opulent families of older Calcutta, fairly often of intermediate-caste origin, had patronized the traditional Brahmin literati, but also a motley crew of multi-caste *kabiwalas,* with such disconcertingly diverse names as Anthony Phiringhi, Nimai Shunri (tapster), Haru Thakur or Keshta Muchi (cobbler). Perhaps somewhat paradoxically, the creators of the 'new' or 'modern' culture would be overwhelmingly upper-caste. In its own eyes this was a middle-class (*madhyashreni, madhyabitta*) or *bhadralok* culture, refined and somewhat puritanical in its norms, whose links with the older culture largely snapped after the poet Ishwarchandra Gupta (1812-59). It distinguished itself from both the luxury and corruption of the old-style Babus, and the superstitious ways of the uneducated masses, whether of city or countryside.

The nineteenth-century *madhyabitta* (middle class) was linked to structures which arose first in Calcutta – the new colleges and schools, the printing press, hospitals and law courts, the new kind of government and business offices – but it was far from being a purely metropolitan phenomenon cut off from the countryside. Many of its members were first-generation immigrants to Calcutta; a significant proportion spent the bulk of their lives outside the city. While relatively few big zaminders achieved prominence in this self-consciously middle-class culture, the typical successful *bhadralok* family would combine service or a profession with tenure-holding in the vast and growing rentier hierarchy created by the Permanent Settlement. 'The *madhyabitta*', said the *Amrita Bazar Patrika* of 9 December 1869, 'have two sources of livelihood: landed property and employment in service.' The suburban towns along the Hugli and in certain parts of East Bengal (like the Bikrampur region, allegedly supplying one-third of Bengal Government clerks) were almost as important for *bhadralok* culture in the nineteenth century as Calcutta. The subsequent decline of many mufassil centres probably helped to intensify the twentieth-century identification of the 'renaissance' image with the metropolis alone.

It seems helpful to make a further distinction within the Calcutta-based *madhyabitta* between upwardly-mobile professional groups (the more successful lawyers, doctors, journalists, teachers, civil servants) and the growing numbers of humble clerks in government and mercantile offices. Here lay, I would argue, the roots of some interesting tensions within 'renaissance' culture.

An adequate survey of the content of 'renaissance' culture is obviously impossible within this brief essay, even if one leaves out imaginative literature, which is being treated in another article in this volume. Any attempt at such a survey would inevitably degenerate into a bald catalogue of scholarly achievements, Brahmo 'reform' and Vaishnava or Shakta 'revival', and a series of conflicts over specific issues of social reform: *sati,* widow-remarriage, women's emancipation, *kulin* polygamy, marriage legislation and the age of consent, caste rules and the sinfulness of sea-voyages. All that can be done, I feel, is to probe a little further the implications, quite often contradictory, of the three institutional impulses that I distinguished at the beginning as crucial to the 'renaissance': Western education, print-culture and the office job.

Western education has always provided the focus for debates on the 'renaissance'. It has been hailed as the principal source of the 'awakening' and 'rationalism', or denounced for its denationalizing and alienating effects. The ferment brought about by sudden contact with a culture both rich and apparently irresistible in technology and power cannot, of course, be underestimated. Yet there is need to avoid a number of simplifications.

The quality or tone of much Christian missionary propaganda should be a sufficient reminder that the influence of the nineteenth-century West cannot be equated with 'rationalism' in any total sense, whether in praise or as critique. Rationalism, again, is not unique to the modern West: Rammohan Ray, before he knew much English, could use the Islamic Mutazilite heritage to write the most uncompromisingly rationalistic of his religious tracts, the *Tuhfat-ul-Muwahhidin* (c. 1804). Colonialism no doubt wanted English education to produce clerks for running the administration cheaply and to create an alienated loyalist group. But much of the spread of 'modern' education came through Indian initiative. Rammohan's letter to Amherst (1823) pleaded for English education a decade before Macaulay, and stressed its

18.5 *Rammohan Ray*

Rammohan Ray

Rammohan Ray (1772–1833) came to live in Calcutta in 1814 at the age of forty-two. Before that he had managed his father's estate and made money in trade and as *diwan* to various British civilians. But he had also left home at fifteen and wandered for years 'in distant lands, over mountains and plains'; studied Sanskrit at Varanasi and Persian at Patna; and gathered the seeds of spiritualism from certain learned teachers of his village boyhood.

In Calcutta, he led the lavish life of the wealthy babu. But he probed deeper into spiritual matters, cultivating monotheism as well as music from association with the singer Kalidas Chatterji (Kali Mirza). He had already published a Persian work on monotheism. He now set up the 'Atmiya Sabha' in 1815, the 'Unitarian Committee' in 1821, and finally in 1828 the Brahmo Samaj, with the support of Dwarakanath Thakur and others. He also learnt Hebrew and debated on the Bible with Christian clergymen, converting some of them to his views. In his day, people of all faiths came to pray at the Brahmo chapel.

Rammohan's zeal for social reform appeared in his active campaign against *sati* or widow-burning. He brought out three journals, in English, Bengali and Persian, and argued eloquently for English learning – principally as a vehicle for mathematical and scientific studies. An internationalist in politics, he would grieve or rejoice over events in Italy, France, Greece or Latin America.

In 1831 he was awarded the title of Raja and sent to England as the Mughal Emperor's emissary. He was fêted in Britain and France, but finally died a lonely death in Bristol. Visiting his solitary grave – for he had refused to be buried in a Christian cemetery – ten years later, Dwarakanath Thakur built him a mausoleum at Arnos Vale.

connection with scientific culture in total contrast to what would be visualized in the latter's notorious Minute of 1835. *Bhadralok* initiative in the late nineteenth century carried English education deep into parts of the East Bengal countryside, a process only tardily helped by ungenerous official grants-in-aid.

Such Indian appropriation tended to push the sytem of Western education in a very different direction, so much so that the 'educated babu' quickly became the principal butt of racist ridicule. 'Surrender' to colonial discourse was seldom total or unambiguous among the new literati – as distinct from many not particularly well-educated zamindars and babus, who mindlessly aped scraps of Western fashion and thus became the target of merciless satire precisely from the men truly steeped in European culture, like Michael Madhusudan Datta or Bankim. Even the Derozians – so often stigmatized as superficial and denationalized Anglicists – evoked ancient Hindu glory to refute those who 'brand us with the infamy of *barbarians* – [as] men born naturally *inferior* to Europeans': thus Pyarichand Mitra in his paper *The State of Hindoostan under the Hindoos,* read at the Society for Acquisition of General Knowledge during 1839-41. The language is already proto-nationalistic; even the clear Hindu slant would persist throughout later nationalist thought.

Education remained the preserve of a small if growing minority, and the foreign medium deepened the cultural divide between 'high' and 'low'. Such barriers, however, were hardly new. Sanskrit and Persian high culture had been very exclusive too. But pre-colonial courts or literate groups had never tried to appropriate printing technology despite fairly intensive commercial contacts with Europe from the sixteenth century onwards.

Printing in Indian languages came in the wake of colonialism, as an adjunct to administration and Christian proselytization – but once again, it was quickly appropriated and extended. The missionaries were prominent among the early creators of Bengali prose, yet 'missionary Bengali' soon became a term of ridicule. A real breakthrough was achieved by the simultaneous innovations of print-culture and vernacular prose – perhaps a more radical breakthrough than was achieved by English education, though strangely little-noticed in our historiography.

Printing has been associated everywhere with a shift towards the vernaculars and towards prose. The mnemonic aspect becomes less important than in cultures based on oral tradition with a limited number of manuscripts; and publishers and printers, to make their trade viable, have to reach customers who are literate but without classical education. Vernacular print can also stimulate national consciousness by forging communication links at a level below the classical language but above the various spoken dialects.

Nineteenth-century Bengal was marked by all these developments along with an explosion of new genres and modifications of older literary forms. Printing, still relatively cheap and not yet controlled by big publishing firms, widened opportunities to some extent for authors of relatively plebeian origin. Biographical literature, for instance, had so long dealt mainly with rulers or saints. But of a recent compilation of sixteen autobiographies written between 1833 and 1916, about half are by little-known men. Four are by women – two of them distinguished because of their husbands or sons, the other two entirely obscure.

Printing, and the periodical literature it made possible, created a form of sociability somewhat different in style and composition from the traditional durbar of princes or zamindars. This was the middle-class *adda,* today considered so typical of *bhadralok* life. It often centred around a periodical: a long and rich heritage, from *Bangadarshan* through *Bangabasi, Sabujpatra* and *Kallol* to *Parichay* and beyond, to mention only some of the best-known.

Print-culture, however, also had other, more ambiguous consequences. It probably contributed to a greater textual focus in religion – at times, perhaps, an emphasis upon a ritual inventory of 'classical' norms. The fluidity of oral traditions diminished and, as at the coming of print-culture in early modern Europe, 'the cake of custom had either to be more deliberately preserved or more deliberately broken', to borrow Elizabeth Eisenstein's words in *Clio and Chronos* (1966). Again, printing extended the bounds of literacy, but simultaneously deepened the gulf between literate and illiterate. So much more of the knowledge relevant for everyday living was now in written form, and formal education was becoming virtually the sole avenue for upward mobility in a colonial Bengal where indigenous entrepreneurship was drying up.

Print-culture may have contributed also to the move, evident among intelligensia of extremely varied orientations, away from popular religious practices that were now attacked as superstitious or immoral. Thus both Rammohan and Bankim seem to have shared a certain aversion for the kind of Vaishnavism, based on the Krishna of the Vrindavan phase, that had been popular in Bengal since the days of Shri Chaitanya. This reaction was a pattern common to both Hinduism and Islam in the nineteenth century, and paradoxically tended to push them apart from each other, for plebeian syncretistic customs could often be condemned in such terms. Community identities were extended geographically through improved communications, and more sharply defined at the same time, setting the scene for modern 'communalism'.

Far from being, as Nirad C. Choudhuri designates it, a 'torchrace' of linear progress, our 'renaissance' consisted of spasmodic efforts at change which were all too often frustrated or recoiled upon themselves; of youthful enthusiasm which, time and again, mellowed and subsided with age. Upper-caste norms and patterns of living changed to some extent, but the fundamental structures of the caste hierarchy did not break down. Untouchability, for instance, never even became a major issue One major factor here must have been the sheer resilience of Hindu orthopraxy, rooted in what the nineteenth century often called *adhikar-bheda*: the practice, and theory, that the various segments of the caste-cum-religious hierarchy could have very different rules of behaviour, rituals and belief. One could get to a roof, as Ramkrishna Paramhansa said, by either staircase, ladder or rope – but the various ways should not be mixed up, each group must stick to its own *dharma*.

This pattern of inclusion-through-hierarchization enabled Hinduism to claim a unique tolerance and catholicity while maintaining its rigidities within each particular segment. Rammohan had directly challenged this doctrine in the specific context of 'polytheistic' image-worship; the Derozians and the more militant Brahmos aroused orthodox fury by publicly violating its practices. The public nature of the protest was often what was most anathema. In

Krishnamohan Banerji's play *The Persecuted* (1831), the orthodox father does not mind his son's eating 'forbidden food', so long as it is *not in public*: 'I care not for the most dissolute life you may lead, but do preserve our caste.' The early Brahmos – and that exceptionally consistent Derozian, Ramtanu Lahiri – aroused anger

18.6 *Above: Henri Louis Vivian Derozio*

18.7 *Below: Ramtanu Lahiri*

103

18.8 Ramkrishna Paramhansa

Facing page

18.9 Ghor Kali. Bat-tala wood engraving. The husband carries his wife lovingly while leading his mother like an animal

by publicly discarding the sacred thread. But fairly soon, Brahmoism came to be accommodated more or less as a new sub-caste with its own appropriate practices.

The 'renaissance' is normally associated with various forms of *bhadralok* social activism: education, social and religious reform, revivalism, philanthropy, eventually patriotic politics. As R. van M. Bauer has noted, new socially-activist meanings were added to the traditional concepts of *dharma* and *karma*. Yet, in a curious and crucial paradox, such activism often alternated with moods of self-critical satire, introspection and passivity. A sense of moving forward in tune with the times was intermixed with evocations of *Kali-yuga* gloom.

This was most noticeable during the last quarter of the nineteenth century, when the dream of progress under British tutelage was fading away, yet the alternative myth of a patriotism that solved all problems simply by driving out the foreign rulers had not yet gathered force. The key figure here was Ramkrishna Paramhansa (1836–86), the rustic *pujari* who had lived virtually unnoticed in Dakshineshwar since the 1850s, but who suddenly in the early 1880s cast a spell on significant sections of the Calcutta *bhadralok* world. His message – in total contrast to that of his best-known disciple, Swami Vivekananda – involved almost total rejection of all forms of social activism, even organized philanthropy.

Yet our present generation, which is witnessing a massive upsurge of obscurantism and communal frenzy, recurrent bride-burning and even a return of *sati,* can hardly afford to be too patronizing or contemptuous towards nineteenth-century intellectuals. The most striking dimension of 'renaissance' discourse was surely the totally unprecedented centrality of the 'women's question' – issues of gender relations which have grown crucial again today, though in new and hopefully more radical forms through the efforts of feminist movements. Familiarity has prevented adequate recognition of how all but unique, indeed mystifying, this centrality was. There can be no question of simple explanations in terms of Western impact or hegemony. Missionary polemics talked of the woes of Hindu women, but equally or more of caste oppression; and women's issues never had even a remotely equivalent importance in nineteenth-century Britain or Europe. Nor can the prominence of such issues be related, as today, to the existence of autonomous women's movements.

One needs to search further for the source of this centrality. Perhaps the English-educated *bhadralok,* still normally married off to a child-bride while in his teens, faced exceptional problems of adjustment. That, at least, was one explanation hinted at by the Derozian Maheshchandra Deb in 1839 while presenting a case for far-reaching reform in his *A Sketch of the Condition of Hindoo Women.* And the 'women's question', along with the whole domain of household and family management, was something the middle class could presumably tackle more or less on its own, a field which could – and should – remain free of foreign control.

Here the implicit, and vitally important, contrast was with the *bhadralok's* place of work, dominated directly or indirectly by the *sahibs* – and most obviously so in Calcutta. Even the most successful of lawyers, doctors, journalists or civil servants could encounter racial discrimination and even harassment at times. And despite repeated pleas for independent entrepreneurship – with sporadic efforts invariably blocked by the British stranglehold on Bengal's economy – a growing number had to crowd into government and mercantile offices as humble clerks. The *dasatwa* (bondage) of employment looms large in the discourse of

Ramkrishna, many of whose disciples were clerks, as well as in much contemporary literature. In Durgacharan Ray's *Debganer Martyey Agaman* (1889), for instance, the *Pauranic* gods on a visit to contemporary India keep meeting 'clerks ... dozing as they return home from office. Their faces are worn out after the whole day's work .... The sahib's kicks and blows the whole day, and when they return ... the nagging of wives...'. Ramakrishna, too, directly associated the evils of *chakri* (employment) with those of *kamini* (sex, woman) and *kanchan* (wealth), and talked of men in *Kali-yuga* having become *'magir das, takar das, maniber das'* (slaves of women, of money, of employers). In an 1880 farce entitled *Kaler Bou* ('The Wife of the Times'), subordination to wives is conflated with political subjection to 'the sons of the London queen', and the figure of the suffering Bengali mother, neglected by sons entrapped by the modern wife with expensive Westernized tastes, becomes a metaphor for the enslaved motherland.

Colonialism had meant an abrupt entry of the discipline of clock-time. For the middle-class Bengali, its principal locus was the office job carried on in the unfamiliar enclosed space of the modern city building under bosses seeking to enforce Victorian standards of punctuality. Through uniform office-routine, so different from the seasonal rhythms of the village, clock-time established its domination over life in the colonial metropolis: the flow of people into and away from the office-district of Dalhousie Square, so crowded in the daytime but deserted at night. This was work over which one could have no control and which one could not really understand. Dickens's Mr Dombey saw himself as one of the masters of the world and sole head of his 'Home Department'; the Bengali *bhadralok* faced a simultaneous alienation of time and of space in his job, and feared intrusions into 'his' domestic

world. This was a sensibility which could produce moods of passivity and introspection, or stimulate patriotic militancy. What it found much more difficult to sustain were drives for radical social change.

LITERATURE AND LITERARY LIFE IN OLD CALCUTTA

Swapan Majumdar

During the early history of the city from 1690 to 1757, the only allusions to Calcutta were either to its deities – Chitreshwari of Chitpur or Dakshinakali of Kalighat – or to its commerce. In other words, though it might hurt the pride of a Calcuttan, Calcutta did not grow like other intellectual centres of medieval Bengal such as Gour or Nabadwip.

Until Siraj-ud-Daula's capture of Calcutta in 1756, an amount of uncertainty hovered over the city. None of the fortune-seekers, whether British or Indian, were inclined to invest or settle in the developing town; but the mock battle at Palashi (Plassey) in 1757 finally sealed the fate of Muslim sovereignty in Bengal and signalled the forthcoming paramountcy of the British power.

Thanks to the new prospects thrown open by the Company, Calcutta became a rendezvous of people irrespective of caste, class, profession or religion, who swarmed there attracted not by its finer spirit but by its flowing purse. The other group of immigrant Indians were the zamindars – the greatest beneficiaries of the Permanent Settlement of 1798, floating weeds devoid of any cultural roots to start with. To an elementary working knowledge of Sanskrit learnt at the village *pathshala,* they added a smattering of Persian, the court language until then, only to be reckoned by the British as educated 'gentoos'. Whatever few vernacular texts they read were almanacs, rhymed fables and legends (*panchalis*) or epics – and those too in the mangled versions disseminated by wandering singers.

Till the middle of the eighteenth century, a few literary talents in Bengal were patronized at the courts of local rulers and aristocrats, especially at Bardhaman, Dhaka, Krishnanagar, Medinipur and Murshidabad. Many other gifted people had to be content with their captive audience among the rural masses all over the 'Bengal Subah'. The latter category of scholar-singers used to move from place to place giving recitals and, in that way, effected an interaction of popular and courtly traditions. It may be surmised that such singers were the earliest entertainers in the new city as well, performing at festivals at the invitation of the local gentry.

The early British settlers, on the other hand, resigned themselves to the culturally arid life of white 'Nabobs'. The size of the community was still too small to form an expatriate culture-group. It was only during Warren Hastings's Governor-Generalship (1774–84) – whose commencement also coincided with the establishment of the Supreme Court in Calcutta – that British factors, lieutenants and clerks began to disembark at the Calcutta port every month. Shipments of books arriving at the docks from around the same time testify to the growing demand for reading matter among the

colonists. This also indicates how their social life was growing more and more self-contained: the rulers and the ruled came to form almost insular endogenous blocks within the city, the 'White' and 'Black' Towns.

However, the Company began to extend its patronage to oriental learning, particularly Perso-Arabic learning in the initial phase. Calcutta began to attract talent from different parts of north India. Although that region was itself in a state of decadence, it lent a new dimension to the city's socio-cultural contours. The establishment of the Calcutta Madrassa by Hastings in 1781, the Asiatic Society by William Jones in 1784, and finally Fort William College in 1800 completed the first phase of Calcutta's emergence as an intellectual centre.

These institutions not only changed the complexion of city life, but called into being a new class altogether. Education now became a surer way to success and position than wealth. For good or bad, however, the Bengali Muslims refused to accept the domination of the English language, far less English education. As a result, they became virtually a third cultural coterie within the city. Their Hindu counterparts, on the contrary,

anticipated the coming of Macaulay by thrivingly speculating in education, so to speak.

The new economic aspirations created a necessity for a new education system to satisfy the eagerness of the 'natives' to be elevated to the new respectable middle class. By the last quarter of the eighteenth century, the emerging urban community – which also comprised a section of absentee rural landlords – grew to form a substantial body that could assert itself in almost all the social activities of the flourishing town. The attempt by a Russian adventurer, Gerasim Lebedeff, to stage two Bengali plays in 1795 was somewhat premature, but it proved that a nucleus of clients ready to pay for public performances had already been formed in the city. Now the entrepreneur and the customer could jointly secure the rise of a class of committed authors.

Under the patronage of the new city rich, there also came into being a class of narrators and wits who drew heavily from both popular and erudite sources in their compositions. They were engaged less to instruct than to entertain the families in question and the local people in the evenings. But their work was still transmitted orally or, if written down, through

19.1 Harisankirtan, the popular song recital, transformed in old Calcutta's literary and musical life. Solvyns

107

private circulation. Literary activity continued to be a matter of performance. Affluent family houses assumed the role of cultural promoters.

The first generation of *nouveaux riches* who founded their fortunes in the 'Company's Town', gradually became the leading aristocrats of the next period, ranging from 1757 to 1800. Their cultural interests were either a continuation of decaying feudal practices or an apish imitation of British colonial diversions. In other words, they divided their private and public lives into two clear-cut segments: tradition reigned supreme in their inner chambers, while the outer sported evidence of Westernization. Like their new masters, they also set up printing presses, started family libraries and organized associations, even if, in the main, only to debate on religious relativism to begin with.

On the creative plane, there was a vacuum caused by the lack of serious endeavour and absence of a creative genius who could provide the fresh impetus required in the new milieu. But the ground lay prepared. The new rich were prepared to spend on books, if not for love of reading, at least for the sake of social status. The void was filled partly by the *kabiwalas (kabials)* or poetic duellists. Their impromptu compositions lacked finesse, but this was amply compensated by a sparkling alacrity: their taste was coarse, and they leaned more towards the grosser and profaner implications of the domestic lives of gods and goddesses. At the same time, they showed a marked tendency towards humanization and mundane reality, brought out through an urbane way of looking at life.

In general, the world of the *kabiwalas* was permeated with jealousy, malice, rivalry and vindictiveness, which indeed made their careers colourful but often dragged them into unhealthy competitiveness. Nevertheless, the first signs of a widening cosmopolitanism, with its concomitant secular love-themes, can also be discerned in their poetry. Their relaxed urbanity and ironic play of wit can be matched from the works of Ramnidhi Gupta (1742-1839) or Nidhubabu. His light classical improvized songs, popularly known as Tappa, with their puns and irony, mirth and melancholy, became the most imitated literary artifice of the times. Nidhubabu may be called the first literary figure of Calcutta.

But poetry was no longer the dominant form: it was subjugated to the spirit of prose. The new interest in prose was generated not by literary aspirants but by administrators. It was Warren Hastings once again who initiated his fellow British bureaucrats into collaboration with 'native scholars' in the vernaculars. Interestingly too, the first specimens of Bengali prose were translations of legal statutes and not religious scriptures. The translation of the *Regulations* (1785) by Jonathan Duncan, or that of the Criminal Code under Neil Benjamin Edmonstone's supervision (1791), or Henry Pitts Forster's edition of Cornwallis's Code in Bengali (1793) laid the foundation of what may be called 'Company Prose'. Even the early Bible translations from Shrirampur or Serampore (1800-09) followed virtually the same model. Above all, they rejected the preponderance of Perso-Arabic diction and endowed the language with the current usage of common speech. Such collaborative efforts bore their finest fruit in the works produced at the College of Fort William.

Truly speaking, literary life in Calcutta began with its emergence as a centre of printing and publishing. (This development has been traced elsewhere in these volumes.) The shift from oral or manuscript tradition to print made it possible to burst easily into authorship, and consequently to fame, for someone stationed at Calcutta: those who lived away from the metropolis were adversely placed. As a result, Calcutta attracted more and more writers who formed into an urban class all by themselves, almost completely divorced from the mainstream of common life in rural Bengal. Henceforth Bengali literature was sharply divided into two parallel forces: one thriving in and around Calcutta, the other forming a satellite culture in the districts.

The College of Fort William emerged as both a centre of research and a publication unit, a cradle of creativity as well as scholarship. Planned originally to train probationer British civilians in the languages and cultures of the subjugated country, the College rendered services tantamount to those of a university in promoting modern Indian literatures, Bengali in particular. The College not only brought British and Indian scholars into close collaboration, but offered undreamt-of opportunities for publication to the up-and-coming generation of Bengali authors. Under the leadership of William Carey, the College could also claim credit for drawing together Sanskrit pandits and Perso-Arabic munshis to reshape Bengali prose.

Needless to say, the Fort William model of prose was far different from the one which had been growing indigenously. The vocabulary was based on classical stems and reflexes as much as loan words from various sources, while an English pattern of syntax was superimposed all along. For the next fifty years or so, Bengali prose maintained a precarious balance between these opposite elements.

The variety of the College's publications also deserves note. From colloquies and popular stories, chronicles and legends, to definitive editions of literary texts – the scholars ranged far and wide with uniform ease. Book prices were prohibitive and the readership highly restricted; yet – or perhaps therefore – these authors were held high in public esteem. This caused a further cleavage between the naïve and the sentimental authors which went on increasing through time.

The cultural calendar of Calcutta became far more eventful with the arrival of Rammohan Ray (1772-1833) in the city in 1814. Social changes, he thought, could only be effected through a reinterpretation of the sacred texts. In the process, he not only compiled the most valuable doctrines drawn from these into the synthesis of Brahmoism, but opened up a new area of literary activity: translations of the scriptures into Bengali. His ideological battles, especially that for the abolition of widow-burning, also elicited some excellent polemical pieces from him, though his immediate purpose, needless to say, was far from literary.

But the time was not yet ripe for the rise of a man of letters. Rammohan remained a pamphleteer all his life. That explains why his readership, like his company of disciples, was confined to the proselytized sophisticates of the Atmiya Sabha (established 1815), the first notable voluntary organization established by a 'native' in the city.

A positive floodtide of ideas now began to flow from individuals and institutions alike. They were not always compatible with each other and hence aroused a lot of confusion and tension among their adherents. A true Calcutta literature was born out of the pangs of such value adjustments, or rather the lack of them.

It was perhaps in the fitness of things that the first work to name the city in its title was

19.2 *William Carey with a Brahmin Pandit, perhaps Mrityunjay Tarkalankar. After a painting by Robert Hume*

Kalikata Kamalalaya (1823), a satiric prose sketch by Bhabanicharan Banerji (1794-1848). The portrayal was not entirely fictional. The tussle between continuity and change could also erupt into personal rivalries, sometimes even into a resort to muscle power. But the prevalent spirit was one of acquisition of knowledge. If the educational institutions inculcated a thirst for knowledge, this was disciplined through the dialectics of debate in various voluntary associations, and finally given lasting shape in printed works, vernacular journals in particular.

To begin with, the Company decided to promote oriental learning. Its advisers on education, though Englishmen all, were openly divided into two factions, the Anglicists and the Orientalists. The popular public demand was for Western education, and found expression in the founding of Hindu College in 1817. A philanthropic product of collaboration between the British and the Bengalis, with David Hare as the binding force, the College saw progressives and fundamentalists united for the first time to establish an institution beyond the bounds of the Company's educational operations. The teachers were not all specialized educationists, but had the right kind of mind to appreciate the spirit of the Enlightenment and instil an admiration for those liberal ideas in the nation's youth. The ideas generated by the

French Revolutionaries, the French Positivists, the British Rationalists from Bacon to Bentham and the American humanist Tom Paine became the new gospel. In spite of the steep tuition fees and the risk of elitist estrangement from the mainstream of society, guardians felt compelled to send their wards to Hindu College.

The College with its army of teachers like Captain David Lester Richardson and Henry Louis Vivian Derozio inspired both the latent creativity and the analytic faculty of the students. The first fruits of the process were seen in the firebrand 'Young Bengal' generation: Tarachand Chakrabarti (1804–55), Rasikkrishna Mallik (1810–58), Krishnamohan Banerji (1813–85), Dakshinaranjan Mukherji (1814–78), Pyarichand Mitra (1814–83). Yet it is somewhat unfair to identify them as the sole products of the Hindu College. A traditionalist like Debendranath Thakur (1817–1905) was also an alumnus. It also needs pointing out that even the most militant 'Young Bengals', almost without exception, returned in later years to the orthodox fold.

In their prime, however, they fought against everything that orthodoxy as well as 'Babu Culture' stood for. Brandy and books were their two enkindling passions. Their Western attire, habitual use of English, derogation of the mother-tongue and everything written in it, disparagement of their ancient religion and culture, and relish in forbidden food often repelled their fellow citizens. They frequently ran into excesses, forgetting in their youthful exuberance that to modernize society did not necessarily imply giving a rude shock to others' beliefs and principles. Yet if they rejected the times or considered themselves persecuted, it was out of frustration at the conflict between reality and their own serious ideals. This doubly proves their anxiety to enlighten and elevate their tribe.

It would be simplistic to ascribe this arousal merely to the borrowed culture of a colonial civilization. The initial motive could well have been one of collaboration; but once they acquired a taste for Western knowledge, it also inspired a spirit of enquiry to search for parallels in indigenous tradition. Western ideas thus impelled them to a quest for native roots. But once rediscovered, this heritage in turn provided a contrast with the as yet minute harvest of the new learning, inevitably creating a conflict of values. The imperatives of life had to be defined afresh. The turmoil generated sweetness and light, but dross and venom as well.

Calcutta society at large was broken into divisive coteries: the propertied and the working class; white-collar workers and manual labourers; country and city-based people; the English-educated and the traditionally learned; the emancipated Brahmos and the ritual-ridden Hindus; the profluent Hindus and the retroflex Muslims; and last but not least, the young and the old – the first evidence of a generation gap operating in society as a whole. In the absence of any dialogue between these opposing groups, the 'we' and the 'they' often ranged themselves in terms of a 'culture-versus-anarchy' syndrome. Rather than seek compromise or withdraw into complacent aloofness, the 'Young Bengals' directly braved the orthodoxies. This was obviously neither safe nor diplomatic.

Hence subsequently, we detect a note of caution in the founding of educational institutions. Besides specialized medical and technical institutions, the Sanskrit College (1824), the General Assembly's Institution (1838; now Scottish Church College), Matilal Sheel's Free College (1843) or the Hindu Metropolitan College (1854) were calculated to offset the 'ill effects' of the liberal education offered at the Hindu College. Even the latter had lost much of its radicalism by the time it was converted into Presidency College (1855). Finally, the foundation of the University of Calcutta in 1857 brought about uniformity in the curriculum. In the latter half of the century, national sentiment also gave rise to more and more Indian-run colleges, turning out a large body of potential consumers of the new literature.

In the early stages, all voluntary associations in the city were restricted to Englishmen. In 1829, the Asiatic Society opened its doors to local members. From the third decade of the century, however, Calcutta became a city of thriving intellectual activity by, of and for the 'natives'. At first, these organizations closely imitated British models. It is interesting to note that though most of them were set up with the goal of religious regeneration, social issues featured from the beginning as the most important item in their deliberations, be they conservative or radical. Until 1829, indeed, the progressives and the fundamentalists remained largely united in these organizations. But after the furore over *sati*, they fell apart and began to hurl invectives at each other through pamphlets. A veritable 'Battle of the Books' was unleashed on the Calcutta literary scene.

From about the same time, the advent of the 'Young Bengal' brought two very different types of associations to the fore. First, a line running from the Academic Association (1828) to the Calcutta Literary Society (1875) clearly indicate a formal shift from religious to socio-educational interests. Secondly, from the mid-1830s many such societies turned to economic and political issues, as manifest in associations from the Landholders' Society (1838) to the Hindu Mela (1867) or the Indian Association (1876). Though their basic premises were derived from the West, their approach to problems was refreshingly indigenous. Even British-dominated associations like the Bethune Society (1851) or the Bengal Social Science Association (1867) admitted discourses on immediate issues affecting the welfare of the native people. Also, perhaps to counter the arrogance of the ruling class, a sense of nationalism found expression in organizations for the propagation of Bengali language, literature and culture like the Bangabhasha Prakashika Sabha (1835), the Bangabhashanubadak Samaj (1850) or the Bidyotsahini Sabha (1853). The line culminated in the establishment of the Bangiya Sahitya Parishad in 1893. In short, although basically a century of storm and stress, it was at the same time an era of expansion and growth in ideas as much as in action.

The spirit of the age was best reflected in the world of Bengali journalism, for which the emergent middle class provided a steady clientele. Gangakishore Bhattacharya (?-1831?) was not only the first to publish a Bengali periodical from Calcutta; he also opened a bookshop and appointed agents to distribute books in the city and suburbs. To support such an establishment, he utilized his press to print popular titles in cheap editions. This was in a way the beginning of the Bat-tala publishing houses, which, however abused for their grossness of taste, played a great role in making books and journals available to a wide reading public.

The contemporary periodicals, opinionated as they were, served the common reader as windows upon the world, providing information and debates on the most vital issues of the day. From *Sambad Koumudi* (1821) and

Bishwakosh Lane

Calcutta is perhaps the world's only city to have a street named after a book. In 1886, before he turned twenty, Nagendranath Basu (1866-1938) assumed the editorship of the 22-volume Bengali encyclopedia *Bishwakosh:* the task took him twenty years. He lived and worked at no. 8 Kantapukur By-lane in Bagbazar. Later, Calcutta Corporation renamed the street Bishwakosh Lane.

Editing this vast work did not exhaust Nagendranath's energies. He also brought out a 13-volume history of the castes and sects of Bengal (*Banger Jatiya Itihas*) and many other archaeological and antiquarian works, editions of old Bengali texts – and a number of plays, for he was no less keen a member of the Darjipara Theatrical Club than of the Asiatic Society and the Sahitya Parishad. He was finally awarded the title of *Prachyavidyarnav,* 'Ocean of Oriental Learning'. The name Bishwakosh Lane commemorates a man as well as a book.

Samachar Chandrika (1822) to *Bangadarshan* (1872) and *Bharati* (1877), this long tradition continued unabated. We cannot claim that their socio-economic views were based on unshakeable beliefs or principles. Clemency, compromise and pressure of circumstances certainly operated. But on literary issues, the new generation could go beyond the confines of their times. The literary controversies were never guided by vested interests or personal gain. Even when they fought a lost battle, they did so out of conviction. The editors of *Sambad Prabhakar* (1831), the *Tattwabodhini Patrika* (1843), *Bibidhartha-Samgraha* (1851) or *Bangadarshan* viewed their task as a religious crusade to recover the lost glory of the mother-tongue.

The 1830s saw not only the growth of Calcutta as a centre of literary activity, but a disproportionate growth, overshadowing the entire literary production in the rest of Bengal. Another almost imperceptible change was the gradual moving of the cultural centre from the north to the new educational complex in the centre of the city. The egalitarian lecture halls along College Street replaced the courtyards of

19.3 Nagendranath Basu

111

the old feudal patrons, classically represented by the Debs of Shobhabazar. The practice of employing proxy scribes or ghost writers declined, and authors became more aware of literary property and rights.

But the event of historic import that decided the city's future literary course was the introduction of English as the medium of instruction at the instance of Lord Macaulay (1835), anticipating the acceptance of English as the official or 'court' language as well (1838). And the very presence in the city of a man of letters like Macaulay or a scholar like Alexander Duff fostered in the Indian mind a reverence for the literary man and his profession.

After the turmoil of the first three decades of the century, the next generation had no option but to face the challenging oppositions between tradition and modernity, Sanskrit and English precedents. Fortunately, despite undercurrents of discord, the makers of the new literature tried their best to reconcile the two. The ambivalence of the new city people, their love-hate relation with both native tradition and the alien modernity, found typical expression in the works of Ishwarchandra Gupta (1812-59). Ishwarchandra was averse to English education, yet could not help being attracted by the innovations it brought. Again, his patriotic sentiment made him extol his immediate predecessors, the late eighteenth-century poets; but his own poems are lyrical, albeit in a witty and sometimes sarcastic vein.

As a journalist, Ishwarchandra encouraged and initiated novices in literary composition. A good many stalwarts of the next generation served their literary apprenticeship under him: Akshaykumar Datta (1820-86), Rangalal Banerji (1826-86), Dinabandhu Mitra (1829-74), Bankimchandra Chatterji (1838-94) and Hemchandra Banerji (1838-1903). A regular school of rhetoric grew up around his journal *Sambad Prabhakar*. Yet every member of the circle struck out in his own direction: their mentor had the catholicity of mind to let them grow in their own ways. With Ishwar Gupta, medievalism breathed its last in Bengali literature and the modern spirit came into being.

As the direction became clear, authors turned to it with rare avidity. The tenor of literature was set for constructive utilitarian purposes. There was a truly revolutionary leap forward under the leadership of Ishwarchandra Banerji (1820-91), better known by his academic title

Vidyasagar. Unlike his senior namesake Ishwar Gupta, Vidyasagar was well acquainted with the English world of letters. Though his basic discipline was Sanskrit, he was independent enough to differ from his fellow-scholars in interpreting the scriptures. After discharging his responsibilities as an academician, and cultivating his passion for social reform and women's emancipation, he found little time for creative writing as such. Yet through the textbooks he compiled, the pamphlets he produced, and of course the retellings of the Indian epics, of Kalidasa's *Shakuntala* (1854) and of Shakespeare's *A Comedy of Errors* (as *Bhrantibilas*, 1869), he set the norm of standard Bengali prose. Akshaykumar Datta's collaborations with him in the pages of the *Tattwabodhini Patrika* complemented what had been lacking in his style. The latter forged a language adequate for precise scientific expression.

One of the finest rational minds of the time, Akshaykumar did not spare to criticize the accumulated evils of Hindu society. But his logical yet suave expositions hardly left any room for misunderstanding and consequent bitterness against him or the group he belonged to, the Brahmos. The two magna opera by Akshaykumar, *Bahyabastur sahit Manabprakritir Sambandhabichar* ('Determining the Relation between External Objects and the Human Mind', 1855) and *Bharatbarshiya Upasak Sampraday* ('The Holy Sects of India', 1870/83) were based on George Combe's or Horace Hayman Wilson's works, but the explorations in newer areas of knowledge and the lucidity of language bore the seal of the author. The widening horizons and mature literary interests of the Bengali intelligentsia were also reflected in other contemporary works like *Bidyakalpadrum* (1846-51), an Anglo-Bengali encyclopaedia compiled by Krishnamohan Banerji.

But the greatest contribution of the period was the systematic formulation of textbooks for schoolchildren. The Baptist missionaries of Shrirampur, the teachers of Fort William College and various authors under the aegis of the Calcutta School Book Society (1817) or the Vernacular Literature Committee (1851; later Society), had endeavoured to set a norm for Bengali textbooks. But Vidyasagar, Akshaykumar and Madanmohan Tarkalankar (1815-57) were the first to envisage texts that would build the character of the new generation without sacrificing literary sensitivity.

Virtually the entire mental make-up of late-nineteenth-century Bengali society was structured through these textbooks.

To achieve this end, Vidyasagar and Madanmohan thought it desirable to establish an independent publishing house, the Sanskrit Press Depository, in 1847. This was the beginning of the modern era of Bengali publishing, where the educated elite emerged as entrepreneurs. This also partly explains the rise of a group of authors like Tarashankar Tarkaratna (?-1858), Ramgati Nyayaratna (1831-94) and Dwarakanath Vidyabhushan (1820-86) – products of Sanskrit College and followers of Vidyasagar.

Although the period may not have been distinguished by great creative flair, it paved the way for the advent of the literary artist. It was also a period when the Bengali literati learnt not to be apologetic about its past heritage and to resist the anglomania of the Young Bengal. The defences of Sanskrit literature by Vidyasagar (*Sanskrita Sahityabishayak Prastab,* 1851) or of Bengali poetry by Rangalal Banerji (*Bangla Kabitabishayak Prabandha,* 1852) point to the change of wind.

In drama too, though the absence of Bengali plays was mostly compensated by translations from Sanskrit and English, original works were inspired by Vidyasagar's anti-polygamy, anti-child-marriage and widow-remarriage movements, which touched the depths of the social psyche. Ramnarayan Tarkaratna's (1822-86) *Kulin-Kulasarbashwa* (1854) marked the beginning of a long tradition where the new breed of dramatist could amply project the dreams and the frustrations, the courage and the cowardice, the foresight and the foolhardiness evident in society.

But the happenings of 1857 completely stupefied the city. Although the first shot fired by the sepoys was discharged only a few miles from Calcutta, the city people remained oblivious of the turmoil and reiterated their fidelity to the rulers, even to excess. Could this bear any relation to the blossoming of creative literature that commences from the very same year? Was the literature of the next period, between 1858 and 1894, a means of escape from reality? Or was it an oblique way of approaching the reality itself? Whatever the cause, a flight of creative imagination now appeared in almost all genres of literary activity. The number of notable works also grew

19.4 *Bhudeb Mukherji*

by leaps and bounds.

Society was already in a ferment. The emancipated new religion, Brahmoism, split into three while still in a process of growth; a popular, yet intellectually and ethically acclaimed version of Hinduism was embodied in a full-fledged religious order that grew up around Ramkrishna Paramhansa (1836-86) and his much-travelled disciple Swami Vivekananda (born Narendranath Datta, 1863-1902). On the political front, the ruthless oppression by the indigo planters almost fomented an upheaval in 1858; the gagging of the Press and censorship of the stage through two infamous laws, the Vernacular Press Act (1868) and the Dramatic Performances Act (1876), exposed the sharp teeth of colonialism. It seemed tantamount to a breach of trust. The imperialist design became so obvious that Bengalis schooled in liberal British ideas thought it wiser to protect their rights through public forums or, failing that, by extremist action.

Whereas the Young Bengal movement was more concerned with the dynamics of social change, their younger contemporaries betook themselves more to literary ambitions. They too came from the new colleges: Michael Madhusudan Datta (1824-73), Bhudeb Mukherji (1825-94) and Rajnarayan Basu (1826-1900) from Hindu College, Bankimchandra from Hugli College. Like their illustrious predecessors, they too began with the wrong priorities but struck the right path through timely advice and self-realization. There was a kind of balance between their different sensibilities: an overweening dandy like Madhusudan against an unpretentious Bhudeb; Rajnarayan's vacillation between extremes against Bankim's rational middle course.

Their works betrayed an intenser as well as a more problematic influence of the West. Richardson's *Selections from the British Poets* acted upon their impressionable minds with a scale of literary values. Shakespeare, Milton and Byron became the triumvirate guiding the destiny of the Bengal muse. A contradiction lay in the choice itself. That is why, even though their works were planned to exercise the head, in practice they turned out more to celebrate the heart. Their vocabulary, images and allusions, mostly culled from Western sources, estranged then from the majority of the reading public. Calcutta literature of this period developed by and large as an elitist product. Creative artists went on endlessly exposing their class-fellows, varying only the angle of portraiture. We may call this a collective exercise in masochistic sadism.

The wave of new literature assumed a dual identity: one of idealism and wish-fulfilment, the other of melancholy or a lugubrious realism, a panorama of caricatures. Even a single text could be rent into two distinct parts: imagination and idealism on the one hand, sarcasm and satire on the other. Pyarichand Mitra's *Alaler Gharer Dulal* (1858), *Hutom Penchar Naksha* (1862) ascribed to Kaliprasanna Sinha (1840-70), Bankimchandra's *Kamalakanta* (1875/85), Jogendrachandra Basu's (1854-1907) *Model Bhagini* (1888) or, at a more popular level, *Haridaser Guptakatha* (1872) in prose; Indranath Banerji's (1849-1911) *Bharat Uddhar* (1877) in verse; the rich line of satiric farces from Madhusudan's *Ekei ki Baley Sabhyata?* and *Buro Shaliker Gharey Roan* (1859), Dinabandhu's *Sadhabar Ekadasi* and *Biyepagla Buro* (1866) to Jyotirindranath Thakur's (1849-1925) *Kinchit Jalajog* (1872) and *Eman Karma Ar Karba Na* (1877) expose the sordid anomalies in different spheres of society.

In the other direction, a rich corpus of writings transport us, as it were, to a land of vision: epics, including Rangalal's *Padmini Upakhyan* (1858), Madhusudan's *Meghnadbadh Kabya* (1861), Hemchandra's *Britrasamhar* (1875/77), Kaikobad's (1858-?) *Mahashmashan*

19.5 *Dinabandhu Mitra*

(1880), Dwijendranath Thakur's (1840-1926) allegorical *Swapnaprayan* (1875) and Nabinchandra Sen's (1846-1909) *Palashir Juddha* (1875) or the first two volumes of his contemplated trilogy of a 'Mahabharata of the Nineteenth Century', *Raibatak* (1886) and *Kurukshetra* (1893); the trumpet-call of Dwijendralal Ray's (1863-1913) patriotic *Aryagatha* (1882) or the lyric ecstasies of Biharilal Chakrabarti's (1835-94) *Saradamangal* (1879); prose romances from Bhudeb's *Aitihasik Upanyas* (1862) to most of Bankimchandra's novels, written between 1865 and 1886, or Rameshchandra Datta's (1848-1909) compendium of four novelettes, *Shatabarsha* (1874-78/79); the mytho-historic deflections in the plays of Girishchandra Ghosh (1844-1912); the *Mahabharata* in Bengali prose (1859-66) edited by Kaliprasanna Sinha, or the funereal epic of Karbala, *Bishad-Sindhu* (1880-85) by Mir Mosharraf Hussain (1847-1922); and the variety of discursive prose by Bhudeb, Bankim, Rameshchandra and Vivekananda, exploring various frontiers of human knowledge and experience.

In spite of the effective social realism of Dinabandhu's *Nildarpan* (1860) and Mosharraf's *Jamidar-Darpan* (1873) in drama, or Taraknath Ganguli's (1845-91) *Swarnalata* (1873) and Bankimchandra's *Bishbriksha* (1873), *Rajani* (1877) or *Krishnakanter Will* (1878) in the new genre of the novel, realism was certainly not the mainstay of the literature of the period. Rather, a text like *Kankabati* (1892) by Trailokyanath Mukherji (1847–1919), with its double-decker structure and overlapping themes of vision and reality, humour and pathos, reflects more faithfully the ambivalence of the age.

Compared to the literature of the Company period, the productions of the Crown era certainly excelled in the imaginative faculty. But – perhaps for that very reason – it was somewhat haphazard in outlook to begin with, though the authors soon methodized their visions. They had indeed to sort out a daunting complexity of stances respecting the home and the world, tradition and modernity, spiritualism and science – in short, between the East and the West. Right from the beginning, English ideas and institutions, language and literature were taken as equivalent to Westernism as a whole. Moreover, the appreciation of these was mediated through books alone. As yet, the Bengali intelligentsia had no direct experience of English culture and society, particularly the relationship between England's social realities and modes of English literary expression. Travel was perfectly possible at this stage, so that a practical comparison was not difficult to make. But the intellectuals of Calcutta were not eager to rectify their notions.

The time had come to take a hard look at both the English model and the state of things at home. And that required leadership. Bankimchandra, through his passionate yet balanced judgement, emerged as the undisputed leader of the new generation of Bengali writers. He moulded the tastes of the readers no less than he provided guiding principles for new writers. In a true and commendable sense, a school of writing grew up around him and his *Bangadarshan*.

Bankimchandra did not consider the ephemera of everyday experiences to be a worthy base for imaginative literature. Nor did he believe, as Rammohan or Vidyasagar did, that human nature or social practices could be changed through legislation. But he was convinced of the efficacy of education in liberating the mind, and of literature as an invaluable means to achieve this therapeutic effect. He was a utilitarian and did not feel shy of putting literature to functional use. But being essentially an artist, he could turn these purposeful writings into objects of art, 'nurslings of immortality'.

Bankimchandra's success and his unbending self-confidence also won him enemies. People were not yet sophisticated enough to accept differences in opinion as distinct from personal animosities. Vidyasagar's followers, the Adi Brahmo Samajists led by the Thakurs of Jorasanko, Christian missionaries like the Reverend William Hastie, or the resurgent Hindus gathered round Ramkrishna – all found threats in Bankim's intellectual interpretation of Hinduism. But they could not argue with him at any length, as none of his opponents could match his mastery over the Sanskrit texts as well as Western rational philosophy. Some branded him communal, others as a conservative; but none could ignore him. This may have been because in fact, Bankim effected a happy coexistence of the best of both East and West in his personality.

Unlike such interaction in the early years of contact, the acculturation now resulted in a much deeper and wider creative urge for expression. The rise of women writers in the city was an event of exceptional importance. Swarnakumari Debi (1855–1932) or Kamini Ray (1864–1933) represented a flourishing generation of educated women writers, discharging with total zeal the responsibilities of their pursuit.

As regards literary form, new genres were

19.6 *Nabinchandra Sen*

explored and new techniques attempted. Travelogues and reviews became two popular and productive areas of literary interest. Experiments with narrative structure enlivened the craft of fiction, making it virtually the most reflective literary form of the period.

Thematically, nationalism not only became a dominant concern, but the sustaining inspiration for almost all sorts of literary activities. As a result, the writers of the city gradually moved out of their self-imprisonment to a more reciprocal relation with their readers. The greatest writers of the age became also the best–selling authors. This wide acceptance inspired writers to extend their range of themes. No human act or thought was discarded any longer as alien to its scope. Literature now began to be viewed in conjunction with other expressive acts like dance and music, painting or sculpture. All these added dimensions of the new literature became manifest in the works of Rabindranath Thakur or Tagore (1861-1941), whom Bankimchandra himself, punning on the poet's name (*rabi*, sun), welcomed as the 'rising sun' of Bengali literature.

That even a genius cannot completely bypass the trends of his time, is well illustrated from the early career of Rabindranath. In spite of his phenomenal powers, his early poems groped in search of an idiom close to Biharilal's yet not the same; his early dramas followed the beaten Shakespearean track; and his early novels were pale shadows beside Bankim's. Between 1878 and 1894, Rabindranath produced no less than two and a half dozen books, a cycle of which the verse-drama *Balmiki-Pratibha* (1881) might be taken as an epiphany, depicting as it does the poetic initiation of the ancient poet Balmiki. Exploring various possibilities of verse drama, he found himself comfortable in the mode attained in *Raja o Rani* (1889), while among his narratives *Rajarshi* (1887) was an enormous success among readers. But he soon struck a finer vein in the short stories which flowed from his pen: *Chhotagalpa, Kathachatushtay* and two volumes of *Bichitra Galpa* all published within a year (1894). And nothing, of course, could match the stream of poetic creations, covering a range of themes and modes from *Sandhyasangeet* (1882) to *Bhanusinha Thakurer Padabali* (1884) to *Kari o Komal* (1886) to *Manasi* (1890) to *Sonar Tari* (1894). More than five hundred songs also gave forth their melody within the same span of time.

Apart from this, Rabindranath made path-finding experiments with the epistolary form and colloquial prose for discussions of serious magnitude (*Europe-Prabasir Patra,* 1881; *Chithipatra,* 1887; *Europe-Jatrir Diary,* 1891/93). In his critical prose, he not only provided valuable evaluations of his predecessors like Madhusudan or Bankimchandra as well as his contemporaries, but through these presented his poetic credo, setting Bengali poetry back on the rails of its inherent formal genius, for the lyric. In this field, he was the undisputed monarch.

Up to this time, publishing in Calcutta had never experienced any crucial economic recession; nor, however, had its financial prospects ever loomed bright. The publishers had failed to acquire true professional expertise. Their trade grew in terms of both investment and production, but could barely attract workers because of the low wage levels. Virtually no steady work-force grew up around the book market. For most people it was either a part-time job or a makeshift pursuit in default

19.7
Bankimchandra Chatterji. Painted from life by Bamapada Banerji

of a better. Skilled technicians preferred to work in mercantile firms or the Crown's Stationery Office rather than in the publishing industry. Advertisements were few and poor. The only prevalent mode of publicity was canvassing. In short, the publishers showed no interest at all in bringing about innovations or improvement.

Their relation with their authors was usually one of mutual distrust. Some writers started publishing their own works; but except for Vidyasagar, they all suffered loss. In fine, writing remained an unremunerative pursuit, and no author could depend on his income from this source alone. A creative writer clung to his vocation only for his passion's sake and for the prestige it brought him. The general discontent implied, however, that things were poised for a change – which ultimately took place about the turn of the century.

In 1894, when Bankimchandra passed away, it was Rabindranath who sounded the last post for the departed leader, even as he assumed the succession. Till then, the epoch-makers of Bengali literature had been born elsewhere, though they chose Calcutta as their intellectual home. Rabindranath was born in the city, and gave it literary recognition the world over. Yet it is ironic that he opted to leave the place. Should we read this decision as a comment by the master on the literary atmosphere of the city?

OLD CALCUTTA
AS PRESENTED IN
LITERATURE

Rabindra Kumar Das Gupta

When Job Charnock set up his residence at Calcutta on 24 August 1690, Bengali literature was more than six hundred years old. English literature was much the same age if we exclude the Old English period. Calcutta and its surroundings were not then known for any literary activity; not did Charnock's arrival inspire any. Indeed, the event seems to have attracted little attention. Even the romantic legends that grew up around Charnock, especially his rescuing a beautiful damsel from *sati* and taking her to wife, passed unnoticed in literature. It was only in 1960 that the romance was made the subject of a Bengali novel, Pratapchandra Chandra's *Job Charnocker Bibi*.

The village of Kalikata had, of course, existed before the British set up their quarters there. Two early Bengali narrative poems make interesting mention of the place. Bipradas Pipalai's *Manasamangal* (1495) has a passage citing Kalikata along with nearby centres like Kamarhati, Ariadaha, Chitpur and Kalighat. Kabikankan Mukundaram's *Chandimangal* of the late seventeenth century also mentions Kalikata and indeed calls it a *mahasthan*, 'great place' or prosperous city. As the poem predates Charnock's settlement by at least fifteen years, this would seem curiously prophetic – were it not that in both poems, the passages in question are held to be later interpolations.

Where Is Calcutta in Eighteenth Century Bengali Literature?

The strange but true answer to this question is, 'Practically nowhere.' The city's growing importance in the British colonial scheme is not reflected in Bengali literature, presumably because the politics of the time did not interest the common man. When it did, as through the Maratha raiders or *bargis*, it provoked the composition of the *Maharashtra Puran*. The devastation of the city by Clive's soldiers in the mid-eighteenth century produced no such reverberations in literature. On the contrary, a village bard, Ramprasad Maitra, welcomed the British merchant as the agent of a divine dispensation:

Listen, all! How wonderfully did the gods of heaven take cane in hand and *topee* on head, and come as merchants to the settlement at Calcutta to the joy of the people of Bengal.

The foundation of Calcutta is similarly a work of providence:

Listen, all! The common subjects of Bengal were under the *subedar* [Mughal governor]. But meanwhile some beneficent dispenser of our destiny created Calcutta, where gods dwell in the shape of Englishmen.

The poem belongs to the second half of the eighteenth century. Not even the most patriotic

Englishman of the day would have invested Charnock or Clive with divinity.

Rammohan Ray on Calcutta

With the city's growth as an intellectual as well as a commercial centre, it began to attract serious literary attention. Raja Rammohan Ray (1772-1833) showed profound solicitude for the city which was the scene of his historic labours for sixteen years. His view of Calcutta as a cradle of intellectual liberty appears in his memorial to the Supreme Court against an ordinance curbing the freedom of the press. Ray's biographer Sophia Dobson Collet has called this piece 'the *Areopagitica* of Indian history'. Rammohan writes:

Ever since the art of printing has become generally known among the natives of Calcutta, numerous publications have been circulated in the Bengali language, which by introducing free discussion among the natives and inducing them to reflect and inquire after knowledge, have already served greatly to improve their minds and ameliorate their condition. This desirable object has been chiefly promoted by the establishment of four native newspapers, two in the Bengali and two in the Persian language, with [accounts of] whatever is worthy of notice at the Presidency or in the country, and also the interesting and valuable intelligence of what is passing in England and in other parts of the world...

Written in 1823, these lines are the first significant statement on the growth of intellectual life in Calcutta in that century. Rammohan was no less enthusiastic about the role of libraries, and set up one in Calcutta in 1824, twelve years before the founding of the Calcutta Public Library.

Satires of Calcutta Life

All serious students of old Calcutta are familiar with Brajendranath Banerji's compilation, *Sangbadpatrey Sekaler Katha* ('The Account of Old Times in Newspapers', 1937-41), where he presents a full picture of Calcutta life in the first half of the nineteenth century through extracts from Bengali newspapers, arranged in five sections: Education, Literature, Society, Religion and Miscellaneous. All these matters have been treated in various articles of this book. Here let us see how, simultaneously with the newspapers, the Bengali literature of the times presents a vivid picture of Calcutta life, especially in its comic and satire-inducing aspects.

These writers loved the city enough to make fun of its follies.

The poet Ishwarchandra Gupta (1812-59) has left behind an oft-quoted couplet on Calcutta:

> *Retey masha diney machhi*
> *Ei taraye Kalkatay achhi.*

[Mosquitoes by night and flies by day: we live in Calcutta with these afflictions.]

Ishwar Gupta also has some telling satire of the 'Babus'; but these targets of censure and derision as well as a kind of awe are held up to the most trenchant ridicule by three prose writers.

The first of these was Bhabanicharan Banerji (1787-1848). In 1823, when he wrote his *Kalikata Kamalalay* – the first Bengali work to name the city in its title – Calcutta had grown into a large city where Rammohan Ray had already worked as a reformer for some ten years, and the early products of Hindu College (founded in 1817) were creating a 'Young Bengal'. Bhabanicharan, however, calls the city *Kamalalay,* the home (*alay*) of Kamala or Lakshmi, the goddess of wealth: the city is a money-makers' submarine paradise, where Lakshmi dwells surrounded by sharks and crocodiles. The author sees this coexistence of divine and infernal as an inevitable consequence of the historical circumstances which created the city:

The sea of Calcutta was churned when the English fought the Nawab and out of it came the gall of sorrow and the nectar of joy. The city became *nirupam,* that is incomparable, and widely known. But there were rapacious sharks too as there was abounding ignorance in the shape of crocodiles.

The work is a dialogue between a Calcuttan and a stranger. The latter castigates the evils of the city, while the citizen points out that things are better than they seem. The citizen obviously represents the author; but he is half in agreement with his interlocutor, whose criticisms are clearly to be taken seriously. He views most Calcuttans as mindless epicureans, heedless of their native language and traditions. The citizen replies that while this is true of many, there are not a few who value Sanskrit and only cultivate English as the official language. Again, when the stranger calls the people of Calcutta factious and vulnerable to flattery, the citizen attributes these traits to their·love of leadership. The work ends with a kind word about the poor Brahmins, who must serve and humour the egregious Babus for their subsistence.

The colophon of the book promises a second part; but Bhabanicharan's next work of the kind has a different title, *Nabababubilas* (1825), 'The Drolleries of the New Babu'. It is a merciless satire of the Calcutta Babu. 'Though the work is highly satirical,' said *The Friend of India*, 'and though some of its strokes of ridicule may be too deeply touched, we cannot venture to pronounce it a caricature.' *Nabababubilas* casts aside the balance and restraint of *Kalikata Kamalalay* to pour scorn on the spoilt-child-turned-hedonist, with no sense of social

propriety, surrounded by self-seeking flatterers. The author describes such a man with a pun on *phul-babu* ('flower-babu'), the Bengali word for a fop or dandy: '*Phul*-babu, that is, the Babu who is a *fool*.' *Nababibibilas* (1831), 'The Drolleries of the New Lady', narrates the career of a wanton girl in this degenerate society, in a prurient but no less hard-hitting manner.

An equally fascinating picture of the seamy side of Calcutta life in that age is presented in the short picaresque novel *Alaler Gharer Dulal* ('The Rich Man's Spoilt Child', 1858) by Pyarichand Mitra (1814–83) under the pen-name of 'Tekchand Thakur'. The hero is the wayward scion of an established family in Calcutta: his experiences take us through the schools, courts and police circles of the city. Of the book's wider descriptive range and down-to-earth vitality, the following passage, recounting the conversation among women by the Ganga at Bagbazar, affords a sample:

Some are speaking of their oppressive sisters-in-law, some are cursing their tyrannical mothers-in-law, some are tired of life because of the kicks they receive from their daughters-in-law, particularly when their sons are too timid to intervene; some complain of the intolerable behaviour of the wives of their husbands' brothers and some say how keen they are to get their ten-year-old sons married.

Alal also gives us interesting glimpses into the city's history, whether true or apocryphal. For instance, we are told for the first time in a Bengali work of the huge tree at Baithakkhana under which Job Charnock is said to have smoked and attended to his business. We also learn how Calcuttans first allegedly acquired knowledge of English:

The Sheths and Basaks ... communicated with the English through gestures, which marked the beginnings of their learning the language. When the Supreme Court was established, the exigencies of legal transactions gave an impetus to the study of English.

An allied vein of satire also runs through *Hutom Penchar Naksha* ('The Screech-Owl's Sketches', 1862), by Kaliprasanna Sinha (1840–70). Bankimchandra Chatterji compared these sketches of Calcutta life to Dickens's *Sketches by Boz*. 'The follies and peculiarities of all classes, and not seldom of men actually living, are described in racy vigorous language, not seldom disfigured by obscenity,' says Bankim.

Kaliprasanna's depiction of the Babu would indeed have been libellous if it referred closely to an actual person:

Bagambar Mitra and the like of him are more terrible than a snake, more violent than the tiger. They are, truly speaking, a kind of dreadful beast. They try to do good to the country to serve their own interests. Their only thought is how to be a big man, how to bring everybody under their feet. They are the least generous, and their charity would never go beyond four annas.

Another such grotesque character, Danu Babu, lays about his own father in a drunken fit, then tells his weeping mother that if the old fool dies, with the blessings of Vidyasagar (the proponent of widow remarriage) he will bring home another father, and the three of them will sit and drink together. Sometimes the vignettes have a disconcertingly modern relevance, like the account of young boys extorting subscriptions for Durga Puja. And of the Puja itself, as practised by the 'Young Bengal':

Instead of feeding the Brahmins they offer wine and rice to their dear friends among whom there are some ladies... . Imported tapers burn in front of the image, and one is allowed to visit the sacred spot with one's shoes on. The image is decorated with finery brought from England. The Mother Goddess wears a bonnet instead of a crown, and takes sandwiches instead of fruits as offering.

This may appear exaggerated or downright fantastic, but we have other testimony of the authenticity of the account. Ramgati Nyayratna, the first historian of Bengali language and literature, values *Hutom* for the accuracy of its depictions of society. A review in the *Hindoo Patriot* observed: 'His pictures are vivid and truthful – they are sometimes so faithful as representations of current weaknesses that many will be pointed at as having sat for their portraits.'

The fidelity is also confirmed by Shibnath Shastri's non-fictional account in *Ramtanu Lahiri o Tatkalin Bangasamaj* ('Ramtanu Lahiri and the Bengali Society of His Times', 1904). Nineteenth-century Calcutta, says Shibnath, was a hotbed of infectious diseases; and further,

Calcutta spread a moral infection too. Men did not hesitate to feather their nests by telling lies, cheating, taking bribes, and committing forgeries and similar crimes; and instead of being looked down upon, they were praised for their cleverness. The rich vied with

each other in extravagance; and they were not ashamed to indulge in open immorality ... . They lived for themselves alone, pleasure being the be-all and end-all of their existence. With faces bearing marks of debauchery, heads covered with a profusion of waving curls, tinged teeth like so many pieces of jet, pieces of thin, black-bordered muslin round their waists, cambric vests made so as to show their figures to best advantage, neatly folded scarves thrown over their shoulders, and shoes ornamented with broad buckles, they strolled down the streets, humming or whistling a favourite tune.

This is Hutom's Calcutta painted in still more vivid colours.

Bankim's Calcutta

During the flowering of the Bengal Renaissance in the second half of the nineteenth century, urban life became a common theme of literature; but the city that was the scene of most such literary labours did not inspire great devotion among the leading writers. Bankimchandra Chatterji (1838–94) lived there as a student of Presidency College, and later for much of his career in the Bengal Civil Service; there, too, he spent his last years. But his perception of the city is no different from that of Bhabanicharan, Pyarichand or Kaliprasanna.

The butt of Bankim's satirical essay *Babu* obviously belongs to Calcutta, though the city is not mentioned by name: 'His God is the Eglishman, his guru is a learned Brahmo, his Veda is the vernacular newspaper, and his holy place is the National Theatre.' Even more hilarious, and more merciless, is the satirical narrative *Muchiram Gurer Jibancharit* ('The Life of Muchiram Gur', 1884). The upstart hero Muchiram leaves his native village for Calcutta,

Facing page
20.1 *The Musk-Rats' Music-Party (Chhunchor Kirtan). Bat-tala wood engraving. Satirizes the Babu's external finery while musk-rats infest his empty house*

20.2 *Kaliprasanna Sinha*

121

as it is in that city that men make their fortunes. His wife Bhadrakali accompanies her husband because she has heard that in Calcutta women decked in finery lend lustre to the streets. On arrival, she finds that such women as go about in this way only pollute the city. She is disillusioned; but Muchiram is overjoyed at becoming a Babu – 'transformed from a rustic monkey into an urban monkey' – and surrounds himself with lewd, drunken parasites who fleece and swindle him. Ultimately, he becomes a Rai Bahadur. Muchiram is Bankim's unflattering answer to the question: 'Who thrives in Calcutta, and how?'

In his novel *Bishbriksha* ('The Poison Tree', 1872) Bankim goes further: Calcutta not only produces Babus, it exports them to the villages. Debendra, a dissolute character, is said to have learnt his ways in Calcutta. Returning to his village, 'he declares himself to be a reformer. He first establishes a Brahmo Samaj. He delivers innumerable public lectures. He tries to found a female school but does not succeed.' Bankim is silent about the genuine Renaissance of ideas and social reform taking place in Calcutta. He sees it only as an instrument of hypocrisy and self-seeking.

Michael Madhusudan Dutta (1824–73) has still less to say about Calcutta – indeed, he is virtually silent about the city, despite having been a student of Hindu College and a barrister of the Calcutta High Court. In a sonnet to Vidyasagar he calls Calcutta 'Hastina-nagar' after the great city of the *Mahabharata* where Yudhisthira is enthroned after the great war. It is the nearest Michael comes to a tribute to the city.

Rajnarayan and Rabindranath

Rajnarayan Basu (1826-99), the father of nationalism in Bengal, writes in a more eager and nostaligic vein about old Calcutta in *Sekal ar Ekal* ('Past and Present', 1874). For Rajnarayan, Calcutta is truly a great city, a *mahanagar*, and he writes with enthusiasm of his student days at Hindu College and of distinguished men like Derozio. It may seem not a little curious that this great Bengali patriot speaks reverently of some English residents as *mahapurush*-es (great men) who contributed much to the welfare of the city. He quotes a Sanskrit distich extolling five great Englishmen: David Hare, John Russell Colvin,

John Palmer, William Carey and Joshua Marshman.

Hare, Colvin, Palmerascha, Carey, Marshmanostatha Pancha gora smarennityang mahapatakanasanang.

(Hare, Colvin and Palmer, Carey and also Marshman: these five white men should be remembered always, for it destroys great sins.)

In a more personal vein, Rabindranath Thakur (Tagore) affords some remarkably sensitive recollections of the life and ambience of Calcutta in the 1860s and 1870s. In his *Chhelebela* (1940: translated by Marjorie Sykes as *My Boyhood Days*) there are passages which almost read like prose-poems about the city:

When I was a little boy Calcutta city was not as wakeful at night as it is now… In those old times which we knew, when the day was over, whatever business remained undone wrapped itself up in the black blanket of the night and went to sleep in the darkened groundfloor premises of the city … In the hot season … the hawkers would go about the streets shouting 'I-i-i-ce'… No-one but myself knows how my mind thrilled to that cry as I stood on the verandah facing the street…. The air was full of the scent of the thickly strung *bel* flowers which the women and girls wore in their hairknots.

Visiting Ahmedabad in his adult years, Rabindranath regretted the absence of old history in Calcutta: 'We are Calcutta people, and history nowhere gives us any evidence of its past grandeur there.' But certain sights in the

20.3 *Michael Madhusudan Datta*

20.4 *Facing page: Mrs Eliza Fay*

city made a profound impression on the poet. The flowing river was one such, as described in his *Reminiscences (Jiban-Smriti,* 1912):

Every day there was the ebb and flow of the tide of the Ganga... the various gait of so many different boats; the shifting of the shadows of the trees from west to east; and over the fringes of the shade-patches of the woods on the opposite bank, the gush of golden life-blood through the pierced breast of the evening sky.

Mrs Fay and Bishop Heber

Most Englishmen in old Calcutta did not love the city. With a sense of exile in an uncongenial clime, they seldom wrote with enthusiasm about the place where profit or conquest had brought them. One of the earliest English writers on Calcutta, Captain Alexander Hamilton (fl. 1688-1723), declared that Charnock 'could not have chosen a more unhealthy place'. Early English poems on Calcutta echo the theme:

Curse on the ship in evil hour that bore
My jolted frame to India's burning shore.
In inauspicious hour, from which I date
The bitter torments of a wretched fate.

Thus an anonymous poem of 1811, one of the earliest English poems on Calcutta. It continues:

On every dish the bouncing beetle falls,
The cockroach plays, or caterpillar crawls;
A thousand shapes of variegated hues
Parade the table and inspect the stews! ...
When hideous insects ev'ry plate defile,
The laugh how empty, and how forced the smile!

Gradually, of course, Calcutta grew into a 'city of palaces'. English sojourners admired its architectural splendours and found them a fit manifestation of imperial power. But for a more intimate English view, which blends the sense of spectacle with personal response and some humour, we cannot do better than turn to Mrs Fay.

Eliza Fay, the wife of a British barrister, lived in Calcutta for about thirty-seven years till her death in 1817. Her *Original Letters from India,* published the same year, are a classic of epistolary literature as well as a unique record of British life in Calcutta in that age. 'She could

write as feelingly as Mrs. Radcliffe or as wittily as Fielding,' says E.M. Forster in his 1925 edition of the *Letters,* adding that they find a charming complement in the Daniells' engravings of the city.

Mrs Fay had looked forward to Calcutta: the city 'for which I have so long sighed, to which I have looked with innumerable hopes and fears, and where I have long rested my most rational expectations of future prosperity and comfort.' Her first glimpse of the riverfront did not belie her expectations: 'the noble appearance of the Ganges which is much wider than the Thames at London Bridge, together with the amazing variety of vessels continually passing on its surface', which 'add to the beauty of the scene'.

But Mrs Fay found herself deserted by her husband, and missed any other felicities of social life in the city:

The custom of reposing, if not of sleeping after dinner is so general that the streets of Calcutta are from four to five in the afternoon almost as empty of Europeans as if it were midnight. Next come the evening airings to the Course: everyone goes, though sure of being half suffocated with dust.

Her amusement lay in visiting the theatre, where she saw 'characters supported in a manner that would not disgrace any European stage', though the taste of the spectators disgusted her: 'many go to see a tragedy for the express purpose of enjoying a laugh.' The expense, alas, prevented her from indulging her pastime too often: 'a gold *mohur* is really too much to bestow on such a temporary gratification.'

Slightly later in date are the recollections of Reginald Heber (1783-1826) in his *Narrative of a Journey through the Upper Provinces of India* (1827). Heber was Bishop of Calcutta from 1822 till his death (at Tiruchirapalli) in 1826. Heber was understandably unhappy about his domestic surroundings in Calcutta:

The lofty rooms swarm with cockroaches and insects; sparrows and other birds fly in and out all day, and as soon as the candles are lighted, large bats flutter on their indented wings. (Letter to the Rt. Hon. Charles W. Williams Wynn, 29 October 1823)

But he admired the larger perspectives of this 'very noble city', and thought the Government House, 'to say the least of it, a more showy palace than London has to produce'. More remarkably, the Bishop knew 'Black' Calcutta too, and has left a vivid description of it:

The native town, deepy, black and dingy, with narrow, crooked streets, huts of earth baked in the sun, or of twisted bamboos, interspersed here and there with ruinous brick bazaars, pools of dirty water, coco-trees, and little gardens, and a few very large, very fine, and generally very dirty houses of Grecian architecture, the residence of wealthy natives. (Letter to Miss Dod, 15 December 1823)

Of these 'sights, sounds and smells', it was the last which chiefly repelled the good pastor: 'the villainous smell of garlic, rancid coco-nut oil, sour butter and stagnant ditches'. But the vigour of his description has seldom been equalled.

Englishmen who did not visit Calcutta could more freely invest it with the grandeur of an ancient city. Landor's Rose Aylmer (1779-1800)

died in Calcutta, and the poet's famous elegy to her is engraved on her tomb in the South Park Street Cemetery. In another lament in 'Abertawy', Landor refers directly to the city:

To those proud halls for youth unfit
Where Princes stand and judges sit.
Where Ganges rolls his widest wave
She dropped her blossom in the grave.

Thackeray's Calcutta

One eminent English writer to be born in Calcutta, on 18 July 1811, was William Makepeace Thackeray. His father Richmond Thackeray (1781-1815) was Secretary to the Bengal Board of Revenue, and died in the city on 13 September 1815. Little William left for England in 1817, when he was six and a half. Consequently, there are almost no recollections of Calcutta in his writings. (Colonel Newcome is perhaps partly based on his stepfather Major Henry Carmichael Smyth.) But he did have a childhood nostalgia for his first home, which he would draw for his maternal grandmother, not omitting 'the monkey looking out of the window, and black Betty at the top drying the towels' (W. W. Hunter, *The Thackerays in India*, p.176). And there is a remarkably mov-

20.5 *Richmond Thackeray and family, with William Makepeace aged three. George Chinnery*

ing reference to his departure from Calcutta in one of the Roundabout Papers in the *Cornhill Magazine*:

remembering in long long distant days, such a ghaut or river stair at Calcutta; and a day when down those steps, to a boat which was in waiting, came two children whose mothers remained on shore.

Perhaps such childhood memories were also at work when, in *The Four Georges* (1855), Thackeray cited Bishop Heber's verse:

I miss thee when by Gunga's stream
My twilight steps I guide.

Macaulay and Trevelyan

Thomas Babington Macaulay (1800-1859) lived in Calcutta from 1834 to 1838 as Legal Member of the Supreme Council. He had no love for the city – in this resembling Sir Philip Francis (1740-1818), author of the *Letters of Junius* (1772), who lived in Calcutta during 1774-80 and disliked it because it was not London.

Macaulay's distrust of Calcutta is disconcertingly close to the archetypal response of the unadaptive Englishman to all foreign places. Within six months of his arrival he was writing

Calcutta is called, and not without some reason, the city of palaces: but I have seen nothing in the East like the view from the Castle Rock, nor expect to see anything like it till we stand there together again. (*Life and Letters*, ed. G. O. Trevelyan, popular edn., 1889, p.277)

The weather was unbearable: 'We arc annually baked four months, boiled four more, and allowed the remaining four to become cool if we can.' (*Ibid.*, p. 307) The local fruits were 'wretched': 'The best of them is inferior to our apricot or gooseberry... . A plantain is very like a rotten pear... . A yam is better. It is like an indifferent potato.' (*Ibid.*, pp. 304-5) He must have been all the more thankful for his expert cook, whom Lord Dalhousie pronounced 'decidedly the first artist in Bengal'.

In brief, Macaulay could not find 'words to tell you how I pine for England, or how intensely bitter exile has been to me' (*Ibid.*, p. 307) The only consolation was that Calcutta was not Dublin. He was reconciled to the local politics, although the Anglo-Indian press attacked him bitterly for his 'liberal' views. Hence he wrote:

We have agitators in our own small way, Tritons of the minnows, bearing the same sort of resemblance to O'Connell that a lizard bears to an alligator. Therefore Calcutta for me, in preference to Dublin. (p.308)

To make the best of a bad job, Macaulay tried to set up a comfortable household in exile. In particular, he seems to have had the Englishman's habitual love for his garden:

I have a very pretty garden, not unlike our little grass-plot at Clapham, but larger... It looks beautiful just now after the rains, and I hear that it keeps its verdure during a great part of the year. (p.304)

Perhaps he cast a lingering look at this garden at least when he left the city for home.

Macaulay's sister Hannah married Charles Trevelyan (1807-86) in St John's Church in Calcutta. Their son George Otto, father of the historian G. M. Trevelyan, visited India as his father's secretary and wrote about his experience in a series of letters published as *Competition Wallah* (1864). Letter VII is 'About Calcutta and Its Climate: With Serious Inferences'. The climate, he says, is 'hateful', involving greater risk to life in a year's residence than 'three battles of Waterloo'. At that time, this may have been statistically correct. He observes dismissively that the city 'can be central only in name', given its geographical location; and ends with a sardonic 'Ode to Calcutta', ascribed to a friend but probably his own:

Fair city, India's crown and pride,
Long may'st thou tower o'er Hooghley's tide,
Whose hallowed but malarious stream,
The peasant's god, the poet's theme,
Rolls down the dead Hindoo.

Kipling's Calcutta

Rudyard Kipling (1865-1936) had much the same view of Calcutta as Macaulay or his nephew, except that as the poet of the White Man's Burden, he was unusually keen on cleaning its filth through British scavengery, so to speak. Not that he was totally dead to the romantic dimension of Calcutta's existence. In 'The Song of the Cities', Calcutta declares:

Me the Sea-captain loved, the River built,
Wealth sought and Kings adventured life to hold.
Hail, England ! I am Asia — Power on silt,
Death in my hands — but Gold.

Top
20.6 Sir Charles Edward Trevelyan

Below
20.7 Rudyard Kipling

20.8 Joseph Sedley, a 'Nabob'. Thackeray's own illustration for 'Vanity Fair'

Kipling's much-quoted description of Calcutta as 'chance-erected, chance-directed' is more typical of his attitude, though curiously neglectful of the imperial labours that went into the making of the city. Of its imperial nature he had no doubt, and had little change for the 'natives' who cast a blot on the scene. In the book of Calcutta sketches published as *City of Dreadful Night* (1890) he observes:

It seems not only a wrong but a criminal thing to allow natives to have any voice in the control of a city adorned, docked, wharfed, fronted, and reclaimed by Englishmen, existing only because England lives and dependent for its life on England. All India knows of the Calcutta Municipality. Has anyone thoroughly investigated the Calcutta stink?

Ghalib's Calcutta

All things are relative; and to a visitor from Delhi, eclipsed in importance in the early nineteenth century, Calcutta could offer happy days rather than dreadful nights. The great Urdu poet Mirza Ghalib (1797–1869) lived in Calcutta for nearly two years, from 20 February 1828 to 29 November 1829. He had reason to be dissatisfied with his stay, for he had come to plead his case for a pension with the Governor-General-in-Council. He returned to Delhi with an unfavourable reply and a heavy load of debts. He was also embroiled soon after arrival in an unpleasant literary controversy. Its bitterness is reflected in one of his Persian poems, a dialogue between the poet and an adviser:

I said, 'Then tell me, what course would you recommend to me?'

He said, 'The course of giving up all thought of poetry.'

I said at last, 'It is in search of justice I have come.'

He said, 'Then run away! Why beat your head against a stone?'

(as in Ralph Russel and Khurshidul Islam, *Ghalib: Life and Letters,* 1969.)

But gradually Ghalib developed a real attachment to the city, which perhaps grew with nostalgia. In a Persian letter written after his return to Delhi, he says:

One should be grateful that such a city as Calcutta exists. Where else in the world is there a city so refreshing? To sit in the dust of Calcutta is better than to grace the throne of another dominion. By God, had I not been a family man, with regard for the honour of my wife and children, I would have cut myself free and made my way there. There I would have lived till I died, in that heavenly city, free from all cares. How delightful are its cool breezes, and how pleasant is its water: How excellent are its pure wines and its ripe fruits!

If all the fruits of Paradise lay there outspread before you,

The mangoes of Calcutta still would haunt your memory.

The substance of this passage enters into one of his short Urdu poems:

Ah me, my friend! The mention of Calcutta's name.
Has loosed a shaft that pierces to my very soul.
Its greenery and verdure take away your breath;
Its women's charms are such that none escapes them whole.

....

All freshness and all sweetness are its luscious fruits;
Its mellow wines are pleasing beyond all compare.

Ghalib found delight in the 'Black Town' that repelled European visitors. The 'cool breezes' and 'pleasant' water provide a happy contrast to the stink that had overwhelmed Heber and Kipling. The people of Calcutta can alone tell how to balance these contrasting aspects caught in the literature that grew around the city.

PRINTING AND THE
SPIRIT OF CALCUTTA

Nikhil Sarkar

In splendour London now eclipses Rome ... and in similar respects, Calcutta rivals the head of empire. But in no respect can she appear so eminently so, as in her publications ... . If in Europe, the number of publications gives the ground to ratiocinate the learning and refinement of particular cities, we may place Calcutta in rank above Vienna, Copenhagen, Petersburg, Madrid, Venice, Turin, Naples or even Rome.

These words were written by William Dune, the editor of *The World,* a journal published from Calcutta, in October 1791. His argument related to the volume even more than the quality of Calcutta's publications. It is therefore curious to reflect that the printing press came to Calcutta only a few years before these words were written.

Leaving aside the achievement of ancient China in this regard, the printing press took over three hundred years after Gutenberg to reach Calcutta. This is all the more remarkable in that on the west coast of India, the Portuguese set up a press as early as 1556, and brought out their first book, a Portuguese Catechism, the next year. Subsequently, Tamil and Konkani books appeared from various centres in south and west India, primarily at the initiative of the Jesuits.

Calcutta, however, had to wait till 1777 for its first printing press. This delay can be explained in part by the political instability in Bengal over the intervening period. British dominance over Bengal became secure not so much after the Battle of Palashi (Plassey) as after the Battle of Buxar (1764) and the acquisition of the Diwani of Bengal in 1765.

Further, political compulsions made the East India Company prohibit the entry of missionaries into Bengal for a long time. It was the missionaries who generally acted as pioneers of printing in India. Until British rule was established, printing was not much required for administrative purposes either. Finally, we may conjecture that the English experience back home had taught the Company that the printing press could be a dangerous and subversive instrument.

But it was an instrument that could not be indefinitely shut out from the community. Even so, it is interesting that the first press in Calcutta was set up, in the words of Graham Shaw, 'at the whim of a bankrupt businessman who whilst in prison resorted to his former calling of printing, simply as a convenient means of paying off some of his debts'. (*Printing in Calcutta,* 1981)

The businessman was James Augustus Hicky (1739?–1802), a man with a colourful if ill-starred life. Bad luck seemed to dog his footsteps. The Government owed him over Rs 43,500 for printing work, but finally made him settle for Rs 6,711. Unable to feed his family, he even appealed to his old target of attack, Warren Hastings, either for a preferment as 'deputy to the clerk of the Calcutta Market' or else for a berth as surgeon (another of his trades) on an Indiaman, which would give the whole family a free passage to England. The same distress and penury clouded his career as a printer.

Besides printing for the Government, Hicky chiefly undertook job printing of various sorts. His first and last excursion into book-printing was a Calendar for 1778. But in January 1780 he brought out his famous weekly *Bengal Gazette or Calcutta General Advertiser* – 'A weekly political and commercial paper open to all parties, but influenced by none'. This proud manifesto is ratified by Hicky's words elsewhere: 'I have no particular passion for the printing of newspapers … yet I take a pleasure in enslaving my body in order to purchase freedom for my mind and soul.'

The authorities were not impressed by these noble principles. Within a year, Hicky was imprisoned and fined on three counts of libel. But he went on publishing the *Gazette* even from prison for all of nine months. Finally in March 1782 the Government confiscated his press. 'Thus curiously,' comments Graham Shaw, 'the first Bengal press had been born and died in Calcutta Jail.'

Hicky's experience foreshadows the later relations between the Government and the press in India. In 1799 Lord Wellesley issued the first 'Regulations for the Control and Guidance of Newspapers published in Calcutta'. It was followed by increasingly harsher measures. In 1878, exactly a hundred years after the first printing from Bengali type, the infamous Vernacular Press Act was passed.

Although Hicky finally recovered his press, he could not set up in business again. He died in 1802 on board a ship to China, in a state of near-bankruptcy. His property, auctioned in Calcutta in 1803, included, in addition to land, house, books and surgical equipment, a printing press 'out of repair', 'a number of printing frames' and 540 pounds' weight of type.

But Hicky's innovation was promptly taken up by others: book followed book, journal followed journal in Calcutta and its neighbourhood. 1778, the year that Hicky published his Calendar, also saw the first book of the Bengali cultural world, Nathaniel Brassey Halhed's (1751-1830) *A Grammar of the Bengal Language,* published from Hugli and written for the training of British civilians as directed by Warren Hastings.

The *Grammar* was written in English, but it carried many excerpts from Krittibas's Bengali *Ramayana,* Kashiram Das's *Mahabharata,* Bharatchandra's *Bidyasundar* and other poems – all printed in Bengali type. Persian *nastaliq* characters were also used at two points. In his preface, Halhed gives the entire credit for designing and making the Bengali type to Charles Wilkins (1749?-1836), 'metallurgist, engraver, founder, printer'. Wilkins's expertise is incontrovertible: he also designed Persian and Devanagari founts later. But there is strong reason to doubt whether the first Bengali type was made by his unaided labours.

Soon after the *Grammar,* the Baptist missionaries of Shrirampur (Serampore) began their historic work in printing and publishing. In their 1807 *Memoir Relative to the Translations* (of the Bible), they report that 'the providence of God brought to us the very artist who had wrought with Wilkins'. His name is given in many other accounts as Panchanan Karmakar (?-1803/4), a native of Shrirampur. Recent research has also brought out the contribution of Joseph Shepherd, a talented engraver who died in Calcutta in 1787 at the early age of thirty-four. On his death-bed he told John Gilchrist, the compiler of *A Dictionary, English and Hindoostani* (1787) that he had 'assisted Mr Wilkins from the first'. There is much evidence of Shepherd's skill to bear out this claim.

In the same historic year of 1778 was set up the 'Honourable Company's Press' – i.e. the Government Press, the most important one in eighteenth-century Calcutta. But there were many others. Graham Shaw has recovered the names of nearly forty printers, 'amateur as well as professional', in at least seventeen presses. Three to five presses were always in operation between 1780 and 1790, and seven to ten in the next decade.

These presses produced not only calendars, grammars and official publications but all kinds of other books, including song-books and picture–books. The pressmen of Calcutta did full justice to the galaxy of painters and engravers active in the city at the time. Balthazar Solvyns's famous album, *A Collection of Two Hundred and Fifty Coloured Etchings Descriptive of the Manners, Customs and Dresses of the Hindoos* (1779), was printed in Calcutta. This world of printing and publishing was

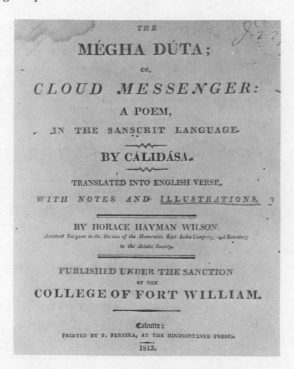

THE

MÉGHA DÚTA;

OR,

CLOUD MESSENGER:

A POEM,

IN THE SANSCRIT LANGUAGE.

BY CÁLIDÁSA.

TRANSLATED INTO ENGLISH VERSE,

WITH NOTES AND ILLUSTRATIONS.

BY HORACE HAYMAN WILSON,
Assistant Surgeon in the Service of the Honorable East India Company, and Secretary
to the Asiatic Society.

PUBLISHED UNDER THE SANCTION
OF THE
COLLEGE OF FORT WILLIAM.

Calcutta:
PRINTED BY P. PEREIRA, AT THE HINDOOSTANEE PRESS.
1813.

brought into being, and kept alive, by a dedicated circle of workers – nearly all Englishmen, but wedded to Calcutta as their place of work and adoptive home. It was chiefly they who built up the necessary infrastructure for the printer's trade. Presses and English (Roman) type could be imported, but type foundries had to be set up for the Indian languages. After Halhed, private printers as well as the Company's Press brought out Bengali and other type. In 1789 the Chronicle Press designed Devanagari as well as Bengali and Persian (*nastaliq*) type. Another type-founder proudly declared in 1793 that he could produce 'faces of the Birmah, Arracan, and other oriental characters ... which never yet passed the foundry'.

Paper was also manufactured locally: We know of at least two paper mills, as well as binding works. Already in the eighteenth century, India's 'city of books' had seen bookshops as well as circulating libraries. The first of the latter was opened by John Andrews, and was soon followed by others. In 1800, one of them boasted of 3,500 volumes.

Two crucial events occurred in 1800. One was the founding of Fort William College by Lord Wellesley; the other the opening of the Baptist Mission Press at Shrirampur by William Carey (1761-1834). Wellesley's aim was to train English officials in local languages; the mis-

sionaries of Shrirampur aimed primarily at preaching the Gospel. But their greatest achievement was to enhance the cultivation of the Bengali language. The College fostered the study of Bengali; Shrirampur brought out books in the language. The two institutions were connected by many ties. Carey taught for some time at the College; the books needed by the latter were supplied by the Shrirampur Mission.

The Mission's historic task was carried out by three men: Carey, Joshua Marshman (1768-1837) and William Ward (1769-1823). They saw a wooden press advertised for sale in 1798, and bought it for forty (or perhaps forty-six) pounds. They pulled the first proofs from it on 18 March 1800, and finished printing the volume in early August. It was a Bengali translation of the Gospel of St Matthew by Ramram Basu (1757-1813) and John Thomas, 125 pages in demy octavo. The type was apparently set by Ward himself, assisted by his fourteen-year-old son and one Brunsdon.

After this start, the stream of books flowed from Shrirampur like a river in flood. Ward describes the scene in the press (of which he was the overseer) in an 1811 letter:

As you enter, you see your cousin, in a small room reading or writing, and looking over the office, which is more than 170 ft. long. There you find Indians translating the scriptures into different tongues or correcting proof-sheets. You observe, laid out in cases, types in Arabic, Persian, Nagri, Telugu, Panjabi, Bengali, Marathi, Chinese, Oriya, Burmese, Kanarese, Greek, Hebrew and English. Hindus, Mussulmans, and Christian Indians are busy – composing, correcting, distributing. Beyond the office are the varied type-casters, besides a group of men making ink, and in a spacious open walled-round place, our paper-mill, for we manufacture our own paper.

Who would believe that these men had set out on their triumphal march just a decade earlier, with a single wooden press? Between 1801 and 1832, the Shrirampur Mission printed a total of 212,000 copies of books in forty languages. The tenth report of the Mission in 1834 claims to have published religious books in forty-seven languages, for forty of which they cast their own type. In designing and casting type, the missionaries were greatly aided by Wilkins's old assistant Panchanan Karmakar and later his son-in-law Manohar

21.1 Title page of H.H. Wilson's translation of the 'Meghaduta', 1813.

Facing page
21.2 Upendrakishore Raychoudhuri

21.3 Stamp of the Bengal Photographers

The Early Days of Photography in Calcutta

Within a year of its invention, a daguerreotype camera was offered for sale in Calcutta on 28 January 1844. The city's earliest camera operator with a known identity was also recorded from 1844: he was Monsieur F. M. Montairo of 7 Wellington Square. Two years later, the *Sambad Bhaskar* became the first Bengali newspaper to advertise the facility of having one's likeness taken by a Mr. Douglas.

Calcutta in the mid-nineteenth century was a witness to the international battle fought between the 'photographers' of Talbot's school of Calotype and the 'Daguerrean artists', operating from 'photographic studios' and 'Daguerrean galleries' respectively. A Mr. Schranzhofer opened Calcutta's first 'photographic studio' at 2 Kyd Street in 1848.

J. W. Newland's 'daguerrean gallery', founded in 1850 at 6 Loudon Buildings, was the most significant and also the longest-lived of the early commercial photographic establishments. Newland was moreover the first man in Calcutta to present a photographic slide-show, entitled 'Dissolving Views'.

However, the two legendary houses that practically ruled over commercial photography in Calcutta for decades were Bourne and Shepherd and Johnston and Hoffmann. Bourne and Shepherd, still continuing under Indian management, claims to be the oldest existing photographic studio in the world. It was originally founded by Samuel Bourne, famous for his photographs of the Himalayas. His first studio was at Shimla; the Calcutta establishment was opened in the 1860s.

The celebrated Indologist Rajendralal Mitra was a camera enthusiast. He was appointed treasurer of the Photographic Society of Bengal on its foundation in 1856. But after some eighteen months, he was expelled on a trumped-up charge by the European members, who were actually enraged by his political speech in defence of the 'Black Act', which sought to permit Europeans to be tried by Indian judges. Almost all the Bengali members resigned in protest. For the next few decades the Society remained a European preserve.

The Bengal Photographers, the first Bengali-owned commercial studio in Calcutta, was set up in 1862 by Nilmadhab Dey. The second important Bengali concern, the Calcutta Art Studio, was founded in 1876 by the lithographer and artist Annadaprasad Bagchi with four of his pupils. The first Bengali lady photographer to open a studio in Calcutta was Sarojini Ghosh, in 1898.

In 1898 too, Maharaja Pradyotkumar Thakur became the first Indian to be elected a Fellow of the Royal Photographic Society. The second was the children's writer Sukumar Ray, in 1922. The first Bengali article on the aesthetics of photography came from Sukumar's pen.

Sukumar's father Upendrakishore Raychoudhuri, writer, illustrator, painter and musician, was also a photographic inventor who brought mathematical precision to half-tone camera work. Nine of his research papers were published between 1897 and 1911 in Penrose's Annual, considered to be the printer's Bible. He also invented a device called the 'Automatic Screen Adjustment Indicator', sold as an attachment to the Penrose process camera.

These are some of the highlights of the wide and indeed innovative role played by citizens of Calcutta in the early days of photography. Nowhere else perhaps were the artistic and technological concerns of nineteenth-century Bengal brought to bear simultaneously on an area of such lively activity.

Karmakar (?-1846). They were able to turn out type not only in Indian languages but others too, such as Malay, Burmese and Chinese.

Needless to say, it was not only Bibles or religious works that were produced in these languages. Grammars of Sanskrit, Bengali, Marathi, Punjabi, Telugu and Kannada appeared from Shrirampur, written by Carey himself. Carey also produced an English-Bengali dictionary and many literary texts. Amazingly, the Shrirampur Baptists were the first to print the *Ramayana* and *Mahabharata* in Bengali; and Marshman brought out a one-volume *Works of Confucius* as well as a Chinese Grammar.

Most remarkably, books were published not only in English, Bengali, Sanskrit or Persian, but even in languages like Armenian. Shaw's *Printing in Calcutta to 1800* (1981) lists 368 books and periodicals; his own subsequent researches have now increased the tally to 667. At least twenty-four periodicals were brought out from Calcutta in the eighteenth century. There were

21.4 Stamp of the Calcutta School Book Society

no daily papers in those days, and Wellesley's puritanical regulations forbade Sunday publications; but one or other journal would come out on every other day of the week.

Most important of all, the first monthly and weekly journals in Bengali appeared from Shrirampur. The monthly, *Digdarshan*, appeared in April 1818, and the weekly *Samachar Darpan* later the same year. (There had been an earlier Bengali journal, Gangakishore Bhattacharya's *Bangal Gejeti;* but no copies of this appear to survive.) Subsequently, Shrirampur also brought out journals in Persian and English.

The Shrirampur press fulfilled its historic task in less than four decades, being formally closed down in 1837. But in actual fact it merged with the Baptist Mission Press set up in Calcutta in 1818 by a group that came out of Shrirampur, led by W. H. Pearce and W. Yeats. This press, like its predecessor at Shrirampur, began humbly with a single wooden press; but within twenty years, it was printing books in

eleven major Indian languages on seven steel presses. It also had its own type foundry. The Baptist Mission Press developed close links with the Calcutta School Book Society founded in 1817 and published enormous quantities of textbooks for it. This historic press was alive till 1970: people going down Acharya Jagadish Basu Road would be awestruck by its proud sign, 'Printers in Forty Languages'.

Upto this point, the story of printing in Calcutta has featured virtually none but Europeans. It is said that Bengalis dubbed the printing press 'the god of the Sahibs'. But now Indians too joined in worshipping this new deity.

The first Indian-owned press was set up in Khidirpur by 'Baburam, a Brahmin from Mirzapur'; its first book was the Sanskrit word-book, *Amarkosh,* edited by Colebrook in 1807. Baburam also printed in Bengali. The press was later taken over by Lallulal, instructor in Hindustani at Fort William College and the father of Hindi Khariboli prose. Under Lallulal, the first book of old Hindi literature appeared in print in 1815: it was Tulsidas's *Vinaypatrika*. But as we know, many Indians had already worked in and for European printers. Panchanan Karmakar and his son-in-law were the first of a long line whom John Gilchrist, founder of the Hindustani Press in 1802, castigated as 'a posse of black unprincipled knaves', but who had grown indispensable to printing in India. Hadjee Mustapha, the eighteenth-century French traveller converted to Islam, wrote:

There are but four Printing Offices at Calcutta, amongst which one only is worked by Europeans; ... the three others, although inspected by a European, are worked by natives, who print in a printing office just as they copy in a counting house, without understanding the language.

Hence there were many practitioners to follow Baburam in the new trade. In the eighteenth century, Calcutta's presses had all been located in the 'White Town': in the nineteenth they sprang up all over the 'native quarters' of north Calcutta – Mathuranath Mishra's press, Mahindilal Press, Pitambar Sen's Press, the Sindhu Press at Shealdah and numerous others.

The first press in this 'Bengali tola' was set up in 1818 by Gangakishore Bhattacharya (?-1831?), already mentioned as the founder of the *Bangal Gejeti*. He was the first Bengali printer, publisher, journalist and bookseller, all in one. From his 'Bengal Gazetty Press or Office' appeared not only the journal of that name but a number of Bengali books. Earlier, Ganga-kishore had brought out the first illustrated Bengali book, an edition of Bharatchandra's *Annadamangal*. Later Gangakishore moved the press to his home village in Bardhaman District: apparently local people still refer to the place as the 'printing-press village', *Chhapakhanadanga*.

The first press at Bat-tala or Bartala was set up soon after by Bishwanath Deb. Sukumar Sen tells us that an arithmetic schoolbook was printed there in 1818. In 1823 they published the *Chandimangal* edited by Ramjay Vidya-sagar. This was the start of the notable contri-bution of Bat-tala to Bengali printing and letters. Till the 1860s, the great printing mart of Calcutta was centred there, at the heart of the Bengali town. The Hindu College was also first set up in this area. It was only later that it moved to what was then called Pataldanga; the Sanskrit College, Hare School, Medical Col-lege and University also came up in the same area, and the printing and publishing centre of Calcutta had necessarily to migrate south-east to what is now College Street.

The Bat-tala printers' network grew like the aerial roots of the very *bat* or banyan tree that gave the quarter its name. Printers and booksel-lers set up their trade from Kumartuli and Bagbazar to Thanthania and Kalutola, with a few outposts even in today's 'bookmen's quar-ters' in Pataldanga or College Street. In other words, Bat-tala books were not produced only in Bat-tala. The name acquired a generic or descriptive significance. Bat-tala books were cheap and often shoddy books produced for the common man. The Reverend James Long has described a typical establishment of 1835: an old wooden press and worn-out type bought at disposal, somehow held together to print on inferior paper. The compositors too were poorly paid: the wages for setting four quarto pages was only one rupee, and that too often in arrear.

Such parsimony had its happy effect in lowering the prices of books. The Shrirampur press charged Rs 24 for its complete *Ramayana;* the Bat-tala printers only Rs 1½. Within Bat-tala itself, the *Chandimangal* sold first for six rupees but thirty years later for only one. More demotic titles like pornographic pam-

21.5 *Frontispiece & title page of the play 'Bidyasundar', 1875*

phlets were even sold for one paisa! Bat-tala was truly a popular institution: it catered for the poorest of the literate population.

The marketing was necessarily popular in orientation. Long wrote:

The native presses are generally in by-lanes with little outside to attract, yet they ply a busy trade. Of late educated natives have opened shops for the sale of Bengali works, ... but the usual mode of sale is by hawkers, of whom there are more than 200 ... The best advertisement for a Bengali book is a 'living agent' who shows the book itself !

These hawkers peddled their wares not only in the city but in village markets, *hats* and fairs. They brought back, both for the publishers and for other interested readers, old Bengali manu-scripts or *punthis*. The huge collection of manuscripts at Calcutta University was nearly all acquired by these hawkers. Nagendranath Basu (1866-1938), the editor of the encyclo-paedia *Bishwakosh,* gathered these manuscripts through the hawkers in an organized way.

What kind of books appeared from Bat-tala? Every kind, from common evidence as well as Long's testimony. But their first and greatest contribution was to the spread of classic literature. Apart from literature with a religious function, like the *Ramayana, Mahabharata* or *Chandimangal,* they brought all kinds of verse and prose writings into Bengali homes. They also brought out Bengali translations of Arabic and Persian classics. Many of the Bat-tala bookmen were Muslims, and some of their

books were printed in 'Islamic fashion' – that is to say, starting from what would be the last page in an ordinary Bengali or English book. Their language too was unusually full of Arabic and Persian admixture. But the total publishing programme of the Bat-tala houses shows remarkable communal exchange and harmony. Hindu publishers brought out the classics of Islam; Muslim publishers engaged Hindu authors to write books for them.

As my account indicates, it would be deplorably wrong to regard Bat-tala, as conservatives of the time and even some later scholars have done, as solely a mart for hack-writing and obscene or vulgar literature. But admittedly, Bat-tala did produce a certain amount of erotica as well as a vast store of popular fiction, drama and sketches, of enormous historical interest. Side by side with formal or classic literature, these products of Bat-tala testify to a flourishing world of urban folk culture. They also provide a fascinating picture of contemporary social and political life. Jayanta Goswami has published a study of nearly five hundred Bat-tala farces that shows how vivid and faithful was this mirror of the times.

21.6 *The goddess Lakshmi. Engraving by Ramdhan Swarnakar from an 1857 almanac*

Folk art can sometimes influence 'higher' art. This can be instanced from Bat-tala as well. The first two formal Bengali novels, Pyarichand Mitra or 'Tekchand Thakur's' *Alaler Gharer Dulal* (1858) and Bankimchandra Chatterji's *Durgeshnandini* (1865) are both said to show the influence of the earlier Bat-tala romance *Hemlata-Ratikanta* (1847). Again, the oft-reprinted Bat-tala work *Kaminikumar* (1856) left its mark on Dinabandhu Mitra's drama and Bankimchandra's novel *Debi Choudhurani* (1884).

Next to the world of books, the Calcutta printers created the world of newspapers and journals. Here again, the field was monopolized by Europeans in the eighteenth century but eagerly invaded by Indians in the nineteenth. After the efforts of Gangakishore Bhattacharya and the Shrirampur missionaries, which have already been cited, many others entered the field. Persian, Urdu and Hindi newspapers sprang up in Calcutta too – the first anywhere in India in these languages. In 1822 Rammohan Ray started his famous Persian journal *Mirat-ul-Akhwar;* it was soon followed by Harihar Datta and Lala Sudha Sukh's *Jam-i-Jahan Numa* and Mathurmohan Mitra and Maniram Thakur's *Shams-ul-Akhwar.* The first Hindi paper, *Udant Martand,* was brought out by Jugalkishore Sukul and Munnu Thakur in 1826.

Calcutta is a major centre of Indian journalism even today. In 1987, there were 54 dailies, 440 weeklies and 1262 other periodicals published in Bengali – most of them, needless to say, from Calcutta, as well as papers in English, Hindi, Urdu and other less probable languages. There are even two daily papers in Chinese.

Things were obviously more difficult early in the last century. Printing was still a recent introduction; there were also greater hazards in journalism under colonial rule. Rammohan Ray had a celebrated controversy with the authorities in these matters. Even so, we find no less than six newspapers set up just between 1824 and 1826: three in Bengali, two in Persian and one in Hindi. An 1830 news item records the existence of five Bengali newspapers and announces the arrival of a sixth.

The names of the journals are significant in their rhetoric: 'The Moonlight of News' (*Samachar Chandrika, Sambad Koumudi*), 'The Darkness-Quelling News' (*Sambad Timirnashak*), 'The Dawn of Knowledge' (*Gnano-*

day), 'The Quest for Knowledge' (*Gnanan-weshan*), 'The Lightning-Flash of News' (*Sambad Soudamini*), 'The Rise of the Full Moon' (*Purnachandroday*), 'The Sun' (*Prabhakar, Dibakar*), 'The Sunrise' (*Arunoday*). Most of them use the metaphor of light or of heavenly bodies: the press is the herald of light, destroying the darkness of ignorance. However we may define the 'Renaissance' in nineteenth-century Bengal, it is unthinkable without the press.

Similarly, the social reforms and movements of the times found in the press a principal weapon. From Rammohan and Vidyasagar to Bankimchandra and Rabindranath, the pioneers of reform found it necessary to set up presses of their own – as did their conservative opponents. The ultimate use of the press as an instrument of change came, of course, during the struggle for freedom.

In the earliest days of printing in Calcutta, the *Samachar Darpan* observed:

As a small stream gradually expands and extends itself till it waters the whole land, so too printed books spread across the nation and elevate the minds of the people. Earlier, even an affluent man scarcely had a palm-leaf manuscript in his house. Since printing began, even humble folk possess a number of books.

According to Long, there were thirty Bengali books published from Calcutta in 1820. Eleven related to the Hindu gods – Krishna, Vishnu and Durga; three were works of fiction and five of erotica, while other categories commanded one title each. Between 1822 and 1826, Long lists only twenty-eight titles. These tallies seem to err grossly on the conservative side: the *Samachar Darpan* of 1822 lists fifteen titles published from Shrirampur alone, and another list in 1825 cites over twenty.

Till mid-century, the publishers concentrated on an incongruous double bill of religion and erotica. After that, tastes changed. The fifty

Bengali books published in 1852 included biographies of Clive and Galileo and versions of Shakespeare and *Robinson Crusoe*. The previous year had seen Bengali manuals on the steam engine and the telegraph. In 1857, the forty-six Indian-owned presses put out 322 books for sale. Long classifies them as follows:

Almanacs   19
History and biography   15
Christian religious works   8
Plays   8
Educational   46
Erotica   13
Fiction   28
Law   5
Hindu legends   85
Religion and morals   19 .
'Islamic Bengali'   23
Natural Science   9
Newspapers   6
Periodicals   12
'Sanskritic Bengali'   14
Miscellaneous   12

The total number of copies printed was 5,71,670. Long did not include Sanskrit and Persian books, or books (chiefly missionary tracts and scriptures) meant for free distribution.

In 1855, Long had already published an invaluable Descriptive Catalogue of some 1,400 Bengali books published between 1795 and 1855. A more elaborate catalogue, carrying the tally down to 1866, was made by Jatindramohan Bhattacharya but remains unpublished: it lists over 10,000 titles. In 1885-86, the year of the founding of the Indian National Congress, Bengal (chiefly Calcutta) had 229 printing presses – the biggest proportion anywhere of the 1,098 in India. The number of Bengali books published that year was said to be 2,414; but the figure has never been matched before or since, and probably includes books in all languages printed in Bengal.

Data on publications is compiled from records under the Press and Registration of Books Act of 1867. It shows that there were 909 Bengali books printed in 1900; 1,194 in 1910;

21.7 *Left: Title-head of 'Sambad Prabhakar'*

21.8 *Right: Ornamental Bengali type-faces printed by P.M. Bagchi & Co.*

1,177 in 1920; 1,029 in 1930; 1,884 in 1940; and 798 in 1950, the sharp decrease no doubt accounted for by the Partition of India. The Delivery of Books (Public Library) Act was passed in 1954. Under it, the National Library received 2,043 Bengali books in 1961-62 but only 1230 in 1971-72. This reduction is not only depressing but puzzling, and suggests that the intake for 1961-62 was inflated owing to some anomaly in recording; for even in the 1980s, the output of Bengali books – very largely from Calcutta – stands at a thousand titles or perhaps somewhat more per annum. This is not a satisfactory rate of increase; but it may be some consolation that Bengali still accounts for the largest number of Indian publications after English and Hindi. The only language that ranks anywhere near is Marathi.

Needless to say, new groups of artisans and professionals have emerged in Calcutta since the early nineteenth century to produce and distribute these books, catering to the new wide market for the wares of learning. Above all, this market has supported more and more authors. Already in 1855, James Long made 'A Return' of 515 Bengali writers excluding journalists. Long's 1859 catalogue lists about 700 names.

Above
21.9 *Sukumar Ray*

Below
21.10 *Composing by hand in a small Calcutta press today*

Apart from compositors, proof-readers, pressmen and binders, the Calcutta press, like any other, has called upon artists, engravers and blockmakers. The first illustrated Bengali book, *Annadamangal,* appeared in 1816; many more followed. Lithography came to Calcutta in the 1820s, and woodcuts and engravings were also commonly used.

In due time Calcutta made its own contribution to printing technology. Towards the beginning of this century, Upendrakishore Raychoudhuri (1863-1915) and his son Sukumar Ray (1887-1923) won international recognition for their innovations in block-making and half-tone printing. Other people's innovations relate specifically to printing in Bengali. I have already alluded to Bengali type design from the days of Panchanan and Manohar Karmakar. The exercise acquired a new dimension when Bengali linotype was inaugurated in 1935, some forty years after the linotype machine came to India. The keyboard was designed largely by the efforts of Sureshchandra Majumdar (1888-1954) of the *Ananda Bazar Patrika;* the typeface was the creation of Sushilkumar Bhattacharya, aided by the well-known artist Jatindrakumar Sen (1882-1966).

Bengali monotype followed in 1939. The type designer was Suhrid Chakrabarti, who is now engaged in designing new Bengali type-faces for photo-typesetting. Printing in Calcutta has, at its higher levels, passed beyond letterpress to planographic processes. But in the warren of little lanes around College Street and Shealdah, as well as elsewhere in the city, hundreds of tiny hand-set presses still keep up the spirit of Bat-tala – a living museum of printing as well as a viable productive activity.

At the same time that the Oxford University Press was celebrating its fifth centenary in 1978, Calcutta's printers and bibliophiles were observing the bicentenary of printing in the city. Calcutta has covered the whole course of printing history in the compressed span of two hundred years: and interestingly if not uniquely, virtually every stage of that progress is still to be found in the living printing practice of the city.

Perhaps nowhere else in the world have the miracles worked by print been so swiftly and so vividly brought to life.

(Translated from Bengali)

ART
IN OLD CALCUTTA:
INDIAN STYLE

R. P. Gupta

In this article I shall try to give an outline of the visual arts, both painting and graphics, in Calcutta between the second half of the eighteenth century and the end of the nineteenth. My aim will be to show how the interaction between the artistic techniques and approaches of the East and the West influenced and modified the works of Indian artists in varying degrees and also initiated them into new forms of graphic art. The article will cover five broad topics: the Company drawings, Kalighat *pats* or paintings, Bengal oils, and two types of print-making – woodcuts and lithographs.

Company Drawings

Mildred Archer says in the introduction to her *Company Drawings in the India Office Library*: 'since the early years of this century the term "Company Painting" has been used by Indian art-historians to denote a special kind of eighteenth- and nineteenth-century Indian paintings done by Indian artists for British patrons'. She does not say who coined the name.

Company drawings began in South India in the second half of the eighteenth century. Within a few years, they spread to different parts of India including, of course, Calcutta. Compared to earlier settlers, the British community from the days of Warren Hastings increasingly included men and women of curiosity, knowledge and taste. These people took a keen interest not only in their own way of life in India – their homes, servants, pets, modes of transport, etc. – but also in scenes and features of Indian life: costumes, crafts, public characters, social customs and manners, religious festivals, urban and rural life, buildings and monuments, flora and fauna.

Indian artists, the so-called Company painters, were commissioned for drawings and paintings on all these subjects. Whatever the regional differences, one fact was central to all Company Paintings. To satisfy their new clients' demands, Indian artists had to adapt their traditional ways to Western tastes and modes. While the British patrons appreciated the copying skill of the Indian artists, they felt that the latter lacked the sense of proportion and were ignorant of the arts of shading and perspective according to Western canons. The Indians quickly acquired these new technical skills, as also the use of water colour in place of the traditional tempera or gouache.

They obtained this training through a number of means. Many of them were employed as draughtsmen to British surveyors and engineers: drawing maps and architectural plans helped them acquire the Western sense of proportion in drawing. As Mrs Archer points out, other painters, under European guidance, 'prepared topographical, archaeological and natural history drawings or made paintings of the local people, their costumes and crafts'. This enabled them to learn the Western sense of perspective and shading. One of their earliest patrons was Lady Mary Impey, wife of Sir Elijah Impey, the first Chief Justice of the Supreme Court at Calcutta. She commissioned three Patna artists, who came down to settle in Calcutta, to make drawings of her own household and over 200 fine natural history drawings, which are now preserved in England.

In Calcutta, some Indians worked as assistants under visiting artists like Thomas (1749-1840) and William (1769-1837) Daniell and Balthazar Solvyns (1760-1824). The Daniells recruited Indian assistants between 1784 and 1786 for their Calcutta edition of *Twelve Views of Calcutta*. Solvyns hired Indian helpers to complete his *A Collection of Two Hundred and Fifty Coloured Etchings, Descriptive of the manners, customs, characters, dress and religious ceremonies of the Hindoos* (1799). In Calcutta, apart from loose prints that were imported in large quantities, Western prints and plates could be studied in such coloured books as William Hodges's *Views in India* (1785-88), Thomas and William Daniells' *Oriental Scenery* (1797-1808) and various other illustrated volumes.

Company paintings continued to be executed till the 1860s. The 1840s marked a high point, with the emergence of some eminent painters including Shaikh Muhammad Amir of Karaya in Calcutta. He was easily the greatest of his kind, with a mastery of Western perspective best seen in his horses, which remind one of George Stubbs or at least of the Currier and Ives print of the thoroughbred Lexington.

Apart from commissioned work, most Company painters (not excluding Amir) made sets of paintings of Indian life, scenes, old Mughal monuments and so on, and hawked them from door to door among British visitors and residents. In the last stages, they took to drawing on ivory and mica instead of in water colour on paper; but the rise of the camera after the 1850s led to their gradual decline.

Apart from their aesthetic interest, the Company drawings shed valuable light on two aspects of the Company Raj. They make a graphic presentation of British life in India; at the same time, they record vividly the life of Indians in that bygone age, which would otherwise have gone undepicted by traditional Indian artists. And most fundamentally, Company Painting marks the first hesitant steps towards the development of modern Western-style painting in India. This has been noted by Mildred Archer.

In the preface to Archer's book, S.C. Sutton says there are 2,750 Company drawings in the India Office Library, spanning the entire history of the mode. This is the largest and

22.1 *Horse and groom. Shaikh Muhammad Amir of Karaya, c. 1845*

22.2 *Worship at a Kali Temple near Titagarh. Anonymous Company painting, c. 1800*

most comprehensive collection in the world. In India, the biggest collection is in the Victoria Memorial, Calcutta.

Kalighat Paintings

From around 1809, when the present Kali temple was built, Kalighat began to draw more and more pilgrims from all over Bengal and India. Hence it became a thriving centre of trade. Many *patuas,* the hereditary scroll painters from different parts of lower Bengal, migrated to Kalighat to make paintings, icons and coloured toys which pilgrims bought as auspicious souvenirs. It is interesting to note that the last lot of Kalighat *pats* – a cache of about 150 – to surface in India in decades, came from South India.

To cope with the increasing demand, as also to earn a reasonable livelihood despite the very low prices of *pats* (two pice or an anna each), the *patuas* modified their old materials and techniques. Water colour replaced the time-consuming gouache and tempera. For economy, they began to use cheap mill-made unglued paper in a rectangular size (generally 17″ × 11″) instead of cloth, and chemical paints in place of home-ground colours.

This brings me to a much debated point: the extent of Western influence on the origin of Kalighat *pats*. Though some deny any noticeable influence, these *pats* actually represent that rare type of painting whose intrinsic identity is happily enriched by inescapable foreign influence. Unlike in the Company paintings, the Western impact here was largely technical. Thematically and stylistically the work remained local and, in the words of Dr Johnson, saturated with local emotions.

For quick execution, the Kalighat *patuas* employed certain stylistic innovations through the entire course of their art. These consisted of an abstract symbolism, a formalized structure and simplicity in composition. An interior scene, for example, was indicated by a stage-like curtain at the top and an outdoor scene by a tree. Unlike in most Indian paintings, faces were shown frontally or in three-quarters profile. The number of figures was generally limited to one to two.

Often, the Kalighat *patuas* first outlined the basic drawing in pencil. They then drew the various elements that went into its composition and filled them in with colours. The grey background of the paper was generally left unpainted. Apart from their glowing colours – red, yellow, blue, green, black, silver, etc. – the strongest point of the 'flat' Kalighat painting, with its judiciously borrowed shadings sparingly used, as in most Indian paintings since antiquity, was its lines. To repeat the oft-quoted words of Ajit Ghosh, the Kalighat paintings present 'one sweep of the brush stroke in which not the faintest suspicion of momentary indecision, not the slightest tremor can be detected.' (*Rupam,* October 1926) This firm and flowing boldness of line is perhaps best exemplified by the lightning-quick brush strokes depicting the black borders and the fall, in concentric circles, of the saris of women in the *pats.* Rarely has a group of painters made such a virtue out of necessity as the Kalighat *patuas* did, turning the need for speed into a superb inner spontaneity.

Like all schools of painting that grew up around famous temples, such as Puri, Thanjavur (Tanjore) and Nathdwara, Kalighat *patuas* began with religious and epic themes. Other such schools remained confined to these themes. Thanjavur, indeed, gave birth to some Company artists. But the Kalighat paintings are unique in the way they developed a vigorous secular aspect. Their religious catholicity was equally remarkable, as evinced by that rare *pat* showing Dul Dul, the Muharram horse. It is, therefore, to this secular aspect that I shall chiefly confine myself.

This secularization has been variously described. In *The Art Manufactures of India* (1888), Trailokyanath Mukherji said the *pats* present 'a few comical aspects of Indian life'. William Archer, in his *Kalighat Paintings,* credited the secular painting to 'a social phenomenon – the "new babu" or the Westernised man about town'. This is inaccurate on two counts. The Babus in the Kalighat *pats* are hardly Westernized; and the period mentioned by Archer (1870-1900) marked not the emergence but the dying spasms of babudom. Elsewhere Archer has said that 'scenes of current life as well as depiction of proverbs and folk tales have always been a part of the patua's repertoire...'. This again is doubtful, because the secular Kalighat *pats* are not as old as Archer imagines. In their recent book *From Merchants to Emperors,* Pratapaditya Pal and Vidya Dehejia say that the *patuas* took their cue from the British tradition of satirical drawing as in *Indian Punch* (i.e. the *Indian Charivari*), as also from the Company school of paintings. I feel that while the Company paintings may have had some influence, to bring in the *Indian Charivari* is too far-fetched. Finally, Hana Knizkova, in her celebrated *Drawings of the Kalighat Style,* says: 'the non-religious Kalighats owed their origin to the secularization of all aspects of cultural life

in Bengal in the nineteenth century, which was even more marked in literature than in the graphic arts'.

Scenes of daily life were depicted on the terracotta temples of Bengal of the sixteenth to the eighteenth centuries. But these apart, I agree that the secularization of the Kalighat *pats* was greatly motivated by the rise of secular literature, particularly the street literature of Bat-tala in north Calcutta. This link has not been sufficiently recognized.

There are remarkable parallels between the evolution of Bat-tala literature and that of the paintings of Kalighat. Both originated in the second decade of the last century to cater to popular taste. The Bat-tala publishers launched their trade with religious literature of all types, just as Kalighat did with paintings of gods and goddesses and scenes from the *Ramayana,* the *Mahabharata* and mythological stories. True, the ordinary Hindu Bengali, like his counterparts all over the country, was thoroughly conversant with the epics and myths through oral tradition. But the Bat-tala publishers first made them available to ordinary Bengali homes through cheap mass-produced books. Similarly, by turning out *pats* in

22.3 *Golap Sundari, the Beauty with the Rose. Kalighat pat, mid-19th cent.*

thousands, the Kalighat *patuas* enabled common people all over Bengal to own pictures of gods and goddesses.

From mid-century, the Bat-tala publishers turned to satirizing the Babus as well as ordinary Bengalis through a flood of cheap novels, plays, skits and lampoons. What the anonymous writers of Bat-tala presented in words, the *patuas* of Kalighat depicted graphically from 1860 onwards. The *patuas* must have been familiar with the Bat-tala literature, and between 1870 and 1900 they almost seem to be working in tandem. Both media castigate the prodigality of the Babus, their drunkeness and profligacy, the sycophancy that attended them, as well as the alleged evils of modernism and Western education, female education and emancipation, and the religious hypocrisy of the times. Again, both groups react to popular events and sensations in Calcutta and Bengal.

Both thematically and aesthetically, some of the finest secular *pats* of Kalighat relate to the Babus and the Bibis. Take the Kalighat gallery of women for instance. They have supplied the Bengali language with the phrase *pater bibi,* a narcissistic beauty. Sometimes they make music on the veena, the violin, the harmonium or the tabla: well-stacked pneumatic women, like earthly versions of the *Surasundaris* or celestial beauties of the Sun Temple at Konarka. Others are seen getting ready for their clients of the evening, giving the last touches to their make-up: one, *Golap Sundari,* putting a rose in her coiffure, another fixing her eardrop, a third finishing her toilette. One beauty fondles her pet peacock as she awaits her Babu, another coyly refuses a drink offered by her lover. A whole series of pictures shows woman as all-dominating. A woman stands like Kali with her foot on a prostrate male; a Babu with bowed head lies at his mistress's feet; in a magnificent line drawing, a Babu massages the feet of his mistress, who is represented as hauteur personified; a woman, Circe-like, has transformed her lover into a sheep; and so on. As Mildred Archer suggests, the *patuas* may have profitably observed the prostitutes that gathered in the neighbourhood of the Kali temple.

Religious hypocrisy was magnificently symbolized in one of the most famous *pats* — a cat, bearing all the marks of a hermit, with a fish in its mouth and an expression that the

22.4 *The sheepish lover. Kalighat pat, c. 1870*

English critic John Day described as 'the quintessence of cattery'. More than one *pat* shows a lecherous family guru being belaboured with a broomstick by the daughter or daughter-in-law of the house for attempting to take advantage of her undoubted charms.

The *patuas* also painted plants and animals, horse-racing and hunting scenes, sahibs with their *sarkars,* quarrels between co-wives, occupational types like fish-women, water-carriers and soldiers, and historical figures like the Rani of Jhansi.

Of the depiction of current events, I shall cite only one instance: the Elokeshi murder case of 1872, a *crime passionnel* that created a greater sensation in Bengal than any such event before or since. Elokeshi, a young wife, was slaughtered by her husband after no less a person than the Mohanta or head monk of the Tarakeshwar Temple had seduced her. The murder produced a mountainous crop of Bat-tala literature, and the Kālighat *patuas* depicted the entire event in a series of sixteen or more paintings in magnificently dramatic fashion.

Like most of the immense bulk of Bat-tala literature, all but a few of the millions of Kalighat *pats* have perished. The survivors are

all over India through millions of cheap lithographs and oleographs, these large-sized, brightly-coloured Bengal oils are still mostly invisible to the public eye. These oils, sometimes over-enthusiastically described as 'Dutch Bengal', are remarkable for their draughtsmanship and masterly handling of the new medium of oil. Unlike Ravi Varma's paintings, which contained hybrid architectural styles and European sartorial and physiological influences, the Bengal oils are a remarkable synthesis of foreign technique with pure Bengali character.

Here I must mention another, almost unnoticed and extremely rare type of painting in Calcutta from the last quarter of the nineteenth century. This was the small-sized oil painting of gods and goddesses on glass window-panes and door-panels. The only examples I know of are in the once-palatial mansions of Nandalal and Pashupati Basu of Bagbazar in north Calcutta. The small anonymous glass paintings bear some resemblance to the Kalighat *pats,* but only in matter of detail. Their colours, glowing gold, red, black, blue etc., and their meticulous finish recall the brilliance and dazzle of Rajasthani miniatures.

Old Calcutta Woodcuts

Printing reached Goa in 1556, exactly a hundred years after John Gutenberg invented printing with moveable metal types. From Goa, it took no less than 222 years to reach Hugli in Bengal. Between 1779 and 1800, however, it took firm root in Calcutta, though not until 1807 was the first press under Indian management set up by a man called Baburam.

1816 saw the first illustrated Bengali book embellished with woodcuts: Bharatchandra's classic *Oonoodah Mongol (Annadamangal),* published by Gangakishore Bhattacharya and printed by Ferris and Company. Of the six illustrations, four are supposed to be woodcuts and two metal engravings, though opinions differ. Only the latter two carry the inscription 'engraved by Ramchand Ray'; but many authorities believe that all six were designed and engraved by the same artist. The illustrations were in Bengal folk style; but the next illustrated Bengali book, *Sangeet Taranga,* a treatise on classical North Indian music, affected a pseudo-Rajasthani style, perhaps out of defer-

mostly lodged in museums in India and abroad, the biggest collection (nearly 650) being in the Victoria and Albert Museum, London. This number does not indicate the range of specific subjects; it includes multiple examples of single themes. The actual number of themes, both religious and secular, amounts to about a hundred.

The changing attitudes to the arts are characteristically reflected in the cases of both Bat-tala literature and the Kalighat *pats.* In their own day, the first was mostly dismissed as bawdry and tawdry and the latter as rude daubs. Today they are prized for their documentary and aesthetic values.

Bengal Oil Paintings

In the 1850s, alongside the Kalighat *pats* the foreign art of oil painting on canvas was slowly and silently taking root. Unknown local painters started painting large canvasses in oil — of gods and goddesses as well as scenes from the *Ramayana, Mahabharata,* Puranas, Krishnalila and so on. Unlike Ravi Varma's later oil paintings, which reached Hindu homes

22.5 Elokeshi and the Mohanta of Tarakeshwar. Kalighat pat. See 22.6, the same theme depicted in Bat-tala wood engraving by Nalinchandra Banerji

ence to the subject. The first illustrated Bengali magazine, *Pashwabali*, devoted to descriptions and tales of animals, was published by the Calcutta School Book Society in 1822. All its illustrations were drawn and also engraved in wood by the Reverend John Lawson; they seem to bear the influence of the great Thomas Bewick.

But Bengali artists learnt the art of woodcut on their own, without British tutelage. Their model seems clear to me. For centuries, weavers in different parts of India had used woodblocks to print coloured designs on cloth, as also *namavalis* or ceremonial wraps printed with *shlokas* on Hari and Krishna. Perhaps the designers occasionally pulled 'proofs' on paper before printing on cloth. Here is a notable precedent for the art of block-making, though using the blocks to print on paper was a technique that Indians first learnt from the Portuguese in Goa and Cochin.

I need not list the various important books, published between 1820 and 1860, to be illustrated with woodcuts. But a point has to be stressed before we leave the subject. Compared to metal engravings and even lithographs, woodcuts were by far the least expensive means of reproducing illustrations and were hence mainly used for popular religious books, almanacs and Bat-tala literature.

The golden age of what has come to be known as Bat-tala woodcuts extended from 1860 to the turn of the century. They were no longer confined to books; they took the form of loose prints, roughly coloured by hand. The relation of these woodcuts to the Kalighat *pats* is so intimate, sometimes virtually amounting to copies, that they can be termed their auxiliaries. Hana Knizkova categorizes them as 'the Kalighat style of drawings'.

Like the Kalighat *pats,* the Bat-tala woodcuts fall into two broad categories: the religious and the secular. They were printed on single sheets of paper, the size of Kalighat *pats,* or sometimes on larger sheets to accommodate two prints side by side with a blank margin in between. Sometimes they were even printed on both sides of a sheet. An interesting feature which I have not seen noted, is the tell-tale marks of screws on certain woodcuts. These indicate how, after electricity came to Bat-tala at the turn of the century, wax moulds were taken from the original woodcuts and copper electrotypes made by immersing the moulds in a galvanized copper bath. The electrotypes were them mounted on wood by means of screws. They remained good for some tens of thousands of prints instead of a few hundred as from the original woodcut.

Like the Kalighat *pats,* the Bat-tala woodcuts were meant for ordinary people. They were produced in large numbers and sold even more

Left
22.6 See 22.5
Below
22.7 Sundar under the bakul tree. Engraving by Ramchand Ray from 'Annadamangal', 1816

Yet we know little about these artists except that, like the Kalighat *patuas,* they had no formal training or general education — lack of this last appearing in the elementary spelling mistakes in their captions. No doubt too, they produced no makers of international standard. But this does not mean that their work is devoid of artistic merit. Their strength lies mainly in their rude vigour and boldness. As in the Kalighat *pats,* architectural, sartorial and other anachronisms add to their quaint charm. And like the *pats,* they were driven out of existence by the shiny coloured oleographs and photographs with their realistic appeal.

Lithographs

The art of lithography, invented by Alois Senefelder in 1798, reached India around 1822 when two Frenchmen, Belnos and Saviagnac, first successfully practised it in Calcutta. The first Bengali lithographic press, the Shura Pathuria Press, was launched soon after in 1829. It printed the images of gods and goddesses as well as maps and charts. None of its works survive; its existence is proved only by an advertisement. But scholars assume that its pictures of Hindu deities were probably painted on stone by some of the Kalighat *patuas.*

Unlike the woodcuts, lithography developed from the 1850s under the auspices of the British by the hand of academically-trained Indians. The most noted Bengali lithographer, Annadaprasad Bagchi, was trained in the Government School of Art, as were many of his colleagues. During their academic days, they helped to illustrate such famous books as Sir Joseph Fayrer's monumental *Thanatophidia of India* (1872) and Raja Rajendralal Mitra's *Antiquities of Orissa* (1875-80). The illustrations of the *Thanatophidia* won high encomiums from eminent British periodicals, while those of the *Antiquities* received wide acclaim at the international exhibition at Kensington in 1871.

But lithographs with real regional flavour were initiated only in 1876 when Bagchi, with four of his colleagues, left the Art School and opened their famous lithographic press, the Calcutta Art Studio, at Boubazar. Almost simultaneously, another group of lithographers also left the Calcutta Art School and started their own firm, the Royal Lithographic Press. Specimens of the latter's work are rare: a few are preserved in the Victoria Memorial,

cheaply than the *pats.* But sadly, they have become even rarer.

While the Kalighat *pats* were anonymous, the Bat-tala woodcuts were mostly signed and further declared their 'provenance' — i.e. the press where they were printed. Among the better-known woodcut artists of the later period are Benimadhab Bhattacharya, Birchandra Datta, Madhabchandra Das, Nrityalal Dutta, Hiralal Karmakar, Panchanan Karmakar, Gobindachandra Ray and Ramdhan Swarnakar. Some only signed their work with their initials in English. But Nrityalal Datta, possibly the most powerful of the lot (active in the 1880s and 1890s) had his own press, and used his full name in Bengali and his initials in English.

Calcutta. It was, however, in 1878, some two years before Ravi Varma's Lithographic Press at Lonavala, that the Calcutta Art Studio started the art of chromolithography in India. As with the Kalighat *pats* and the woodcuts, their main output consisted of images of gods and goddesses and themes from the Puranas.

The art of these mythological chromolithographs has been treated in detail in the next article. Although T. N. Mukherji referred to them in disparaging terms, they display considerable virtuosity in both drawing and reproduction. In fact, these pictures became so popular that according to Raja Rajendralal Mitra, 'Some English chromolithographers took advantage [of it] and made exact copies of Calcutta Art Studio pictures, and sent a large consignment for sale at one-tenth the normal price'. The Government soon banned such imports. The Calcutta Art Studio also produced a series of fine monochrome lithographic portraits of the great men of Bengal, which at one time adorned many Bengali homes.

Various other lithographic presses were also set up: the Kansaripara, Shankharitola and Chorbagan Art Studios, P. C. Biswas and Co., and others. Apart from the inevitable deities and *Pouranic* themes, these studios produced portraits of beauties *à la* Kalighat. But Arya Chitralaya, run by Chandicharan Ghosh of Simla Street, produced a series of didactic lithographs, accompanied by long poetic texts, to propagate traditional Hindu values and morals.

Company painting died out after the 1850s, chiefly owing to the spread of photography in India. The main function of these pictures had been to record the environment, whether for scientific or general interest. This the camera could do more quickly, cheaply and accurately.

The Kalighat *pat,* too, declined in competition with lithographs, oleographs and finally photographs. It survived in a fashion till the 1920s, because of a few traditional masters like the brothers Nibaran and Kalicharan Ghosh. But gradually the fall in demand led to a fall in quality and at last to total disappearance.

Lithographs, the successful intruder, were in turn dislodged by oleographs, photographs and finally letterpress printing with half-tone blocks. By a kind of Gresham's Law, bad lithographs drove good lithographs from circulation. The Bat-tala woodcut, too, survives only in crude posters and engravings for electrotypes to illustrate cheap books.

It is difficult to recapture the innovative vitality of these outmoded arts in their heyday. But something of that exhilaration revives as we view the surviving specimens. And, of course, they provide us with vivid insights into the religion, society and general life of Calcutta in the last century.

Facing page
Above
22.8 Hara-Hari, the combined image of Shiva and Krishna. Bat-tala wood engraving by Nrityalal Datta

Below
22.9 Lithograph by Annadaprasad Bagchi from 'Antiquities of Orissa', 1870

ART
IN OLD CALCUTTA:
THE MELTING POT OF
WESTERN STYLES

Tapati Guha Thakurta

Segregation and seclusion were keynotes of British social life in old Calcutta. Its culture, tastes and values shaped themselves in opposition to the traditional ways and practices of the 'Black Town'. Yet there was constant interpenetration: the European fascination with the 'exotic' and 'oriental' was matched by an emulation of Western mores by the rising Bengali gentry and middle class, with repercussions across other social strata. The story of art and artists in nineteenth-century Calcutta reflects both the polarity and the convergences, the seclusion and the cross-currents of change.

The 1830s and 1840s marked a period of brewing debate in England concerning the 'utility' of the arts. The contemporary crisis in English industrial design bred a powerful reformist movement among leading designers like Owen Jones, Henry Cole and Richard Redgrave, which reasserted the importance of the 'decorative' *vis-à-vis* the 'fine' arts. The Great Exhibition of 1851 in London, on 'The Industry of All Nations', brought special attention to bear on the wealth of 'art-manufactures' that India had to offer. Indian handicrafts were seen as an example for the degraded, industrialized tastes of the West.

But the British appreciation of Indian artware had a double edge; for India's talents were thereby relegated to the realm of the 'lesser' or 'applied arts' as opposed to the 'fine' or 'higher' ones. This distinction between the 'higher' and 'lower' arts was crucial in the context of Empire, particularly in the structure of art education introduced in India in the 1850s. The first Schools of Art, including the one set up in Calcutta in 1854, were concerned purely with a technical craft-based training. The 'fine arts' of painting and sculpture were a negligible concern. They had come to be synonymous with the Western Academic style, particularly with oil painting and three-dimensional illusionism, and excellence in this sphere was thought to be a monopoly of the West.

Long before the establishment of the Art Schools, a stream of European portrait and landscape artists had heralded dramatic changes in the practice and patronage of art in India. First and most prolific of the landscape painters was William Hodges (1744–97), whose travels during 1781–84 bore fruit in a set of aquatint engravings, *Select Views in India* (1786), and then in *Travels in India* (1793). Hodges was followed by the famous team of uncle and nephew, Thomas (1749–1840) and William Daniell (1769–1837), who made Calcutta their first base in 1786–87 before setting out across the country. Their *Oriental Scenery* (completed 1808) was preceded by *Views of Calcutta* (1786–88), a series of engravings which recorded in vivid and meticulous detail the vistas, buildings, roads and riverside of British Calcutta. With time, these panoramic visions yielded to more intimate, on-the-spot recording of 'Indian' scenes among amateur sketchers and visiting professionals like George Chinnery (?–1852), Charles D'Oyly (1781–1845), Balthazar Solvyns (1760–1824) and James Baillie Fraser (1783–1856).

Simultaneously, Calcutta also became a lucrative venue for European portrait painters. The power, status and wealth that the city generated found its most self-gratifying representation in life-size, pompously-posed oil portraits which showed off the patron in palatial mansions, surrounded by 'native' servants, indulging in special 'Indian' pastimes like the *nautch* or (in a different setting) the *shikar*. Such portraits became vital records of the experience of empire.

One of the earliest and most successful of painters to visit India, Tilly Kettle (1740–86) found important patrons among the Indian royalty. In Calcutta, however, both he and the more renowned John Zoffany, R. A. (1733–1810) who stayed here from 1783 to 1789, worked almost solely for the European

host of other European painters through the early and mid-nineteenth century. The more important among them were Thomas Hicky (1760–90), Robert Home (1751–1834), Arthur William Devis (1763–1822) and George Chinnery.

The growing presence of European artists would influence and transform the Indian art scene in two major ways, at different social levels. The first affected the painters of the dying Nawabi culture. Displaced from the courts of Murshidabad or Lucknow and reduced now to 'bazaar' painters, their chief new clients were the 'nabobs' of the East India Company, who wanted records of their own grand life-style as well as of various Indian 'trades and castes', local scenes, flora and fauna. Simultaneously, the painters were introduced to the 'correct' conventions of naturalistic drawing, shading and perspective. The outcome was the hybrid genre of 'Company paintings', which the colonial masters would

23.1 *Town and Port of Calcutta. D'Oyly, colour lithograph, 1848*

residents and captured for posterity the nascent imperialist ethos. Zoffany, in particular, created a special visual type in power and poise: Warren Hastings and his wife with an Indian maid against the imposing spread of their Belvedere Estate; Lady Hastings seated in dramatic opulence with the window framing palm trees; or the Chief Justice Sir Elijah Impey as Justice Incarnate. Such works established the prestige of oil painting in Calcutta, attracting a

carry home as Indian mementos.

There were many ways, direct and indirect, in which local painters were gradually schooled in Western art conventions. In general, direct training and drilling seem to have been less important than emulation, example and the pressure of competition. The success of Hodges and the Daniells encouraged a proliferation of near-identical views of scenery and architectural monuments. Caught in these changing

23.2 *The Charak Festival. Solvyns, colour engraving, 1808*

demands, the traditional painter was reduced to a mere copyist, draughtsman or 'artisan', while the British painters occupied the hallowed place of 'artists'.

At quite a different level, the concept of 'art' and 'artist' acquired new social weight and aesthetic connotations in Indian society through Western example. Over the nineteenth century, Calcutta saw the making of a new category of Indian 'artists', who set themselves the same roles and standards as the European artists: Academic oil painting, commissions for portraits, participation in 'fine art' exhibitions, and the technical skills of engraving and lithography. Some of these artists were wealthy amateurs privately trained by European tutors; others middle-class *bhadraloks* turning to vocational training in the arts as an alternative to a literary university education. Both groups found it essential to distance themselves from the milieu of 'bazaar' art. The ultimate goal for most of them was entry to the city's exclusive domain of 'high art', centred around exhibitions, commissions and private collections.

Exhibitions played a crucial role in propagating the new model of 'fine arts', chiefly through the works of visiting European artists and copies of Old Masters. The first 'fine art' exhibitions, held at the Calcutta Town Hall during 1831 and 1832, were organized by a group of British artists and art-enthusiasts called the Brush Club. The exhibits were exclusively European: alongside Hodges, Kettle, Zoffany, Chinnery and Beechey, there hung, as symbols of greater prestige, the works of Royal Academy stalwarts like Joshua Reynolds and Benjamin West, the Venetian landscapes of Canaletto, and copies of seventeenth-century masters like Guido Reni, Rubens and Van Dyck.

This Europeanized art world first began to admit Indians not as artists but as patrons and collectors. In course of time, wealthy Bengalis like Raja Ramanath Thakur (1801-1877) and Jatindramohan Thakur (1831-1908) emerged as influential art patrons of the day, featuring as both donors and purchasers of European paintings in these exhibitions, and also extending their favours to the few Indian practitioners of the Western style.

A taste for Western art, architectural styles and interior decor had become a major signifier of wealth and status among the new Bengali aristocracy. Over the nineteenth century, Dwarakanath Thakur's Belgachhia Villa, the 'Tagore Castle' of the Pathuriaghata Thakurs, the Marble Palace of Raja Rajendra Mallik, Raja Manmathanath Mitra's house at Shyampukur, and the palaces of the Bardhaman Maharajas flaunted the largest collections of Western art in the city. The highest value was always accorded to European 'classical' art: the Neoclassical

paintings of Royal Academicians like Opie, Eastlake or Alma-Tadema; duplicates of Raphaels, Titians, Rubenses and Guido Renis; and an array of Venuses, Cupids, Apollos, Minervas and Mercuries in marble and bronze.

The works of European artists in India was supplemented by a flow of works from abroad. Certain European ateliers like that of L. Pompignoli of Florence specialized in copies of antique sculpture and Renaissance painting, catering to the pervasive taste for 'classical' art in nineteenth-century Europe and its outpost in colonial India. Regular shipments of engravings, mostly of nineteenth-century British painting, also arrived in Calcutta. And the city had its own channels for the circulation of European art. The Tagore Castle, for instance, owes part of its collection to the good offices of George Chinnery and later of W. H. Jobbins, Superintendent of the Calcutta School of Art from 1887 to 1896. There were also local sales occasioned by shifting tastes or fortunes. Part of the collection of Belgachhia Villa passed on to the Tagore Castle with the sale of the former estate; European oils disposed of by the Jorasanko Thakurs moved to the neighbouring Marble Palace; and when E. B. Havell began to Indianize the curriculum of the School of Art, the sudden dispersal of European paintings from the Government Art Gallery in 1905 provided an opportunity for wealthy collectors.

Such private collections viewed local artists primarily as copyists. Supplies of Western art could always be augmented cheaply by locally-made copies of Old Masters and antique sculpture. Oil portraiture was another field where

Above
23.3 Left: Elijah Impey as Justice Incarnate. Platinotype after oil painting by Zoffany, 1783

23.4 Right: Warren Hastings and his wife. John Zoffany, oil, c. 1785

Below
23.5 Maharaja of Bardhaman, Bijoychand Mahatab

149

23.6 *Maharaja Jatindramohan Thakur*

distinction between the Indians and the Europeans. The former were seen primarily as students and trainees, relegated to life-studies, landscape sketches or architectural drawings and to second-tier occupations like those of drawing-masters, draughtsmen, engravers or lithographers. The awards they won in exhibitions were almost invariably those earmarked for 'native' art alone. In the competition for favours, they lagged far behind their European counterparts.

A gap between aspiration and reality was largely inherent in the training programme of Calcutta's new artists. The Calcutta School of Art was caught between the two contrary priorities of British art-education policies in India: its self-avowed mission of inculcating in Indians a taste for the 'higher arts' – which would imply producing a number of Western-type artists – and its practical aim of providing the majority of trainees with some useful and employable skills. A central objective of the Art Schools was the preservation and tutelage of the country's dying tradition of handicrafts. In practice, however, the schools became important less for the resuscitation of traditional craftsmen than for the training of a new stratum of semi-clerical, skilled professionals who could be absorbed within the network of British services.

The School of Industrial Arts in Calcutta, converted to a full-fledged Government institution in 1864, had its focus on the 'applied arts' offering courses in Drawing, Painting, Modelling, Lithography and Engraving. Yet within a few decades, the same School acquired a parallel status as an Academy inclining to the 'fine arts', on the strength of an adjoining Art Gallery, stuffed with specimens of European oil paintings and copies of antique sculpture. Founded by Lord Northbrook in 1876, the aim of the Gallery was chiefly educational – to train students through examples in the 'right' way of observation and representation.

The ambivalence between 'fine' and 'industrial' arts was reflected in a sharp dichotomy in attitude and policy. From the 1880s, the Applied Arts Division showed a marked interest in Indian crafts, design and architecture; but the Drawing and Painting classes remained strictly European and Academic in outlook. The curriculum remained clearly polarized between Western 'fine arts' and Indian 'decorative arts'. This line of divide persisted in Art School

Indian skills were in some demand. But in a city crowded with European artists, only a few Indians landed big commissions and most had to content themselves with copying or repainting the works of their European peers. From the 1870s, a new chain of Government-sponsored exhibitions first saw substantial participation by Indian artists and art-students. Occasional private collections, like that of the Tagore Castle, also opened up to some oils and water-colours by Bengali artists like Girishchandra Chatterji, Harishchandra Khan, Bamapada Banerji (1851-1932) and Jaminiprakash Ganguli (1876-1953). *(See page116, Bankimchandra by Bamapada Banerji)*

But there remained always a subtle line of

policy through the turn of the century, even under E. B. Havell's celebrated programme of Indianizing the modes and models of teaching.

By the end of the nineteenth century, the Calcutta School of Art had successfully engendered a new notion of art as a 'respectable' vocation and career. Since the 1870s, a main mark of success among graduating art-students seems to have been their employment as teachers within the School itself. A wide range of commissions was also open to them through both official and private patronage, often while they were still at the School. There was a growing demand for ethnological clay models and for illustrations to lavish British publications such as the Records of the Geological Survey, the Annals of the Royal Botanic Garden, Sir Joseph Fayrer's book of snakes, *The Thanatophidia of India* (1872), or Raja Rajendralal Mitra's monumental two-volume *The Antiquities of Orissa* (1875-80). In all such commissions, the demand was less for 'art' than for skilled copying and draughtsmanship. The role of the copyist acquired new respectability and refinement through official training and patronage.

The most prized skill, however, was proficiency in oil painting and the art of realistic portraiture. This field attracted others besides Art School students, including privately-trained gentlemen-artists from aristocratic families. From the Mallik family of the Marble Palace, there came Debendra and Nagendra Mallik; from the Pathuriaghata Thakurs, Jaladhichandra Mukherji (a daughter's son) and Shoutindramohan Thakur (1865-98), the latter one of the first Indians to have studied at the Royal Academy; from Jorasanko and its extended branches, Abanindranath Thakur's grandfather and father Girindranath (1820-54) and Gunendranath (1847-81), his cousin Hitendranath (1867-1908) and his nephew Jaminiprakash Ganguli. Jamini Ganguli was perhaps the most gifted and prolific of these painters, specializing in a genre of dusky landscapes and romantic studies of peasant life.

Oil painting, especially portraiture, was also the source of success and renown for the few Art School products who made a name for themselves as 'artists'. Among them were Annadaprasad Bagchi (1849-1905), appointed teacher of oil painting and Head Master at the School of Art in 1870; Shashi Hesh (1869-?), who was sponsored for further training at the

Academies of Rome and Munich and returned home in 1900 as a prominent portrait artist; or Bamapada Banerji, who built up a flourishing career in portrait-painting in northern India. These painters measured most closely to the model of the successful Western-style artist which the British had impressed upon Indian society

Yet the careers of these same artists also illustrate the opposite process of transformation sweeping Calcutta's art world. From their 'respectable' careers as teachers and portrait painters, they branched out towards indigenous commercial art work and mass picture production, in response to the wider changes in visual tastes that were penetrating all layers of urba society. While elite patronage remained a narrow circuit, the popular market for prints, illustrations and religious pictures offered a more sustaining base. The very status of 'artist' had involved a rejection of 'bazaar' art. But the pressures of livelihood and the commercial potentials of their skills drove a number of these new artists to bridge the gap between 'high' and 'low' art and enter the domain of popular tastes.

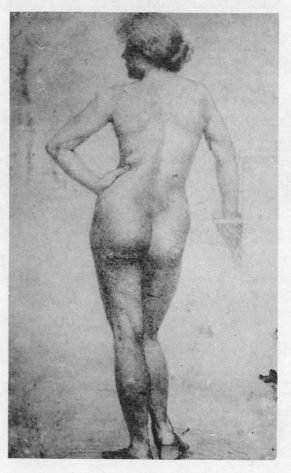

23.7 Nude Study.
Shashi Hesh

This paradox leads us to the phenomenon of 'Westernization from below' – the extension and absorption of Western norms and techniques beyond the insular world of 'high art'. The new artists introduced new competitive standards of style and technique in mass picture production. But simultaneously, these new skills were adapted in various ways to the popular demand for a kind of picture that presented Indian religious and mythological themes within the loose framework of an Academic realistic style. Colour prints became one of the main meeting-grounds of 'high' and 'bazaar' art.

By the mid-nineteenth century, the traditional popular picture-trade of Calcutta was in a state of flux. Outside the direct reach of Western demands, groups of 'bazaar' artists like the *patuas* of Kalighat or the metal engravers of Bat-tala were also being drawn into the cross-currents of change under different degrees of pressure and volition. The Bat-tala engravings

in particular display a novel assertion of individuality. Many of them carry the engraver's name, and some even a declaration of copyright. A few engravers like Nrityalal Datta or Ramdhan Swarnakar became entrepreneurs and press-owners. But the Bat-tala artisans never became 'artists' in contemporary esteem. Even in the arena of mass picture production, success and status derived from the School of Art.

In the 1880s, a dramatic new intrusion on the market came in the form of chromolithographs on Hindu mythological themes from the Calcutta Art Studio. This press at Boubazar was set up around 1878-79 by Annadaprasad Bagchi with four compatriots from the Art School. It found its most solid source of profit and success in the 'Hindu Mytho-pictures' (as they were called), which it churned out for a mass market. The arrival of these pictures augured a general transformation in the iconography of popular religious pictures. Both the Kalighat paintings and the Bat-tala engravings had been singularly

23.8 Lovers (Nayak-Nayika). Bat-tala wood engraving by Madhabchandra Das

resilient to Western Academic styles of representation. Western influences worked their way in only through certain images out of the visual vocabulary of British Calcutta: top-hatted sahibs and Westernized babus, European furniture seating *nayaks* and *nayikas,* or winged angels hovering around the Mother Goddess.

By contrast the Art Studio mytho-pictures stood out for their marked adaptation of a realistic style. Figures were given the tactile quality of flesh, muscles and volume; backgrounds acquired depth and dimension; costumes simulated the feel of velvet and silk; and scenes from mythology were now set against contemporary mansions or copy-book landscapes. The affinities with Western neo-classical painting are also apparent in the hybrid imagery: a half-draped Venus-like figure of a sleeping Damayanti, or a dramatic shaft of light revealing a muscular Yama in a picture of Savitri and Satvavan.

Yet realism itself suffered much dilution in mingling with conventional iconography. This is clear if one contrasts the realistic finesse of the portraits of famous men circulated by the same Calcutta Art Studio with the shoddy naturalism of the mytho-pictures. The rigours of life study lapsed as gods and goddesses had to retain their multiple arms or mythical blue complexions. The loud and dazzling colour of the costumes and landscape settings evoked a world of mythic fantasy.

By the end of the century, there was a large turn-out of cheap chromolithographs from a host of small presses around the Bat-tala locality: at Kansaripara, Chorbagan, Pathuriaghata and Boubazar. The trappings of a Western Academic style, however crude, had become the staple of urban commercial art. The illustrations in the almanacs and cheap novels of Bat-tala began to move towards more naturalistic representations and more refined printing techniques through the use of electroblocks. Over the late nineteenth century, a superior

23.9 Savitri and Satyavan. Colour lithograph from the Calcutta Art Studio, c. 1880

middle tier of Bengali books and magazines made their appearance, half-way between the expensive Western publications and the cheap Bat-tala books reflecting the same trends in illustration and design. Among them were the first Bengali satire magazine *Basantak,* several children's magazines like *Sakha o Sathi* and *Mukul,* and literary magazines like *Balak* and *Sadhana.* Their art work was chiefly excuted by Art School alumni and their kind.

Even oil painting, that hallmark of 'high art', saw a collapse of barriers between 'high' and 'low', the studio and the bazaar. Large oils on Hindu religious and mythological themes were being produced by anonymous 'bazaar' painters from Chitpur and Garanhata, as well as other parts of Bengal such as Chunchura and Chandannagar. They combine illusionist techniques with the iconographic attributes of divinities and the decorative designing of costumes and ornaments. The mix of styles and degree of refinement vary widely in these oils: it appears they were produced over a long period of time, probably spanning the whole of the nineteenth century and beyond, responding continuously to new techniques and emerging popular stereotypes in imagery.

Along with European neo-classical painting and statuary, these indigenous oil paintings also found their way into Calcutta's rich homes. But they were viewed more as religious pictures, objects of devotion, than as 'works of art'; they seldom found their way out of the household altars into the great halls. Although the forms of these paintings were gradually modernized in keeping with changing tastes and demands, they could not constitute 'high art' from the collector's viewpoint.

Once again it was the participation of gentlemen-artists which gave this genre of oil painting an elevated status. A member of the aristocracy of Travancore, Raja Ravi Varma (1848-1906), achieved all-India fame and enjoyed widespread patronage for his oils on mythological themes, painted in an accomplished Academic style in the manner of European 'history' paintings. From an oleography press which he set up with German collaboration on the outskirts of Bombay, glossy colourprints of these paintings invaded the popular art market in the 1890s, superseding other existing varieties.

In Calcutta, Ravi Varma's career found a striking parallel in that of Bamapada Banerji, an alumnus of the Art School. From oil painting and portraiture, he diversified into mythological painting with the specific intention of massmarketing these through oleograph prints. Even for such established artists, the popular art market was obviously more lucrative than the patronage of the elite. In 1890, before Ravi Varma's pictures arrived in Calcutta, two of Bamapada Banerji's paintings – 'Arjun and Urvashi' and 'Abhimanyu and Uttara' – were sent to Germany to be reproduced as oleographs.

By the last decade of the nineteenth century, Ravi Varma and Bamapada Banerji's pictures had taken over the local art market. There were clear variations in refinement and finesse between the two, as between the latter's work and mytho-pictures from the Calcutta Art Studio. But the gradations of training, style and competence were often levelled out by the uniformity and ubiquity of the colour print and the semblance of a realistic style. There emerged a standardized type of new 'realistic' picture, continuously reproducing itself through certain stereotyped images and set gamut of naturalistic conventions.

Nonetheless, new waves of aesthetic exclusiveness were emerging even in the sphere of

23.10 *Arjun and Urvashi. Oleograph by Bamapada Banerji, 1890*

154

prints and mass-produced pictures. This can be seen in the 'discovery' of Ravi Varma by the Bengali cultural elite, as his mythological paintings appeared in prestigious literary journals like *Sadhana, Pradip, Prabasi* and *The Modern Review*. A range of new intellectual and aesthetic concerns were now projected by critics around the special 'Indian' and 'aesthetic' quality of these paintings. This coincided with an advance in colour printing technology, the use of the new half-tone process block by Upendrakishore Raychoudhuri (1863-1915). It served to create a new distinction between the print as 'art' and the print as 'bazaar' picture or religious oleograph.

The nature and reach of such changes in the form, practice and idea of art in Calcutta underline the need to reassess the phenomenon of Westernization. The very categories of 'Western' and 'Indian', 'modern' and 'traditional' grow fluid: they acquire new, open-ended definitions at different levels of interaction. The Westernized art world of 'high art'; beneath it, the milieu of the small-time portraitists, drawing-masters, draughtsmen and engravers; and further below, the widespread diffusion and appropriation of Western styles and techniques that transformed conventional iconography as well as the popular commercial art of the city. Calcutta's new stock of gentlemen-artists straddled this entire range of art activity. Forces that operated at one level as alien Western influences were made to serve very different ends within the framework of popular pictures. The new realism, far from being dismissed as a Western intrusion, was seen as an essential ingredient of 'art' and of the Indian iconography of the time.

The turn of the century brought new ideological factors into the painting of 'Indian' pictures. The rise of Abanindranath Thakur and his nationalist art movement polemicized the notions of 'Western' and 'Indian' styles and drove a deep wedge between them. Rejecting the current standing of the artist as a trained

23.11 *Damayanti and the Swan. Oleograph from oil painting by Ravi Varma, 1899*

professional, Abanindranath embodied a new romantic image of the artist as genius. In a conscious break with Western norms and training, he experimented with the recreation of a new 'Indian style' that came to symbolize the recovery of tradition and a lost identity. A new nationalist concept of 'high art' was thus established, ideologically reliant on a sharp break with the past. But a long-range view of the artistic changes and encounters of the preceding century helps to place Abanindranath's movement within an ongoing and far-reaching process of change, generated by colonial contacts and indigenous adaptations.

TRENDS IN
CALCUTTA ARCHITECTURE
1690-1903

Dhriti Kanta Lahiri Choudhury

Most architectural reviews of Calcutta have been by Europeans taking, understandably, a European point of view, seeing the architecture of Calcutta chiefly as an extension, often debased, of European idioms. The 'Black Town', for all practical purposes, did not exist for such writers: from J. Fergusson (*History of the Modern Styles of Architecture,* 1863) through H. B. Hyde (*Parish of Bengal,* 1899; *Parochial Annals of Bengal,* 1901) and Katherine Blechynden (*Calcutta Past and Present,* 1905) to Sten Nilsson (*European Architecture in India,* 1968), Jan Morris (*Stones of Empire,* 1983), Philip Davies (*Splendours of the Raj,* 1985), and M. Archer in *Country Life.* Even H. E. A. Cotton, despite his understanding of the city and deep knowledge of the established Bengali families, does not note the architectural details of their great houses in his *Calcutta Old and New* (1909).

In this article, a fresh exploratory look will be taken at Calcutta's earlier buildings, to show how a genuine 'mutated style' was evolved through interaction between Indian and European idioms of architecture. This made the face of Calcutta typically colonial, and therefore representative of the city's origin and moving spirit – namely, commerce – and the middle-to-low-brow cultural heritage which it is colonialism's peculiar privilege to breed.

A city consists of buildings, roads, space and people. Buildings do not stand by themselves. They react, positively or negatively, with their environment. In *The Design of Cities* (1968), Edmund N. Bacon traces some recurrent patterns in the growth of cities which we may use as points of reference: (1) by accretion with space as the connector; (2) by a system of interlocking axes of large and prominent buildings; (3) with mass acting as the connector, bringing together various parts of a many-angled composition, especially important in congested city streets; (4) growth by accretion around rectangular spaces (as in early Calcutta) with interlocking space and/or the vertical force of towers or spires, visually interlocked, binding the accretions; (5) by tension between various landmarks in the city.

It may be useful to link this account of the architecture of Calcutta to an assessment of her growth and overall planning, as well as the chief currents of her history and culture.

The period covered by the present study can be divided into the following phases: (1) 1690 to 1756; (2) 1757 to 1803; (3) 1804 to 1863; (4) 1864 to 1903.

1690 to 1756

The settlement founded by Charnock was palisaded after the insurrection of Raja Sobha Singh in 1696. By January 1697 its nucleus was a bastioned and walled yard facing the river. Its eastern boundary was the age-old pilgrim-path running parallel to the river to Kalighat temple, a few miles further south. The movement path led east along what is now Lalbazar and B. B. Ganguli (formerly Boubazar) Street, terminating at Charnock's famous banyan tree at Baithakkhana. To the north of the English town lay the established settlements of weavers and yarn merchants in Sutanuti and Chitpur; to the east, the Salt Lakes; to the south, the flourishing village of Gobindapur; then Kalighat, and beyond that the mangrove forests and swamps of the Sundarbans.

Charnock cannily chose the site, protected by natural barriers on all sides, with an eye to the security of his factory. But the growth-potential of the city was severely limited by the very barriers that protected it. The death of Aurangzeb in 1707 and the unsettled political situation that followed fuelled the self-protective insularity of the settlers, and the existing bastions were extended. The three-mile Maratha Ditch was excavated by 1742 as a protection against marauding Marathas who never came, only to prove useless when Siraj-ud-Daula eventually did. About the same time, the palisades around the settlement were strengthened and each exit guarded by a gate, creating in effect a 'white ghetto'.

By this time, a psychological barrier had also sprung up: the distinction between the 'White' and 'Black' Towns. The Black Town lay to the north of the English settlement in the villages of Sutanuti and Chitpur and to the south in Gobindapur. The 'White' settlement was restricted to Kalikata, mostly on the northern side of the old Fort: 'rising,' as Hamilton aptly remarked, 'like [the town] about a baronial castle in the medieval times'.

The sharp division between the White and Black Towns was sealed by a gradual withdrawal of the English from Sutanuti, presumably considered more vulnerable because of its northerly location. From that day to this, planners and developers have battled with only limited success to eliminate the contrast between the original Black and White Towns, to break through the tangled mass of unplanned growth to the north and east of the planned and fortified European settlement. The city's growth has been dogged from the outset by the basic contradiction of colonialism.

It is true that the rulers also showed a recurrent urge to expand the city northward, beginning with Clive, who preferred to live in Dumdum. But all such efforts failed because of

the basic contradiction on which the city was founded.

Not many buildings survive from this period. Indeed, Cotton goes so far as to observe that modern Calcutta began in 1757. The early drawings show the old Fort from the riverside, indicating what was in those days the settlement's 'front'. The Governor's House in the early drawings is an imposing structure, but without much distinction. Notable are the pedimented windows showing the early influence of Neoclassicism.

The earliest structure from this period, as generally accepted, is the mausoleum of Job Charnock (d. 1693), erected, probably in 1695, by his son-in-law Charles Eyre, who succeeded him as the Company's agent. The style is Islamic, except for rounded arches on the doorways. We need not ascribe the borrowing to either Charnock's or Eyre's known addiction to 'country habits and customs'. A simpler explanation would be that the settlement did not as yet have the benefit of military engineers, or of engineers' manuals and design-books. Eyre fell back on the only local idiom for the construction of tombs, the Islamic, and had the work executed by an indigenous master-builder. A later picture of St John's Churchyard shows several massive domed structures of similar conception.

Miss Blechynden has pointed out a large house in the map of 1742 at the site of Sir Elijah Impey's house, now occupied by Loreto House in Middleton Row. This, she feels, must have been the mansion of a 'native'; and we may assume that it continued the Islamic tradition of architecture, as perhaps did the 'lofty mansion' of the Faujdar or military governor of Hugli who had his official residence in Calcutta at the crossing of Chitpur and Kalutola.

Early paintings of Calcutta show temples in the Bengal terracotta style, indicating the presence of a third tradition: that of the Hindu temple. The foundations of many temples in Chitpur and Sutanuti date back to this period; but few of them retain their original shape.

The villas of Gobindaram Mitra the 'Black Zamindar' and Umichand the merchant were both located at Halsibagan in north-east Calcutta. One assumes they must have contained civic architecture of some importance. Umichand's house lodged Siraj-ud-Daula himself when he descended on Calcutta in 1756. We do not know anything of

the style of this building; but two of the nine *mahals,* the reception area and the kitchen area, have survived of Gobindaram Mitra's residence in Kumartuli – probably the oldest civic building still standing in the city, very likely contemporaneous with Gobindaram's *nabaratna* temple of 1731 (see below). The celebrated house of Banamali Sarkar, whose ruins were still extant in the mid-nineteenth century, has disappeared. Other extant buildings in the Chitpur-Kumartuli area may be as old, but to this writer they are not architecturally significant.

Even at this early stage, the reception area of Gobindaram's house sports columns. They are of the 'giant' or 'colossal' order, rising up to the top of the lofty second storey and clearly meant to impress. But the space is too limited for the huge columns: they only line a narrow courtyard, instead of commanding the vista that columns of such proportions demand. The entablature is crude, but it shows an acquaintance with the details of classical idiom.

This difference in rendering between columns and entablature is a distinctive feature of Calcutta Neoclassical architecture, as columns were status symbols while entablatures were not. The lintels are of wood, plastered over, and the Ionic capitals have terracotta cores: examples of early adaptation of local technology to an imported mode. There is no façade, only a narrow entrance leading to the courtyard, a space-division followed in all early buildings in Calcutta.

On the other hand, when the same Gobindaram used his ill-gotten wealth to construct his famous *nabaratna* ('nine-jewelled', i.e. nine-towered) temple in 1731, the city's most prominent landmark at that date, he observed architectural decorum by choosing the traditional Bengal temple style. The temple was overthrown in the terrible earthquake and cyclone of 1737, but a small tower, much plastered over, still survives. The other temple of architectural significance which David McCutchion dates before 1757 is on Kebalkrishna Sur Street in Kumartuli, built according to one oral tradition by Banamali Sarkar. This is an *atchala* (eight-roofed) construction, illustrating the other line of Bengal temple architecture.

Significantly, Gobindaram chose a novel style for his residence, particularly the public reception area, and a traditional one for his temple, guided apparently by what would be appropriate or decorous in each case. The choice, at the end of this particular phase, lay between three architectural traditions side by side: the Islamic tradition; the style of the Bengal temples in two variant forms; and the pseudo-Neoclassical style introduced recently by the British.

As early as Charnock's mausoleum, we find in the round arches the first impact of European style on a basically Indo-Islamic conception. In Mughal architecture, round arches appear as moulded design framing pointed arches. Sixty years later, in the monument to Charles Watson (d. 1757), the classical orders are in, and the composition is essentially Neoclassical. We can use these two contrasting structures to mark the opening and close of this phase in the development of architecture in Calcutta.

1757 to 1803

To the English the Sack of Calcutta in 1756 by Siraj-ud-Daula was a total disaster. A large part

24.1 *Gobindaram Mitra's house at Kumartuli*

of the palisaded English settlement was either demolished or gutted by fire. Apart from the imposing Governor's House, the buildings destroyed included the houses of Edward Eyre and Edward Cruttenden; the Mayor's Court; the Company's house southeast of the Fort; and St Anne's Church, which had survived the disastrous flood and earthquake of 1737.

Barabazar, then probably a conglomeration of shanties, was also put to fire by the Nawab's army. (The precedent had been set by the English themselves a few days earlier in Gobindapur.) For the rest, the Black Town was largely unaffected. The picture one gets, on the whole, is of a disciplined army carrying out an operation without unnecessary damage. We can compare this with Captain John Brohier's ruthless demolition job at Chandannagar in 1757 on Clive's orders, which 'left only a few indigent widows' huts standing' in a town of 100,000 inhabitants.

As one would expect, the destruction was followed by intense building activity, specially though not exclusively in the White Town. The village of Gobindapur was cleared, and the lines of the new Fort William laid there by Clive in August 1757. Work began in October 1757 and was completed around 1773. Nabakrishna Deb ('Nubkissen' to the British) and other residents of Gobindapur received compensatory land in Sutanuti, and 'Nubkissen' must have started building his *thakur dalan* (hall of the deity or hall of worship) at Shobhabazar well before August 1757.

The southerly location of the new Fort and the shifting of the original population from Gobindapur to Sutanuti reinforced the southward thrust of the more organized part of the city. The original idea, it seems, was to have an enlarged and strengthened version of the former palisaded White Town within the vastly enlarged fortifications. This would enclose all public buildings, but free private settlement – by whites only, of course – was encouraged. The perspective changed with the political situation: by 1780, according to Mrs Fay, 'no person [was being] allowed to reside in Fort William but such as are attached to the Army.' We are here witnessing an unconscious movement towards the plan of the later cantonments all over India, so much a part of the nineteenth-century Raj heritage: in Calcutta, the Maidan, cleared of jungles and hutments, becoming the parade ground – as it

24.2 *The Esplanade. After a painting by T. Allom*

still is – with the 'lines' on one side and officers' bungalows scattered all round it.

The second major change lay in abandoning the old front on the river and taking up a new front facing the land: the south face of the Esplanade, as it then was, running straight from Dharmatala to the river. The most important public buildings and imposing private houses lined the northern side of the Esplanade, facing the Maidan on the south, all looking remarkably Neoclassical with their pillars and pediments. 'Esplanade Row,' wrote Mrs Fay, 'seems to be composed of palaces.'

The inevitable corollary followed: the city turned its back to the north, including Chitpur, Sutanuti and part of Kalikata itself. True, Clive probably had a house (later occupied by Philip Francis and described as the finest house in Bengal) at the site now occupied by the Royal Exchange; the much-married Begum Johnson reigned over the area till her death in 1812; the town house of Warren Hastings was in the older central part of the town at 7 Hastings Street (now Kiranshankar Ray Road); and even in 1780, says Cotton, Tank Square (now B.B.D. Bag) was 'still the centre of fashion'. But the areas to the south of this and to the east along Chourangi were emerging as preferred haunts. At the beginning of this period, there were only two buildings of importance on Chourangi Road; by 1794 there were twenty-four. Simultaneously, the areas around Writers' Buildings as well as Baithakkhana (Boubazar), Dharmatala and Janbazar went down in estimation and were gradually taken over by 'the rest', which included half-castes, Portuguese, Armenians and so on, to become a grey area between the Black and White Towns.

In other words, the eastward thrusts along Dharmatala and Boubazar Streets (Lenin Sarani and B. B. Ganguli Street) were overshadowed by two parallel southward axes, one along present-day Chourangi and Jawaharlal Nehru Roads, the other across the recently-cleared Maidan to Alipur.

The temporarily deposed Mir Jafar took up residence in Alipur in 1760. The property, it is claimed, eventually passed to Warren Hastings, who used it as his country residence. In June 1763, Hastings obtained the Company's permission to build a bridge across 'Collighaut Nullah' to his villa. Philip Francis occupied his 'lodge' nearby, and Colonel Tolly purchased what, after much renovation and alteration, came to be known as the Belvedere, once the residence of the Governor of Bengal and now the National Library.

What we see emerging here is a system of accretion by 'squares' or open spaces: the houses of the well-to-do standing in their own spacious grounds, not interlocking among themselves but connected to the main centre, the Tank Square, by a radial system of shafts or expanses of space and thrusting roads, each having its outer terminal point fixed by geographical barriers. The major new eastward thrust was along the old Burial Ground Road (now Park Street), terminating in the Park Street cemeteries.

South-east of the city proper, Garden Reach – the city's 'oldest and best-known' garden suburb between 1768 and 1780 – stretched along the river bank for two miles. The 'white' character of the suburb changed only after 1856, when Wajid Ali Shah, the deposed Nawab of Awadh, moved with 'his swarm of followers' into the house formerly occupied by Chief Justice Sir Lawrence Peel. 'Nativization' of the locality ruled out planned development for the future.

It is Calcutta's misfortune that the Company squashed Lord Wellesley's grandiose plans, during his Governor-Generalship (1798-1805), for a new Government House at Barrackpur: a grand palace to be set in a park of 250 acres, estimated to cost Rs 34 lakh. Soon afterwards, Wellesley was recalled and the Court of Directors in London scotched the idea. Only the ground floor of the basement storey had been built. If completed, the palace would have

played Versailles to Calcutta's Louvre, the new Government House, and provided a firm terminal point to a highly desirable northward axial thrust to the city's future development.

Wellesley's master plan for the city's development is reported to have included a great avenue linking the palaces, along what is now the Barrackpur Trunk Road. The rich took the hint and started building along the river, then the main approach to Barrackpur, as well as along the projected avenue: at Emerald Bower, acquired and extensively renovated by the Thakurs of Pathuriaghata and now housing the Rabindra Bharati University; the complex now housing the Indian Statistical Institute; Cossipore Club (purchased by the Sheel family from a European lady); Belgachhia Villa, which passed from Lord Auckland to Dwarakanath Thakur and finally to the Sinhas of Paikpara; etc. However, the impetus slackened and finally died out when Shimla replaced Barrackpur as the Viceroy's summer residence in 1864. With the Viceregal touch gone, commerce quickly moved in to fill up the vacuum, and both banks of the river were taken over by the jute industry. The counting house scored over the palace once again.

Architecturally, this period saw the expansion and consolidation of the Baroque Neoclassical style in Calcutta, the seeds of which had been sown in the Governor's House in the old Fort. When the new Fort was being built, a large number of skilled workmen were sent out from England by the Court of Directors. They were often enticed away by private employers at higher wages, despite repeated infructuous prohibitions of the practice. Most of the private employers were undoubtedly in the White Town, but the effect of these workmen's presence must have been considerable even in the Black part. The results can be assessed by analysing individual buildings of both European and Indian affinities.

The most important public buildings of this phase, the old Council House and Government House – the latter rented from the Nawab of Chitpur – were pulled down to accommodate Wellesley's new Government House. But St John's Church, consecrated in 1787, remains. Designed by Lieutenant James Agg of the Bengal Engineers, it followed the prototype of James Gibbs's St Martin-in-the-Fields; but with many modifications, not all of them happy.

The main entrance and porch were transferred to the eastern end. One full tier was left out from the tower supporting the spire, and the other tiers were made flatter. The side porches and carriage-porch, added later in deference to the climate, increased the horizontal spread of the building and further dissipated the steeple's upward thrust.

Other departures are also significant. The order was changed from Corinthian to Tuscan, the plainest and cheapest of the Roman orders: it dominates almost all Calcutta buildings in the eighteenth and early nineteenth centuries. All in all, St John's appears a penny-pinching copy of an opulent model. Agg used Chunar stone for the steeple, and Chunar and other stones for the stairs and floors; but the 'stones of Empire' were commonly brick-and-mortar, in the laudable cause of economy. Probably for the same reason, a part of the stone used to build St John's was obtained by despoiling the ruins of the ancient capital of Bengal at Gour.

Hastings House in Alipur (c. 1776) – probably the house described by Mrs Fay as a 'perfect bijou' – became the prototype of many such 'bungalows', single or double-storeyed, all over the subcontinent. It has a simple arrangement of space: a central hall with two flanking rooms; a carriage-porch; an alignment designed to catch the southern breeze, and a 'verandah to the southward'. Tuscan columns dominate the elevation on the ground floor, and superimposed Ionic columns with plain shafts on the first.

The Government House in Fort William (1773, or 1781 according to Curzon), now called Amherst House, has undergone many changes, but the Palladian temple-front in the north façade is still there. The building establishes many features of standard Calcutta Neoclassic: the three-cube division of the Neo-Palladian front; the central temple part on the first floor, forwards of the other two, and surmounted by a pediment supported by half-columns; the lower storey or basement clearly separated from the top; the large casement windows with double shutters; and the fanlights on windows framed in keystone arches.

In the charming Kitchener House in the Fort, so called now after one of its illustrious past occupants, the idea of the Palladian loggia merges with the functional conception of the Mughal arcaded terrace and the open-on-all-

sides *hawa-khana* (wind-chamber) of western India. The climatically appropriate 'verandah to the southward' here emerges out of the fashionable, but in England functionally useless, Italian loggia. Around this time, terms

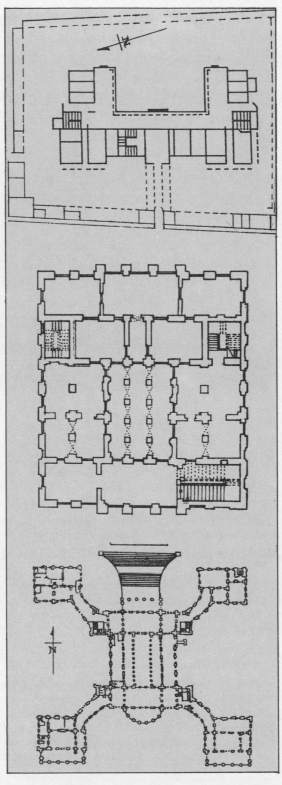

24.3 *Ground plans of three successive Government Houses: (a) in the old Fort; (b) Amherst House in the present Fort William; (c) the present Raj Bhavan*

like *bungalow* and *verandah* emerge, indicating a new Anglo-Indian conception of architecture, despite a surface homage to the fashion at 'home'.

The Baroque-Neoclassical phase culminates in the new Government House of Wellesley (1803: now the Raj Bhavan, residence of the Governor of West Bengal), designed with Kedleston Hall in Derbyshire in mind. The architect-engineer was Captain Charles Wyatt of the Corps of Engineers. The building cost Rs 1,300,000; the original plot of land (about six acres) reportedly Rs 80,000 and the furniture Rs 50,000. Wellesley has been variously called the 'Augustus of Calcutta', the 'Shah Jahan of the Company', 'the last of the Great Mughals', and a 'Sultanized Englishman'. Unfortunately, such lavishness left the Company's Court of Directors aghast; and Wellesley lost his job.

More than anything else, the new Government House was an ocular demonstration of the splendour that could be achieved without expensive stonework. The orders within and without are the simpler ones: Tuscan or Tuscan-Doric and Ionic, dictated perhaps by economy more than by purist severity of taste. Fittingly, the chandeliers were second-hand, from Claude Martin's palace-tomb in Lucknow.

The Government House had a seminal influence in the White as well as the Black Town, despite its plethora of architectural blemishes and debasements: among others, plaster replacing Derbyshire sandstone; the 'four little dingy miserable staircases', as D'Oyly put it, in place of the central grand staircase at Kedleston Hall; the lack of height; and a non-functional dome. It firmly established the concept of the facade, especially one with a pedimented porch. Also, it came to terms with the local climate by providing cross-ventilation through numerous openings in the walls set opposite one another, and a wide colonnaded verandah on the south.

Finally, and most importantly, the Government House authenticated the idea of functionally divided vertical arrangement of space, though combining it with the traditional horizontal spatial spread: a significant step towards urbanization of building style. In colonial Calcutta, the 'garden houses' set in extensive grounds, simulating the manorial life-style at 'home' – an exercise in wish-fulfilment by the burgher class – slowly gave way to a 'vertical living-idiom', as pressure on space increased and the price of land soared. In the specifically Indian context, it led to a gathering together of the sprawling *mahals*, horizontal blocks or units of distinct functions, into a consolidated single-block arrangement of space at different levels. Wyatt's building added a third storey to Kedleston's two. Space was functionally divided among the five component blocks, practically separate houses – a lingering vestige of the *mahal* system; but within the blocks, there was vertical floor-wise division of function. The kitchen, like the stables etc., was outside the palace grounds altogether – 'somewhere in Calcutta', in the vague but ladylike words of Lady Dufferin. (It was actually in Government Place North till Lord Minto's time.)

The ceremonial grand staircase placed outside, ostentatious to a degree, added to the emblematic character of the building and was imitated in many palaces and pseudo-palaces, as were the four Adamitic entrance-screens or gates. The addition of 'verandahs to the southward' indicates recognition of the demands of local weather.

Let us move to the Black Town. The *thakur dalan* of Raja Nabakrishna Deb's mansion at Shobhabazar is held to have been completed in three months with a huge labour force, and Durga Puja performed there with great ceremony in 1757, attended by Clive and others in celebration of the victory at Palashi. Nabakrishna made two houses, one on either side of the road that now bears his name: the earlier, to the north, was left to his adopted son Gopimohan, the other built for himself *c.* 1789 after a son, Rajkrishna, was born to him late in life. The first house eventually passed on to Gopimohan's son Radhakanta, whose additions to the original design will be considered later.

A comparative study of the two houses is rewarding. The old house has two chief parts: the *thakur dalan* facing south and the *nach ghar* (dance room, levée room). It was 'Nubkissen' who introduced the fashion of entertaining Europeans lavishly at Durga Puja. The two portions are linked by double-storeyed wings, forming a rectangular courtyard of impressive proportions (109 by 66 feet).

This introduces to the Black Town the crucial development noted above: the double-storeyed hollow-cube design of consolidated space, the wings incorporating different functions, instead of the traditional sprawling *mahals*. But the concept of the *mahal* lingers, while that of the facade is still absent.

The *thakur dalan* shows little European influence. The compound piers with their cluster of tapering shafts support cusped, slightly ogee arches, topped by a decoration of bouquet motif, long sanctified in Mughal and medieval Bengal temple architecture. Instead of European balusters we have a solid parapet decorated with terracotta plaques, now mostly lost. The wooden arcaded gallery running on brackets or corbels along the sides of the courtyard is again of indigenous inspiration.

The levée room, on the contrary, is entirely Mughal in conception: tapering columns with their cushion base, slightly flared foliated capitals, alcoves in the wall, a round floral design atop ogee arches. The roof collapsed some five years ago; but the intricate stucco-work in the frieze, owing nothing to Adam, still remains. Here is an architectural style as self-conscious as European Neoclassicism: all of one piece, without any trace of the ersatz. The later incongruous additions probably belong to Radhakanta's time.

Developments in the *thakur dalan* in the new house are striking. The cusped arches have become more round. Slender tapered pillars of traditional design still support the imposts; but the patera in the corners above the arches, sanctioned by Mughal usage, are gone. Paired half-columns between the arches support an entablature of classical European origin. The moulding of the cushions is Vitruvian, the acanthus leaves crowning the whole common in Roman Corinthian entablature; but just below is a row of what looks uncommonly like the 'spear-head' design in Islamic architecture. There are many other such amalgamations. The new house signifies a transitional phase in Calcutta's architecture, when Western influence was being gradually absorbed. *See page* 164

The course of this process is clearly charted in the two houses of the Malliks in Darpanarayan Thakur Street. The first, premises no 32, is older, probably dating from the last decades of the eighteenth century. Raja Rajendralal Mallik was born here. The street-front is typically inconspicuous and belies the opulence within. The house is in five *mahals*, strung in a row from front to back, and stylistically allied to the older house at Shobhabazar. What is striking, however, is the 'Adam design' in the frieze of the *thakur dalan* with its wavy lines and central vase, stylistically not incongruous if we ignore the historical anomaly.

The *thakur dalan* of the later house (no 33) is most strikingly innovative. The spatial

24.5 & 24.6
Thakur dalans of Nabakrishna Deb's old (above) and new (below) houses, Raja Nabakrishna Street

arrangement is still the same, the sanctum separated from the open courtyard by an arcade; but the round arches with accentuated moulding encasing a second arch within now speak a different idiom. The piers still have

slender clustered pillars; but these are now straight, with European-style, almost Gothic capitals. An Adam 'shell design' has replaced the traditional bouquet motif on top of the arches. The bases of the columns have mouldings unknown in Rajasthani or Mughal style. The paired columns are Ionic at first-floor level and plainer Tuscan on the ground floor, a 'correct' arrangement which the Neo-Vitruvians could not have faulted. It is fascinating to observe the slow metamorphosis of a traditional style which as yet does not touch the total conceptual design and, particularly, the spatial arrangement. The same stage may be observed in the *thakur dalan* of the Dattas of Hatkhola, of the same period according to family tradition.

As David McCutchion observes in *Late Medieval Temples of Bengal* (1972), many of the eighteenth-century temples of Calcutta have been so modified subsequently that they are of little historical value now. One of the few exceptions is the Shiva temple at Hatkhola. The pillars in the porch, their plaster off, reveal the traditional Bengal bonding with tiles. The dome-construction over the sanctum, borrowed from Islamic architecture, is also typical of the temples of medieval Bengal. It seems the traditional style was still preferred at this stage in temples meant purely for worship; but in *thakur dalans* designed for ostentation and the entertaining of sahibs, the imported idiom

was used, the hallmark of which was the column but not, as yet, pediments.

Similarly, Nawab Muhammad Reza Khan of Chitpur (d. 1798) laid out his house and gardens sumptuously in English style; but the mosque

he built on the northern bank of Chitpur Creek – probably the oldest mosque in Calcutta – is orthodox in concept and design (probably modelled on the Katra Masjid of Murshid Kuli Khan in Murshidabad), with many elements associated with the later Mughal period: a cusped ogee arch, slender tapering Rajasthani-type half-columns flanking arched doors and niches, three onion-shaped domes in a row constricted at the bottom, set on drums to separate them from the cube or rectangle below. Yet where the plaster has crumbled away, one can see that the construction of the arches is round and in the new mode, and the decorative ogee outlines are just plaster. Reza Khan must have employed some of the English workmen brought over to build the new Fort William.

At the end of this phase, then, we see a European style trying to come to terms with the local climate; following assiduously the fashion at 'home' at the lowest possible cost, achieving thereby an effect which is perhaps best described as 'pariah Palladian', while consciously eschewing the indigenous idiom. The Indian styles, on the other hand, were more receptive to the external ornaments of European architecture than to any total conception drawn from it. Indian architecture has always been eclectic in temper, and no breach of decorum was perceived in this. But the new elements were more pronounced in

24.7 & 24.8
Thakur dalans of old (above) and new (below) houses of the Malliks on Darpanarayan Thakur Street

24.9 '*Bengal bonding' from the Hatkhola Shiva Temple*

24.10 *Reza Khan's mosque*

places of public display or reception than in places of private residence or purely religious worship.

Most buildings of the age in the White Town are mere copies, cheap in both senses of the term. But from time to time – most successfully in Nabakrishna's new *thakur dalan,* minus the pillared surround – there is a genuine fusion of styles, whether in delineation of space or use of ornaments. It is at points like this that a new quickening excitement enters the architecture of Calcutta.

1804 to 1863

The beginning of the nineteenth century saw White Calcutta decked in stuccoed couture of classical Baroque or Neo-Palladian inspiration, with an emphasis, perhaps after John Nash, on the designing of the exterior rather than a full treatment of the interior, and an insistence on grandiose facades. Starting at the Esplanade, this architectural scheme for the city's front was pushed westward by the Town Hall, the Government House becoming the centre-piece of the arrangement. (It had not yet been obscured by its screen of trees.)

Appropriately, the Town Hall was designed under Wellesley and completed in 1813 (architect: John Garstin, Colonel of Engineers). In its main (southern) facade, a magnificent flight of steps, inspired by the new Government House next door, leads up to the great hexastyle Palladian portico in the usual Tuscan order. A covered carriage-porch was provided without spoiling the grand effect of the wide staircase, by extending the tall porch at the northern end. This became the standard solution to a weather-problem. Lofty French windows with wooden Venetian shutters provided the necessary ventilation. *(See page 233.)*

The effect consciously aimed at was the monumental and the emblematic. What one misses here is a pediment crowning the porch. The heavy running frieze, the copybook entablature, the by now characteristically Calcuttan row of single-bulb balusters – all emphasize the horizontality of the roof-line, and by contrast the loftiness of the Government House dome, the height of which was tinkered with several times 'to increase the impact of the elevation' (Davies).

The formula of Gibbs, vulgarized in St John's Church, reached its finest moment in Calcutta in St Andrew's Church (1818), the focal point of the newly created vista along Old Court House Street and Red Road, as well as of the older shaft of space along Boubazar (now B.B. Ganguli) Street. This Scottish church particularly wanted a steeple higher than St John's – and achieved it, crowned by a cock 'to crow over' the Anglican Bishop Middleton, who tried to block its creation. But while the church effectively copies the outline of St Martin-in-the-Fields, a closer inspection reveals the plainness of the skimpy structure in brick and plaster, devoid of any textural subtlety and variation, and lacking as usual in the baroque richness of the original. (Funds, as always, were the problem: the Government had to step in with Rs 80,000.) A far better example of the Gibbsian prototype is St Andrew's Church in Madras (1821).

The cenotaph (1817) in St John's Churchyard commemorating the Rohilla War is thought to be based on Sir William Chambers's Temple of Aeolus at Kew, England. Faithful to the design-books, it achieves an effect of order, porportion and poise that makes it perhaps the finest example of Neoclassical style in the city.

Numerous other ill-maintained and weather-beaten examples of Neoclassical funerary architecture can still be seen in the South Park Street Cemetery.

As the century progressed, new European fashions in architecture made themselves felt in Calcutta: the Greek Revival – a stricter form of Neoclassicism shorn of all baroque elements – and the Gothic Revival. Both remained by and large restricted to public buildings in the White Town and outlying white settlements. When the Doric order was tried out in domestic architecture in the Black Town, the effect was often unhappy.

One of the earliest examples of the Greek Revival in Bengal is the external design of the so-called Temple of Fame in Barracpur (1815; architect, George Rodney Bane). A more prominent landmark is the Ochterlony Monument, now Shahid Minar (1828; architect, J. P. Parker). It shows a remarkably successful fusion of different architectural styles and elements: a fluted Doric column, not of strict Vitruvian proportions; a pedestal which has been called 'pure Egyptian'; a metallic cupola hinting at Turkish influence. The two viewing galleries on top and the spiral stairs within leading to them recall the Qutb Minar in

24.11 *Above: St. Andrew's Church*

24.12 *Below: Rohilla War Cenotaph, St. John's Churchyard*

Delhi. The hybridization is so effective that even Cotton did not notice that it was basically a column of classical order, free-standing in the Roman tradition, but with parallels in Ashokan pillars and Egyptian obelisks, set on a pedestal having antecedents in Palladio, with viewing galleries and a *chhatri* added. Set at the south of the Esplanade, the Monument consolidated the centripetal forces that turned the White Town's organized growth inward upon itself, reinforcing the 'White Ghetto' mentality.

At the centre of the city, the finest examples of Greek Revival are the Silver Mint and Metcalfe Hall. Other examples from this period are the Calcutta Madrassa (1824), the Catholic Church in Dumdum, and the original building of the Calcutta Medical College (1852), now under orders of demolition.

The Doric Silver Mint (1831) was designed by Major W. N. Forbes, R.E. The main portico facing the Strand copied in half-size the Temple of Minerva in Athens. The facade is placed against more colonnades. Three successively broader rows of columns in a dipteral arrangement should have given a feeling of airiness; in fact, the massive columns, compressed frieze and unusually weighty abacus leave a heavy impression that is characteristic of Calcutta's

24.13 The Ochterlony Monument, now Shahid Minar

Greek Revival. We may compare the use of 'even heavier forms' (Nilssen) of the Doric order in the Catholic Church at Dumdum (commenced 1822).

In the square Mint building with a central court, the idea of a large hollow single-block structure seems to take a definite shape. The arrangement of internal space is remarkable: a downward vertical growth, with rooms as deep as 26 feet. The building lacks the eminent location such a structure demands, and the view from the river (which has moved farther west) is blocked today by the unsightly Posta Bazar.

Metcalfe Hall (1844; architect, C. K. Robinson) copies the order of the Temple of Winds in Athens. (So does the Cossipore Club.) More fortunately located than the Silver Mint, Metcalfe Hall still has an imposing presence, helped by the ten-foot-high ornamental podium – now, alas, hidden by a protective wall. Typically, the peristyle was left incomplete because of the paucity of funds.

The earliest Gothic building in Calcutta is St Peter's Church in Fort William (1835), now housing the Fort Library. It looks pleasant enough from a distance, and was obviously considered good enough for the troops in the tropics, though it is doubtful whether Ruskin would have approved of it. It is interesting to observe, however, how the carriage-porch has been incorporated in the imitation-Gothic scheme. This is also a conspicuous feature of St Paul's Cathedral (1847; architect, Major (later General) W. N. Forbes of Bengal Engineers; construction by Mackintosh Burn). Cotton's words aptly describe such buildings: ' "Indo-Gothic", that is to say, spurious Gothic adapted to the exigencies of the Indian climate'. Again, in St. Paul's the climate had primacy over stylistic decorum; for when seen from the road, the western porch hides the view of the west window by Burne-Jones, the Cathedral's chief glory.

Neither the Greek nor the Gothic truly interacted with Indian building traditions. The Gothic in particular denied the vital climatic advantage of a flat roof. And preference in the Black Town was emphatically in favour of Baroque classicism rather than the stricter classicism of the Greek Revival.

A number of temples have survived from this period to show how temple architecture in Bengal was reacting to the various imported building styles. Of the temples of the Ghosh family in Tollyganj, the earliest dates from *c.* 1788 and the largest, founded by Baburam Ghosh, from *c.* 1807. The basic details of the *atchala* construction are the same, but the terracotta work has deteriorated over the twenty years. This agrees with McCutchion's postulation of a decline in temple terracotta art after 1770.

Though the *atchala* design continued right up to the 1930s, plaster and moulding, or occasionally coloured tiles with floral and other decorative motifs, gradually replaced terracotta ornamentation and treatment of surface. In the later temples, even the traditional narrow entrance-porch was replaced by a wide verandah, perhaps modelled on the lavish *thakur dalans* in rich men's houses.

The renovated *nabaratna* temple of the Mandal family in Chetla is the largest and most important temple of this type in south Calcutta, its counterpart in the north being Dakshineshwar temple constructed by Mackintosh Burn. A detailed study should be most revealing of the interaction of European and indigenous building modes at Dakshineshwar. The date of the Chetla temple is uncertain: an old date-plaque gives Saka 1718 (A.D. *c.*1796), with a postscript dated 1731 (A.D. *c.*1809). Its form

remains traditional and the proportions are noble; but plaster and stucco have replaced terracotta – perhaps through later renovation – in the treatment of the surface. The traditional polygonal design of the pillars of the entry-porch has been replaced with tapered round Western-Indian-type columns – a common feature in Calcutta after Nabakrishna's *thakur dalan* and dance hall – set, however, not in clusters but in pairs.

Above
24.14 *Cossipore Club*

24.15 *Left: Prince Ghulam Muhammad's mosque, Tollyganj*

24.16 *Right: St. Peter's Church, Fort William*

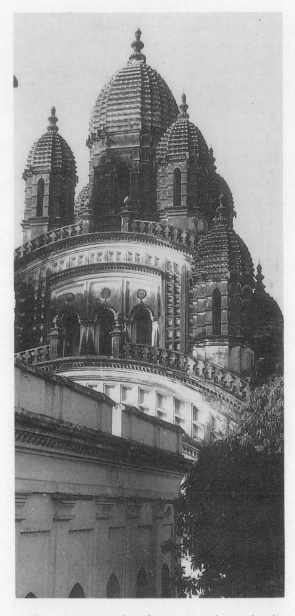

24.17 *Above: The Nabaratna temple of the Mandal family, Chetla*

24.18 *Below: Terracotta from a temple of the Ghosh family of Tollyganj, c. 1788*

subsequent repairs.) The *nat mandap* in front – undoubtedly of much later date – uses round arches and vulgarized Tuscan-Doric columns.

What we are witnessing is not a successful hybridization but the contamination of a traditional style. Because of the medium, plaster and stucco, orders and ornaments can be changed easily. The columns of the *nat mandap* in the Chetla temple sported the Ionic order even twenty-five years ago; it has since been altered to a very plain Tuscan, supporting a flat roof with no pretensions to a classical entablature. The change was dictated by cost. The Hon'ble Company's Directors would have approved.

There are surprisingly few architecturally interesting mosques dating from this period. The two built by Prince Ghulam Muhammad, at Tollyganj (c.1830) and Esplanade (1842), therefore deserve special attention. The interaction of the imported and the indigenous styles is clearly marked, not to the latter's advantage. The Palladian 'Serliana' (an archway or window with three openings, the central one arched and wider than the others); the doors topped by fan-lights designed in stucco; the round arches; the half-columns in the Tuscan order; the entablature with its acanthus-leaf motif – these are straight from European practice. It is in the upper part, in the octagonal minars arranged round ten domes (not the traditional three), arranged in two rows of five each, the Indo-Islamic *chhajja* (overhanging cornice or eave) and the *guldasta* (a small turret-like construction) that the Islamic touch continues. Even here, the recesses on the minars use Gothic, not Islamic pointed arches.

The colonial culture thus resulted in a quick degeneration of the indigenous religious building styles, both Hindu and Muslim. In the case of Hindu religious architecture, a new hybridized form appears on the scene: the *thakur dalans* with a court, required by the 'Babu Culture' for display of wealth and pomp at festivals.

The main building activity now moves in a new direction, towards a city of 'palaces' – that is, residential mansions of the rich. The impact of British culture replaced the tradition of Indian and Indo-Islamic religious architecture by a new idea of secular urban civic architecture.

The Lottery Commission (1814) and its successors the Lottery Committee (1817) and Fever Hospital Committee (1836) opened up

The transitional phase is also clearly demonstrated in the temples at· Barisha (c.1809), where the surviving traces of terracotta decoration illustrate the middle stage of the decline of terracotta work in Bengal temples. Careful restoration may allow more precise conclusions.

The Kalighat temple, of *atchala* design (1809), much restored in later years, shows a different conception of surface decoration emerging: it now has coloured tiles of floral or geometric design throughout, though there might have been terracotta tiles earlier. Also interesting here is the use of dentition as an ornament under the eaves. The ogee arch has given way to the round arch. (This too may be owing to

the Black Town and hence stimulated its architectural expansion. The inspiration was Wellesley's, in his famous Minute of 1803. The main axial thrusts created by the new roads were from south to north, parallel to the existing Chitpur-Chourangi alignment and the newly metalled Circular Road. The Strand Road, completed in 1828 on land reclaimed from the river and not yet disfigured by warehouses, saw some of the most prestigious new public buildings of the period: Metcalfe Hall, the Silver Mint and Prinsep's Ghat (1848), as well as the Bank of Bengal building.

The most important achievement of the planners was the axial thoroughfare from south to north along Wood Street, Wellesley Street (now Rafi Ahmed Kidwai Road), Wellington Street (now Nirmal Chandra Street), College Street and Cornwallis Street (now Bidhan Sarani). The third partial parallel thrown out, farther east, was Amherst Street (completed *c*.1824; now Raja Rammohan Sarani). This central axis met the Circular Road where the old Dumdum-Murshidabad Road and the alignment of Wellesley's new avenue to Barrackpur also converged, at the present Shyambazar crossing.

It was along these new avenues, flanked by squares and freshly excavated tanks, away from the garden-suburbs of Chourangi and Alipur, that Calcutta's urbanization now progressed without the dubious benefit of the guidance of military engineers. Planned urban growth for the entire city seemed realizable at last: but sadly, this was not to be.

Raja Radhakanta Deb's additions to his ancestral house reflect the spirit of change. Either Radhakanta or his father superimposed upon Nabakrishna's *nach ghar* the Palladian scheme of a loggia in the Tuscan order on the first floor and round arches on the weight-bearing ground floor. The plastered terracotta lions flanking the gate are unintended caricatures of the animals guarding Wyatt's new Government House. Gateways were becoming status symbols; unfortunately, here it had to be squeezed in at a right angle to the house. The building is now crumbling; the portion to give way first was the loggia, showing that the columns were not integral parts of the main structure.

An even more glaring example of architectural solecism is provided by Radhakanta's *nabaratna* temple, tucked away

behind a flat-roofed parapeted *natmandap* or reception hall of classical style, sporting a tetrastyle carriage-porch in the Tuscan order. In Nabakrishna's buildings, the *thakur dalans* had been the centres of focus. The Palladian stucco fanlight designs on the *natmandap* doors – among the earliest examples in Calcutta – were later used extensively. The main tower of the temple is gone; the small surviving towers are traditional in form, but their openings are pure Queen Anne. The whole construction vividly illustrates the suppression of an indigenous idiom by an exotic secular civic style.

In Rajendralal Mallik's Marble Palace (begun 1835), the new ideas seen in Radhakanta's temple crystallize further. The idea of the facade is established once and for all. The Palladian formula of the new Government House is ignored. The break with convention is clear in the use of elaborate Rococo stucco work and the Corinthian order. The architect, according to family tradition, was a Frenchman. The construction was by Mackintosh Burn.

The main building complex consists of two functionally separate squarish compact blocks, each with a central court. The first one, facing the road, develops the idea embedded in Radhakanta's *mandap*. Its intended function was entirely public: to house a collection of art objects for display. The *mandap* within faces west rather than south as ritual demanded, because the building plan had to be reoriented after failure to obtain a frontage on Chitpur Road. Hence the *mandap* is not actually used for pujas, though the image of Jagannath, the family deity, is brought there on certain days of the year. But the deity's own temple is extremely modest, without a *mahal* or court of its own, set in a corner of the grounds. In the older family complex in Darpanarayan Thakur Street, Jagannath has a regular *dalan* with a separate court.

The second block lies immediately behind the first, and is vertically designed according to function: the upper floor is the family residence, with a shrine for private worship, while the ground floor houses the kitchen, community dining hall, servants' rooms etc. Hence the Marble Palace provides one of the earliest examples of the new direction which Calcutta's buildings have already been seen to take: compact, usually rectangular residential houses, divided vertically by function, around a

24.19 *Atchala temple of the Ghosh family at Tollyganj*

171

central courtyard; of palatial proportions, and with suitable ornamentation when funds permit.

Instead of the hollow square round a courtyard we sometimes find a more compact block, as in the rather unattractive example of Raja Rammohan Ray's son's house (*c.* 1856) on Amherst Street, with its barrack-like row of rooms, all facade and no body. There is a pedimented verandah on the first floor; but the grouping of the columns is clumsy, and the total effect is of a conscious imitation of the outer trappings of a foreign style.

1864 to 1903

1864 saw the formal inauguration of Shimla as the summer seat of the Imperial Government.

Till then Barrackpur had served as the summer residence of the Viceroy. In 1864, almost symbolically, the trees lining the road to Barrackpur were devastated by a storm. The decline of Calcutta's position in the national scheme of things began at this time.

To this period belong two important examples of Gothic Revival in the city: the High Court (1864–72; architect, Walter Granville), inspired by the Town Hall at Ypres, and the new Municipal Market (Sir S.S. Hogg Market, 1874), supposedly in Moorish-Gothic style. Wooden *jhilmils*, lack of height, an insignificant clock-tower, and a flimsy carriage-porch, all combine in the market building to create an effect as un-Gothic as possible.

One laudable feature of the High Court is the extensive use of stone, particularly in the richly carved capitals, which preserves more of the spirit of the Gothic Revival than any of the churches in Calcutta in the same style. Despite its stumpy tower, this is perhaps the only Neo-Gothic building in Calcutta worth serious notice at all.

One of the most important buildings of the Greek Revival, the University Senate House (architect, Walter Granville) also belongs to this period (1873; pulled down in 1961). It was a stately peripteral building with a Palladian hexastyle portico, and used the Ionic order. In the true spirit of the Greek Revival, the entablature had few ornaments, and the frieze was plain. The flat roof had a solid parapet interspersed with antifixa.

The Neoclassical or Georgian character of the White Town undergoes a qualitative change during this period. The houses on Esplanade East gradually shed their columns and put on a new make-up; the Neo-Palladian face of Esplanade West is drastically altered by the Neo-Gothic High Court, as well as the eclectic new red-brick Treasury Building and Imperial Secretariat, which use ornaments from the Italian Renaissance. The Government House itself slowly disappears behind its screen of tall trees. Writers' Buildings acquires a new eclectic façade (1882) using the Corinthian order and combining a hexastyle pedimented dummy porch at the first floor level with the ornamented red-brick style of the Government buildings of the period. Baroque statuary is introduced on top. The new facade of Writers' Buildings links up visually with the front porch of the Government House along the shaft of

24.20 *Calcutta High Court*

space from the latter down Wellesley Place (now Red Cross Place) and across the Great Tank: a deliberate piece of town planning, now frustrated by the construction of the Telephone Bhavan. The façade of the Government House was also reflected in the three separate Palladian hexastyle pedimented porticos which Writers' Buildings had acquired by 1832.

The construction of public offices gave the central part of the city a new, unmistakably Victorian look. The chief among these buildings were the Treasury Building and Imperial Secretariat next to the Government House – the most opulent of them all, barring the new façade of Writers' Buildings; the Central Telegraph Office in Wellesley Place (commenced 1873); the Surveyor-General's office in Wood

naissance ornaments, showing a typical preference for 'bright colours, contrasted materials, and coarse strong sculptural shapes' (Peter Kidson *et al*, *A History of English Architecture*, 1962), with a marked predilection for Italian styles and motifs.

Some prominent public buildings of the time, however, stick to classicism. The Small Causes Court or Bankshall Court (partially completed in 1879; architect, W. M. White) has been called 'French Palladian seen through Victorian eyes'. Walter Granville's GPO (1864–68, constructed by Mackintosh Burn) in the classical style combines a Renaissance dome with a Corinthian colonnade punctuated with rusticated pylons, and a Baroque outline. Granville's Indian Museum (1875) with its

Street (the 1880s); the East Indian Railway's office in Kailaghat Street (1882-84); and, the culmination of the style, the Calcutta Collectorate (1890). The main surface decoration and variation in texture were achieved by the use of moulded tiles.

The diversity of architectural styles in Victorian England cannot be put under strict period labels. Eclectic methods were taught in the Royal Academy as early as the eighteenth century. Some official buildings of Calcutta sought to achieve a stylistic unity by embellishing frankly red-brick buildings with Re-

monumental façade and vast courtyard lined with galleries and niches in the outer walls, reminds one of the Roman heritage of Classicism. The Renaissance Italianate style is especially noticeable in the Returned Letter Office (1874), complete with campanile.

The Indo-Islamic style suffered from the impact of this spurt of building activity in the White Town. No mosque of any importance was built during these years, and the Madrassa made by Prince Ghulam Muhammad's descendant Prince Rahimuddin in 1865 shows a disconcerting readiness to compromise in style.

24.21 Treasury Building, Council House Street

24.22 *The General Post Office (centre) and Collectorate (right)*

24.23 *Some late Calcutta capitals' stucco work*

The tradition of Bengal temple architecture becomes so debased that only the outer shell, the outline of the *atchala,* is retained in the insignificant little shrines built during these years.

But while the new influences suppressed what was best in local tradition, it also released new forces and created new classes with new aspirations which found expression in urban domestic architecture as distinct from the villa or bungalow. Historians from Bernier to Abdul Haleém 'Sharar' have agreed that under the Mughals, displaying one's wealth was considered imprudent. The British, by guaranteeing the right to private property – at least to their collaborators – released a new urge to flaunt wealth, and set new norms for the standard of living. Perhaps for the first time in Bengal, domestic architecture became a status symbol. It also achieved fully the structural integration begun earlier, a single unified architectural presence marshalled behind a planned facade and divided vertically by function.

The typical products of this efflorescence are on the new roads: Amherst Street and Cornwallis Street (now Rammohan and Bidhan Sarani respectively) and their surrounds. Representative examples are the palaces of the Lahas, the freakish 'Tagore Castle' off old Chitpur, and the Jhamapukur Rajbati off Amherst Street. The trend culminates in Burdwan (Bardhaman)

House in Alipur (1903): 'Gothic, Corinthian, Colonial and Mackintosh Burn,' as Desmond Doig put it in *Calcutta: An Artist's Impression.*

Unbridled eclecticism is the only principle that holds these edifices together. Architecturally, they are not great or even significant; but they have charm, and present the idea of a life-style India had not known before. Despite their jumble of Western ornaments, these buildings are Calcutta's own, and set the pattern or formula for future constructions. Intricate stucco work, especially in surface decoration, probably an inheritance from Wajid Ali Shah's Metiabruz; a marked preference for the ornate; extensive use of the flamboyant Corinthian order in stucco; mouldings, often of mixed character; ornaments copied from everywhere without any consciousness of solecism: these mark the important buildings of the period in the Black Town, and the guiding spirit behind it all was Mackintosh, Burn and Company, architects and civil engineers, the acknowledged purveyors of off-the-peg splendour.

The real hybridization takes place around the thirties of the present century in the houses in and around the newly-made Central Avenue (now Chittaranjan Avenue) and Vivekananda Road, where we have verticality dressed in *jaffrey* work, so suited to the climate, and pointed with Western ornaments, yet achieving

24.24 *177A*
Chittaranjan
Avenue: the last
phase of Barabazar
architecture

n effect which is entirely Indian. Many of the
ouses on Central Avenue (constructed 1912-
4) carry on the tradition of frenetic eclecticism
en in Pareshnath Temple (1867) and the
urdwan Raj Palace in Alipur, using for
xternal decoration elaborate and heavy Baro-
ue ornaments in plaster, including plaster
opies of curtained opera boxes.

But gradually, as on Vivekananda Road
completed 1928), a different kind of architec-
ural composition emerges. The problem of
weather – fierce wind and rain, strong sun –
which the colonnaded loggias created, and
which was sought to be solved with wooden
jhilmils shutting off most of the opening (sometimes completely enclosing a verandah and
making a room out of it), is now resolved by
the use of extensive *jaffrey* work of intricate
design in plaster on iron frame. Without the
openings, the columns lose their importance.

Calcutta buildings now acquire a new texture. Buildings no longer try to stand in their
own ground; the last vestige of the 'garden
house' syndrome is shed; separate gates or
entrance screens are out, as the ground to
accommodate them is no longer affordable.
There is a reversion to the old Calcutta design
of a narrow entrance leading to a central
courtyard. Several courtyards, as in the *mahal*
system, are replaced by a vertical growth, now
often of four storeys. The arrangement of
rooms remains, as always, simple: a single row
of rooms around a central court with a surrounding gallery or verandah to ensure max-
imum cross-ventilation. The *jaffrey* work outside combined ventilation with protection from

sun and rain, and allowed privacy: a move
away from the view of private residences as
status symbols, and towards a functional,
vertically arranged, introverted use of space.

It is in these buildings that Calcutta Baroque
finally comes into its own, shuffling off its
colonial bondage. But that was after a new
rising class of vigorous rustic stock, unencum-
bered by the old pretensions or the urge to keep
up with Their Excellencies the Joneses, had
taken over the city from the Babus of comprador Calcutta.

THE MARBLE PALACE

Jaya Chaliha and Bunny Gupta

In the mid-nineteenth century, three merchant-philanthropists of the Subarnabanik community pledged their wealth to the people of Calcutta. Motilal Sheel (1792-1854) endowed a free college. Sagarlal Datta (1821?-86?) built a charitable dispensary and hospital at Kamarhati. Both their dreams have sadly faded; but Rajendralal Mallik's (1819-87) dedication to the arts and to feeding the hungry has left a lasting legacy. The Trust he set up is still ably managed by his descendants. His art gallery is open to the public free of charge; and 500 poor people are fed every day.

Rajendra was the adopted son of Nilmani Mallik of Pathuriaghata. The Malliks were an established family of bullion merchants whose wealth lay in the maritime trade in silver, gold and sugar. Nilmani died when Rajendra was only three. His widowed mother moved with him from Pathuriaghata to Chorbagan, where his philanthropic father had his *thakurbari* or place of worship and a permanent kitchen for feeding the poor.

Because of litigation over the inheritance, Rajendra became a Ward of Court. The Supreme Court appointed James Weir Hogg his guardian. Rajendra's pious mother and Hogg guided their ward to become one of the most remarkable men the city has ever known.

A student of Hindu College, Rajendra's chief interests were natural history and the arts, both Western and Oriental. He was musically inclined; the hymns he composed were occasionally sung in his *thakurbari*. He also continued, and enlarged, the paternal tradition of philanthropy. His relief efforts during the famine of 1865-66 earned him the title of Rai Bahadur; and in 1878, Lord Lytton endowed him with the title of Raja, along with the ceremonial gift of a large diamond ring.

None of these achievements was unique among the aristocratic Bengalis of the day, though seldom were they combined on this scale by one man. Rajendra's distinction lay in building a lasting edifice to embody all his interests and ideals. His Palace to the Arts at Chorbagan was commenced when he was sixteen. It was completed in about five years, and named the Marble Palace by the Viceroy Lord Minto when he visited it early this century.

Rajendra is said to have personally directed the 500 artisans, both Indian and foreign, who executed the plan. The architecture is a mixture of exuberant Rococo and the three European classical styles, imposed on the oriental quadrangle pattern of introverted space. This became the model for many contemporary mansions. But Rajendra's remains the only well-maintained edifice of its kind, one of the last true palaces left in the erstwhile City of Palaces.

Part of the extensive Baroque garden was devoted to a menagerie of rare birds and imals, Calcutta's first zoo. The Raja also sent animals and birds to various zoos in Europe: the Zoological Society of London awarded him a medal for introducing the Himalayan Pheasant to England. The tradition carries on. A black buck, spotted deer, monkeys, and birds still occupy the cages, although import restrictions have ended the exchange of animals with foreign zoos.

The menagerie spills over into the palace itself. From a corner of the wide verandah around the open courtyard, an aviary of cockatoos, hyacinthine macaws, mynahs and an albino crow sends sounds of life to the art galleries within, while a wayward pelican waddles in from the tank outside.

We enter the palace through a long colonnaded carriage-porch into the billiard room. This is the visitor's introduction to a kaleidoscope of marbles on floors, walls and table-tops through the museum. Rajendra

Mallik himself designed the floor of the reception hall, a combination of multi-coloured marbles patterned to render carpeting redundant. The etched Venetian glass panes on the doors afford a view of the green lawn where sarus cranes and white peacocks strut between marble lions and statues. Ravi Shankar played in this hall at a specially arranged musical soiree, amid marble and bronze statuary, while incense from the enormous Chinese burner filled the air with fragrance.

On an earlier evening, in 1858, a thousand and one candles glowed in the Venetian chandeliers on the upper storey as wigged and powdered gentlemen led their crinolined partners to a quadrille down the length of the ballroom. On either side, the gilt-framed Belgian mirrors from floor to ceiling created a million parallaxes. The red carpet is now rolled up. The floor has been re-set with green and white marble tiles, laid by the present

25.1 *The Marble Palace*

25.2 The young Victoria: rosewood statue by Benjamin in the Marble Palace. Sketch by Desmond Doig

generation of Malliks. The sunlight falls through the translucent alabaster sea-horses atop a pair of tall vases, to settle on the dust-covered period settees and whispering chairs.

For most Calcuttans, the Palace affords their only chance to view the art forms of Europe. A rosewood Queen Victoria stands larger than life beneath a Florentine ceiling in the red-veined marble room named after her. A delightful pair of children carved in wood by Grinling Gibbons ride on goats beside the Grecian pillars in green marble flanking the arched doorways. The largest Chinese vase in India sits on the floor.

In the face of criticism, Rajendra Mallik placed figures from the Greek and Roman pantheon in the *thakur dalan* or house of worship. In the niches on the wall behind, figures from the *Ramayana* and more recently the *Mahabharata* stand in happy harmony. Paintings of the Italian, Flemish, Dutch and English Schools cover every inch of wall space.

The paintings of two Indian painters i[n] particular, Shashi Hesh and Bijay Chandra have also been prominently displayed. At th[e] head of the southern staircase, the Raja himsel[f] presides, painted in oils by Chinhing, a Chines[e] artist and protégé of the Raja.

The norms of modern museums do not apply to the Marble Palace. Air-conditioning would not only be out of the question but, the family feels, unnecessary. Ventilation and lighting in each room have been planned according to the exhibits housed there.

The Rubens Room is the only one to present the modern concept of uncluttered exhibition. Connoisseurs, scholars and students come to see the enormous 'Marriage of St Catherine' by Rubens and 'Child Hercules and the Serpents' by Sir Joshua Reynolds. This gallery has recently been renovated. The mosaic inlay on the walls has been refurbished, original frames repaired and re-touched, and the paintings cleaned and preserved according to family formulae.

A member of the Asiatic Society and a trustee of the Indian Museum, the Raja held meetings in the Durbar or Meeting Hall. Cultural meetings continue to be held in this room, where Landseer's 'Shoeing of the Bay Mare' hangs half-hidden. 'This is inevitable,' says Hirendra, a sixth-generation Mallik who has carefully catalogued the contents of the Palace. 'Six such palaces would not be adequate to display to advantage the family's art treasures.' As housed at present, there is careless profusion in the display, at times almost a heedless and undiscriminating bounty. But everything in this amazing collection, hidden down a narrow street in old Calcutta, calls for awe and not flippant criticism.

Not mere dilettantes, each succeeding generation of Malliks has produced creative artists and conservationists. On museum holidays, a Mallik nephew plays the piano while a grandchild feeds the birds and an uncle paints in a quiet corner of the garden. And so the heritage of Rajendra Mallik is carried on.

MUSIC IN
OLD CALCUTTA

Rajyeshwar Mitra

Even before the foundation of the British city of Calcutta, the old villages on its site – Sutanuti and Gobindapur in particular – were established settlements and trading centres. They undoubtedly shared in the general culture of contemporary Bengal. It is necessary to grasp this background in order to understand the development of music in old Calcutta.

From the days of the Delhi Sultanate, imperial control over Bengal was commonly lax, owing to its remoteness from the capital. This measure of political and administrative freedom helped to preserve a distinct cultural entity as well. Right through the period of Muslim rule, Bengal retained the remnants of Hindu traditions fostered by the Pala and Sena dynasties. Hence, while western and northern India were being initiated into various new types of melodies and musical patterns – which came to constitute the noble tradition of North Indian classical or raga music – these were practised in Bengal only within a limited circle. The generality of people enjoyed various forms of indigenous and folk music which were not classical or raga-based.

These forms, technically known as *Prabandha* songs, existed in many varieties all over India. There were important versions in Bengali and Maithili as well. It was Jaideb who, in the twelfth century, first made a significant departure from these traditions by devising an original style of music for the lyrics of his *Gita Govinda*. He employed several ragas and va-

rious measures (*talas*): although highly sophisticated, they proved immensely popular, influencing musical composition even up to the eighteenth century. It was only in that century that a great new upsurge of creativity brought out radical innovations in the music of Bengal.

After Jaideb, the other important personality was Vidyapati of Mithila (born c.1374). He created the *Padabali* songs, composed in his own Maithili language and set to raga music. Hence the reliance on Sanskrit was relaxed, and raga-based songs came to be composed in the new vernaculars.

Maithili *Padabali* songs became highly popular in Bengal, where Vaishnav lyricists arose to carry on Vidyapati's tradition. Narottam Das founded the classical *Padabali Kirtan* after Chaitanya's death in the sixteenth century, and chose *Padabali* songs for his recital at the Vaishnav festival he instituted at Kheturi, the village of his birth. This tradition continued for centuries after Narottam, during the period of the settlement of Calcutta.

Bengal entered the mainstream of Hindustani raga music during the cultural upsurge of Akbar's reign (1556-1605). This was when the musicians and intellectuals of Bengal invited North Indian masters to their province, or made trips to North India themselves, to imbibe the forms of raga music like *Dhrupad*, *Dhamar* or *Khayal*. But such contact was limited by the difficulty of travel to North India and the absence of adequate patronage in

26.1 *A group of musicians. Mrs Belnos*

180

Bengal. One important centre was the court of the Rajas of Bishnupur. The 'Bishnupur *Gharana*' reached Calcutta in the nineteenth century through maestros like Kshetramohan Goswami (1813?-93) and Jadunath Bhattacharya.

But meanwhile, musical culture had sprung up in the newly-founded but already prosperous city of Calcutta. The wealthy residents of the city and its neighbouring districts patronized music along with other forms of culture; the musicians too refurbished their old practices and conventions to please this new clientele. Thus a distinctive musical culture began to grow up in the city in the eighteenth century. This may be divided into three classes: religious, social and purely entertaining.

At the end of the seventeenth century, music was incorporated with the *Kathakatas* and the *Mangalkabyas* or mythological poems in praise of gods and goddesses. *Kathakata* was a form of rhetorical narration and exposition of the Puranas or old epics, interspersed with songs. These songs were not of a high order, but usually adequate to the basic demand of the melodic structure. Later they grew more sophisticated, even incorporating *Tappas* (to be explained later) of a high order, as in the creations of Shridhar Kathak of the nineteenth century.

We should not forget the early audience for such songs: migrants newly arrived from the villages and keeping up something of their rural community life. It was only some decades later that new norms and patterns evolved, to meet new sophisticated demands from a truly urban population.

Initially, musicians came from the traditional rural schools: Vaishnav *Kirtan* singers from Murshidabad, Birbhum and Bardhaman, exponents of *Kheurs* (a type of love song) from Shantipur and Nadia, and Shakta singers from all over the state, who presented the compositions of Ramprasad Sen (c.1720-1781) and Kamalakanta Bhattacharya (c.1772-1821). At first they rendered these songs in conventional style. This was gradually modified to please the new generation, as evinced by the introduction of lighter *Kirtans* and, later, the stylized *Dhap Kirtans* of Madhusudan Kinnar (c.1813-68), popularly known as Madhu Kan. The songs of the old *jatra* or rural theatre also underwent modification. This is seen in the Krishna-*jatras* of Gobinda Adhikari (c.1800-72) and the plays of Nilkantha Mukherji (1841-1912).

But these were modifications of traditional forms. Entirely new forms also came into existence. The most novel was the *Kabi* song, an important new social entertainment that sprang up in Calcutta. The *Kabi* song was a long lyric on a mythical subject, partly recited and partly sung. One *kabial* would confront

another, the two composing parallel lyrics to carry on a kind of debate. The points made by the first would be challenged by his adversary, often leading to hot words and sometimes to bitterly acrimonious duels.

Although the products of the *kabials* were undoubtedly a species of song, they depended for their success chiefly on poetical or verbal talents of improvisation and rejoinder. But in between the long poetical duels came some portions rendered into beautiful song, coming under the category of *baithaki* music or concert recitals. Celebrated *kabials* like Rasu Nrisingha (1728?-1800?), Haru Thakur (1738-1813), Ram Basu (1786-1828), Bholanath Modak or Bhola Maira ('Bhola the Confectioner', 1778?-1851?), and the Portuguese-born Antonio Cabral ('Anthony Phiringi' or 'Anthony the European', ?-1836) are still remembered for these interludes in their long and otherwise unpolished lyrics.

Kabi songs were followed by the *Panchali,* whose closest predecessor was the *Kathakata.* But whereas the *Kathakata* was basically a prose narrative, the *Panchali* was composed in verse, with sporadic songs sung by trained singers. As with the *Kathakata,* mythological subjects formed the staple of the *Panchali;* but important social issues and events could also be treated, generally in simplified or even unsavoury form.

Dasharathi Ray (1806-57), the famous *Panchali* composer, even carried on a vilifying attack on Ishwarchandra Vidyasagar over the latter's campaign for widow remarriage.

But the most remarkable musical development in old Calcutta was the rise of the *Tappa* in the late eighteenth century under the genius of Ramnidhi Gupta or 'Nidhu Babu' (1741-1839), revered as the father of lyric song in modern Bengal. He was a resident of Kumartuli, near the very point of Sutanuti where Charnock is said to have landed in 1690. Ramnidhi was a well-educated young man, in Sanskrit, Persian and even English; but the source of his musical training remains untraced. What is known is that he was already an accomplished singer and composer by the age of thirty-five, when he left to take up a post in the Collectorate at Chhapra, Bihar. He remained there for eighteen years.

Chhapra was a lively musical centre. Ramnidhi had the opportunity of improving his range in classical music under notable *ustads.* In particular, he became a master of *Tappa,* a popular form in those days. *Tappas* were composed in Punjabi. It struck Nidhu Babu that if the form were to be recreated in Bengali, it would be an immense benefit to the music of his own region. This was his sole occupation after retirement, when he spent forty-five

26.2 *Musical recitation of the Ramayana (Ramayan-gan). Solvyns*

181

26.3 *Left:*
Atulprasad Sen

26.4 *Right:*
Lakshmiprasad
Mishra

productive years back in his old house at Sutanuti, dying at the ripe age of ninety-eight. His mental alertness in his last days is attested by the beautiful Brahma Sangeet *Param Brahma tatparatpar* that he composed shortly before his death at the special request of Raja Rammohan Ray.

Nidhu Babu's *Tappa* and *Khayal* were not only of the highest order musically: they also provided fine specimens of poetry. Above all, he showed remarkable modernity in that age, so that his influence reigned over composers for a century after his death. We should also remember his contemporaries Radhamohan Sen (fl.1818-39) and Kalidas Chatterji, known from his command of Persian as 'Kali Mirza' (1750?-1820?): notable creators of *Tappa,* though Nidhu Babu was its chief architect.

Besides *Tappa,* Nidhu Babu also established the *Akhrai* song, in which he introduced an orchestra: this was probably the first time the violin was used in North Indian music. But the *Akhrai* proper proved too highbrow for general acceptance: it yielded to the '*Half Akhrai*', devised by Nidhu Babu's own disciple Mohanchand Basu of Bagbazar. Mohanchand lightened the tone of *Akhrai* by introducing the type of love song called *Kheur* at the end. But even the *Half Akhrai* did not last long, for want of efficient exponents. It went out of fashion in the mid-nineteenth century, when the taste turned to newer fashions.

The *Tappa* assumed special importance in the music of Bengal by its distinctive development there, which exercised an influence on the rest of the country. But there were various other lighter styles to evoke sheer pleasurable responses in the audience. We may particularly mention the innumerable songs that enriched the *jatra* or popular theatre of the day, above all the '*Ar Khemta*' type of song immortalized in the jatra *Bidyasundar* by the great Gopal Urey (Oriya). These were remembered long after their time: even Rabindranath Thakur's music owed greatly to *Tappa* and other traditional forms.

But amid this amorous exuberance, Raja Rammohan Ray introduced a strain of piety and sobriety in the notable body of *Brahma Sangeet*, the devotional songs of the Brahmo Samaj. Some of the earliest were composed by Rammohan himself. Brahma Sangeet was sung by established singers appointed by the Brahmo Samaj, and became popular with the more

intellectual and refined class of society. The words were not always remarkable; but the raga music to which they were set elevated the taste of the musical public, and still remains memorable by its chaste and distinguished level of composition.

The higher reaches of classical music did not, of course, remain inaccessible to Calcuttans. Nawab Wajid Ali Shah of Lucknow was brought to Calcutta in 1857 and remained at Metiabruz as an august prisoner till his death in 1887. He was a noted patron of classical music: the *Thumri* was evolved at his court. *Ustads* from all over India came to Calcutta to woo his patronage, which would assist their all-India reputation. Their presence generated a wider interest in raga music in Calcutta. Local singers devoted to raga music gained from the presence of these *ustads*, becoming their disciples and cultivating their music in a wider perspective than was earlier possible in Bengal.

Of the Nawab's court musicians at Lucknow, the famous Bindadin and Kalka Prasad did not come to Calcutta; but their fame did, and they influenced Bengali music as late as through Atulprasad Sen (1871-1934), who lived in Lucknow. And to Calcutta, in the Nawab's entourage, came singers like Ali Bux and Taz Khan. The Nawab also patronized local singers like Aghornath Chakrabarti (1852-1915), Pra-

mathanath Banerji (1868-1956), Bamacharan Banerji and Kaliprasanna Banerji (1842-1900) – men who went on to achieve all-India fame.

At the Nawab's court there also sang the legendary Jadunath Bhattacharya or Jadu Bhatta (1840-83). He came to Calcutta from his native Bankura at the age of fifteen; and after a hard struggle, even involving domestic service, became the disciple of the famous *Dhrupad* singer Ganganarayan Chatterji (1806-74). Later he spent years in North India to master classical music, which he subsequently taught and sang in Calcutta. Rabindranath was his pupil; so was Bankimchandra Chatterji, whose song *Bande Mataram* was first set to music by Jadu Bhatta. His fellow disciple, under Ganganarayan, was Haraprasad Banerji.

It was at this time that local singers learnt to recognize the different schools or *gharanas* of classical music, and even to identify themselves with various styles according to the *ustad* who taught them. In this way, singers in Calcutta became exponents of different styles or 'houses' of music hailing from various parts of India.

Other centres of patronage arose in Calcutta too. The most important was perhaps the branch of the Thakur (Tagore) family at Pathuriaghata. Their house musicians were Kshetramohan Goswami from Bishnupur and Lakshmiprasad Mishra from Varanasi. Trained and influenced by men like these, Shourindramohan Thakur (1840-1914) became a musicologist of international fame, loaded with honours from various European nations as well as from the Shah of Persia. He set up the Banga Sangit Bidyalaya in 1871 and the Bengal Academy of Music in 1881. His elder brother Jatindramohan (1831-1908) was also a notable enthusiast and patron. It was at Pathuriaghata that the use of an orchestra was first cultivated in Bengal. Western music, and its union with Indian traditions, was also cultivated by men like Krishnadhan Banerji (1846-1904), Kaliprasanna Banerji and Nabinkrishna Haldar, disciples of Kshetramohan and members of the Pathuriaghata circle.

Again, when the musically active state of Betia in Bihar went into decline, some of its leading *ustads* like Shivprasad Mishra and Guruprasad Mishra came to Calcutta, and trained a generation of singers like Radhikaprasad Goswami (1863-1924), Shashibhushan Dey and Gopeshwar Banerji (1880-1962). Big musical soirées were arranged by rich patrons

26.5 *Above: Gopeshwar Banerji*

26.6 *Below: Aghornath Chakrabarti*

of Calcutta like the Thakurs of Pathuriaghata and Jorasanko, the Debs of Shobhabazar and Shimulia, the Malliks of Sindurpatti, the Nandis of the Kashimbazar Raj Palace and many others only slightly less exalted in rank. But there were other, humbler houses too which held soirées and informal gatherings of the highest order: the home of the eminent singer and artist Girijashankar Chakrabarti (1885-1948), for instance, or the Boubazar home of the famous musical family of the Barals.

Out of such musical meetings there gradually emerged the elaborate public soirée or 'Conference', a regular (usually annual) meet, continued through several evenings, featuring a range of leading artistes. The way was paved by relatively small and informal gatherings like the Murari Sammelan and the Shankar Utsab. The earliest of these, the Murari Sammelan, was started in 1905 by Durlabh Bhattacharya at his house in Shibnarayan Das Lane in honour of his *mridanga* teacher Murarimohan Gupta (1821?-1901). Durlabh kept it up until his death in 1938. The Baral brothers, Raichand, Bishenchand and Kishenchand ran a Conference for some years from 1928 in memory of their father Lalchand.

But the first full-fledged Conference was the

All Bengal Music Conference, organized by Bhupendrakrishna Ghosh (1886-1941) of Pathuriaghata. The Conference became a byword not only for the quality of the musical fare, but for Bhupendrakrishna's reputation as an organizer and gracious host to the musical elite of India. The rival All India Music Conference was set up by Damodar Das Khanna ('Lalababu'). Though run on more commercial lines, its musical level and range of participants was no less remarkable. Hence the high point was reached at which local singers as well as *ustads* from elsewhere viewed recognition in Calcutta as the key to all-India fame.

It is worth noting the respect that Bengali songs commanded in the most advanced musical circles of the time. Hindustani classical songs had come to occupy their esteemed position; but the local *ustads* did not eschew the artistic lyrics in their own tongue. At a soiree or social gathering, they would render a song of Nidhu

26.7 Rabindranath and Jyotirindranath Thakur

Babu or some other Bengali composer in the same recital as a Hindustani *Dhrupad* or *Khayal* in a different *Darbari* style.

But unsurprisingly, at the more popular level, less rigorous forms of music ruled the day. With the establishment of the theatre, songs came to play an important function on the stage. Local theatre groups would refurbish popular plays with additional songs and present them as *gitabhinay* or musical drama. Their popularity, and that of the *jatra*, was not lost on the formal theatre. Songs abounded in the plays of the time, and operas were composed specially with a view to attract the audience by their music.

At first such songs did not depart radically from the traditional types prevailing in *jatra*; only the lyrics had to be remodelled in some cases to suit the new demands of the Western-style stage. Even Michael Madhusudan Datta composed the songs in his plays in the well-trod path of Nidhu Babu. Nor were the traditional moulds broken by the memorable songs placed by Bankimchandra Chatterji in his novels.

It was only with Girishchandra Ghosh that stage songs acquired a character of their own. He composed about twenty operatic plays: some religious or mythological, others like *Abu Hossain* or *Aladin* drawing on the Arabian Nights. Amritalal Basu drew on the same two sources for his musicals, as did Kshirodeprasad Vidyavinode, perhaps most successfully in *Ali Baba*, still remembered and sometimes acted today. But it was left to Dwijendralal Ray to refine the model and create consummate literary lyrics – comic, romantic and spiritual or philosophical – in the early days of the present century. He also succeeded, more easily and totally than ever before, in blending Western elements with Indian, even earning the opprobrium of purists on that score.

At this stage too, we find the rise of a celebrated line of musical and dramatic culture in the house of the Thakurs (Tagores), which was much more polished and enlightened in character than most other such houses. The chief architect of this development was Jyotirindranath Thakur (1849-1925), Rabindranath's elder brother. Although the entire process emanated from an aristocratic circle, the songs obtained wide circulation in society generally. Indeed, their greatest service was to create a common taste for refined lyrics relying on a polished and dignified melodic line. The perfection of this course of development lay, of course, in the work of Rabindranath Thakur (1861-1941). By the end of the nineteenth century, when he was about to enter the middle point of his life, his reputation was secure as the leading composer in this chaste and elevated vein of music. Other notable practitioners in this line were Atulprasad Sen and Rajanikanta Sen (1865-1910). The former lived at Lucknow and the latter at Rajshahi in East Bengal, but their songs were an integral part of the Calcutta musical scene.

The great nationalist movement sparked off by the Partition of Bengal in 1905 also witnessed a spate of new creations, the patriotic Swadeshi songs composed by all recognized poets of the time. Nationalistic songs had indeed been composed much earlier; but after 1905, they acquired a unique spirit of national awakening and came to constitute a distinct category in the musical history of Bengal. Apart from their political, cultural and frequently literary value, they also had an important significance in purely musical terms in that they incorporated various types of folk tunes. Elements of Western music were also used to make them more arousing. These songs were sung with immense enthusiasm at the street gatherings in Calcutta which came to form a chief vehicle of the anti-Partition movement. Rabindranath's famous patriotic songs like *Ek bar tora Ma boliya dak* ('Only call once, "Mother"') were sung at a huge gathering on 7 August 1905, and his *Banglar mati Banglar jal* ('The soil of Bengal, the water of Bengal') became the hymn of the famous Rakhi-tying festival on 16 October that year. In the middle of the same year, a barefoot procession went down Cornwallis Street (Bidhan Sarani) singing Rajanikanta Sen's *Mayer deya mota kapar* ('The coarse cloth given us by our mother'). The great poet-composers – Rabindranath, Rajanikanta, Dwijendralal Ray – were supported by host of minor talent, like the prolific Kaliprasanna Kavyavisharad (1861-1907).

These various developments ushered in a modern age in music by the dawn of the present century. Already before the First World War, music in Calcutta was a great institution, enriched by different types of songs emanating from almost every branch of society. On the one hand, there was the contribution of eminent poet-composers like Dwijendralal Ray, Atulprasad Sen and Rajanikanta Sen, apart from Rabindranath himself; on the other, the output from *jatra, Kirtan* and variety entertainments. All this was made possible by the vigorous and receptive nature of the musical public of the city.

Hence as one might expect, great enthusiasm greeted the emergence of the record age in Calcutta, at the start of the twentieth century. The Gramophone Company of India played a crucial role as patron and compiler, bringing together the best of classical as well as light music, as practised by artistes of all schools and persuasions throughout the country. In a new way now, Calcutta came to be a meeting-place and uniting bond for the entire nation's music.

The early days of the Gramophone Company mark the culmination of old Calcutta's musical life; but obviously, it denotes the start of a new era as well, not only by virtue of technical innovation. A change was also under way in the social history of Calcutta's music. The story of that music from this time onward must be told in a separate chapter.

26.8 *Dwijendralal Ray*

CALCUTTA THEATRE
1835–1944

Kironmoy Raha

Like the city itself, Calcutta theatre was a British creation, and Bengali theatre took shape under the influence of European drama and dramatic techniques. But it could scarcely have taken root as firmly and rapidly as it did if it had been wholly an alien transplant. Classical Sanskrit theatre had declined even before the Islamic invasion of India, and died thereafter; but various forms of popular drama and folk entertainment survived and flourished. In Bengal, this was embodied in the *jatra,* which, by the late eighteenth century, had acquired a basic dramatic form and, more important, an embryonic secular temper.

Tastes nourished by the *jatra* served to dictate the themes, treatment, dialogue and acting style of Western-style Bengali theatre. Perceptive critics and playwrights also recognized the deeper potential of the *jatra* form. 'I like the *jatra* of Bengal,' wrote Rabindranath Thakur in *Bangadarshan* in 1902. 'In *jatra* there is no forbidding separation of the actors from the spectators. There is an easy bond of mutual trust and dependence...' And Shishirkumar Bhaduri, doyen of Bengali actor-directors, said regretfully in his old age, 'If our theatre had evolved from the *jatra,* it would have been a different sort of theatre, a true national theatre. But our theatre has grown under foreign influences.' (*Natyalok,* 10 December 1951).

But for a hundred years before Shishirkumar, the English-educated upper crust of Bengali society had looked down upon the lowly *jatra*

and considered the English theatre as the only fit model for the educated to follow. For their knowledge of English theatre, they did not have to rely only on reading or report. The first of many Engish playhouses, the Calcutta Theatre, had been built as early as 1775 in what is now Lyons Range. (There had been a short-lived playhouse earlier still, set up in 1753 and destroyed by Nawab Siraj-ud-Daula in 1756.)

A series of English theatres opened and closed through the next eighty years. Among them was the famous Chowringhee Theatre (1813–39) which gave its name to Theatre Road (now Shakespeare Sarani), and the Sans Souci, set up in 1839 and moved in 1841 to the present site of St. Xavier's College on Park Street. These companies enjoyed a steady inflow of experienced, even renowned actors and actresses, sometimes from the London stage: Emma Bristow, Esther Leach, James Vining, Mrs Deacle, Miss Cowley. At first the audience was exclusively European – even the ushers and doorkeepers at the Calcutta Theatre were Englishmen – but Indians gained entry from the early nineteenth century, and the English theatre became a haunt, and sometimes a source of serious interest, of the emerging English-educated Bengalis. A minor landmark was set up when 'Prince' Dwarakanath Thakur became one of the founders of the Chowringhee Theatre; a more memorable one in August 1848 when a 'Native Gentleman', Baishnabcharan

27.1 *The Chowringhee Theatre. William Wood Jr*

Adhya, played Othello at the Sans Souci. Yet the *Calcutta Star's* notice of 'a real unpainted nigger Othello' suggests the ambiguous, even offensive nature of such accommodation.

By the early nineteenth century, the cultural leadership of Bengal had passed firmly to the emerging class of landowners and wealthy merchants, and the new middle class of smaller traders, rentiers, salariat and professionals. They took eager advantage of the schools teaching English and soon became ardent admirers of English ways, ideas and institutions, drama and theatre being among them. The 'Young Bengal' generation would act Shakespeare at the David Hare Academy and the Oriental Seminary. Inevitably, the New Bengalis came to conceive the idea of a new Bengali theatre.

Interestingly though, the first Bengali plays had been staged well before this, not by a Bengali but by a remarkable Russian scholar-adventurer, Gerasim Lebedeff (1749-1818). With the help of his Bengali tutor Goloknath Das, he made free adaptations of *The Disguise* by an 'M. Jodrelle' and Moliere's *L'Amour Médecin.* This double bill was presented on 27 November 1795 and 21 March 1796 at a 'New Theatre in the Doomtulla [now Ezra Street] Decorated in the Bengallee style.' The 200-seat house was 'overfull' on both nights; but Lebedeff left India soon after, and his pioneer efforts bore no fruit.

At last in 1832, Prasannakumar Thakur built a makeshift auditorium at his house in Narkeldanga, but only a few English plays were staged there. The first Bengali production was in 1835, at Nabinchandra Basu's home theatre where the Shyambazar tram terminus now stands. The play was *Bidyasundar,* based on a traditional story popular with *jatra* companies.

More and more private stages (usually temporary structures) came to be built; and though the audience was restricted to invitees, it could sometimes be sizeable – 900 at a performance in July 1858, according to the *Sambad Prabhakar.* The plays were translations, chiefly from Sanskrit. Nandakumar Ray's translation of Kalidasa's *Abhignan Shakuntalam,* played on 30 January 1857 at the house of Ashutosh Deb (Satu or Chhatu Babu) in Shimulia (Simla), was the first play to be staged after *Bidyasundar.* Among original Bengali plays, Taracharan Sikdar's *Bhadrarjun* and Jogendrachandra Gupta's *Kirtibilas* were written in 1852 but never staged. That honour went to Ramnarayan Tarkaratna's *Kulin Kulasarbasya,* published in 1854 and acted in March 1857 on a makeshift stage at Ramjay Basak's house in what is now Tagore Castle Road. Significantly, this was not a mythological play but a satire on contemporary social evils like the caste system and polygamy.

Two private theatres stand out in importance. One was the Belgachhia Natyashala built by the enlightened Rajas of Paikpara. It was inaugurated on 31 July 1858 with a production of Ramnarayan Tarkaratna's *Ratnabali,* adapted

27.2 *Above: The Sans Souci Theatre*

27.3 *Below: Ardhendushekhar Mustafi*

from a Sanskrit play. The other was set up by the Thakurs at Jorasanko. It lasted for some decades; on 21 February 1881, it saw the first production of Rabindranath Thakur's early play *Balmiki Pratibha*.

The rich man's private theatre provided the incentive for 'amateur' theatres set up by 'societies' and 'clubs' among the stage-struck middle class. These too were private affairs, but they helped to focus the rising demand for commercial theatres open to the public. A crucial role was played by the Bagbazar Amateur Theatre (later the Shyambazar Natyasamaj), among whose members were such pioneers of Bengali theatre as Girishchandra Ghosh, Ardhendu Mustafi and Nagendranath Banerji. It also had the services of the pathbreaking dramatist Dinabandhu Mitra. His social comedy *Sadhabar Ekadashi* was the society's first production, in 1868, and in 1872 his *Lilabati* scored another major success.

The demand for a public theatre was succinctly expressed by the journal *New Essays* in August 1868. It appealed to the amateur groups: 'Please get together, build a playhouse, engage actors and actresses on a salaried basis, sell tickets and with the sale proceeds meet the expenses.' Not all got together, nor was a playhouse built, nor for that matter were actresses engaged. But the watershed in the

history of Bengali theatre was about to be crossed.

Some of the enthusiasts got together and formed a group. They called it the National Theatre, hired the courtyard of Madhusudhan Sanyal's mansion in Jorasanko at Rs 40 a month, built a stage and announced their opening performance for 7 December 1872. This was another play by Dinabandhu Mitra, *Nildarpan,* a powerful protest against the tyranny and exploitation of the indigo planters. *The Englishman* fumed and threatened, but other papers acclaimed the production – Nabagopal Mitra's *National Paper* called it 'an event of national imporance' – and the play was staged again a fortnight later. The Rev. James Long brought out an English translation of *Nildarpan,* written perhaps by himself or by Michael Madhusudan Datta. Long was imprisoned for his pains, but gradually Europeans too turned to the play. A special performance was held for them on 19 April 1873, after which the same *Englishman* wrote: 'The really conspicuous talent for histrionic art possessed by the Bengali cannot be seen to better advantage than in this drama.'

The public theatre grew rapidly from this start. Many new groups were formed. Girish Ghosh had at first dissociated himself from the National Theatre, objecting to the sale of tickets – ironically in view of his own later commercial success. He joined it later, only to see its other stalwart Ardhendu Mustafi leave it to form the Hindu National Theatre. This was launched with a production of Michael Madhusudan Datta's *Sharmishtha* on 5 April 1873 at the Opera House, a former English theatre on Lindsay Street. It was an unsuitable venue for a Bengali playhouse; it ran into loss and took to touring the districts.

.The split in the National Theatre was symptomatic of the squabbles, splits and clashes of personality endemic throughout the history of Bengali theatre. The basis of patronage also underwent a change. Wealthy donors continued to lend support, but the crucial sustenance, financially and artistically, now came from the rising middle class. Gradually, hardheaded businessmen moved in. The Minerva Theatre was funded by a Rajasthani businessman, and the Star Theatre rebuilt by another businessman. The new importance of the box office actually acted as a boon to overcome several deficiencies.

Permanent playhouses were soon in demand. The first, in August 1873, was the Bengal Theatre at No. 9 Beadon Street, where the Beadon Street Post Office now stands. (Beadon Street has now been renamed after the legendary actor Surendranath Ghosh or Dani Babu). It cost Rs 15,000, a considerable sum at the time, was flimsily built and looked outwardly like a poor man's copy of Lewis's Lyceum Theatre on Chourangi. The Bengal Theatre made history in another way, by engaging actresses from the red-light areas – where else could they be found in those days? Predictably, there was a storm of protest, but within a couple of years almost all other companies followed suit.

The most popular theatre, with the greatest number of star actors, was the Great National, with its ramshackle theatre opened at No 6 Beadon Street on 31 December 1873. The company folded up in October 1877, and was followed by various changes in name and ownership. Finally, the Minerva Theatre was built there in 1893. The present structure dates from 1922, after the old one was gutted by fire.

The Great National Theatre played another important role in Indian theatrical history. During the Prince of Wales's visit to Calcutta in January 1876, a leading Indian lawyer, Jagadananda Mukherji, had brought his womenfolk

Government Ord(i)nance,

মশা মারিতে কামান

out of purdah to greet him. The shocked reaction in conservative society found expression in a farce, *Gajadananda and the Prince,* staged at the Great National in February. To stop it, the Viceroy Lord Northbrook passed an Ordinance on 29 December 1876 empowering the Government to prohibit plays 'which are scandalous, defamatory, seditious, obscene or otherwise prejudicial to the public interest'. This was ratified later in the year by the Dramatic Performances Act – the first law of censorship of the arts in India.

The other lasting seat of drama in Calcutta was the Star Theatre, first built at no 68 Beadon Street in 1883 and later moved to grander premises at Cornwallis Street (now Bidhan Sarani). Girish Ghosh masterminded the project. His protégée Binodini Dasi has left a vivid account of how it was partly built by their own hands, Binodini herself carrying hods of earth and paying the labourers speed money to work faster.

The Minerva and the Star symbolize the rise and consolidation of Bengali commercial theatre. The latter, in particular, has kept alive the tradition of mainstream Bengali theatre for over a hundred years. But other theatres came up, and often changed names and owners. The original Star in Beadon Street became successively the Emerald, the Classic, the Kohinoor,

27.4 *'Firing a cannon to kill a mosquito': contemporary cartoon on the Dramatic Performances Act*

the Manmohan and the Natyamandir, before it was pulled down to make way for Central Avenue.

Bengali theatre established its acting style, production methods and managerial structure in the short space of three decades. By then, it had become an important medium not only of entertainment but also for the propagation of views and beliefs among the Bengali gentry and middle class. This was reflected in the coverage it received in both English and Bengali newspapers, and the hot debates it provoked in most Bengali households. Another measure of its impact was the hostility it evoked among puritanical social reformers; but they fought a losing battle. A curious variant of their reaction is seen in the efforts of that simple and good man, Rajkrishna Ray. He built the Bina Rangabhumi at 38 Mechhuabazar Street in 1887 to stage morally unexceptionable plays with men playing female roles and with ruinously low rates of admission. Not surprisingly, he won much praise but little success; after many changes of hand, the Bina was taken over for 'moving pictures', which it shows to this day.

Obviously, an expanding theatre relies on a steady supply of plays. When the Bengali theatre began, this supply did not exist, and producers had to fall back heavily on adaptations and translations, chiefly from Sanskrit and English. But the demand for theatre created playwrights. The pioneer was Ramnarayan Tarkaratna (1822-64). In his footsteps came the poet Michael Madhusudan Datta (1824-73) with six plays to his credit including two fine satirical farces. Dinabandhu Mitra (1830-73) was a better craftsman than either, and with a deeper social involvement. He, more than

anybody else, gave Bengali drama a solid foundation.

Needless to say, there were also 'instant' plays devoid of literary merit, as well as dramatizations of novels and narrative poems. Bankimchandra Chatterji's novels were a ready source, like Rabindranath Thakur's short stories later on. But worthwhile drama continued to be written, as by Manomohan Basu (1831-1912), Jyotirindranath Thakur (1845-1925), Amritalal Basu (1853-1929), Girishchandra Ghosh (1844–1912) and Rabindranath Thakur (1861–1941).

Manomohan Basu introduced operatic music in his plays; in various forms and degrees, this came to be almost an essential ingredient of Bengali plays. Jyotirindranath Thakur chiefly translated Sanskrit plays and French comedies. Amritalal Basu was closely associated with the theatre from its inception as actor, producer, manager and playwright. His thirty-odd plays, chiefly popular comedies, earned him the title *Rasaraj,* 'king of humorists', though their literary merits do not bear close scrutiny.

Rabindranath's *Raja o Rani* was first produced at the Emerald Theatre in 1890. From then on, his early plays and comedies were staged intermittently at various public theatres. But of about sixty plays that he wrote, only some fifteen were performed there in his lifetime. Producers clearly found his major drama too difficult and indeed too alien to stage. Of his great symbolic plays, there was

27.5 Left: The Manmohan Theatre

27.6 Right: Amritalal Basu

190

only one performance (of *Grihaprabesh*) in his lifetime, at the Star.

What the stage demanded was a simple formula to satisfy the middle-class thirst for entertainment and vicarious emotion. These were best provided by Girishchandra Ghosh, arguably the most towering figure in the history of old Bengali theatre. Among his eighty-odd plays are farces and burlesques, musicals and fantasies, social drama, and plays based on religious and quasi-historical figures like those from the Hindu epics. In the serious plays, the burlesque and comic interludes (sometimes in questionable taste) provided entertainment, while religion, patriotism and high moral purpose satisfied the higher aspirations of the audience.

Not the least of Girish Ghosh's contributions was his expansion of dramatic language by innovative variations of metre and rhythm, affording a wider range of modulation for the actors. He once remarked that Shakespeare was his ideal. After months of preparation, he staged a skilful translation of *Macbeth* at the Minerva on 28 January 1893. It was rejected by the public: as Girischandra ruefully remarked, they only wanted songs and dances – a point he took care of in his later plays.

Girishchandra entered the theatre in its 'amateur' days and dominated it for four decades after it had gone public, as an outstanding actor, producer, playwright, manager and teacher. He was fortunate in his gifted colleagues. Pre-eminent among them was Ardhendushekhar Mustafi (1850-1909). In that first production of *Nildarpan,* he amazed the audience by acting four different parts including a female one. He was an incomparable comic actor; and, as significantly, a fine teacher of acting skills.

There were others, like Amritalal Basu, Mahendralal Basu (1853-1901) the 'tragedian of Bengal', Sharatchandra Ghosh, Motilal Sur and Amritalal Mitra (?-1908). Of the many reputed actresses, Binodini Dasi (1863-1942) was surely the greatest. It was no easy climb for her against older and more experienced actresses like Sukumari Datta or Golapbala (fl. 1873-90), Kusum Kumari (?–1948) or Kshetramani (fl. 1874-1903). Her triumph may be explained not only by her inherent genius but also the guidance of Girish Ghosh and the models in the English theatre that Ghosh sent her to see, though she did not know a word of English.

This galaxy of outstanding actors and actresses was supported by devoted talents in other branches of the theatre. There was Dharmadas Sur (1852-1910), painter, set-designer and architect; Nagendranath Banerji (1850-82), an organizer of exceptional ability; and Bhubanmohan Niyogi, ever ready with money and time. Away from the footlights and the applause, they and many others laboured to enable Bengali theatre to stand on its feet. And, as already noted, persons with business acumen came to secure it a commercial foundation.

The formative decades of the Bengali theatre were also decades when diverse religious, social, political and intellectual ideals were agitating the minds of the educated Bengalis. There were fierce debates and reform movements against the entrenched orthodoxies. English education and scientific thought had struck roots, and nationalist

27.7 *Left: Binodini Dasi*

27.8 *Kusum Kumari*

impulses were beginning to stir. The early Calcutta theatre reflected these profound movements of the Bengali spirit; it seemed set to function as a powerful medium of the Bengal Renaissance.

The tragedy was that it failed to consolidate this early start. This was partly a matter of formal influence. The theatre had to contend with the contrary forces of *jatra* and the English stage. The Bengalis of Calcutta were, after all, migrants from the countryside, and did not leave their villages wholly behind even after they had settled in the city. The hold of *jatra* lay

27.9
*Kshirodeprasad
Vidyavinode*

far too deep in their psyches to disappear wholly; and the lure of English theatre, while far more superficial, was for that very reason directed towards crude second-hand copies. Neither influence could be denied. What Girish Ghosh and others succeeded in doing was to fuse these contrary components into a popular form of entertainment and mimetic art.

But by the turn of the century, the average theatre-goer had wearied of the crude and heavy fare: the hamming, the simplistic religious themes, the overdose of songs and clowning. A reprieve came when Amarendra Datta (1876-1916), a youth of barely twenty, started the Classic Theatre in 1897. Within a few years he made it the most popular theatre in the city, a place of uninhibited fun, though by means not always seemly or ethical. But he was an innovator in production methods, and not unmindful of the serious side of theatre – as borne out by his pioneering theatre journals, *Saurabh* and *Rangalaya*. It is a measure of his acumen that his *Hariraj* (1897), a somewhat free Indianization of *Hamlet,* was a resounding success where four years earlier, Girish Ghosh's translation of *Macbeth* had flopped.

The first decade of this century saw the appearance of two great playwrights. Dwijendralal Ray (1863-1913) is remembered as a dramatist for his historical plays. His

Rajput and Mughal heroes, legendary princes and warriors, were shaped by the rising nationalism of the day, given new impetus by the Partition of Bengal in 1905. There is something specially modern in this refashioning of old patriotic myths, as in Ray's keen sense of theatre, in spite of his poetic prose and a somewhat rhetorical literary grace. Yet significantly, his plays grew famous in print, and few were staged during his lifetime. It would be another two decades before they overcame the conditioned responses of the audience and the play-safe commercialism of the theatre owners.

Kshirodeprasad Vidyavinode (1864-1927) also had to wait till the 1920s for due acclaim for his best plays, like *Raghubir* or *Alamgir*. His early successes were colourful romances like the blockbuster *Alibaba*. His language was more varied and less rhetorical than Dwijendralal's, and less long-winded than Girish Ghosh's. He also avoided vulgar clowning. These qualities have earned him an important place in Bengali dramatic literature.

Plays were lengthy affairs in those days. Starting late in the evening, they dragged on till the early hours of the morning. At the beginning, Saturdays were 'theatre days'. Later Sundays were added. Later still, the length of the plays was shortened and mid-week performances on Thursdays, with an additional show on Sundays, were started. This pattern, with some variations, still continues in the commercial theatres of Calcutta.

From the outset, Bengali theatre was actor-oriented. This stemmed from its twin sources of inspiration, English theatre and the *jatra*. Girish Ghosh and his peers drew sustenance from the English tradition of grand acting set up by Garrick, Irving and Ellen Terry. *Jatra* too had evolved a style of loud, boldly–drawn 'heroic' acting. Aggravated by the limitations of stage space and bad acoustics, 'star acting' became the hallmark of the Bengali stage, and actors and actresses were not lacking to meet the demands of such a mode.

By contrast, other components like sets, costumes and make-up were grossly deficient. They may have escaped notice in the early days; but by 1910, the shortcomings were blatant enough for Manomohan Goswami, a playwright, to say that 'one could not make out from the costumes whether the character was a Bengali, a Bihari, or a Rajput or a Sikh, a Jat, a Marathi or a South Indian'. The sets were crude copies of London models, imbibed through local English playhouses, pictures or plain hearsay. Dhananjay Mukherji, in his book *Bangiya Natyashala,* notes ludicrous misapplications: 'we see a castle instead of a fortress, a villa instead of gardens, corridors instead of verandahs, and drawing rooms in place of royal courts'. Amarendra Datta's reforms did no more than correct some glaring inconsistencies. The sets served little purpose, either imaginative or functional. The great achievement was to create 'magical' effects: actors vanishing through trapdoors, toy trains trundling across the stage, or 'close combat in chariots'. No doubt they drew crowds, as more sophisticated gimmicks do now. But it is worth remembering that even the biggest hits rarely ran for more than thirty shows.

Girish Ghosh died in 1912. The next decade was a barren one for Bengali theatre. It had used up the store of passion that had sustained it for so long. Some plays like *Siraj-ud-Daula* and *Balidan* continued to draw full houses, but these were exceptions. Generally, the theatre was sustained by the sheer size of the potential audience, by wider publicity, and by a few outstanding actors like Surendranath Ghosh or Dani Ghosh (1868-1932), Girish's son, and Aparesh Mukherji (1875-1934) and actresses like Tinkari Dasi (1870?-1917) and Tarasundari (1878?-1948). But the decline could not be concealed. Shrikumar Banerji, in his memoir of the actor Shishir Bhaduri, has given a clear account:

Acting and stagecraft had adopted the romantic sentimentalism and unreal fantasies of the nineteenth century. One saw the gaudy dresses of kings and princes, the revelling in patriotism and cheap idealism, the unrelieved roar of heroic passion, the excess of grief with its tears and ululations in cracked voices, the unchecked and indecent bouts of laughter.

Such attacks had already been made in the 1920s by discerning critics like Hemendrakumar Ray, who edited the theatre journal *Nachghar.* The intelligentsia grew contemptuous, the common playgoer unenthusiastic. It seemed nothing could rescue Bengali theatre from a slow fade-out. But rescued it was, and by one man.

Shishirkumar Bhaduri (1889-1959) came of an educated and affluent family. His friends included some of the leading scholars and intellectuals of Bengal. He took an MA degree in English and taught for seven years at Vidyasagar College before resigning to become a professional actor – an astounding decision for a Bengali *bhadralok.* He joined the Cornwallis Theatre, a relatively small unit owned by a Parsi, and made his debut on 10 December 1921 in Vidyavinode's *Alamgir.*

The play was an instant success. But in order to have a more amenable playhouse, Bhaduri took over the Manmohan Theatre on lease, renamed it Natyamandir (Temple of Drama), renovated it thoroughly, and opened on 6 August 1924 with Jogesh Choudhuri's *Sita.* The re-designed playhouse and production were like a triumphant manifesto: a new age of the theatre had come into being.

The Star Theatre (though not the Minerva) responded to the winds of change: it revamped its management, saw to the comfort of the audience, and chose plays more judiciously than before. The change was heralded by the production in 1923 of *Karnarjun* by Aparesh Mukherji, and the new owners, Art Theatre Ltd., fostered many fresh talents like Ahindra Choudhuri (1895-1974), Naresh Mitra (1888-1968), Durgadas Banerji (1893-1943) and Sushilasundari.

But the lead remained with Shishirkumar. Before *Sita* completed its hundredth performance in July 1925, he had won the acclaim of the learned and the elite, as well as tumultuous praise from the public and the press. He created an excitement among the intelligentsia such as no theatre man has done before or, probably, since.

All the same, Shishirkumar had to leave the Natyamandir, chiefly through financial impru-

27.10
*Girishchandra
Ghosh*

27.11 *Ahindra Choudhuri and Naresh Mitra in Manmatha Ray's 'Chand Sadagar'*

dence. He took the Cornwallis Theatre on lease in 1926, and his four years there marked the high point of his career. *Sita* was soon followed by new plays like Kshirodeprasad's *Naranarayan* and Jogesh Choudhuri's *Digbijayee,* besides D.L.Ray's plays and other old favourites. Significantly, Shishirkumar also staged several of Rabindranath's plays – though these often failed at the box office, *Tapati* being the biggest flop.

In 1930, Shishirkumar took his troupe to the USA – the first time a Broadway impresario had invited an Indian company. The trip was a disaster, though Shishirkumar won high acclaim for his own powers. On his return, he continued to move from one theatre to another, with spells of inactivity in between. Finally, he took out a lease on the Natyaniketan in 1941, renamed it Shrirangam, and produced a wide range of old and new plays. But here too, despite his own brilliance and a few popular successes, Shrirangam steadily declined. He was ejected in January 1956 and died three years later, a poor, bitter, disillusioned man.

There is no doubt that Shishir Bhaduri was a great actor by any standards. He had eminent predecessors, but none with his theatrical sense and intellectual underpinning. But perhaps he contributed still more to the rejuvenation of the Bengali stage as a director than an actor. He was indeed the first Bengali director, as we now understand the word. Girish Ghosh had laid the foundations of the Bengali theatre. Amarendra Datta gave it a mass base. It was Shishirkumar who endowed it with prestige and respectability. Treated till then with an ambiguous, almost contemptuous affection, it was now recognized as a fit pursuit for an artist and intellectual.

But again by the mid-1930s, the theatre was falling into a rut. In the countryside, the situation grew worse, and nationalist sentiments were reshaped by a new social awareness. The theatre gave no sign of being even aware of these changing realities. The chronic shortage of good plays became, if anything, more acute. A few competent playwrights, responding to the reality around them, did of course appear: Manmatha Ray (1899-1988), Shachin Sengupta (1891-1961), Bidhayak Bhattacharya (1907-86). Their plays, with dramatizations of popular novels, concealed the decline for a time, aided by the talent of rising actors like Nirmalendu Lahiri (1891-1950), Chhabi Bishwas (1900-62), Bhumen Ray, Sarajubala Debi and Shanti Gupta (fl. 1930-60). There was also the presence of Shishir Bhaduri and the sheer professionalism of seasoned actors like Ahindra Choudhuri, Durgadas Banerji and Prabha Debi (1903-52) to give the theatre a deceptive look of health.

In 1942 the country was thrown into a turmoil following the Quit India movement. Meanwhile, Japan had occupied Burma, and panic ruled alongside frenetic military preparations in Calcutta and all of Bengal. And in 1943-44, the infamous Bengal Famine claimed close upon three million lives. The Bengali intelligentsia, bewildered and fragmented, seemed to have lost the power to respond to these cataclysmic events. Nowhere was this paralytic inertia more in evidence than in the theatre. The plays of the early 1940s still evoke a weird sense of unreality. By 1944-45 the playhouses had become dull, shabby and penurious.

Even Shishir Bhaduri, now an old man, could not bring about a second rejuvenation. Trapped in the past, the effete Bengali theatre grew more and more remote from changing conditions and concepts. Drastic action was required, and the Bengali commercial theatre lacked the vigour to promote it. Remedy was at hand; but it came, as it had to, from outside the professional theatre.

SCIENTIFIC STUDIES
IN CALCUTTA:
THE COLONIAL PERIOD

Partha Ghose

By the time Calcutta appeared on the map of India, the ancient glory of Indian science and technology had faded. The wealthy and learned classes had abandoned the scientific method of thinking, backed by experiment and observation, in favour of barren orthodoxy. In the absence of intellectual guidance from above, the crafts and skills of the common workmen also became a matter of routine. The spell of religious dogmas and superstitions was almost complete. The results of modern science were largely viewed as 'the outlandish notions of alien and casteless unbelievers'. Hence Western scholars and administrators like Macaulay readily concluded that Indians were incapable of scientific enquiry.

The actual history of the Indian response to Western science belies this hostile view. Despite the intellectual stagnation and religious dogmatism, the Indian mind remained receptive at a deeper level to fresh cultural influences, and responded positively when they came from Europe. During the sixteenth and seventeenth centuries contact with Western science was sporadic and limited. But by the end of the seventeenth century, British interests had shifted from mere commerce to territorial acquisition and empire-building. Within a hundred years, colonial activities in the natural and physical sciences – although undertaken for ultimate economic gain or for political and military reasons – became the nucleus of modern science in India. Many of the European

fortune-hunters of the late eighteenth century were professional people – surveyors, plant collectors, mineralogists, doctors, surgeons and engineers in the civil or military service of the Company. They introduced steam vessels, steam railways, the electric telegraph and the printing press; they built bridges and started wide-scale surveys. For all this they needed support from the local people, who responded swiftly and positively.

Calcutta became a natural centre for such activities. In 1784 Sir William Jones (1746–94) established in Calcutta one of the world's first societies for the scholarly study of Asia, particularly India. Modelled on the Royal Society of London, the Asiatic Society concerned itself not only with history and literature but also with the scientific study of the region – in fact all the works of 'Man and Nature, whatever is performed by the one, or produced by the other'. It thus provided the nucleus for much scientific activity in the future – primarily, it is true, among European naturalists rather than Indians.

Topography

Lord Clive was perhaps the first European who encouraged topographical surveys in India, chiefly for military and fiscal purposes. These surveys started almost immediately after the Battle of Palashi or Plassey (1757). Hugh Cameron was encouraged to survey the regions

The Asiatic Society

Next to the Batavian Society (1779), the Calcutta Asiatic Society is the oldest institution of oriental studies in the world, founded by Sir William Jones, (1746-94), Sanskrit scholar and judge at the Supreme Court at Calcutta. It was in the Grand Jury Room of the Supreme Court that Jones brought together thirty enthusiasts in oriental studies to found the Society on 15 January 1784. (The first Indian members, Dwarakanàth Thakur and Ramkamal Sen among them, were admitted in 1829.)

In 1808, the Society moved to its own quarters at the west end of Park Street. Much of its early activities was scientific. The Calcutta Medical and Physical Society was founded on its premises in 1823, and the Indian Museum grew out of its collections. But its chief glory and since long its dominant concern lies, of course, in oriental studies, with a priceless collection of 40,000 manuscripts and some 1,00,000 books, plus coins, works of art and archaeological material.

Among the Society's earliest scholars were Charles Wilkins, Nathaniel Halhed, Henry Thomas Colebrook, John Herbert Harington and William Carey; a little later, James Prinsep, and later still Rajendralal Mitra and Haraprasad Shastri. Its remarkable series of publications include *Asiatic Researches* (1788-1839), the invaluable *Bibliotheca Indica* of oriental texts, and of course the Society's Journal. At the Society again, James Prinsep, assisted by Kamalakanta Sharma, undertook his pioneer work on early Indian scripts; and Haraprasad Shastri carried out his historic collection and study of old manuscripts.

The Society has passed through some troubled times in recent years. But with its treasure-house of materials, its new building (opened in 1965) and the assumption of its financial responsibilities by the Government of India, there is no reason why its future should not be as distinguished as its past.

28.1 *Above: Sir William Jones*

28.2 *Below: 'Park Street, the Asiatic Society's house.'* Wood Jr

adjoining the 24–Parganas. On 10 October 1765 James Rennel was asked to make a quick map of the whole of Bengal; in 1767 he became the first Surveyor-General of India. But it was only in 1818 that Colonel William Lambton (1756–1823), an expert trigonometrist, geographer and geodesist, founded the Great Trigonometrical Survey of India.

Lambton began with a sorry set of instruments. But better ones soon arrived, including a hundred-foot steel chain, theodolites, telescopes, thermometers, astronomical telescopes and chronometers. Indians got the first glimpse of Western science through these topographical and trigonometrical surveys, which were of strategic importance for politics and profit. Although initially Indians were only employed as flagmen and carriers, the British soon realized that extensive and proper surveys could not be made without 'training the natives'. A survey school was started at Guindy (Madras) in 1794, and later mathematics and trigonometry were introduced in the Hindu College and the Madrassa in Calcutta. The results appeared in the mathematical achievements of Radhanath Sikdar (1813–70) who worked under George Everest and Andrew Waugh, and the mechanical skill of Mohsin Hussain, appointed the mathematical instrument-maker after the departure of Henry Barrow.

Botany

By the 1780s the British had consolidated their position in India as administrators. The latest inventions in technology back home made them look more systematically for raw materials from the new colonies, particularly India. Thus began a period of 'plant imperialism'. At the suggestion of Robert Kyd (d. 1793), the Governor-General Lord Cornwallis established the Royal Botanic Garden at Shibpur, across the river from Calcutta, in 1787 with a fourfold purpose: to extract economic benefit from plant trade, to increase the resources in food and raw materials, to import new plants of economic importance from other parts of the world, and to extend and popularize botanical studies in India. Kyd was appointed the first Superintendent.

Kyd's successor Dr William Roxburgh (1751–1815) was the first botanist to attempt a systematic account of the plants of India. Based on the Linnaean system, his *Plants of the Coast of Coromandel* became the basis of all subsequent works on Indian botany. Roxburgh built up a small team of Indian artists who acquired great skill in the exacting task of natural history drawings. Roxburgh was followed by Dr Buchanan Hamilton in 1813 and by Nathaniel Wallich in 1815. Wallich (1786–1854), a Danish

28.3 Advertisement of surveying and mathematical instruments, c. 1925

botanist, had been taken prisoner at the siege of Shrirampur (Serampore) but released because of his distinguished scientific record. One of his greatest achievements was to extend tea plantations in the Himalayan Valley with the help of Chinese tea planters.

The Botanic Garden at Shibpur has a herbarium which houses almost all the dried plant materials of the whole of the Indian subcontinent, Asia, Europe and Australia. The present Botanical Survey of India was established in 1890 by George King (1840–1909) who became its first Director and later Director of the Royal Botanic Garden at Kew.

Geology

Geology remained practically unknown in India until its importance was recognized by a Physical Committee of the Asiatic Society, formed in 1808 to prepare plans to promote the knowledge of natural history. In the beginning geological mapping was carried out by members of other professions. Dr H. W. Vosey, a surgeon attached to the Great Trigonometrical Survey, submitted the first geological map to the Court of Directors of the East India Company in 1820.

Geological researches gained momentum with the rise in demand for coal and iron after the coming of steamships and railroads. Dr Thomas Oldham (1816–78), a geologist of unparalleled talent and a mining engineer, arrived on 4 March 1851 with a five-year contract as Geological Surveyor to the East India Company. His recognition of the Talcher Formation as of glacial origin laid the foundation of the concept of 'Gondwanaland' as a 'great Southern Continent'. In 1859 he rendered advice on the railway alignment between Calcutta and Patna. That was the beginning of engineering geology. His classic work on the great Assam earthquake (1897) laid the foundation of modern seismology in the world.

Under Lord Canning, geological research was brought under a government department. The Geological Survey of India was established in January 1857; the Museum of Economic Survey (set up in 1840) moved to no 1 Hastings Street and was placed under the Survey.

The first Indian to be appointed to the Geological Survey in a graded post was Pramathanath Basu (1855–1935). He was probably also the first Indian scientist to have published original research in his own field. Other eminent geologists associated with the Geological Survey were H. B. Medlicott, W. T. Blanford, H. F. Blanford, William King and T. H. Holland.

28.4 *The Indian Museum*

Zoology

Compared to botanical and geological exploration, the colonists' zoological work was restricted by its limited commercial value. Nevertheless, private interest led some European naturalists, formally attached to botanical or geological expeditions, to carry out zoological investigations in their spare time, collecting specimens and writing commentaries upon them. Official patronage began with the appointment of Edward Blyth (1810–73) as Curator of the Asiatic Society's Museum in 1841. He is considered the founder of the school of field zoology in India: Darwin made use of his papers in British journals. Finally, the Zoological Survey of India was established in 1916.

The Indian Museum

In 1814 Nathaniel Wallich had pleaded for the establishment of a Museum to house objects of science as well as relics which 'illustrate ancient times and manners'. The Asiatic Society complied. Its museum in Calcutta was divided into two sections: one for archaeological, ethnological and technical exhibits, the other for geological and zoological research. Dr Wallich assumed charge of the latter.

In 1856, the Asiatic Society submitted a memorandum to the Government of India to establish an Imperial Museum in Calcutta. Acting on this proposal, the Indian Museum Act was passed in 1866. The Society accordingly transferred its valuable exhibits to the Board of Trustees. The Museum building was completed in 1875, and the Museum opened to the public in April 1878. It has six sections: Zoological, Geological, Archaeological, Art, Industrial and Anthropological.

The Museum can rightly claim to have inspired all early research in India in zoology, geology, meteorology, archaeology, botany and chemistry. It also took the initiative in starting the Indian Science Congress in 1913 and, with its help, founded the National Institute of Sciences of India in January 1935 with its headquarters on the Museum premises. This has now become the Indian National Science Academy and is located in New Delhi.

Meteorology

The importance of meteorological data was early recognized by European seamen, astro-

28.5 *Cyclone at Calcutta: old engraving*

nomers, engineers and even administrators. As far back as 1784 one Henry Trail at Calcutta kept a meteorological diary and Thomas D. Pearse recorded the observations of the barometer, thermometer, hygrometer, wind direction and rainfall during the period 1785-88. During 1805-28 James Kyd prepared the register of tidal observations relating to day and night tides in the river Hugli at Khidirpur, and G. T. Hardwick maintained a meteorological register at Dumdum from 1816 to 1823.

The year 1864 was a turning point for Indian meteorology. That year a major cyclone devastated the Calcutta region, killing 80,000 people. This was followed by the Bengal Famine of 1866. A meteorological committee was set up in Calcutta in 1865 'to consider the best means of establishing a system of observations for the protection of that port'. The committee recommended the appointment of recorders from the Telegraph Department to telegraphically transmit data to the observatory attached to the Surveyor-General's office in Calcutta.

28.6 *Above: The Medical College, Calcutta*

28.7 *Below: Madhusudan Gupta*

Henry Francis Blanford (1834-93), Professor of Natural Science at Presidency College, was appointed Meteorological Reporter to the Government of Bengal in 1867. 1875 saw the establishment of the Indian Meteorological Department; and Blanford became Meteorological Reporter to the Government of India. Under his able guidance the Department made rapid progress, preparing daily weather charts, issuing weather summaries, and carrying out studies in seismology, solar physics and terrestrial magnetism all over India.

Other Scientific Societies

Several other scientific societies also came into existence in Calcutta in the 1820s. In September 1820 William Carey founded the Agricultural Society in Calcutta to disseminate scientific information among Indians and train them in the use of imported seeds and plants and agricultural machinery. Carey also developed his own botanic garden and herbarium at Shrirampur. A Medical and Physical Society was opened in Calcutta in 1823 'to promote co-ordination among the medical men, scattered far apart from each other, over a vast extent of the country'.

Scientific Education

These academic and field studies progressed *pari passu* with technological innovations, especially the coming of the steamship, railway and telegraph: these have been treated elsewhere. Both scientific study and engineering works were undertaken by the British for strategic, political and commercial advantage; and Indians were trained only as attendants and mechanics. But the process triggered off an intellectual response of far-reaching consequences.

One of the first to realize that modern science was essential to rejuvenate his country's ossified traditions was Raja Rammohan Ray (1772-1833). In 1816 he raised a private subscription to establish a Vidyalaya in Calcutta to promote Western learning. Dwarakanath Thakur (1794-1846) also gave liberally in the cause of scientific education. Medical classes began to be held in the Calcutta Madrassa and the Sanskrit College; Sanskrit translations were made of the elementary European medical texts. But the teaching was entirely through oral lectures and wax models: no practical demonstrations were given. In 1822 a Medical School was opened in

Calcutta 'with a view to the military and civil service under European doctors'.

The British were at first apprehensive of the Hindu reaction to scientific education. Rammohan lashed out at this vacillation in a memorandum to the Governor-General Lord Amherst in 1823. The British plans, as he saw them, were 'of little or no practical use to the possessor [of such education] or the society', and were 'best calculated to keep this country in darkness'. He pressed for 'a more liberal and enlightened system of instruction, embracing Mathematics, Natural Philosophy, Chemistry, Astronomy, with other useful sciences'.

many years this was the only institution in India with facilities for real laboratory science. (Anatomy classes at the Sanskrit College and the Calcutta Madrassa had been purely theoretical.) On 10 January 1836 Pandit Madhusudan Gupta (1800-56), instructor at the Calcutta Medical College, took the daring step, in a caste-ridden society, of dissecting the human body. Guns were fired at Fort William to mark the occasion. Madhusudan thus initiated a process that broke down the age-old barriers that had led to the degeneration of the Ayurvedic system.

The same year, Dwarakanath Thakur donated Rs 2,000 for each of the following three

28.8 Bishop's College, Shibpur: later the Bengal Engineering College. D'Oyly

For decades to follow, however, the British considered it 'premature to establish separate classes for any of the several branches of European science in India'. Inevitably, a stage came when 'training the natives' in the useful sciences became imperative. Even so, the colonial government began – about the middle of the nineteenth century – to prepare Indians for subordinate civil service positions and as flagmen, overseers and apothecaries rather than as engineers and scientists.

By 1880 there were four institutions in Calcutta teaching modern science through the medium of English. The first was the Medical College of Bengal, established in 1835 to train Indians irrespective of their caste or creed. For

years as prizes for Indian medical students. He also offered to pay the entire cost of sending two students to England for higher studies in medicine. In 1839 four students, Bholanath Basu, Dwarakanath Basu, Gopalchandra Sheel and Surajitkumar Chakrabarti went to England. All four distinguished themselves, becoming members of the Royal College of Surgeons.

The second notable institution was Presidency College, which gave courses in natural philosophy, astronomy, natural history and geology as well as in civil engineering. The third was St Xavier's College, established by Belgian Jesuits in 1860. It probably imparted the best scientific instruction in the whole

28.9 *Sir Ronald Ross*

Calcutta College of Civil Engineering, started in the Secretariat or Writers' Buildings in 1856. It moved to Presidency College in 1864, and finally to Shibpur as the Bengal Engineering College in 1880.

Sir Ronald Ross

However, the most important piece of scientific research in old Calcutta was not carried out at any of these four institutions but in a small laboratory in the Presidency General (now SSKM) Hospital. Here in 1897 Ronald Ross (1857-1932) discovered the malarial parasite in the gastro-intestinal tract of the Anopheles mosquito, and a year later came to the conclusion that human malaria was transmitted by Anopheles mosquitoes. This life-saving discovery won Ross the Nobel Prize for Medicine in 1902.

We have reached a point where the pursuit of science in Calcutta has passed beyond survey and training to significant new discovery. The leading figures so far have chiefly been Europeans. But the stage was being set for a new course of learning and discovery with Indians in the vanguard. I shall trace this latter phase in the second volume of this book.

country at that time. Its Rector, Father Eugene Lafont, became renowned for his public lectures and demonstrations in physics.

The fourth institution of importance was the

TRADERS AND TRADES
IN OLD CALCUTTA

Sabyasachi Bhattacharya

The economic history of Calcutta is too often equated with that of Bengal. This is scarcely satisfactory. To get around this tradition in historiography, let us begin by looking at the morphology of early nineteenth-century Calcutta, as might have been seen by someone walking through different quarters of the city, and relating this to the history of economic activities there. Such a method may also render my story more readable, though obviously it has its limitations.

On 20 February 1828, the poet Mirza Ghalib was impressed with the greenery of Calcutta while riding into the city after a long and dusty journey on horseback from Varanasi. (He came by boat up to Varanasi from his home in Delhi.) He stayed in Calcutta for almost two years, in vain pursuit of a 'pension' of Rs 750 a year.

In some of the poems written during his stay, he talks not only about the charms of Calcutta's women but also about its 'greenery and verdure which takes away your breath', its 'cool breezes'. It was indeed, in the 1820's, a city with a lot of open spaces, tanks, villages and vegetation. Even the more densely inhabited and built-up parts contained more huts than brick-and-mortar buildings. In the latter category, according to the Magistrate's Surveyors of 1819-20, there were a few 'upper roomed houses' (8.3 per cent) and 'lower roomed houses' (13.4 per cent); whereas straw huts constituted 54.2 per cent and tiled huts

24.1 per cent. A glance at J.A. Schalch's map of Calcutta shows numerous ponds and tanks dispersed uniformly even in thickly populated parts of the town. On 8 August 1822, the newspaper *John Bull* estimated the area of the city to be $4\frac{1}{2}$ miles from north to south and $1\frac{1}{2}$ miles from east to west. Of this, the southern part and the areas north of Mechhuabazar were 'thinly covered with habitations', leaving only a middle part between Dharmatala and Mechhuabazar comparatively densely populated.

If you took a walk through the city at that time, the central place to start from would have been Barabazar on the northern side of Dihi Kalikata, adjoining Dihi Sutanuti. It was the central and most densely populated part of the city, the locale of the business activities we are concerned with. We observe a bipolar system spatially segregated into the European business quarters on the one hand, in the 'White Town' near Fort William, and on the other the heart of the Black Town, the Barabazar area (sometimes englished as the 'Great Bazaar') where the *kothis* and *bazaars* were located.

The bazaars are graphically described in various European accounts of Calcutta. In 1774, P.D. Stanhope, in his *Genuine Memoirs of Asiaticus,* spoke of the Calcutta bazaar with some disdain: 'streets of miserable huts and every Indiaman who occupies one of these is called a merchant'. By the 1820's the bazaars were better built and administered. W.

29.1 *'Native shop on Jan Bazar Street'. William Simpson*

Hamilton reported in his *Geographical, Statistical and Historical Description of Hindostan* (1820) that

the greater number of the bazaars are the property of individuals who pay a certain assessment to the Government.... The total number of this description is 13, and their collective assessment rupees 10,050. Grants [of land] were made to encourage the construction of substantial buildings, adapted for the convenience of the market dealers in the different parts of the town.

However, the laws and regulations against the sale of goods outside designated market premises or on the streets were never very effective, and streets continued to be, as of old, a place of business transactions. A correspondent of *Samachar Chandrika* (6 November 1843) complained of the nuisance caused by retail traders' activities on the streets, converting public thoroughfares into bazaars.

A conglomeration of bazaars, Barabazar was the central point of the market network in the city, and connected the city with its hinterland. In all probability, Barabazar was already an important market place in the mid-eighteenth century. The Great Bazaar which, according to Orme, Nawab Siraj-ud-Daula's solidiers set on fire, has been identified as Barabazar. A hundred years later, Colesworthy Grant's *Anglo-Indian Sketches* (1850) provides a fine

description of what Barabazar became in the mid–nineteenth century:

For oriental traffic, oriental tongues and oriental heads, commend me to the Burrabazar, a mart tailed on to the north end of the China bazar and occupied and visited by merchants from all parts of the east. Here may be seen the jewels of Golkanda and Bundelkhand, the shawls of Cashmere, the broad cloths of England, silks of Murshidabad and Benaras, muslins of Dacca, Calicoes, ginghams, Chintzes and beads of Coromandel, firs and fruits of Caubul, silk fabrics and brocades of Persia, spices and myrrh from Ceylon, Spice Islands and Arabia, shells from the eastern coast and straits, drugs, dried fruit and sweetmeats from Arabia and Turkey, cows' tails from Tibet and ivory from Ceylon; a great portion of these and various other articles too numerous to mention are either sold or bought by natives from the countries where they are obtained who together with visitors, travellers and beggars form a diversified group of Persians, Arabs, Jews, Marwarees, Armenians, Madrasees, Sikhs, Turks, Parsees, Chinese, Burmese and Bengalees.

It is not fortuitous that the Bengalis are mentioned last of all. They were steadily marginalized through the late eighteenth and early nineteenth centuries. More about that later. As regards the great variety of commodities metntioned above, what appeared to the casual observer as one vast cornucopian

medley was actually a hierarchized conglomeration of highly specialized bazaars, each concentrated in a particular area within Barabazar according to the commodity it traded in. Thus a buyer would go to Dhoti-patti or Fancy-patti or Pagia-patti for apparel, to Suta-patti for imported thread or cloth, to Tula-patti for hessian and cotton, to Chini-patti for sugar and so forth. There was further specialization within each branch of trade, creating subdivisions like the *katra, chowk* or *kothi.*

If one element in this inner order was spatial concentration by commodity, another was ethnic specialization in particular lines of business along with strong ties of personal-cum-business relations within that ethnic group. The pattern to which Clifford Geertz draws attention (in *Peddlers and Princes,* 1963, a study of Indonesian society and economy), the fragmentation of the flow of commerce into a multitude of person-to-person transactions, made room for a great number of participants. Hence large client groups could form around a big merchant; such groups were often predominantly of the same ethnic origin as the latter. The interface between ethnicity and business activity is too complex to be reduced to the cliche 'Marwari versus Bengali'. It is true that as early as 1830, the conflict of interests

between Bengali and Marwari *mahajans* finds mention in Bengali newspapers. At the same time, it has also been observed that, as Pradip Sinha puts it in *Calcutta in Urban History* (1978), there was a 'withdrawal of the Bengali merchant from the macro-Indian bazaar', creating space for North Indian business groups with 'a sound hold on inter-regional money circulation and the flow of imported cloth and spices'.

The emergence of the Marwaris was more the outcome of an adjustment than of a struggle. Well-entrenched in indigenous banking and up-country trade, the North Indian merchants also expanded into the growing areas of internal trade in Bengal: the marketing of imported cloth, and procurement of agricultural commodities such as jute on behalf of English business houses. Indigenous Bengali captial, meanwhile, turned towards rentier-type investments while retaining a hold on some traditional lines of business (e.g. the gold merchants' trade, petty money-lending, purely local trade in grain, oil seeds, etc.) which had little growth potential.

In the first half of the nineteenth century, the North Indian trading groups of Barabazar, quietly expanding their activities, offer a sharp contrast to the social visibility and conspicuous consumption of the opulent *banians, diwans* and merchants of Bengali origin. N.K. Sinha, in his *Economic History of Bengal, 1793-1848,* points out that as early as 1816-17, there were only twenty-three Bengalis among the fifty-nine prominent cotton dealers in Barabazar. However, it seems likely that large-scale purchase of land in Barabazar by Marwari, Gujarati and Khatri businessmen took place only later, in the last decades of the century. The up-country merchant-houses who maintained *kothis* and operated through *munims* in Barabazar began to make Calcutta their headquarters and place of residence in the second half of the nineteenth century. The Reverend James Long noted the development of Barabazar as a distinctively Marwari quarter as early as 1872. H. Beverley in his 1826 Census of Calcutta found that only 11 per cent of the population of Barabazar were native to Calcutta. While there was scarcely any province of British India not represented among the residents, the Marwaris undoubtedly dominated. This domination was due not only to business acumen but to the ability of the community to organize itself – first in the form of the Marwari *Panchayat;* in voluntary bodies (The Perseverance Society of 1847, including the Bengalis of Barabazar); through informal pressure-group activities in response to taxation and other government policies; and finally in trade associations like the cut-piece merchants' and jute bailers' associations, the Marwari Association of 1898, and the Marwari Chamber of Commerce founded in 1900. The role of ethnic identities in the culture of the traditional bazaar was invested with new functions and norms in the context of modern business activity in colonial Calcutta.

Bengali Business Aristocracy

If one took a walk north of Barabazar in the early nineteenth century roughly along the old pilgrim road of Chitpur, or along one of the new roads northwards made by the Lottery Committee, one would have found on the left and right mansions of the Bengali business aristocracy, rapidly moving into estate-owning rentier status. Between Barabazar and Shobhabazar, for instance, there were the house of Ramdulal Dey at Sutanuti, the palace and bazaar owned by the family of Raja Nabakrishna Deb at Shobhabazar, Ruplal Mallik's mansion on Chitpur Road, the houses

of Raja Sukhamay Ray of Posta and of the relatively impoverished descendants of the famous Sheths and Basaks of Sutanuti.

The families of some of these legendary Bengali business tycoons continued to have business ties in the second or third generation. For instance Radhakrishna Basak (d.1846), descendant of Shobharam, was Diwan to the Bank of Bengal; or again Raja Sukhamay Ray (d.1811) of Lakshmikanta Dhar's family became director of the Bank of Bengal. But an essential trait of the Bengali business aristocracy is captured by a historian of Calcutta, Pradip Sinha, in the phrase 'comprador-Maharaja'. Through a study of wills and the documents of succession-rights lawsuits, he has ably shown how fortunes once made in business were rapidly transformed into estates. A few instances: the Malliks of Sindurpatti, who were gold merchants and *banians,* owned in 1807 a total of ninety-six premises in Calcutta. The Sheths and Basaks of Sutanuti, the leading business families of the eighteenth century, trading in cotton piece-goods, opium, and money-lending with Europeans, switched to investment in urban property. Shobharam Basak left thirty-seven houses to his heirs in 1780, while Ramkrishna Sheth in 1770 left sixteen houses in Barabazar alone. The family of Lakshmikanta Dhar, who made his money as banker to Clive, became mainly rentiers; likewise the Deb family of Shobhabazar. There were some families which were deeper into rural estates than urban property, like the Thakur (Tagore) family after the time of that great entrepreneur, Dwarakanath.

One set of explanations cite social values and cultural traits. If one were to look for that austerity, abstemiousness, and work ethic which Max Weber associated with the accumulation of capital, one would find little evidence of it among the Calcutta business aristocracy. A pattern of conspicuous consumption and waste of resources was characteristic of the new rich of Calcutta. This made the 'comprador-Maharajas' conspicuous and created an impression in public memory of great wealth – while eroding the very basis of wealth. Another explanation, put forward by N.K. Sinha, is that the decline of the rich business families was caused by the litigation following the death of the *karta* under the *dayabhaga* system of succession law peculiar to eastern India. It is true that numerous instances of this kind have been documented. But this does not seem to provide a sufficient explanation for the failure of entrepreneurship in an entire class. It may account for the fall of particular families, but why was their place not taken by others in the arena of commerce?

A third explanation is that capital was diverted from business towards land purchase after the institution of the Permanent Settlement. It has also been said that this was a means of acquiring social status to set the seal on the new wealth earned in business. This hypothesis raises a number of questions. Was the rate of return in *zamindari* higher than that in alternative business opportunities, so as to make *zamindari* a preferred investment choice? We do not yet know enough about the rates of return to answer the question. Moreover, were there many businessmen among the buyers of *zamindaris* after 1793? M.S. Islam's study (*Permanent Settlement in Bengal, 1790-1819,* Dhaka, 1979) suggests that in the period 1793-1819 very few such buyers were businessmen. If land acquisition was a means to social status, was disesteem for business part of Bengal's culture? If so, the law of 1793 should have made little difference. Finally, was purchase of *zamindaris* a cause of the failure of entrepreneurship, or was it a consequence of that failure?

The Artisans' Quarter

A walk through nineteenth-century Calcutta from the thickly populated middle belt to the less densely inhabited northern extremity of the city would have passed by a number of localities named after trades: Kansaripara, the braziers' quarter; Darjipara, the tailors'; Sutanuti, the cotton market; Beniatola, the spice merchants' quarter; Darmahata, the bamboo market; Jeletola, the fishermen's quarter; Kumartuli, the potters' village, and so forth. Steady erosion of those communities in course of the late nineteenth and early twentieth centuries left little except the place-names to mark the former habitation areas of artisan communities. Anthropologists' findings about the Pathuriaghata-Jorabagan area may be typical: in that north-central zone of Calcutta, in the middle of the eighteenth century, there were settlements of *Kangsabaniks, Tantubays* and *Shunris* (manufacturers or dealers in bell-metal, cotton textiles and liquor respectively); but in the late nineteenth century most of them

29.3 *A Shankhari or conchshell-worker. Solvyns*

were gradually pushed out by invasion from Barabazar (see Meera Guha in *Man in India,* 1964, and A. Raychoudhuri, *ibid.,* 1965). Likewise in Dihi Bhabanipur in the extreme south, along the Adi Ganga river (Tolly's Nulla), there were settlements of artisans who were supposedly immigrants from Gobindapur, dislodged from there by the construction of Fort William. Hence the place-names which have survived to this century: Kansaripara, Shankharipara (after the conch-shell workers), Telipara (from the oil-pressers), Potopara (after the makers of earthenware images and the justly famous *pats* or 'bazaar paintings'). With the decline of the traditional crafts and the expansion of the city southwards, these communities yielded place to the middle-class professionals who developed modern Bhabanipur.

The numbers of artisans in Calcutta in the pre-Census period can be guessed from the licences obtained under the Licences Tax Act. In the financial year 1868-69 this number was approximately 3,600. (As against that, there were 6,406 shops for food and drink; 4,919 shops of other kinds; and 4,946 pedlars and itinerant vendors.)

The ratio between the percentage share of the tertiary sector (services and ancillaries to industry) and the secondary sector (industrial production) in the working population (Sabolo's index) is used as a measure of the strength of industrialization or, alternatively, tertiarization. This index reveals that, according to the Census of 1872, Calcutta had a higher ratio of its work-force in the tertiary sector than smaller towns in the hinterland such as Mirzapur, Allahabad, Kanpur or Lucknow. It seems very likely that at the beginning of the nineteenth century artisanal activities in Calcutta, particularly with respect to cotton textiles and connected trades, was in a more flourishing state. The infamous Inland Transit Duty (2.5 per cent to 10 per cent *ad valorem*) was levied between 1801 and 1834 on not less than 235 commodities, including a very large number of artisanal products. Along the Hugli river, the main thoroughfare of commerce, there were sixty *chowkis* or stations within fifty miles of Calcutta for collection of Inland Transit Duty and tolls (apart from stations which collected duties on salt and opium). I have elsewhere described the consequence of this as follows:

From 1813 English goods, excepting liquor, were imported at 2.5 per cent (metals were duty free); hence arose the anomaly of foreign goods enjoying a preference in the home market over the produce of native industry. Secondly, whereas the pre-British system levied a duty proportionate to the distance goods travelled, from 1810 the consolidation into standard rate meant an increase of tax on the great mass of business which consisted of small transactions between town and country. Thirdly, this allowed a scope for chicanery by petty officials and delay in transit. Further, each time goods underwent a change of form (e.g. raw material through various stages into goods for final consumption) a duty was payable - somewhat like a modern value added tax. The foreign imports were granted a waiver. (*The Cambridge Economic History of India,* Vol II, pp. 276-77).

While the increase in Calcutta's population expanded the local market for artisans, the effect of the Inland Transit Duty and the inreasing import of foreign manufactures did not allow the artisanal industry to reap the benefits of these new opportunities. In some areas of artisanal work, the immigration of skilled craftsmen also appears to have affected the conditions of traditional indigenous artisans. John Crawfurd, in his *Sketch of the Commercial Resources ... of British India* (1837), noted that Chinese carpenters were paid almost four times the wages of native artisans, and the few European artisans who were available in Calcutta would earn at a rate incomparably higher: 'While the Indian earns no more than £3 and 12 Shillings to £6 per annum, the Chinese will earn £48' and Europeans in the same trade as much as £100. The *Samachar Darpan* commented on 9 January 1830 that foreign *mistris* having taken up the trade, many native *mistris* had been completely ruined. This was also said to be true of masons, builders, carpenters, tailors etc.

According to John Crawfurd, the lack of skilled industrial labour was a major hindrance in setting up industrial manufactures in Calcutta under English management: 'We may safely consider that the attempt to introduce the complex manufactures of Europe into India, notwithstanding cheapness of raw-material and low price of wages, may be looked upon as a signal commercial blunder.' However, Crawfurd also mentions what appears to be a more weighty reason, the lack of protective tariff: in contrast, he said, 'in St. Petersburg and Moscow...manufacture is conducted under the protection of an enormous duty.' The new industrial establishments that slowly came up in Calcutta, not so much in the period we are concerned with but between 1860 and 1880, involved processing rather than advanced manufacture. H. Beverley in his 1876 survey of Calcutta recorded twenty oil mills, eighteen flour mills, thirteen jute screws etc. Manufactories of a more advanced kind included only five iron foundries and a few cotton and jute mills which developed mostly in the 1870s. The story of the development of modern manufactures in the last half of the nineteenth century belongs to another chapter in this volume.

The decline of artisanal industries was accompanied by an increasing hold of usury and merchant capital over artisans. The artisans' dependence on a *mahajan,* on the middleman's advance of cash or *dadan,* allowed the middleman to dictate terms to the artisans. It is possible that in some non-traditional industries, such as fabrication from imported pig-iron and the incipient small-tools industry (for example, in Haora), there were instances exempt from this general trend.

On the Waterfront

If one sailed up the river Ganga in the middle of the nineteenth century one would pass on the river-front north of Fort William a number of major ghats; some of these were embarkation points. There were the Clive Street Ghat, Rammohan Mallik Ghat and Ruplal Babu Ghat, all roughly opposite the Barabazar and Armanitola areas; and further north or up-stream, the Sutanuti and Rathtala ghats, opposite the Ahiritola and Kumartuli area. Around the end of the nineteenth century Thomas Twining, describing his arrival in Calcutta in 1792 in *Travels in India,* recalls the busy traffic on the river. He sailed up the river in a 'budgerow' towards Calcutta, leaving the English ship about sixty miles downstream. He was impressed with the sight of 'the City of Palaces, with its lofty detached flat-roofed mansions and the masts of innumerable shipping'. Twining's boat, having 'cleared the Esplanade arrived opposite the old fort' – that is, north of the new Fort William.

Along the shore in front of the wharf, and to the north as far as I could see, were a great many ships, all manned with native sailors but commanded principally by English captains, and chiefly belonging to these captains or to British Houses of Trade established in Calcutta. These vessels called country ships were employed in Indian seas exclusively... I quitted the boat at a spacious sloping *ghaut* or landing place.

Beyond the clutch of country ships seen by Twining at the main wharf near Fort William, there would have been smaller boats anchored near the northern *ghats,* less frequented by Englishmen. These smaller boats plied along the Ganga river system, the lifeline of Bengal's commerce until the railways were built. These low-tonnage boats carried the goods pouring into Calcutta: apart from the staple items, jute (from the 1830s) and rice, they brought coarse sugar and molasses, oil seeds, tobacco, raw silk, fish, vegetables and, up to the early decades of the nineteenth century, coarse cloth. These imports into Calcutta through internal trade were immense by the standards of the day. Major Ralph Smyth in his statistical survey of

29.4 *'Pykars or pedlars'. Mrs Belnos*

the 24-Parganas District in 1857 estimated that from that district alone, fish worth Rs 2,000 was despatched to Calcutta daily, vegetables worth Rs 80,000 annually, *gur* amounting annually to 20,000 maunds, and so forth.

The *mahajan* in interior districts, through the agency of the *ghat majhis,* would commission the services of the *majhis* or boatmen of the cargo boats. The *mahajans* or *aratdars* in turn obtained their commodities from *paikars, dalals,* and brokers of various categories, as well as through direct purchase in the *hats* or village marts and fairs. Till the 1850s it was the small country boats which linked the great bazaar of Calcutta with the hinterland. In *The Cambridge Economic History of India,* I have described the complex hierarchized market network in nineteenth-century Bengal.

When we turn from internal trade to the overseas export trade of Calcutta, we enter an arena already hegemonized by the British in the late eighteenth century. It is true that in the early nineteenth century there were some native ship-owners and participants in overseas trade; Ramdulal Dey (1752-1825) and Matilal Sheel (1792-1854) have become part of Bengali folklore as great merchant princes. Actually, however, the Indian share of the total tonnage of ships over 80 tons registered in the port of

Calcutta was small: 5.2 per cent in 1805, 4 per cent in 1817, and 8 per cent in 1825. And of these only one-third on an average were owned by Bengali Hindu ship-owners. In contrast, in Bombay half or sometimes more than half of Bombay-registered shipping tonnage was owned by Indian ship-owners.

With the increasing use of modern ships with iron hulls and steam engines, the construction and use of timber-built sailing vessels declined drastically, in both Calcutta and Bombay: This happened in the last three decades of the nineteenth century. As late as 1861-62, 803 sailing vessels visited Calcutta port against only 89 steam vessels; the ratio changed in favour of the steamers in the 1880s. The technological level of Calcutta shipping also remained low. For example, it did not have a modern wet dock till the 1890s, despite the efforts of the Bengal Chamber of Commerce since 1843; and the Calcutta Port Trust for administration and development of the port was set up as late as 1870. It sufficed for the Government in the first half of the nineteenth century if Calcutta port served as a funnel for export of textiles, metals, minor manufactures and bullion. However, the engine of external commerce, controlled by British hands, did leave space for Indian business interests in a subordinate position in the interstices of that system.

The European Citadel

'The Black Town is to the north of Calcutta, and contiguous to it,' wrote the French visitor L. de Grandpré, in *A Voyage in the Indian Ocean and to Bengal* (1803). 'Calcutta' for him consisted of Fort William, the Esplanade fronted with a series of European mansions, the Square (later Dalhousie Square, now B.B.D. Bag) and a few churches:

As we enter the town, a very expansive Square opens before us, with a large expanse of water in the middle, for the public use... . The Square itself is composed of magnificent houses which render Calcutta not only the handsomest town in Asia, but one of the finest in the world. One side of the square consists of a range of buildings occupied by persons in civil employments under the Company, such as writers in the public offices.

Close by were lesser buildings housing the British business houses, declaring by their proximity the happy marriage between British administration and British business.

It is easy to elaborate on the rise and growth of the White Town and British business; the literature on that subject is immense. I have preferred to give more attention to the 'native' part of the city. The essence of the British story in the first half of the nineteenth century was the establishment of the hegemony of British capital in the colonial metropolis through the subordination of native capital on the one hand, and the curtailment of the outmoded monopoly privileges of the East India Company on the other. The Company's monopoly, greatly eroded by the late eighteenth century under the onslaught of the Free Merchants and the private trade of the Company's servants, was finally terminated in respect of Indian trade in 1813 and China trade in 1833. Thus the Agency Houses – born out of wedlock, so to speak, in an alliance between the private trading interests of the Company's servants and the Free Merchants – won freedom from the legal restrictions which had earlier limited them to 'country trade', that is Indian and Asian trade.

'The government of an exclusive company of merchants is perhaps the worst of all governments for any country whatsoever': thus Adam Smith. However, the separation of sovereignty from commerce by the Charter Acts of the early nineteenth century brought about a regime of 'Free Trade' characterized by three features: systematized inequality between native and British participants in that trade; gross speculative malpractices often amounting to fraud; and the growth of a collective monopoly of some leading British business houses. Apart from these three broad trends, the role of the state-backed banking system was also crucial in lowering the status of indigenous capital *vis-à-vis* British.

The source of the inequality was the access of the British business interests (organized in the Bengal Chamber of Commerce, founded in 1834) to decision-making processes in the Government owing to commonality of interests, as well as pressure-group activities and the long reach of British businessmen to those who held political power in London. The malpractices in colonial business were possible owing to certain infirmities in the British Indian legal system till the middle of the nineteenth century. The consequences were disastrous for the indigenous capitalists, who suffered more losses than their European principals – for instance, in the business crises from 1830–34 to the failure of the Union Bank in 1848.

The monopolistic control of a handful of British business houses developed fairly early. For example, in 1830 only six Agency Houses of Calcutta owned or managed 65 per cent of the vessels belonging to the port of Calcutta, all the dockyards used by the larger ships, all the collieries and the only textile mill in Bengal. This monopoly was intensified by their access to the financial support of the government in the form of loans at times of crisis and, of course, their control of overseas import-export trade in Calcutta.

'A subject race under an alien rule cannot attain welfare.' Such was the title of a remarkable essay in 1855 in the journal *Sarbashubhakari* (with which Ishwarchandra Vidyasagar was associated). It observed:

Racial prejudice and self-interest are strong forces among all men, and therefore alien rulers will first attend to their own interest and the welfare of their own race before paying attention to the welfare of the subject people.

English rule, the author said, had ruined the business of the natives: because of this decline of business, hundreds of people in Calcutta were supplicants for petty jobs, and as their numbers increased their salary declined. 'The white masters treat the employees with greater disdain than they would treat inferior animals' (literally 'jackals and dogs'). Although the essay ends by advising Indians to return to business, it generally conveys a sense of despair. Perhaps it was the same oppressive alien presence that Mirza Ghalib sensed and expressed in a poem on Calcutta: 'What calling would a man do best to follow here? There is no calling you can follow free from fear... .'

WEALTH AND WORK
IN CALCUTTA
1860–1921

Amiya Kumar Bagchi

Calcutta, the Capital City

Calcutta was the seat of the government of British India until 1911, and the commercial capital of the British Indian empire down to the First World War. Except for two decades – the 1850s and 1860s – when Bombay overtook it, Calcutta was throughout the nineteenth century the point of largest outflow of exports from India as well as imports into the country. Until the development of the railway network in Punjab and Sind, and the rise of the port of Karachi, it was through Calcutta that the agricultural exports of the whole Gangetic basin, part of the Indus basin, and central India found their way to East Asia, Europe and the USA. From the 1870s and 1880s, exports from Punjab, Sind and Rajasthan, as well as parts of central India and Uttar Pradesh, increasingly found their way abroad through Karachi and Bombay. But Calcutta added new exports to the list: tea, raw jute and, increasingly, jute manufactures. Calcutta was the *entrepôt* for imports of cotton piece-goods and other manufactures into its hinterland, consisting of Assam, Bengal, Bihar and Orissa, most of today's Uttar Pradesh, large parts of central India and, in the beginning, British Burma and parts of the Madras Presidency as well.

Most of these exports and imports were controlled by British firms from the point of their entry into Calcutta and, in the case of such commodities as jute, tea, opium, mica and manganese, from the point of production or extraction as well. Many of those firms were domiciled in Calcutta, but not all. For a long time, tea companies registered in the UK controlled more acreage than those registered in India. These 'sterling' companies as they were called had their own marketing networks; their finances were handled mostly through banks registered in Britain. Moreover, the profits made in the Anglo-Indian rupee and sterling companies were regularly transmitted abroad, and contributed only a trickle to the accumulation of capital assets in India or to the disposable incomes of Indians. Hence the impact of the operations of the British (Anglo-Indian or sterling) firms was much smaller than might be guessed from the figures of the foreign, coastal or inland trade of Calcutta.

In order to understand the changing structure of the commercial and financial world of Calcutta, it is necessary to have some idea of the distribution of wealth and incomes in the city, for the character of local commerce was greatly influenced by that of local purchasing power and local custom.

The memory of Calcutta as the seat of Empire inspires visions of grandeur and riches. Grandeur there was and riches too. But as H.E.A. Cotton put it at the time when its colonial glory was coming to a close, Calcutta was a 'queen of two faces : a city of startling contrasts, of palaces and hovels, of progress and reaction, of royal grandeur and of squalor that beggar[ed] description'. For eight months in the year, the seat of government was Shimla and not Calcutta: an annual transplantation begun in the days of Sir John Lawrence and lasting right through the period we are covering.

The rich Europeans lived in the central part of the city. As the bureaucracy expanded and the wealth of the Europeans grew, the squalor in their part of Calcutta was removed, and the face of the city changed noticeably. But concomitantly, the poor were moved out to the periphery of the city – not only the suburbs which were later incorporated within municipal limits but also to more outlying areas. Public amenities in Calcutta were very unequally distributed between the 'native' or 'Black' Town (chiefly the north of Calcutta, and the more southerly portions of the southern part) and the parts where Europeans lived; also, within the Black Town, between those which harboured the mansions of the rich and those which only housed the poor.

Changes in Population and Occupational Structure

Originally, the 'town' of Calcutta, for which the various Municipal Acts were designed, consisted of 20 mauzas or 19 wards. From 1888 onwards the Calcutta municipal area came to incorporate parts of Chitpur, Ultadanga, Maniktala, Beliaghata, Entali, Kashipur, all of Beniapukur, Baliganj, Watganj and Ekbalpur, and parts of Garden Reach and Tollyganj. The population of Calcutta as enumerated by official censuses between 1872 and 1921 is given in Table 1.

By the Municipal Consolidation Act of 1888, the area under municipal jurisdiction was increased from 11,954 acres to 20,547 acres, that is, by nearly 72 per cent; but the population added thereby was only 45 per cent. By and large, the density of population decreased from the centre of Calcutta to the more outlying wards. But the population density within the central area also varied greatly. It was far higher in wards inhabited mainly by Indians, such as Kalutola, Barabazar and Jorabagan, than in wards where Europeans lived such as Park Street, Waterloo Street and Victoria Terrace (formerly Bamun Bustee). Moreover, in the successive slum-clearance drives, the 'European' wards generally gained most in terms of space per resident at the cost, of course, of the bustee-dwellers who were expelled from the area.

While some of the northern wards were inhabited by families which had come there in the eighteenth or early nineteenth centuries, in

TABLE 1 The Population of Calcutta 1872-1891

	(a) Old Town			(b) Calcutta Municipal Area		
	Males	*Females*	*Total*	*Males*	*Females*	*Total*
1872	299,857	147,644	447,601			
1876	282,506	147,029	429,535			
1881	288,817	144,402	433,219			
1891	318,739	149,813	468,552	446,746	234,814	681,560
1901				562,596	285,200	847,796
1911				607,674	288,393	896,067
1921				617,590	290,261	907,851

Notes : (a) including the population of the Fort and the Port area.
(b) including the population of the Fort, the Port area and the canals.
Sources : Maguire, *Report on the Census of Calcutta*, 1891, pp. 16-18; Census of India, 1911, Vol. VI, *City of Calcutta*, Part II, *Tables* by L. S. S. O'Malley; *Census of India*, 1921, Vol. V, Bengal, Part II, *Tables* by W. H. Thompson.

The Census of 1872 was considered to be unreliable; hence a special, more carefully conceived Census was carried out in 1876. Again, the Census of 1891 has been adjudged to be defective as compared with that of 1901; hence the growth of population between the two dates may have been overestimated by the Census figures. However, the figures will serve for our present purposes.

most wards the immigrant element was very visible. The immigrants included Europeans, but also traders from Rajputana and other north Indian states, and general labourers and artisans from Bihar, the United Provinces (earlier called the North Western Provinces), Orissa, the Central Province and Madras. The immigrants were mostly male adult workers: taking immigrants and residents together there were two males to every female, and there were far fewer children than in a population of normal, balanced age-structure. As a result, Calcutta's population failed to replenish itself through growth within the city: it was only the stream of immigrants that kept the population growing.

The high mortality rate also contributed to the situation; and here too, different Calcuttans faced different degrees of risk. Cholera took a toll every year, as did various unspecified 'fevers' including 'Burdwan fever', that is malaria. The northern or 'native' part of the town had far more than its fair share of these visitations. For example, out of 697 deaths from cholera during the fourth quarter of 1882, 'no less than 540 occurred in the north of the town,…against 157 in the nine wards of the south of the town. Only two deaths occurred in the Park Street ward and only four in the Waterloo ward.' (*The Statesman,* 5 February 1883) When sanitation work was taken up in earnest and water supply improved, the European quarters and, to a lesser extent, the central district benefited more than the outlying wards. More glaringly than ever, spatial patterns reproduced the inequality of the human condition.

Most Calcuttans made a living from work, in trade, industry, transport and other services. Some made a living openly as rent-receivers; some others must have been 'agriculturists' (according to census returns) only in the sense of owning enough land or *zamindari* rights to preclude their having to work for a living. Successive censuses indicate the changes in the occupational structure of the city. But the concepts and schemes of classification differed from census to census. In Table 2, we have attempted a summary of the changes between 1891 and 1921 in the number of persons engaged or dependent upon two major occupations: trade or commerce (including banking, momeylending, etc.), and secondary industry, that is the production of material substances

other than agricultural products from the soil. The censuses of 1911 and 1921 conveniently separated the pure traders from manufacturers or manufacturers-cum-sellers. In 1891 and 1901, such separation had not been made consistently. Hence I have regrouped the data, adding the pure sellers of material substances to the category of general merchants, grocers, etc. and, conformably, grouping together all persons engaged in secondary industry as defined above.

The occupational structure of Calcutta changed under pressure of four different kinds. First, Calcutta had a surprisingly large industrial population for an imperial capital, where we might have expected the apparatus of government and the residential demands of the bureaucrats to push most industries to outlying areas. Some industries catered to local demand, especially from the rich: carriage-makers, saddlers, jewellers, dress shops, ice factories, and shops turning out innumerable items of food and house furnishings. Building firms catered to the growth and improvement of the city. But there were also industries connected with exports, such as jute presses. The near-total lack of town planning regulations allowed any enterprise to be located anywhere: there was no separation of residential and industrial zones. As late as 13 September 1890, a correspondent to *The Statesman* complained about a chimney belonging to Mackintosh Burn & Co. belching out black smoke in the Bentinck Street area.

When the European wards of the town were improved, the more noisome industries moved to other parts of the city. In his 1914 plan for the improvement of the city, E.P. Richards, Chief Engineer of the Calcutta Improvement Trust, described the industrial belt of Calcutta as follows:

The larger [manufacturing area] is formed along and between the railways and canals of north east Calcutta. It extends north in a broad band…from south of Sealdah station, right up to the north limits of Calcutta. Still unbroken, it then turns west and continues south some distance down the Hooghly bank. It is of horseshoe shape with the arms of unequal length, having the end of the long arm on Sealdah, the curve on Cossipore Bridge and the short arm finishing on the river bank near Aheeritollah Ghat. From the east, the Cornwallis Street residential area is now being seriously eaten into by this growing manufacturing district, which deals mostly with jute, cotton, ropes and flour manufacture.

TABLE 2 Industry and Trade in the Occupational Structure of the City of Calcutta, 1891-1921

		Actual workers			Total no. of workers and dependants
		Males	Females	Total	
1891					
(1)	Engaged in trade	54,135	3,480	57,615	116,263
(2)	Engaged in industry	67,562	2,172	69,734	120,496
(3)	All occupations	329,203	68,882	398,085	681,560
(4)	Percentage of (1) to (3)			14.5	17.1
(5)	Percentage of (2) to (3)			17.5	17.7
1901					
(1)	Engaged in trade	86,890	5,970	92,860	179,062
(2)	Engaged in industry	90,135	6,944	97,079	169,521
(3)	All occupations	441,969	66,236	508,205	847,796
(4)	Percentage of (1) to (3)			18.3	21.2
(5)	Percentage of (2) to (3)			19.3	20.0
1911					
(1)	Engaged in trade	88,102	6,530	94,632	169,286
(2)	Engaged in industry	97,156	5,925	103,521	172,929
(3)	All occupations	482,277	61,177	543,454	896,067
(4)	Percentage of (1) to (3)			17.4	19.0
(5)	Percentage of (2) to (3)			19.0	19.3
1921					
(1)	Engaged in trade	91,893	6,335	98,228	184,537
(2)	Engaged in industry	75,073	4,561	79,634	132,179
(3)	All occupations	476,006	52,660	528,766	907,746
(4)	Percentage of (1) to (3)			18.5	20.3
(5)	Percentage of (2) to (3)			15.1	14.0

Source and Notes : Computed on the basis of Census Reports and accompanying *Table* volumes, cited under Table 1. The occupations had to be regrouped for 1891 and 1901, so as to separate, as far as possible, the pure sellers from makers and sellers, or makers of material substances.

This probably demarcates the greatest extent of manufacturing industries in the city proper. Apart from some new war-related engineering and other units, industry was henceforth slowly displaced from the heart of Calcutta by the demands of trade and the professions. However, the displacement was a long-drawn process and has not yet been completed. Manufacturing brought riches to a few and subsistence-level wages to others; but the crudeness of the manufacturing processes, and the near-total absence of regulations on permitted processes, posed serious problems to the residents of the city.

The second factor that influenced the occupational structure of Calcutta was the character of the immigrant population. This in turn was doubtless influenced by pressures in their place of origin as well as the varying nature of demand for their services in the city. The Census Report of 1911 undertook a special return for 289,566 immigrants belonging to twenty-six large and representative castes. Here are some of their findings :

There are only 2 females to every 5 male immigrants; over two-thirds of the latter are actual workers, but only one-fourth of the females are engaged in any occupation. Prostitutes alone account for one-fourth of the female workers, and their number is equal to one-seventh of the women of adult age. Altogether 15 per cent of both sexes are under 15 years of age. Half the women and two-thirds of the men are adults, i.e. aged 15 to 40; at this age period there are three males to every female. Trade engaged the energies of 19 per cent of the male workers. While 14 per cent are employed in domestic service, 13 per cent are day labourers and 7 per cent are clerks. Domestic service accounts for the largest population of female workers, viz., 42 per cent, and then come prostitutes with 25 per cent.

In fact, this census of immigrants in 1911 foreshadowed the direction of changes in the occupational structure of the city population as a whole between 1911 and 1921. For example, the proportion of traders among the immigrant workers was six times that of workers in mills and factories. At a more disaggregated level, we find in 1911 the domestic servants among immigrant workers outnumbering the prostitutes virtually in a proportion of 2 : 1.

The Census authorities were almost obsessed with caste at this time, creating new mischievous rigidities of segregation, and even generating new traditions and status symbols on an immense scale. Yet census after census found a number of castes to be engaged in every occupation: 'superior' castes such as Brahmins or Kayasthas were carrying out all kinds of menial or lowly tasks such as domestic service, daily-wage labour, begging and so on. Mills and factories provided employment for immigrants belonging to all the listed castes except the 'trading' castes of Agarwala, Gandhabanik, Maheshwari and Subarnabanik, and the Baidyas, the Shunris and the Dhobis. Prostitutes seemed to have come mainly from West Bengal districts, from typical peasant as well as uppercaste backgrounds.

Calcutta obviously acted as a melting-pot for all castes and communities, mixing and merging them in respect of occupations or

avocations. Trading, for example, could be undertaken by almost any caste: in 1911 the Brahmins and the Kayasthas formed a third of the traders and outnumbered 'the members of all the mercantile castes, viz., Agarwalas, Gandhabaniks, Maheshwaris, Subarnabaniks and Telis taken together'.

However, 'traders' could designate both the haughty merchant princes or magnates of British business houses and banks, and the lowly pedlar hawking a basketload of wares on his head. In between came a whole range of shopkeepers, moneylenders and bankers, spread all over Calcutta but concentrated in the central districts. Increasingly, the wealthiest element among them was constituted by the Jains and the Hindu traders from Rajasthan. Between 1901 and 1911 the largest supply of immigrants, after the Bengal districts, Bihar, Orissa and the United Provinces, was provided by Rajputana, chiefly from Jaipur (8,000) and Bikaner (7,000). According to the 1911 Census report, emigration to Calcutta from this area was growing in popularity: the number rose from 15,000 to 21,000 in the preceding ten years.

Calcutta's popularity with the Marwaris and North Indian traders continued to grow in the decade 1911-21. In the latter year, as many as 23 out of every 1000 Calcuttans were found to have been born in Rajputana. According to the Census report of 1921, they absorbed much of the piece-goods trade and were brokers in many other commodities. Their clerks and servants also generally came from Rajputana: 'They are almost the only Indian race which really favours the town life,' said the report, 'and those who have settled in Calcutta are well off and have usually brought their families with them.' But their habit of saving space and preserving communal confidentiality by crowding into the areas where their clansmen had already settled doubtless increased the congestion of the central business district and adjoining areas.

Briefly, it can be said that the city passed the peak of its manufacturing and administrative functions by 1921, thereafter becoming more a city of traders, moneylenders, professionals, and of course labourers. As the population became more settled and the sex ratio less unfavourable, the demand for prostitutes declined and that for domestic service increased. The departure of many Europeans after the

30.1 *Marwari merchants of Calcutta: old engraving*

transfer of the capital to New Delhi doubtless brought down the demand for many types of luxury goods, as of European prostitutes.

Living Space

How was the growing population of Calcutta accommodated? In terms of both space and civic amenities, the population fared poorly in most wards. The urban rich, who generally provide funds for improvement of most cities, did not want to part with money at the best of times. According to the statistics cited by A.K. Ray in *A Short History of Calcutta* (1902) the revenues of the town administration (including ground rent) grew from Rs 2,84,000 in 1821 only to Rs 4,19,167 in 1850, in spite of the increasing need of funds for sanitation and public utilities of various kinds. Between 1875 and 1901, the municipal revenues (including ground rent) increased from Rs 21,79,589 to Rs 57,86,580. (Ground rent formed an increasingly unimportant part of the total, being Rs 18,000 in 1821 and Rs 19,113 in 1901.)

The increase in total revenue looks impressive until we remember that the backlog of public utility works in the pestilential city had accumulated at least since the late eighteenth century, and that both the overcrowding and the wealth of the central districts were increasing much faster than the population. To take just one instance of the increase of wealth, it has been estimated that the real value of jute manufactures from Bengal, which contributed so mightily to the wealth of the Anglo-Indian firms, was virtually doubling every ten years between 1880 and 1910. A similar story could be told about Anglo-Indian firms in the tea, coal, and jute trading sectors: the bigger firms, of course, dealt in practically all those commodities. But the Europeans were birds of passage though their firms were not. They often left their families at home, visited them on furlough, and returned to them when they retired or took over as London (or Edinburgh or Manchester or Glasgow) partners of the firm. In any case, the British businessmen and bureaucrats, civil or military, had their children educated at 'Home'. Calcutta was not home for them, and they were not going to spend more money on it than they could help.

The European businessmen, of course, wanted a better infrastructure for carrying on their trade. In particular, they wanted better port facilities. When at one stage, there were proposals for combining the municipal and port facilities, the businessmen and their representatives protested through the newspapers controlled by them as also through the Bengal Chamber of Commerce, and made their voices heard in the consultative councils of the Governor-General and the Lieutenant-Governor of Bengal.

A separate Port Trust with its own finances was created in 1870. It improved the docking, berthing, loading, unloading and warehousing facilities of Calcutta as a port, but left the civic facilities strictly alone. In the 1880s, there was a proposal to build a warehouse at the port exclusively for tea. The Municipal Commissioners and the British Indian Association protested, presumably on civic and environmental grounds, although the tea industry was almost wholly under British control. The warehouse was erected nonetheless.

The constitution of the Calcutta municipal administration was almost entirely bureaucratic, with the government nominating the Commissioners and civil servants serving as Chairmen. From the 1870s onward, the elective principle came to be more pronounced. As Indians acquired a stronger voice in the municipal administration, the implicit conflict of interest grew more and more apparent between the predominantly Indian owners of houses (including slum dwellings rented out at exorbitant rates but with no civic amenities) and the European businessmen and bureaucrats. The Europeans wanted more spacious houses, wider streets and more sanitary conditions – for themselves – but were not prepared to pay for them in proportion to their wealth, income or exalted requirements. The Indians could not see much point in beautifying the European part of the city at a direct cost to their pockets: they would have to fork out higher rates, while losing as slum landlords if the *bustees* were demolished. The slum dwellers would lose out either way. If they remained where they were, they lived miserably and died like flies from cholera, smallpox, malaria and other fevers, and plague (though the last was a minor curse

compared to its incidence in Bombay or Kanpur). When they were pushed out, they moved to equally noxious slums, and had to travel farther and spend more to go to work.

The natural solution for a city such as Calcutta was for the supreme government to spend generously for civic improvement. As Richards pointed out in his report of 1914, Calcutta did not have the financial resources 'to carry out, unaided, the reformation of fifty years of neglect.' Calcutta was neglected even when it was a capital city, and the neglect has continued ever since.

The Europeans now exerted *force majeure* to get what they wanted – mostly at the cost of the Indians. From the 1890s, the elected element in the municipal administration was virtually eliminated, and the Europeans (including representatives of their major commercial associations, the Bengal Chamber of Commerce and the Calcutta Trades Association) came to be the controlling element. The densely-populated Bamun Bustee, for example, was removed to make way for Victoria Terrace; roads were widened in the mainly European wards (which included, in 1921, Baliganj-Tollyganj as well as Park Street, Waterloo Street and Victoria Terrace), and the benefits of sewerage and municipal water supply were more heavily concentrated in those wards. The unequal endowment of space per inhabitant in Calcutta can be gauged from the density per acre in the different wards between 1881 and 1921 (Table 3).

From Table 3 it can be seen that whatever increase in population took place in the half-century from 1872 to 1921 was mostly accommodated in those northern and central wards which were regarded as Indian quarters or in the low-density peripheral wards. The European-dominated wards hardly gained any population and in some cases actually lost it. The only Indian-dominated wards to lose population significantly towards the end of one period were Kalutola and Watganj – the former because of the driving of the Central Avenue through the area and the latter because of a temporary depression of trade (owing to Non-Cooperation?) at the time of the 1921 Census.

Patterns of Ownership and Management of Industry

The above account would already indicate that

Table 3 Density of Population Per Acre in the Different Wards of Calcutta 1872-1921

Ward	1872	1881		1901	1911	1921
1. Shyampukur	71	70	90	115	130	139
2. Kumartuli	157	118	123	139	152	157
3. Bartala	74	72	90	125	136	152
4. Sukea Street	78	76	109	131	150	173
5. Jorabagan	161	149	161	202	214	216
6. Jorasanko	138	125	159	202	227	219
7. Barabazar	108	96	95	146	141	152
8. Kalutola	227	211	227	282	255	172
9. Muchipara	95	95	108	139	138	151
10. Boubazar	160	147	154	184	170	184
11. Padmapukur	123	124	125	169	181	197
12. Waterloo Street	27	27	28	30	30	34
13. Fenwick Bazar	140	135	148	163	148	136
14. Taltala	137	132	148	163	162	160
15. Kalinga	71	66	74	94	64	66
16. Park Street	30	32	30	40	35	25
17. Victoria Terrace	51	48	36	43	24	25
18. Hastings	48	47	45	55	51	40
19. Entali	25	24	31	35	41	43
20. Beniapukur	24	23	28	34	46	43
21. Baliganj Tollyganj	11	10	11	13	19	25
22. Bhabanipur	45	47	52	61	67	70
23. Alipur	16	11	12	14	16	18
24. Ekbalpur	20	17	17	23	24	34
25. Watganj	32	38	37	52	60	47
Calcutta Municipal Area average	51	48	54	68	72	74

Source : Census of India, 1921, Vol. VI, *City of Calcutta,* Part I, *Report,* p.16.

Calcutta was a colonial city, dominated by an alien minority, and with a highly heterogeneous Indian population constituting the other strata of society. At the top of the European society, as the fount of honour and patronage for the Europeans and even more for the Indians, were the Viceroy and his Council. The Viceroy's salary was Rs 10,000 a month, and that of the members of his council appropriately graduated. The real incomes of the senior bureaucrats and judges were generally far higher than their official salaries (which ranged above Rs 2,500), as they were usually provided free or subsidized housing and an elaborate retinue of servants.

The European merchant princes, of course, earned considerably more than most of the civil servants. But their status was measured by the kind of honour which they received from the Government Houses at Esplanade or Belvedere. The expenditures made by the European merchant princes and civil servants helped to maintain retainers and, as we have already indicated, numerous mostly small-scale luxury industries. *The Friend of India* remarked that Calcutta was regarded as the 'Paradise of Swells'. But a major part (perhaps half) of the incomes of these grandees regularly leaked out to Blighty, to pay for the upkeep of their wives and children and for the accumulation of a fortune.

Even after such remittances to Britain, the Europeans managed to control larger and larger values of manufacturing, mining, planting and banking capital in eastern India, Calcutta in particular. Table 4 gives some idea of the distribution of control over enterprises above a certain size in Calcutta in 1911 and 1921. It must be remembered that most of the bigger enterprises were controlled by registered companies, the majority of which had Europeans as directors. And these companies employed a

TABLE 4 Ownership Pattern of Establishments in Calcutta and Suburbs Employing 20 or More Persons in 1911 and 1921

	Total number of establishments.	Those directed by government or local bodies.	Those directed by registered companies.	Those owned by private persons		
				Europeans or Anglo-Indians	Indians	Others
1911	572	24	105	85	351	7
1921	643	20	180*	55	361	7

Source : Census of India, 1921, Vol. XI, *City of Calcutta*, Part I, *Report*, Chapter IX, Subsidiary Table VI.

Note : * So printed here, although 190 in other tables.

much larger number of persons on an average than an ordinary establishment. In 1911, for example, out of the 105 registered companies, 94 had Europeans (with a few Eurasians) as directors; 4 had a combination of European, Eurasian and Indian directors, and only 7 had Indian directors alone. In 1921, the number of registered companies was 190; of these 119 had directors who were Europeans or Eurasians, 40 had only Indians as directors and 31 had a mixed board of Indians, Europeans and Eurasians.

In some establishments, mainly the larger ones demanding newer types of technology, the managers were European or Eurasian even where the ownership was Indian. Among the Indians, the Bengalis – especially Hindus – were more in evidence than most other groups. Between 1911 and 1921, the number of enterprises owned or managed by Marwaris or other north Indian trading groups grew; but even at the later date, the presence of these groups in industry of any kind was rather feeble.

Table 5 throws some light on the changing management pattern of industrial enterprises

TABLE 5 Management Pattern of Establishments in Calcutta and Suburbs, 1911 and 1921

	MANAGED BY						
	Europeans and Anglo-Indians	Hindu bhadralok groups (a)	Bengali trading groups and other Hindus (b)	Marwaris or North Indian trading groups (c)	Muslims (d)	Others (e)	Total
1911	202	160	134	8	22	47	573
1921	218	202	440	29	95	23	1007

Sources: Census of India, 1911, Vol. VI, *City of Calcutta*, Part II, *Tables,* p.114 (Table XV-E); and Census of India, 1921, Vol.VI, *City of Calcutta*, Part II, *Tables,* Table XXII, Part III.

Notes: (a) This is the classification used in 1921 but not in 1911; we have grouped the Baidyas, the Brahmins and the Kayasthas in 1911 as the *bhadraloks* for this is how the census authorities seemed to have grouped the castes. This may overstate the importance of this group since some 'Kayasths' may have been of non-Bengali origin.

(b) The 1921 Census gives 'Bengali trading classes' and 'other Hindus' separately; we have clubbed them and taken this category to be comparable to that of the total of 'Banias, Kalus, Kansaris, Chasi Kaibarttas, Sadgops, Subarnabaniks, Tantis, Telis and Tilis', whose numbers among managers are shown separately in the 1911 census.

(c) For 1911, the only group shown was 'Marwaris'; we have taken this figure to be comparable to that of 'upcountry trading classes' in the 1921 census.

(d) For 1911, the category given was of 'Sheikhs'; we have taken this to be synonymous with Muslims.

(e) 'Others' included Chinese and Parsis.

between 1911 and 1921. In interpreting the data in Table 5, it has to be borne in mind that only 623 out of the 1,007 enterprises in 1921 were at all comparable to the 573 enterprises of 1911; the rest were much smaller in size, and it is mostly these latter that were owned or managed by Indians. Considering their later record, the Bengali *bhadralok* and Bengali Hindu traders owned and managed a surprisingly large number of industrial enterprises. From more detailed data gathered in the censuses of 1911 and 1921, we know that Bengali Hindus were to be found in large numbers as managers and owners of printing presses, oil mills, bakeries, flour mills and rice mills; also, more surprisingly, iron foundries, iron and steel works, and a few tanneries or leather works. The Kalus were the only caste which seemed to have adhered to their ascribed calling: all the seventeen owners or managers among Kalus in 1911 ran oil mills.

So the enthusiasm for *swadeshi,* fed both by the official propaganda of men like George Birdwood, E.B. Havell, and Trailokyanath Mukherji (1847–1919) and the nationalist efforts of Jogendrachandra Ghosh, Manindrachandra Nandi (1860–1930), Satyasundar Deb (1880?–1971) and nationalist ex-officials such as Pramathanath Basu (1855–1935), had a wide social base. But this base was about to crumble in at least two of its bastions. The Bengal Tenancy Act of 1885 and the successive survey and settlement operations which limited the arbitrary rent-enhancing powers of the landlord, hit the old *zamindars* or lesser landholding gentry very hard. So did the agricultural depression of the 1920s and 1930s. From the other side, the Marwaris and other North Indian traders gradually came to capture the inland trade of Calcutta's hinterland, including that in jute – the source of greatest lucre for the traders and greatest misery for the Bengal peasantry in bad years.

Willingness to take risks and appropriate technical education were not equipment enough for lasting business success in a colonial economy where the government for a long time refused to patronize large-scale industry under Indian control. Only prowess in finance and marketing could have allowed any businessmen to ride out trade cycles in such an economy. The weakness of the Bengalis in business had already been evident to discerning onlookers in the 1870s, when the 'young hopefuls' were advised by the editor of *The*

Slum Life in Old Calcutta: Some Statistics

Year	Number of Kutcha Houses		
1706	8,000		
1726	13,300		
1742	14,747		
1756	14,450		
1794	13,657		

	Tiled huts	Thatched huts	Total
1821	15,792	37,497	53,289
1831	19,419	35,354	54,773
1837	20,304	30,567	50,871
1850	48,314	...	48,314
1866	43,575	...	43,575
1872	18,421	...	18,421
1876	22,860	...	22,860
1881	20,667	...	20,667
1891	24,191	...	24,191
1901	49,007	...	49,007

Notes:

(a) Thatched huts were prohibited by law in 1837.

(b) The sharp decline in the number of huts after 1872 seems likely to be caused by differences in the basis of enumeration more than by actual civic uplift.

Source: A. K. Ray, *A Short History of Calcutta* (1902).

Statesman to buy land and combine landholding with the calling of a *bania.*

The 1890s and early 1900s seem to have still provided the Bengali upper classes with opportunities for small-scale industrial investment in the interstices of an agrarian economy. But when the Marwaris captured 'the commanding heights' of trade from the Europeans, the more enlightened form of capital of the educated Bengalis was overwhelmed by the less progressive form which could better integrate itself with the changing demands of a late-colonial economy. A finer analysis of the data would reveal the symptoms of change already between 1911 and 1921.

The Muslims, whether Bengalis or from outside Bengal, fared badly as industrialists or traders. They constituted a much smaller proportion of factory-owners than of the popula-

30.2 A horse drawn tram in front of the High Court. An old sketch

tion. There were some rich Nakhuda merchants who traded mainly with West Asia, but most others operated on a small scale. There were practically no bankers of importance among them. This was a major source of their weakness *vis-à-vis* the Marwaris, who combined both trade and banking. The latter financed the operations of the Nakhudas, to whom (as to Bengali traders) they offered worse terms than to the members of their own community. Of course there were rich Muslims such as the descendants of Tipu Sultan or of the Nawabs of Lucknow, the Nawab of Murshidabad or the members of the Nawab family of Dhaka, who all maintained establishments in Calcutta. But few of these wealthy men engaged openly in trade, industry or banking, although the chief shareholders of the Dacca Bank (later absorbed by the Bank of Bengal) had belonged to the Dhaka Nawab's family. In the jute trade, Adamji Haji Dawood, a Muslim merchant from western India, became one of the biggest traders after the First World War, and his firm went on to found the Adamji Jute Mills. But one Dawood could not alter the relative positions of Hindus and Muslims among Indian businessmen.

The Condition of Wage-earners

Our attention has so far been confined to the owners of land and capital. How did they fare who owned mostly nothing but their bodies (and sometimes not even that) and constituted the vast majority of Calcutta's population? A connected history of the labouring poor of Calcutta is still to be written, and we will not try to encompass the task here. Let us first try to figure out how much they earned and how their earnings varied over time. An idea of the monthly earnings and the cost of living can be obtained from Table 6.

In Table 6, syces or grooms are taken to represent unskilled workers and common masons etc. are taken to represent skilled workers. We take the price of common rice as a major component of the cost of living of ordinary workers, who spent most of their meagre earnings on food. On this basis, the cost of living almost doubled between the 1870s and the end of the century, whereas the earnings of unskilled workers increased in much smaller proportion. Thus the real income of such people, already low in the 1870s, fell by the end of the century.

TABLE 6 The Monthly Wages of Syces and Common Masons, Carpenters or Blacksmiths in Calcutta, 1871-1899

| | Average monthly wages (in Rs.) of | | |
	Syces or grooms	Common masons, carpenters or blacksmiths	Average price of common rice in Calcutta in terms of seers to the rupee
1871	-	-	20.00
1873	6.5	7.5 to 10.0	-
1876	6	15.55	12.28
1881	7	12	16.80
1886	7	15	14.24
1891	6	15	13.38
1896	8	15 to 16	10.95
1899	8	18 to 20	11.85

Source : *Prices and Wages in India,* Seventeenth Issue, compiled under the supervision of the Director-General of Statistics (Calcutta, Office of the Superintendent of Government Printing, 1900), Table Nos 1 and 52.

With skilled workers the trend was apparently different, since their money earnings according to Table 6 rose in greater proportion than the cost of living. However, the figures are a little suspect. The publication from which the figures are taken also gives the figures for skilled and. unskilled workers in a paper mill (probably the Bally Paper Mills). The wages of 'coolies' in that mill are almost identical with those of syces in Table 6. But the wages of mill carpenters and blacksmiths, while higher than those of the skilled workers in Table 6 in the beginning of the 1870s, show virtually no trend thereafter and are lower than those of skilled workers as given in Table 6 in 1899. Weighing the evidence, it is reasonable to conclude that skilled artisans may have just about maintained their real earnings but were very unlikely to have improved their condition in the Calcutta of the 1890s. This is consistent with the stagnation of wages of jute-mill workers in Bengal after 1900.

How did the wages of unskilled workers in Calcutta relate to the cost of items other than food? I shall only cite the cost of internal transport. Horse-drawn tramcars appeared in Calcutta in the 1880s. In 1881, the fare from Kalighat to Tank Square (today's B.B.D. Bag) was 2 annas; but the fare from any intermediate point, such as Dharmatala, to Tank Square was also 2 annas. As the daily wage of an unskilled labourer then was about 4 annas, one ride would cost him half a day's wage, and a journey out and back his earnings for the day. The fare was reduced in late 1881, but it still cost a minimum of one anna.

The reduction in fare was preceded by a drastic cut in conductors' and drivers' salaries: for conductors, from Rs 20-25 to Rs 14 per month. For both conductors and drivers, the company resorted to payment by trips: in order to earn Rs 20 per month under the new system, a conductor would have to work from 6 a.m. to 10 p.m., that is, 16 hours at a stretch. Such actions of the Tramway Company provoked repeated strikes by the staff.

Workers in factories, steam-powered mills and other establishments resorted to strikes in protest against alterations in working conditions and wages, even though there were as yet few organized trade unions. For example, workers of Dykes & Co., a coach-building firm, went on strike in March 1881 because they were forbidden to go out to smoke a hookah. Several strikes by municipal sweepers, and by the workers of Union Jute Mills (near Shealdah Station) and other establishments were reported in the newspapers of 1880.

Most Calcuttans — which obviously means most common workers — still lived in *kutcha* houses in 1891. Through their wretched living conditions and endemic poverty, apart from conditions in their places of work, the labouring men and women felt the brunt of a colonial, authoritarian rule even more keenly than did others. European foremen could kick them to death; policemen could beat them black and blue or warn them off public paths and gardens, under threat of an arrest or a beating. Slum dwellers could be evicted by landlords, beaten up by their musclemen, and thrown out by the municipal administration bent on improving the city.

Not all workers actually had work. Technical and organizational changes were continually threatening the livelihood of workers, who had little job security. The advent of motor cars threw carriage-making firms out of business and along with them, the thousands of workers engaged in the trade. Improvements in the port took away the jobs of thousands of porters, whose place was taken by hydraulic cranes and their few operators. Porters had been engaged earlier on to carry dignitaries from their boats to dry land, since there were virtually no jetties at many places. The advent of Portland cement took away the business of *surki* (brick-dust) works. The growth of Calcutta's population and the construction of palatial buildings partly compensated for these dislocations; but immigrants were steadily adding to the supply of workers, while the demand grew sluggishly or in fits and starts. Workless people satisfied the desire for vicarious acquisition of virtue (*punya*) of rich Jains who hired them to feed bedbugs on their own blood at the rate of 2 annas for 2 hours. Work in the factories was also affected by trade cycles; workers thrown out by trade depressions might go back to the villages or hang around in a half-starved condition in the hope of getting a job in some other establishment.

Calcutta's history is as much a story of the plight and struggle of such people, and their enjoyment of life snatched from the jaws of misery, as of the doings of the great sahibs, maharajas and nawabs. But that story is yet to be told.

CIVIC AND PUBLIC SERVICES
IN OLD CACLUTTA

P. Thankappan Nair

Old Calcutta was divided into a White Town and a Black Town. The division was officially recognized, though there was no racial segregation. Up to 1757, the White Town was confined to the environs of the Tank Square (today's Binay-Badal-Dinesh Bag) and the old Fort William. The European business quarters remained in this area till 1911 and later. But after the new Fort was completed in 1774, the residential White Town extended to Chourangi, and thence spread south and east progressively. The Europeans also had villas in Garden Reach, Alipur, Baliganj and elsewhere in south Calcutta, but these were sparsely populated areas.

The level of amenities in the two sections of the town differed greatly. Those who castigate the civic services of Calcutta today are often unaware of the appalling conditions in the city generally, and the Black Town in particular, in the eighteenth and nineteenth centuries.

In the early years, there was no civic or municipal authority in Calcutta. (The 'Mayor's Court' set up in 1726 had judicial functions alone.) The East India Company had no legal obligation to render civic services. However, it did undertake some such works to attract settlers to the new city.

On 12 August 1765 the Company was granted the Diwani of Bengal. This bestowed judicial and revenue-collecting functions upon it, but also implied a moral obligation to

provide civic services. These were placed in charge of the Collector of Calcutta. The demand for municipal services grew after 1773, when Calcutta was elevated as the capital of British India. Effective measures began to be taken at last.

But statutory civic services began only in 1794, when municipal administration was shifted from the Collector to the Justices of the Peace for the Town of Calcutta. The Justices were none other than the Governor-General, the members of his Council, and the Judges of the Supreme Court. The day-to-day running of municipal affairs was entrusted to the Chief Magistrate, who combined the roles of today's Municipal Commissioner and Commissioner of Police.

Only in 1876 was the elective system introduced: two-thirds of the Municipal Commissioners (i.e., Councillors) were henceforth elected, the rest – including the Chairman – being nominated by the Government. The first elected Mayor assumed office in 1924.

Uptil 1765, the East India Company confined its attention to the White Town exclusively. The building of the new Fort William meant uprooting the native population from Gobindapur in the mid-eighteenth century. Around the same time, the English began to build the magnificent houses on Chourangi that earned Calcutta the title of 'City of Palaces'. But the Company was not authorized to levy taxes for

civic improvement; the English merchants were solely concerned with making money, and the Indians were by and large lacking in civic awareness. Hence William Mackintosh wrote on a visit to Calcutta in 1779: 'an undistinguished mass of filth and corruption, equally offensive to human sense and health, compose the capital of the English Company's government in India.' Eight-five years later, the President of the Sanitary Commission for Bengal in 1864 found even the White Town 'offensive and objectionable', the Black Town such that 'no language can adequately describe its abominations', and the whole 'unfit for the habitation of civilized man'. Viewed from this perspective, the municipal history of Calcutta appears to exemplify progress rather than decline.

The progress had in fact commenced from the eighteenth century. Let us trace it, step by step.

Water Supply

After May 1870, even the most orthodox Hindus were attracted to Calcutta by the assured supply of Ganga water at the turn of a tap. The scientist Praphullachandra Ray, arriving in the city as a boy in August 1870, found them agonizing as to whether the holiness of the water was impaired in transit; but 'the superior quality of the water carried its own recommendation; by slow degrees, reason and convenience triumphed over prejudice'.

How did Calcuttans obtain their water before 1870? The devout Hindus, of course, used nothing but Ganga water from the Hugli River. Baishnabcharan Sheth of Barabazar made a fortune by supplying the holy water to far-off places: Ramraja, the Prince of Telengana, was a regular customer! The water would be stored in Pegu jars for as long as a year. Wealthy Hindus even sent upstream to Hugli Town or downstream to Khulna for the supposedly purer flow there. The water would be filtered through sand and charcoal, after immersing a red-hot iron rod in the jar.

Europeans had an understandable aversion to the river water, polluted by corpses and the filth of the city. They preferred rainwater and the supply from tanks, digging several tanks for the purpose. The Great Tank in front of the Old Fort (called *Lal Dighi* by the Indians, in today's Binay-Badal-Dinesh Bag) was dug in 1709 to serve both the White and the Native Town. The tanks in the Maidan were dug in the last two decades of the eighteenth century. Guards were posted to prevent washing and bathing in these sources of drinking water.

The Lottery Committee excavated a number of tanks between 1808 and 1837, chiefly along the arterial road it constructed from Lower Circular Road to Shyambazar. The Black Town too had a number of private tanks,

31.1 *See also* 31.2 *The contrasting settings of the White and Black Towns. Sketches by D'Oyly. (But note the adjutant stork even in the White Town.)*

sometimes open to the public. The total number of tanks within the Maratha Ditch stood at 1043 in 1847; in the suburbs, Bhabanipur alone had 823 in 1888!

A steam engine was installed at Chandpal Ghat around 1822 to lift unfiltered water into open masonry aqueducts for watering some important streets. The public tanks were also replenished in this way in the summer; and as ever since, poor Calcuttans used the unclean supply for domestic and personal use.

A plan for filtered water supply was submitted in 1847 by F.W. Simms, Consulting Engineer to the Government of India and Director of the Railway Department. He proposed Palta, 30 kilometres upstream from the city, as the intake point. Chemical analysis also favoured either Palta or Chunchura; the former was preferred so as to benefit not only Calcutta but also Barrackpur, Dumdum and other military concentrations. The project was sanctioned in 1860 and completed in 1870 at a cost of Rs 70 lakh. From May that year, 6 million gallons of filtered water flowed to Calcutta daily through a 42-inch iron main.

Conservancy

An entry in the Company Accounts for October 1703 shows that *hollocores* or sweepers

had been engaged to clean the White Town by that date. Their activities were supervised from 1760 by a 'Scavenger' or Director of Conservancy, the first incumbent being Edwards Handle, a former arrack farmer. The Scavengership was a lucrative office, but not it seems a very effectual one. William Mackintosh in 1779 and the Comte de Grandpré in 1789 both describe jackals, kites and vultures as the only functioning city cleaners. The state of the Black Town, needless to say, was by far the worse.

In 1785, the town was divided into thirty-one thanas for municipal as well as police purposes, and a new system of conservancy service introduced. The English Town had four bullock-carts per thana, and the Black Town two per thana, to remove garbage. By 1802 there were eighty-five carts, and two municipal depots to house them and their bullocks.

More excitingly, a railway was built in 1867 to carry the town's refuse to the municipal square mile at Dhapa. The 'Dhapa Mail' ran from Theatre Road (now Shakespeare Sarani) to Bagbazar along the Circular Road, with the main loading platforms at Shealdah. The railway was dismantled as late as 1950: the tracks could be discerned at Shealdah for many years more.

31.2 *See* 31.1

Drainage and Sewerage

Grandpré in 1789 found most of Calcutta's streets to have a 'small canal on each side', which conveyed not only storm water but the flow from the river during 'great swells'. The channels, upto 3 feet deep and 2 feet wide, were 'reservoirs of filth' and even dead animals.

Such as they were, small surface drains had been introduced in 1695 when a trench was dug round the Sutanuti factory. A deeper trench, '16 or 18 foot broad and 12 foot or more deep', was begun in 1710 to separate the British settlement from 'native' Sutanuti and keep the former dry and wholesome. The ditch ran from Lalbazar probably to Babu Ghat. It was palisaded, with drawbridges and a guardhouse – for needless to say, it served for defence no less than drainage. Defence was also the chief purpose of the Maratha Ditch, commenced in 1742 – first from Bagbazar to Park Street, then extended to Alipur; but it served also as the grand drainage outlet for the whole city till 1801, when it was filled up.

By 1857, Calcutta had surface drains everywhere; but their repellent state has been described. The only effective solution was underground drainage. William Clark, Chief Engineer of the Calcutta Municipality, submitted a plan for this in 1855. It was sanctioned in 1859, completed within fifteen years, and still serves as the Town System for drainage and sewerage within the ambit of the old Maratha Ditch. The system has been described in the article on 'Drainage, Sewerage and Waste Disposal' in Volume 2.

Clark's scheme was a 'combined system' for storm water and sewage. Till 1864, one of the most revolting practices in old Calcutta had been the dumping of 200 tons of nightsoil daily into the Hugli. This was collected by privately-engaged *mehtars* (sweepers), taken to nightsoil depots and thence by bullock-cart to the Nightsoil Ghat near the Old Mint. From there, boats hired by the municipality carried it out beyond Bajbaj and dumped it in the river at ebb tide. Repellent enough as laid out, the system was rendered more objectionable still by lax execution, the greater part of the filth being thrown into the public drains under cover of darkness.

After acquiring land at Dhapa in 1864, the Justices of the Peace arranged for trenching part of the nightsoil there. Several other trenching sites were opened between 1864 and 1896, and the collection of nightsoil by the *mehtars* brought under municipal control. With the progress of underground drainage-cum-sewerage works, as well as the piped water

31.3 *The Great Tank. T. & W. Daniell*

supply needed for flushing, the whole earlier system could be phased out. But this happened lamentably slowly: only in very recent years has the manual collection and disposal of nightsoil been totally abolished in the Calcutta Municipal area.

Another repugnant practice in old Calcutta, as in old-time India generally, was the consignment of dead bodies to the Ganga. Owners of riverside villas had to employ *Doms* to keep the bodies away from their ghats; the Government also employed boats to float corpses that got stuck or entangled.

Orthodox Hindus would immerse their dying kinsmen in the holy stream, and even hasten their death by blocking their nose, mouth and ears with Ganga clay. Those who survived these ministrations were considered dead for all purposes: these wretches consorted in a colony at Sukh Sagar, the ironically-named 'ocean of happiness'.

Hence the establishment of municipal and other burning ghats came as an untold boon. The Nimtala Burning Ghat dates back to the 1820s if not earlier, and was twice enlarged by private donation. The present building dates from 1876. The Sahanagar (Keoratala) Ghat, originally leased by an individual, was conveyed by him to the municipality in 1872. Privately-run too was the Kashi Mitra Burning Ghat, dating from 1774, once the exclusive cremation-ground for wealthy Hindus.

Public Health

April to November were the 'killer' months for the English in old Calcutta. Every year on 15 November, they would celebrate their survival at a gathering called the 'Reunion'. Captain Alexander Hamilton wrote in 1710 how, of the 1,200 Englishmen in the city in August, 462 had been buried by the end of the year. The high mortality rate made the Government itself look after public health till 1857, when it became a municipal responsibility.

The first hospital in Calcutta was begun in 1709, with the Company contributing Rs 2,000 and European inhabitants and sailors the rest. This was the Presidency General (PG) Hospital (now Seth Sukhlal Karnani Memorial Hospital). Its original site was in Garstin Place; in 1769 it moved to a larger building brought from the Reverend J. Z. Kiernander, the first Protestant missionary in Bengal. It was perhaps fitting that the original building should have stood next to the old burial-ground: for as Hamilton said of it, 'many go in to undergo the Penance of Physick, but few come out to give Account of its Operations'.

The PG Hospital was strictly for Europeans.

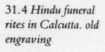
31.4 *Hindu funeral rites in Calcutta. old engraving*

Indians could be hospitalized from 1874 in the newly set-up Campbell Medical School and College (now Nilratan Sarkar Medical College). This had earlier been the Police or Pauper Hospital, in existence by 1789 as an asylum and refuge for dying destitutes picked up from the streets. Meanwhile, the Calcutta Medical College had been established in 1835, and its first twenty-bed hospital added in 1838. The Government had also started a public dispensary at Bhabanipur in 1840. In 1896, this was moved to a commodious new building (provided by the Corporation) and renamed the South Suburban Hospital. In 1898 it became Shambhunath Pandit Hospital, after the first Indian judge at the Calcutta High Court.

Roads

There were practically no roads in the villages of Sutanuti, Gobindapur and Kalikata. The one probable exception was Chitpur Road (now Rabindra Sarani) connecting Halisahar in North 24-Parganas with Kalighat: it was accordingly called the 'Pilgrim Road' by some writers. It was kept in repair by the Sheth family; Janardan Sheth planted it with trees on both sides. The Sheths also maintained a highway connecting their garden (Jora Bagan) through Barabazar with the old Fort William, along the line of today's Netaji Subhash Road (formerly Clive Street).

The following table traces the pace of road construction (and digging of tanks) in the days of the Zamindar or Collector of Calcutta:

TABLE 1

Year	Streets	Lanes	By-lanes	Tanks
1706	2	2	–	17
1726	4	8	–	27
1742	16	46	74	27
1756	27	52	74	31(?)*
1794	163	520	517	61

*Given as '13' in A.K. Ray, *A Short History of Calcutta* (1901), p. 58.

In 1721 the Company began work on new roads around the Old Fort to allow 'the wind's free passage into the White Town' and drain the 'low ground between Calcutta and Govindpur by making a high road across it', corresponding to the Council House Street-Government Place West axis. As till 1794, the Company could not levy taxes for municipal services, road-building

was chiefly carried out through private contributions of labour and money. The Maratha Ditch was both excavated, and later filled in to create the Circular Road, by such means. As late as 1828, fifty-eight persons contributed Rs 1000 each towards the Rs 64,000 needed to build Circular Garden Reach Road (now Karl Marx Sarani).

Roads in early Calcutta seldom had names; they were designated by cumbersome phrases like 'Road to Dumdum', 'Avenue leading to the Eastward' or 'Street from Omichand's house to Mir Bahar Chouki'. Most of the roads received names after the recovery of Calcutta from Siraj-ud-Daula in 1757: they are indicated in the map prepared by Lt. Col. Mark Wood in 1784–85 and published in 1792.

Most of the roads from Calcutta to the suburbs were built by the Collector after the acquisition of the Zamindari of the 24-Parganas in 1757. By 1766, these included 'Shyambazar Road', 'Dullendaw Road' (Bhabanipur Road), 'Manickchurn [Maniktala] Road', Gopalnagar Road and Beliaghata Road. In the next century, the Lottery Committee built some major arterial roads with tanks along them. Chief of these was the north-south corridor along today's Wood Street, Rafi Ahmed Kidwai Road (Wellesley Street), Nirmal Chandra Street (Wellington Street), College Street and Bidhan Sarani (Cornwallis Street). The Lottery Committee also built the Strand Road from Prinsep Ghat to Hatkhola; Amherst Street (now Rammohan Sarani), Hare Street, Waterloo Street, and the Kalutola-Mirzapur axis (now Surya Sen Street), as well as the group of exclusive streets named after the various titles of the Governor-General Lord Hastings and his wife: Rawdon Street, Moira Street, Hungerford Street and Loudon Street.

The major roads farther south, as also in the Phulbagan-Kankurgachhi area to the east, are the work of the Calcutta Improvement Trust (CIT), founded in 1911. Its most important work, of course, is the Central Avenue from Esplanade to Shyambazar, and other merciful outlets in congested North Calcutta like Vivekananda Road, B.K. Pal Avenue and Girish Avenue.

One of the problems in Calcutta is that roads are built and maintained by various authorities with little co-ordination. The roads along the canals – Canal East, West and South Roads, Galiff Street etc. – are still under the State

31.5 Bhistis watering the street. Old engraving

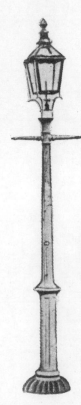

Irrigation Department. The State Government also owns Diamond Harbour Road, Bajbaj Road and some others. The roads constructed by the Port Trust are owned and maintained by it, and those in the Maidan are the property of the Defence Ministry of the Government of India.

Needless to say, the streets of old Calcutta were all *kutcha,* made of pounded brick until Pakur stone became available with the coming of the railways. *Bhistis* would be employed to keep down the dust – at first only on 'the Course', a rendezvous for the elite now engulfed by the Race Course, then in other important streets. The practice was kept up after the roads were macadamized, but has been sadly discontinued in recent decades.

The first road to be macadamized was Chitpur Road, in 1839. Pavements began to be provided from 1858 – first on Chourangi, in front of the old Corporation Office, to facilitate the erection of gas lamps. Traders objected as their customers would have to park their carriages at some distance from the shop doors.

Most lanes and by-lanes in old or inner Calcutta have no pavements to this day. No room had been allowed for them, as the lanes were not meant for wheeled traffic.

Street lights

As in London, street lighting in old Calcutta was a private responsibility. House-owners were obliged to maintain gate lamps, and *mashalchees* would meet their masters with flaming torches. The duty of providing gate lamps was commuted in 1856 for a 2 per cent lighting rate. But there was already limited municipal lighting earlier in the century – in the European quarters. The entire city had 313 oil lamps in 1836 and 417 in 1854. The poor quarters went totally unlit. Even a central point like Champatala (the Bowbazar-Amherst Street crossing) was without lights as late as 1887. Table 1 gives the progress of street lighting in Calcutta.

TABLE 2 Number of Street Lights in Calcutta

Year	Oil	Gas	Electric
1864	677	1,064	Nil
1870	621	2,711	Nil
1880	151	3,859	Nil
1890	1,158	5,397	Nil
1900	2,295	6,811	a few
1910	2,192	10,185	a few
1920	1,170	13,612	206
1930	1,005	18,693	2,412
1941	355	18,844	8,518
1951	333	19,001	10,669
1961	Nil	3,818	39,748
1971	Nil	Nil	75,816
1977	Nil	Nil	74,354
1987	Nil	Nil	132,250

In March 1823, Bathgate and Co. demonstrated the gas light at their showroom in Old Court House Street. But it would be twenty-four years before gas lights appeared on Calcutta's streets. Only in March 1841 did the Justices of the Peace call for tenders for commercial gas supply; and only on 6 July 1857 did the Oriental Gas Company – started by Frenchmen but gradually taken over by Englishmen – commence supply. That evening, Chourangi was lit by gas lights, though some lamps had been set up by the Company in November 1854 in order to demonstrate the superiority of gas over oil. The subsequent progress of gas lighting for once shows little or no discrimination between 'European' and 'native' localities.

The Gas Company's plant was at Gas Street (now Dr M. N. Chatterji Sarani) near Narkeldanga, and the distributing station at Halliday Street, now lost in Chittaranjan Avenue and Muhammad Ali Park. The progress and decline of the Company is reflected in that of gas-fuelled street lights as shown in Table 2. The 'sick' Gas Company was taken over by the Government of West Bengal in November 1960. Only very recently has it been able to contemplate a brighter future, with the setting up of a new gas plant at Dankuni; but needless to say, the fuel will now feed households and industries rather than street lights.

Amritalal Basu commented in 1928 that even outlying 'native quarters' like Baranagar and Shibpur scorned the gas lamp in favour of the electric. Initially, however, electricity had to compete tooth and nail with gas. The first Calcutta street to be lit by electricity was the newly-built Harrison Road (now Mahatma Gandhi Road) in 1891. Kilburn and Company undertook its lighting from dynamos set up at Halliday Street Pumping Station; the municipal consultant was Jagadishchandra Basu. But in 1905 the authorities reverted to gas, and the Halliday Street plant was sold off.

Needless to say, the cheap and powerful electric lights could not but triumph in the end. The CIT favoured electricity for lighting the streets and parks it constructed. In 1914, high-power Keith lamps of 1000 candle power were fixed on Corporation Street (now S. N. Banerji Road) and Chourangi: the Calcutta Electric Supply Corporation bore the cost itself to demonstrate the advantage of electricity. The same year, electric street lamps were installed in Maniktala, then a separate municipality. Finally, at Garden Reach in 1924, electric lights were installed directly without the preliminary stages of oil or gas. But the latter took a long time to fade. The last oil lamps were extinguished only in 1958, the last gas lamps in 1970.

Chitpur in Flood

The flooding of Calcutta streets in the monsoons is not a recent phenomenon but a feature as old as the city itself. An exasperated Rabindranath Thakur wrote in 1917 in his essay *Kartar Ichchhay Karma*:

The moment a monsoon breeze blows, our lane gets flooded right up to the main road. The wayfarer's shoes must be carried over his head like his umbrella, and it becomes clear that the inhabitants rank no higher in the struggle for existence than amphibious beasts. I have grown grey with watching the same sight from our balcony since my childhood days. ...

The moment the rains break, they start repairing the tramway. All laws ordain that what begins must have an end, but the unlawful ways of the tramwaymen seem never to end. This year, when they dug up the tracks again, I saw the flood of water contending with the flood of humans on Chitpur Road and at last began to ponder deeply. Why do we put up with it?

That we need not put up with it, and that it is better not to do so, becomes obvious if we once set foot in Chourangi. It is part of the same town under the same municipality; the only difference is that we put up with it and they do not.

31.6 *'Flood at Kalitala'. Cartoon by Alex Taylor, 1928*

Other Municipal Functions

The Calcutta Corporation provides many other services, and provided still more in earlier times. From 1861 to 1912, for instance, it had charge of the city's fire brigade. Fires were extremely frequent in old Calcutta: the first one recorded, on 18 December 1694, burnt down Job Charnock's own house. The poor people's huts were made of highly inflammable materials, though thatch was prohibited in 1837 after 7,174 huts were devastated between January and April that year.

The Corporation was first authorized in 1871 to use municipal funds for building markets. Before that, trading was chiefly conducted at the *ganj,* where a particular commodity was sold, and the *hat,* held on particular days of the week, often without permanent buildings. Of *bazaars* in something like the present-day sense, the Barabazar (mentioned in Company records from 1703) was pre-eminent. J. Z. Holwell, the celebrated Collector of Calcutta, mentioned fourteen other bazaars in 1752; Sterndale added another ten as being extant in 1768. All these were privately owned by Indians. Europeans also set up markets, like Edward Tirreta's in 1783; and the Government of India itself built a modern market in Khidirpur sometime before 1859 for the support of the Military Orphan School. The Orphanganj Market was transferred to the State Government in 1956 and is now managed by the Collector of 24-Parganas (South).

The first municipal market, the New Market, was opened on New Year's Day 1874. Simultaneously, the Corporation purchased and re-organized the nearby Dharmatala market to ensure the viability of the New Market. The Lansdowne Market followed in 1903, Sir Charles Allen Market in north Calcutta in 1910, and the College Street Market in 1917. Today the Corporation owns 19 markets and has 167 private ones within its jurisdiction.

The Corporation also runs slaughter-houses (the main one, in Tangra, dates from 1869); *dhobikhanas* or washermen's depots (the first set up in 1897); and, most importantly, primary schools. It funded a few favoured schools from 1888 and later set up schools of its own: it now runs 317. It also has dispensaries and maternity homes, though (unlike in Bombay) the public hospitals in Calcutta are a government, not a municipal, concern.

Calcutta's parks are also chiefly under the Corporation, though the biggest open space, the Maidan, is part of the Fort William complex under the Defence Ministry. The unplanned growth of the city allowed no room for public parks or gardens: even today, Calcutta is notoriously deficient in this respect. The first planned parks were set up by the CIT after 1911: it is responsible for virtually every open space in the city outside the circle of the Maratha Ditch, as well as several within it. Among its creations are the Park Circus Maidan and the Deshapriya and Deshbandhu Parks. But its most impressive contributions in this line are the two large artificial lakes: Rabindra Sarobar at Dhakuria, excavated between 1926 and 1939, and Subhash Sarobar at Beliaghata, planned in 1938 but completed only in 1962.

In the old city area, a number of parks were created by sanitary filling of old tanks after

The Adjutant Stork

The old emblem of Calcutta Corporation (replaced in 1961) showed two adjutant storks with serpents in their mouths. The adjutant stork is a large ungainly scavenger bird. Its heraldic elevation throws a curious and unflattering light on early municipal services, for such birds once thronged the city and fed on the uncleared garbage. Bishop Heber wrote in 1824 that they 'share with jackals ... the post of scavenger, ... lounge about with perfect fearlessness all day long, and almost jostle us from our paths.'

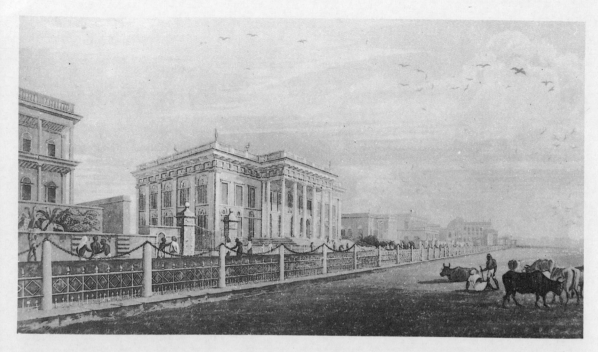

piped water supply began. Rabindra Kanan (Beadon Square), Muhammad Ali Park, Marcus Square and Jatin Das Park (Hazra Park) were created in this way. Elsewhere, the tanks were retained and beautified, as with Binay-Badal-Dinesh Bag, College Square, Azad Hind Bag (Hedua) and Padmapukur. Most of Calcutta's public swimming pools have been set up in these tanks.

Finally, a word must be said about the Town Hall. Old Calcutta had few halls for public functions and entertainments. Indians chiefly held their festivals in open spaces. Europeans used the Old Court House (adjoining Writers' Buildings), where the old Supreme Court and Mayor's Court used to sit. When this was demolished in 1792, Calcutta was left without a public hall.

Funds were therefore raised through lotteries for building a Town Hall. The noble building, completed in 1814, was first in charge of the Government and after 1864 of the Justices of the Peace. Until Independence, the hall was used for public functions; since then it has accommodated the Municipal Magistrate's Court and other offices. It still stands at the time of writing, and a strong citizens' movement has grown up against its proposed demolition.

Public Transport

The earliest forms of public land transport in Calcutta were *thika* (public-hire) palanquins and horse-drawn carriages. There were special screened palanquins for women. There was also a lighter open palanquin somewhat like a sedan chair, called a tonjon.

Needless to say, palanquins disappeared long ago, though there were 606 of them as late as in 1891. Some horse-drawn carriages – thirty-three in 1987 – still ply their trade, chiefly in the Rajabazar and Khidirpur areas and for joyrides on the Maidan and the Strand.

Before we leave the more primitive modes of transport, we may note that the rickshaw was quite a late introduction in Calcutta. The Chinese brought it to the city around 1900 to negotiate the flooded streets. Some of them

began to run rickshaws commercially, with Chinese pullers, from 1913–14; but by the 1920s the trade was almost completely Indianized.

The only form of mass transport in old Calcutta was by water. After Haora Station was opened in 1854, launches and country boats ferried railway passengers across the river to the central business district. (The practice has recently been re-introduced on a larger scale.) A three-horse omnibus plied briefly between Dharmatala and Barrackpur in November 1830. Horse-drawn buses were introduced more extensively, though not always more

31.10 Early transport in Calcutta: bullock-cart, horse-carriage, palanquin and sedan chair. J. B. Fraser

31.11 The tank in College Square, now a public swimming pool

successfully in the commercial way, from 1864. The early Fathers of St Xavier's College ran some, and girl students commonly used horse-buses to travel to school. In 1873, writes Mrs Mitchell, the girls of Duff School came 'in large, close omnibuses, under the charge of careful servants'.

But the truly successful horse-drawn public vehicle was the tramcar. An experimental horse-drawn tramway was built by the Justices of the Peace for Calcutta in 1873 from Shealdah Station through Boubazar and Dalhousie Square (today's Binay-Badal-Dinesh Bag) to Armenian Ghat. This municipal tramway operated from 24 February to 20 November 1873, but closed down in view of a monthly loss of Rs 500. The prospects grew particularly depressing after the Government, reneging on its earlier promise to the Municipality, allowed the East Bengal Railway to set up a goods yard at Chitpur. This deprived the tramways of the lucrative jute traffic between Shealdah Station and the Docks during off-peak hours.

It was thenceforth decided to leave tram services to private enterprise. Parish and Souttar, the experienced British tramway engineers, submitted a tender for an eight-route system in 1878. After construction, the firm sold its concession to the Calcutta Tramways Company Limited (CTC): on 27 October 1880,

horse-drawn tramcars began to run from Shealdah to Dalhousie Square. One by one, tram services were opened on Chitpur (March 1881), Chourangi (November 1881), Dharmatala (March 1882), Strand Road (June 1882), Shyambazar (November 1882), Khidirpur (1883) and Wellesley Street (January 1884).

In 1882, the CTC obtained municipal permission to run steam-powered cars – first along Chourangi Raod to Kalighat, then to Khidirpur. But in both cases, the tracks ran through the Maidan, which was (and is) under the Defence authorities. The latter insisted on the withdrawal of steam-car services – except for five days during Durga Puja, when such cars plied round the clock to carry pilgrims to Kalighat temple.

Finally in 1899, the CTC entered into an agreement to introduce electric traction. On 27 March 1902, the first electric tramcar ran from Esplanade to Khidirpur, and on 14 June that year to Kalighat. By the end of the year, the entire system had been electrified: no doubt to the relief of the wretched Waler horses, which died in great numbers each year, especially during heat waves as in 1881.

Subsequently, tracks were laid on the Tollyganj, Belgachhia and Harrison Road (now Mahatma Gandhi Road) sections in 1903, Bag-

bazar in 1904, and Lower Circular Road, Alipur, Behala and Haora In 1908. Later extensions were to Rajabazar (1910), Park Circus (1923), Rasbehari Avenue (1928), Upper Circular Road and Galiff Street (1941), and Gariahat (1943). Tracks were also laid along the new Haora Bridge in 1943. More recent changes have been noted in Vol. II

Tramcars were for long virtually the only form of mass transport in Calcutta. Although the first motor car appeared in Calcutta in 1896, and a car rally with eleven vehicles was held in

31.12 *One of Calcutta's last horse-drawn carriages waits outside the Victorial Memorial today*

31.13 *Early electric trams on Chitpur Road*

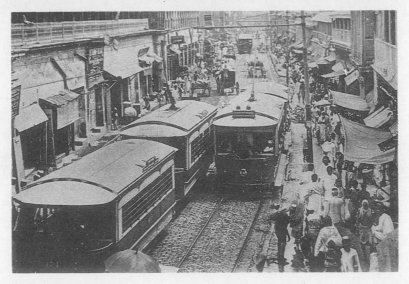

1904, motor bus services only began in 1920 and gained momentum from a prolonged tram strike. The first two 'buses', run by A. A. Subhan, were merely trucks fitted with benches, one running from Metiabruz to Khidirpur and the other from Beliaghata to Shealdah. The CTC also began bus services, as did Walford Transport Limited, the latter introducing double-decker buses in 1926. There were only 55 buses in the city in 1924, but 280 a year later.

From 1935, the services came to be dominated by private owners under the aegis of the Bengal Bus Syndicate. The Syndicate first operated from the eastern suburbs to the business district. Some of today's routes, such as nos 3, 12 and 12B, survive virtually unchanged from 1937. Taxis appeared in Calcutta in 1906. Rules governing their operation were framed in 1910, by which time seventy-six had taken the road.

The recent history of Calcutta's transport system is being told in Vol. II. Let us turn to another means of communication.

Telephones

On 12 March 1878, Father E. Lafont lectured on the telephone at St Xavier's College; but for a demonstration of this 'greatest wonder of the age', Calcuttans had to wait till 23 April that year for the watchmakers Black and Murray to arrange an exhibition. Remarkably, the Viceroy Lord Lytton refused permission to intending telephone companies. His successor Lord Ripon was more progressive, and the Oriental Telephone Company Limited obtained their franchise in June 1880. The 'Central Exchange', on the magneto system, was opened on 28 January 1882, simultaneously with exchanges in Madras and Bombay. The Calcutta exchange had 300 lines but only seventy-nine subscribers: the sole Indian among them was the philanthropist Sagar Datta.

In 1883 the concession was bought by the Bengal Telephone Company Limited For Rs 7,60,000. By then there were 107 lines; in 1899, 748, and by the end of 1912, 3,363. Haora was brought within the system in 1884, and Bajbaj in 1892.

In 1918, the Bengal Telephone Company moved to the premises at no 8 Hare Street which still house the commercial offices of Calcutta Telephones. On 31 May 1922 the concern became the Bengal Telephone Corporation Limited. It was acquired by the Government of India on 1 April 1943.

The story of the telegraph is being told elsewhere, and that of Calcutta's gas supply has emerged from my account of street lighting

31.14 *Man washing the streets. Basanta Ganguli*

above. Let me conclude with an account of electric supply to the city.

Electricity

Electric lights were first demonstrated in Calcutta by P. W. Fleury and Company on 24 July 1879, and then by Dey, Sheel and Company on several occasions. But the first regular use of electricity in the city was to light the newly-built Harrison Road in 1891, as recounted above.

Public distribution of electricity, generated from thermal stations, began on 30 May 1899. The Indian Electric Company Limited had been incorporated in England on 14 January 1897, and renamed the Calcutta Electric Supply Corporation (CESC) Limited the next month. Their first generating station was at Emambag Lane near Prinsep Street. Then, in succession, came stations at Alipur (March 1902), Haora (May 1906) and Ultadanga (September 1906).

These were all Direct Current (DC) units. The first Alternating Current (AC) plant came up at Ultadanga Station in September 1910. Plans were already afoot for a large central AC station: the Kashipur (Cossipore) station was finally commissioned in July 1912. The old DC plants were now converted into sub-stations. Other large plants followed: Southern (Garden Reach), Mulajore and New Kashipur. The story of these and later developments is being told in the article on Power Supply in Volume II

As with gas, the earliest major use of electricity was to light the streets – and then,

from 1902, to power tramcars. By 1901, there were only 708 domestic subscribers. Even in the 1930s, the CESC engaged canvassers to enlist subscribers, apart from promotion through advertising. Perhaps the cost acted as a deterrent at first: 8 annas per unit in 1901, reduced by 1937 to only $2\frac{1}{2}$ annas.

A CESC advertisement of 1940 asked: 'Were the "Good Old Days" really good old days?' The allusion, needless to say, was to the pre-electric era. With regard to civic services and public amenities as a whole, the question is not merely rhetorical. Civic services in old Calcutta functioned within manageable limits, catered much more openly and exclusively to the affluent classes and particularly the Europeans, and were undoubtedly laudable in many respects – as in watering the roads, which has acquired a nostalgic symbolism for elderly Calcuttans. But this account may indicate the deficiencies of those times as well, and convince today's citizen that his lot in the daunting overgrown city of 1990 is less dismal than he may believe.

THE RAILWAY COMES
TO CALCUTTA

Sukanta Chaudhuri

On 16 April 1853, the Great Indian Peninsular Railway ran the first train in India, for twenty-one miles from Bombay to Thane. The East Indian Railway (EIR) had been formed long before that, in 1845; but for various reasons – among them the delayed trans-shipment of engines from England and the loss of the first batch of coaches in a shipwreck – the first train in Eastern India steamed out of Haora Station experimentally on 28 June 1854. It went up to Pandua, though the line had been sanctioned to Raniganj. From 15 August 1854, the company ran a regular service, morning and evening, between Haora and Hugli with stops at Bali, Shrirampur and Chandannagar. The fare ranged from three rupees by first class to seven annas by third class. The service was extended by stages, reaching Raniganj on 3 February 1855. The opening run to Raniganj was flagged off by the Governor-General Lord Dalhousie, whose enthusiasm had been largely responsible for the execution of the project.

It was the railway that first raised Haora above the status of a small village. The main booking office was on the Calcutta bank, at the Armenian Ghat, and the fare covered the ferry to the station. At the Haora end, the station consisted of a tin shed and a single line flanked by narrow platforms, somewhat to the south of the present station building. This was constructed between 1901 and 1906 on the site of a former Catholic orphanage.

The line was extended north and westward along the route now known as the Sahibganj Loop, reaching Varanasi by the end of 1862. But it was only in 1865 (again on 15 August) that a bridge was opened over the Ganga at Allahabad, and in 1866 over the Jamuna at Delhi, allowing through services between the old capital and the new. Services to Bombay via Allahabad commenced in 1870 when the last link, west of Jabalpur, was completed. Today's Main Line (then called the Chord Line) via Patna was opened to through traffic in 1871; but the quickest northward route, via today's Grand Chord, had to await completion till 1906, though surveys had been undertaken as early as 1850.

Meanwhile in 1887, the Bengal Nagpur Railway (BNR) had been set up to take over an extant line in Central India and extend services eastwards to Asansol. This was achieved in 1891, but only in 1900 was the link with Haora through Kharagpur completed. The BNR had no station at Haora, and does not to this day. It operated from a siding in Tikiapara, and was later permitted to use the new Haora Station of the EIR. By that time, it had built another line westward to Cuttack and acquired the next stretch of track, up to Vijaywada, from the East Coast Railway.

In 1857, the East Bengal Railway (EBR) was formed to lay a track along the east bank of the Ganga to Kushthia and then across the river to Dhaka. The line to Kushthia was opened in

1862, ending at Calcutta at a tin-roofed station room at Shealdah. A proper station building was erected in 1869, but had to await expansion till the 1970s with the phenomenal rise in suburban traffic.

In 1862 also, the Calcutta and South-Eastern Railway opened a line southward from what was then called Beliaghata Station to Port Canning. This was taken over by the Government in 1863, as was the EBR (which had meanwhile opened its own southern line to Diamond Harbour) in 1887. Services east of the river were henceforth unified under the Eastern Bengal State Railway and, after further amalgamation in 1942, the Bengal Assam Railway. The Government also acquired the assets of the EIR in 1879, though the management remained with the company.

The development of the railways in Bengal had created an anomaly whereby the link with the rest of India, across the river, was controlled by one company but rail access to the Port by another. After much deliberation, the Jubilee Bridge linking Hugli (Bandel) and Naihati was opened on 21 February 1887, so that up-country freight traffic could run through to the Port, a charge being paid to the EBR for the use of its tracks.

The bulk of today's suburban lines have been traced in the account above. Of the rest, on the Haora side the Tarakeshwar line was opened in 1885, the Haora-Katwa line in 1912 and the Haora-Bardhaman Chord in 1917. On the

32.1 *Haora Station with the old bridge. Ramendranath Chakrabarti*

Shealdah side, the line to Bangaon was constructed between 1882 and 1884, and the Calcutta Chord to Dankuni over the Willingdon (now Vivekananda) Bridge only in 1932. To the south, the Bajbaj line came up in 1890 and the Lakshimakantapur line in 1928.

Special mention must be made of the light railways which provided a substantial support system for both suburban and rural traffic in pre-Independence days. Their disappearance is now widely regretted; and only occasionally have they been replaced by broad–gauge lines – fully between Barasat and Hasanabad, but only very inadequately between Haora and

Freight Equalization Then and Now

The rail link between Calcutta Port and India's interior, set up via the Jubilee Bridge in 1887, had grown imperative after 1881, when through traffic between Bombay and the Delhi-Agra region commenced by a metre-gauge link across what is now Gujarat and Rajasthan. This made Bombay and Calcutta Ports virtually equidistant from Agra, while Bombay proved closer to Delhi by 65 miles. The EIR offered cheaper rates for freight traffic to Calcutta. This was sought to be neutralized by something like today's Freight Equalization Policy, whereby certain goods are transported throughout India at uniform rates.

A Government despatch of 19 May 1882 opined:

…if the Government ruled that the rates from Delhi and Agra to Bombay and Calcutta were to be the same, such ruling would be distinctly favouring Bombay at the expense of Calcutta, and placing an artificial restriction on the East Indian Railway traffic, thereby depriving the districts served by it of the natural advantages of their position.

A decision was postponed till 1887, when it was settled that the laws of the market and free competition should prevail, subject to certain controls. This decision has not been emulated in later times, even when an open and competitive trade policy has been professed in other respects.

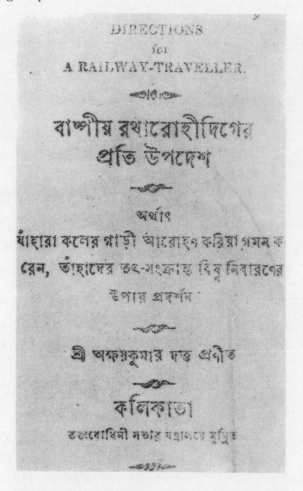

DIRECTIONS
for
A RAILWAY-TRAVELLER.

বাঙ্গীয় রথারোহীদিগের
প্রতি উপদেশ

অর্থাৎ

যাঁহারা কলের গাড়ী আরোহণ করিয়া গমন ক
রেন, তাঁহাদের তৎ-সংক্রান্ত বিঘ্ন নিবারণের
উপায় প্রদর্শন

শ্রী অক্ষয়কুমার দত্ত প্রণীত

কলিকাতা

তত্ত্ববোধিনী সভার যন্ত্রালয়ে মুদ্রিত

Bargachhia. This last stretch is the only result so far of the promise to compensate for that vanished institution of rural Haora district, the light railway network run by Martin Burn and Company from Haora to Amta, Champadanga and Sheakhala. The principal terminus was moved after Independence from Telkalghat to Haora Maidan, but the entire service wound up on 1 January 1971. The Kalighat-Phalta Light Railway had been closed just before Independence, and the Shyambazar Light Railway in 1955.

Although it did not touch Calcutta, we should make space to mention the Bengal Provincial Railway, from Tarakeshwar to Tribeni, unique among pre-Independence railways in being entirely built and financed by Indians. The brain-child of Anandaprasad Ray, it was opened in 1894 and closed in 1956.

As for the major railways, they soon became what they have always remained, part of the mythic content of modern Indian life. Their role in breaking down caste barriers and ensuring all-India mobility of population is part of a wider context of social history. So is the mystique of old first-class travel, not to mention the special trains of the Maharajas. So in a different way are the reported conditions of plebeian travel. The old 'fourth class' (later third class) had no seats to begin with: benches were introduced only in 1885, and lavatories in 1891, after long campaigns.

Three thousand people applied for tickets on the first train out of Haora in 1854: only a small portion could be accommodated. Thousands of men and women lined the whole stretch of track to see the fire-breathing iron horse. Later, the movement of trains would provide a sort of rural clock, while suburban trains made Calcutta more attractive than ever as a place of employment and contributed to an unhealthy decentralization, to be exacerbated many times after the Partition. The demographic consequence of the Partition, indeed, radically altered the balance between long-distance and suburban traffic on the Calcutta railway system, adding to the general pressure of increased trade and travel.

THE CALCUTTA POLICE
FROM CROWN
TO ASHOKE PILLAR

Sidney Kitson

A question seldom asked at the Police Training School, Calcutta is: 'How did we begin? When did it all start?' In Mughal times and earlier, law-enforcing bodies were basically ruler-oriented. Among the common citizens, self-protection was the rule, every man his own policeman. A police force even remotely along modern lines is, as everywhere in the world, a relatively recent development.

The Calcutta Police began as protector of the early English settlement. The semblance of a force with police powers existed in 1704, though the Justices appointed to administer the city were preoccupied with fiscal and municipal duties. Predators, both human and animal, abounded in the surrounding jungles; violence and lawlessness flourished in the periphery of the city. As life in England at this time was equally lawless and violent, there was little precedent to go by. The important tasks that could broadly be called police work were the repression of highwaymen, watch over anti-social elements, and control of the sale of liquor.

Wealthier citizens employed their own watchmen. Balthazar Solvyns has a painting of the 'Chokedar' (*choukidar*) in *Les Hindous* (1807-12). 'His accoutrements are most formidable,' observes Solvyns; but 'their cowardice renders them quite useless and except the Company no Europeans employ them.'

The Company had 64 watchmen in 1720.

This paltry number was replaced by 1779 with 31 Thanadars and 700 Pykes under a Superintendent of Police paid for by levy of a house tax (commuted for a municipal tax in 1793). The Company had now perforce to assume responsibility for administering the growing town, with burglaries and violence increasing. The European section had its own demands, as did the 'Black' Town.

Courts were set up in Warren Hastings's time, but collection of revenue was their first priority. The police were adrift on an uncharted sea. Districts were demarcated and redivided into Divisions in an attempt to find a workable system. Cornwallis, in 1793, established Darogas and Thanadars, but they still did not provide more than a semblance of protection. The Frenchman L. de Grandpré, who travelled in these parts in 1789-90, observed: 'So considerable a town ought to possess a vigilant police; but in this respect it is very defective.'

However hard the police tried to keep pace with the growth of the city, they were always a step or two behind, more from inadequacy of forces than lack of effort. In 1800, a Committee was appointed by Lord Wellesley to examine the working of the police; it resulted in the Justices getting magisterial powers. This being still found inadequate, another committee was formed by Lord Bentinck in 1829. There now came to be forty Thanadars with twenty to thirty choukidars under each, an Armed Reserve (Town Guard) for European offenders,

From Crown to Ashoke Pillar

33.1 *'Two Police Chuprasees or Constables'. Emily Eden*

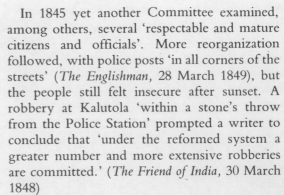

In 1845 yet another Committee examined, among others, several 'respectable and mature citizens and officials'. More reorganization followed, with police posts 'in all corners of the streets' (*The Englishman,* 28 March 1849), but the people still felt insecure after sunset. A robbery at Kalutola 'within a stone's throw from the Police Station' prompted a writer to conclude that 'under the reformed system a greater number and more extensive robberies are committed.' (*The Friend of India,* 30 March 1848)

The year following the upheaval of 1857 saw the introduction of Appointment Certificates, changes in uniform, outlining of duties and a system of inspections and reports introduced by Sir Stuart Hogg, Commissioner of Police as well as Municipal Commissioner. It was also debated at this time whether the Calcutta Police should be placed under the jurisdiction of the West Bengal Police. The issue has often been raised since; but the city police functions independently to this day.

The list of police duties was already staggering 130 years ago: dealing with suicides and accidental deaths; attendance at large fires; operations under the Vagrancy Act, Lunacy Act, Immigration Act and Gaming Act; issue of Bills of Health, and of passes and licences concerning arms, gunpowder, inflammable oils and fishing rights, as well as all shops dealing in food, drink and drugs; orders regarding interstate property; payment of allowances to court witnesses from the districts; control of pounds; regulation of boats and carriages; and administration of the Maidan, where thieves of both races flourished in the 1860s. The Commissioner of Police or his nominee was (and is) visitor or inspector of all kinds of public institutions. Even the water supply to shipping was controlled by the Police till 1900, and the Fire Brigade till as late as 1950. Next to this daunting list, the central policing activities seem dwarfed: the preparing of Crime Returns and enquiry into 'cases of heinous nature'.

Then as now, the shortcomings of the police in their monumental task were roundly condemned, while their achievements usually went without praise. There was frequent criticism in the papers about the inactivity and failure of the police, at both thana and higher levels. 'Pray, what is Mr. Macfarlane doing as Chief Magistrate? Surely he ought to be more active...'. The commonest grievances were

and a River Police set up to cope with piracy and thefts from boats but often themselves involved in such crimes. River Thugs were active, but little was known about them. They were finally put down only in the 1850s under Sleeman's operation against the Thugs.

On 6 August 1840 newspapers reported the appointment of a Daroga for every four thanas. *The Friend of India* justified the appointment by reporting that 'the number of larcenies and burglaries committed in Calcutta seem to render some vigorous measures ... necessary...' In 1842 J. H. Patton (one of the Commissioners who replaced the Justices by an Act of 1840) became Chief Magistrate, and it was in his time that the Calcutta Police began to take its present shape: three Divisions, each controlling a number of Section Houses with Outposts or Watch Houses under them. But the Chief Magistrate was still so preoccupied with municipal affairs that a Superintendent was appointed to assist him in his police duties.

about thefts and robberies, and the proliferation of grog shops and punch houses licensed by the Police, the source of sailors' brawls and drunks littering the streets. European drunks, drifters and vagabonds posed a special embarrassment. European constables were recruited to deal with them, and to protect the .young sahibs from Writers' Buildings on their forays into the 'establishments' on Boubazar.

Punishments were barbaric in the early days: hanging (there was a gibbet at the crossing of Lalbazar and Chitpur Road), the stocks, the pillory, mutilation and whipping, from which even women were not exempt.

The *Hindoo Patriot* complained in July 1885 that of a total of 2,121 personnel, there were 82 Bengali officers and 141 Bengali constables in the Calcutta Police. (The number of Hindustanis was much larger.) The reason, suggested the paper, was that 'the duties of watch and ward are so distasteful to Bengalis'. *The Englishman* countered (8 July 1885) that it was low pay that kept the Bengalis away: certainly the jute mills offered more lucrative openings.

Two branches of the Calcutta Police deserve special mention. The Mounted Police, first set up (by 1840) to carry messages, is now chiefly used to control sporting crowds. Their use to control mobs elsewhere, with rubber shin-pads for the horses, did not prove very successful. They also appear in parades and ceremonies, and did so more extensively till 1950. The Commissioner of Police would himself appear on horseback to inspect parades, and (with his Deputy) ride alongside the Governor's coach at the opening of the Assembly.

Selected originally for heft rather than intellect, the Sergeants (formerly European Constables) were another pride of the Calcutta Police. Their tall contingent literally stood out head and shoulders above the rest in a parade or a crowd. They were the visible establishment. Vigorous training, with emphasis on body-contact sports like boxing and rugby, produced a brash but disciplined body of men, numbering about fifty. They were generally deployed in and around Esplanade and Dalhousie Square, and were of course in the vanguard of the force during demonstrations and riots. The supervising Inspectors went on their rounds on powerful motorcycles, with a Sergeant in the side car. They were no less formidable on foot. Old-timers still recall a

33.2 *Old constable's uniform with the famous red turban*

33.3 *European Sergeants, early 20th century*

33.4 *The Police out-post at Chourangi, 1913*

Facing Page
33.5 *John Palmer's house at Lalbazar, where the Police Headquarters now stand*

very tall Sergeant who used to plod slowly down the middle of the road on Chourangi or the Haora Bridge – and not a taxi, bus or rickshaw dared to leave its lane.

The Sergeants and constables were symbols of the Raj – objects of awe but not respect. The average citizen had little direct contact with them, unlike the carters, drivers, coolies and petty traders who had reason to fear and avoid them. They still do, and for the same reasons.

In 1950 the first batch of Bengali Sergeants passed out, and proved the equal of their predecessors. Later, Sergeants were posted to all police stations; they also form the anchor of the Reserve, Traffic and Armed Police. But the imported cork helmet has gone, and the helmet spike of the Mounted Inspector and Sergeants is confined to ceremonial dress. The 1950s even saw the demise of the constable's famous *lal pugree* (red turban), magnificent to view and excellent protection against blows and brickbats. It was replaced by the French beret. Kurta and knickers gave way to shirts and trousers, and the gurgabi (without socks) and knee-length puttee were replaced by boots.

From 1857, the writing on the wall was becoming clear. The 'Black Act' of 1836, and later the IIbert Bill of 1883, which sought to

The Policeman's Lot

From *The Englishman,* 4 July 1889:

From a Resolution of the Government of Bengal on the Report of the Police Administration of the Town of Calcutta and its suburbs for 1888, we find that in 1888 the total number of cognizable and non-cognizable cases reported was nearly ten thousand in excess of 1886 and eight thousand in excess of 1887 … . The number of persons arrested and summoned during the year was 69,377 as compared with 55,175 in 1887, and the number of persons convicted was 61,865, against 48,334 in 1887 … . The value of property stolen was Rs. 1,22,523 against Rs.1,32,347 in 1887. Property to the value of Rs. 59,401 was returned. There were six murders, against two in 1887. Four of these cases were brought to justice, but no clue was detained in regard to two of them … . Hardly a day passes that the loss of a child with valuables on its person is not reported to the Police … . The number of upcountrymen in the Police was 1,957 against 1,942 in 1887, and the number of Bengalees was 181, against 143 in 1887 … .

allow European British subjects to be tried by Indian judges, brought howls of protest from the English, who thought of Calcutta as 'our city'. The police were still preoccupied with protecting European interests and tackling the growing nationalist movement. Nevertheless, they had signal success in simple law enforcement, using what were then the most modern methods of investigation, together with a network of informers and excellent detective work. The city was safer than ever before. This was the era of the legendary Commissioner Charles Tegart. The Calcutta Police had come of age. Meanwhile the present Police Headquarters at Lalbazar had also been erected, in 1919, where earlier there stood the residence of John Palmer, a popular and charitable merchant.

Since then the city has grown at a staggering pace. Like the citizens they serve, the police – now expanded to some 21,000 officers and men – have lived through the traumas of Partition, the swelling migrant population, burgeoning and declining industries and extremist politics. No less of a challenge than the Thuggee or the Terrorist Movement was the extremist activity of the late 1960s. But there is little that is new

under the sun. The situations faced by the force in the last forty years were largely known to their predecessors in some form or other. The rules may have changed somewhat, but the problems remain the same.

CALCUTTA'S INDUSTRIAL ARCHAEOLOGY

Siddhartha Ghosh

Industrial Archaeology is a recent but estab-lished study in the West. It is devoted to investigating, recording and where possible preserving monuments and artefacts related to the Industrial Revolution and its aftermath. In India, such study is still practically unknown. In Calcutta there has been a recent spate of interest in old architecture – only its styles, to the sad exclusion of the materials, processes or expertise involved. Old street furniture has been melted down or consigned to municipal junkheaps: roadside iron drinking-troughs for horses, ornamental gas or electric lamp-posts, fire brigade call-boxes ('In case of fire break glass and turn handle'), old metal tram-stop signs ('Tram cars stop here on request'), lion-headed cast-iron water-taps, hexagonal cast-iron 'Penfold' pillar-boxes.

The giant retorts of the old gas works near Narkeldanga, the brick chimneys topped with

34.1 *A roadside drinking-trough for horses, now used for bathing*

iron fencing at the Palmer Bazar pump-house, the semaphore-cum-time-ball tower at Fort William – these are as essential to Calcutta's cityscape as the temples, mosques, churches, and buildings of the Raj. Behind these defunct and silent monuments lies a remarkable story of endeavour and ingenuity – a native absorption of Western technology no less remarkable than the cultural and literary interactions of the 'Bengal Renaissance'.

Building Bridges

Old Calcutta scenes painted by D'Oyly, Jump or Wood show picturesque suspension bridges, all of which have disappeared today. According to Captain A.H.E. Boileau in 1842, the first iron suspension bridge in India was built at Kalighat by Captain Schalch in 1823, and 'the largest and finest bridge yet created in India' was the old Hastings Bridge.

The most memorable name in this connexion is that of Colin Shakespear, the Superintendent-General of the GPO. In 1822, he put on display a model of a lightweight rope suspension bridge, prepared and assembled at the Calcutta GPO. This was to support his bid to undertake the construction of such bridges. He also advertised to that effect in the Calcutta Gazette of 27 May 1824 – asking, interestingly enough, about locally available construction materials.

Bishop Heber in his Indian Journal wrote at length about Shakespear's bridges, especially

dismantlable ones made of such local materials – 'likely to be most useful, in this country at least'. At Lord Amherst's Durbar on 7 February 1824, Heber also met Ramchandra Ray, who was 'about to build one of Mr Shakespear's rope bridges' over the Karmanasha River. Here is the first of many Indian participants in these endeavours that we shall meet.

A Windmill Shows the Way

In the history of Indian shipbuilding, Calcutta trails behind Bombay in the absence of a family like the illustrious Wadias of the latter city. All the same, the first modern engineering industry in Calcutta – i.e., powered by an agency other than human or animal – was connected with shipbuilding. In 1779, Colonel Watson began to set up shipbuilding docks in the present Watganj area; and here were erected two large sail windmills, the first in Bengal. They were exactly alike: 114 feet high, of five floors, the upper ones for grinding grain and the ground floor for sawing timber with a circular saw.

Sadly, the windmills had a brief life. Watson's enemy Richard Barwell induced an influential local resident, Gokul Ghoshal, to file a suit claiming ownership of a narrow strip of land running right through the site of the windmills. The Supreme Court upheld Ghoshal's claim, and the machines were pulled down. Ghoshal also reportedly pleaded that the windmills overlooked his *zenana*. 'This,'

comments James Long, 'was a suit of Windmill versus Nuisance!'

'Guru' Jones and 'Goluk Chunder'

The literary achievements of William Carey, Joshua Marshman and William Ward have

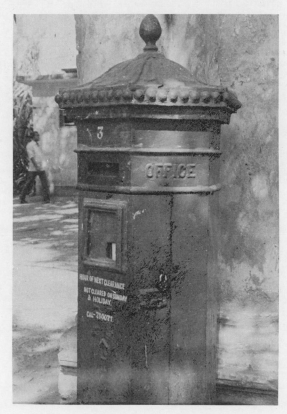

Above
34.2 Old bridge at Khidirpur. William Wood Jr

Below
34.3 An old pillar-box still in use

eclipsed their industrial efforts. It was they who set up India's first self-contained industrial complex at Shrirampur (Serampore) in the early nineteenth century. It included a type foundry, printing presses and also a paper manufactory. Paper-making at Shrirampur commenced in 1809, but the real breakthrough came in 1820 with the introduction of steam power – the first use of steam in India for any kind of manufacturing activity. The man who guided the Shrirampur missionaries in the matter was William Jones (not to be confused with the orientalist).

Jones, an outstanding multidisciplinary engineer and a typical product of the Industrial Revolution, reached Calcutta in 1800 – at least sixteen years before the supposed Calcutta pioneer of steam, Captain William Nairn Forbes. After ten years as a working mechanic, Jones set up a canvas manufactory at Albion Ghat in Haora. A resident of Shibpur, he spoke fluent Bengali and was called 'Guru Jones' by the local people.

Jones also set up a small paper manufactory. As a builder, he is said to have designed the first Gothic building in India, the Bishop's College in Shibpur (now part of the Bengal Engineering College); but he died of fever in 1821, at the early age of forty-four, before it was completed.

Most important, Jones was the first man to work a coal mine in India, at Raniganj. He did not win commercial success; but the same Raniganj mine was the first to be acquired by Carr, Tagore and Co. in 1836, and paved the way for operations on a bigger scale. There is also little doubt that Jones used steam power to drain the mine. Hence his link with the steam engine at Shrirampur, whose name-plate and a possible replica are preserved in the Carey Museum at Shrirampur College.

From its inception, the 'machine of fire' became virtually an object of pilgrimage for Indians and Europeans alike. Some Englishmen attempted to copy it; but the man who did so successfully was a Bengali blacksmith, 'Goluk Chunder of Tittygurh' (Titagarh). His steam engine was exhibited at the Annual Exhibition of the Agri-Horticultural Society in 1828: a curious flower of iron among the fruits, vegetables and a dairy cow of enormous yield. The machine won a prize of Rs 50 for its usefulness in irrigation.

Nothing else is known about the life and labour of Golak Chandra. He seems to have had no further opportunity to exercise his talents. The Shrirampur Paper Mill itself, which upto 1865 was the only mechanized paper mill in Asia, was gradually 'crushed by the expensive and unsatisfactory contracts made at home by India Office,' as George Smith says in his book *William Carey: Shoemaker and Missionary*.

Prince Dwarakanath and Hanif Serang

The most venerable industrial relic in Calcutta is a patriarchal beam steam engine of the 1830s that greets visitors as they enter the Birla Industrial and Technological Museum. The engine belonged to the Calcutta Steam Tug Association, run by the managing agency Carr, Tagore and Co., of which the dominant partner was 'Prince' Dwarakanath Thakur or Tagore (1794–1846). The majestic engine, with a flywheel nearly ten feet in diameter, is of unknown manufacture. It differs only in minor detail from James Watt's first commercially successful machines.

Messrs Boulton and Watt of Soho supplied many machines to India: the portfolios are preserved in the Boulton and Watt Collection of the Birmingham Public Library. To Calcutta came machines for the Cannon Foundry (later the Kashipur Gun Foundry); two saw mills and an oil mill, as well as four engines supplied to the Calcutta Mint (opened in 1831). This magnificently-columned Old Mint, designed by Captain Forbes, still exists as the Silver Refinery on Strand Road near Haora Bridge. Its massive foundations went 26 feet below ground to accommodate heavy machinery, and tunnels conducted water from the river for the condensers of the steam engines. The building needs urgent preservation – for more than its architectural style.

In the early 1820s, the Bowreah Cotton Mills at Fort Gloster, fifteen miles south of Calcutta, began to use steam power. (They also brought over English girls to impart machine-spinning techniques, but some moved to 'easier, if less virtuous, means of livelihood'.) The mills closed down in 1837; but were re-opened as the New Fort Gloster Mills Company, in which Dwarakanath Thakur held one-twelfth of the shares. By 1840, this was a major industrial complex: a cotton-twist factory, a rum distillery, an iron foundry, an oilseed mill and a paper mill, all powered by five steam engines.

In 1829, the Fort Gloster Mills built a small steamer for their own use, designed like the 'baulea' type of country boat and fitted with a 4-horse-power high-pressure engine built entirely at Fort Gloster by one Mr Macnaught: the first boat engine manufactured in the East. Macnaught built at least one other engine, of 6 horse-power. Jessop and Co., who had built the first steamboat in India (with an imported engine) in 1818, had also by 1830 built two condensing engines in their Phoenix Foundry.

The first practical steamboat on the Hugli, the gunboat 'Diana', was launched from Khidirpur Dockyard by Kyd and Co. in 1823. Its usefulness in the First Burma War of 1824–25 eased the way for inland steam navigation. The 'Diana' was powered by imported Maudslay engines.

In December 1825 the first steamship (aided by sails) reached Calcutta from England.

Between 1823 and 1829, of the twelve steamers employed on the Hugli, eight were built at or near Calcutta by J. Anderson of Khidirpur, Kyd and Company and the Howrah Docking Company. Only the engines were imported from England. The 'Lord William Bentinck' was the first iron steamboat to appear on the Hugli in 1834.

But after the advent of iron steamers, shipbuilding activity in Calcutta came to be confined to the mere assembling of knocked-down parts sent from England. The great age of the steamship was about to begin, and the Indian shipbuilding industry had ample prospects of a superb period of growth. That these prospects did not materialize was owing to the well-documented apathy of a colonial administration. At the same time, once the Government Dockyard had been set up, private firms like Jessop and Co. were not allowed

34.4 The beam steam engine now in the Birla Industrial and Technological Museum

even to repair steamboat engines, let alone make them. Thus government policy crushed a vast potential engineering industry.

Jessop and Co. was the largest engineering firm of the day in Calcutta, with a huge range of manufactures. They offered to build a railway from Calcutta to Diamond Harbour in 1825. They also arranged for Calcutta's first regular water supply. About 1822, the company set up steam pumping machinery at Chandpal Ghat at a cost of nearly Rs 25,000 for delivering water into an aqueduct for further transmission. For many years, the company operated the pump at a monthly charge of Rs 360. In a painting of Chandpal Ghat by D'Oyly, a tall chimney identifies the engine-house.

But to revert to the steam engine with which we began this section: it was discovered in 1976 in a junkpile of the Central Inland Water Transport Corporation at the Rajabagan Dockyard. It belonged to the India General Steam Navigation Co. Ltd. (IGSN), and before that to the Calcutta Steam Tug Association – owned, as said before, by Carr, Tagore and Co.

In 1836, Mackintosh and Co., which ran a tugging service between Calcutta port and the river mouth, went out of business. Dwarakanath purchased their steamer 'Forbes' and set up the Calcutta Steam Tug Association. Only a month earlier, he had purchased the Raniganj Colliery. Other collieries were gradually bought as well. Thus, with rare foresight, he founded a commercial empire whose solid basis was the guaranteed sale of coal: to the Steam Tug Association, the Calcutta Docking Company, the IGSN, the Fort Gloster Mills, and above all the government steam vessels. In 1840 there were nine of these, with a total of 600 horse-power, consuming ten pounds of Raniganj coal per horse-power per hour of running time: 7,500 tons a year at a conservative estimate.

The Bengali obsession with the cultural role of the Thakur family has made us overlook Dwarakanath's achievement as industrial pioneer and even spread canards about his luxurious lifestyle, mounting debts and bankruptcy. Few know of his intensive tours of the mines, dockyards, steel plants and engineering factories of Europe. He was also a pioneer and generous patron of medical and engineering education in Calcutta, personally attending dissection classes to help Hindu students overcome their taboos.

Most important of all – yet strangely overlooked by all Dwarakanath's biographers – he wrote to the Council of Education on 21 February 1844 advocating the teaching of Civil Engineering and Architecture at a Normal School proposed to be attached to Hindu College. He even offered Rs 150 a month towards a Chair in Civil Engineering. The proposal, like many of his dreams, was not taken up.

The first proposal of informal engineering training for Indians was made in 1830 by a Mr Henderson, engineer of the government steam vessel 'Burhampooter'. He asked permission 'to select for his assistants two country born lads whom he will engage to instruct to the best of his abilities as Engineers'. The proposal was approved; but by 1838, the 'country born lads' comprised only two Muslim engine drivers and a Chinese carpenter. The rest were all Anglo-Indians.

At last in 1876, the first Indian assumed command of an inland steamer in eastern India. He was Hanif Serang, master of the ISGN's tiny 20-ton 'Nazeerah'; then, around 1822, the bigger 'Sultan'; and finally the newly-renovated 'Barisal' on the Calcutta-Cachhar line. Hanif and others of his ilk ensured that the occupational surname 'Serang' (from Persian *sarhang*, commander of a vessel) became the common Indian term for the captain of an inland vessel in particular.

At the turn of the century, Alfred Brame, Superintendent of the ISGN, wrote of 'the large body of serangs now employed in the Company's service'; but up to 1899. they were restricted to small 80-horse-power vessels. In this connection, I may cite a newspaper item of 1875 warning against the employment of Indians as locomotive drivers, in case there was a 'repetition of the outbreak of 1857'.

Hearteningly, there were still Indian entrepreneurs to give such Indian functionaries their due. From 1884 to 1889 Jyotirindranath Thakur (1849-1925), Dwarakanath's grandson, ran a fleet of steamers on the inland waterways of Bengal. He has left behind portraits of some of his staff: Haricharan (engineer), Shashi (clerk), and an unnamed *mistri* or mechanic, as well as Bijiram, a chauffeur. Thus some humble but indispensable servants of

technology obtained their tribute from an aristocrat's brush.

O'Shaughnessy, 'Nundy' and the Telegraph

The Postal Museum and Philatelic Library in the Calcutta GPO has many interesting exhibits including a flag-hoisting machine used in semaphore telegraph, rescued from the Mud Point Post Office near the mouth of the Hugli. In 1827, a series of semaphore towers was set up at 8-mile intervals all the way from Calcutta to Chunar, to relay messages by mechanical signals aided by telescopes for viewing. It was followed by two others, one to Barrackpur and the other to Kaikhali Lighthouse, near Khejuri, 20 miles below Diamond Harbour.

A semaphore tower – better known as the time-ball tower – still stands at Fort William: circular, four-storeyed, tapering slightly at the top. A ball was dropped from the top of the tower, landing on a charge of gunpowder. So infallible was this cannon-clock that a correspondent in *The Statesman* complained on 11 May 1887 when the ball 'dropped yesterday about 2 seconds after mean 1 p.m.'

The electric telegraph that ultimately replaced the semaphore had an early start in India, but the government promoted it on a large scale only after noting its crucial value in military communication in the 1857 uprising. The telegraph was the first major application of electricity, and gave birth to the profession of electrical engineering.

William Brooke O'Shaughnessy (1809-89: afterwards Sir William O'Shaughnessy Brooke) came to the Calcutta Medical College as Professor of Chemistry and Materia Medica around 1835. A true Renaissance man, he was also Chemical Examiner and Master of the Mint, Joint Secretary of the Asiatic Society, and finally father of the telegraph and of electrical science in India.

In 1839, O'Shaughnessy laid his first experimental telegraph line, 21 miles long, within the Botanic Gardens at Shibpur and successfully transmitted messages. This almost coincided with the world's first experimental telegraph, from Washington to Baltimore. But it was only in 1850 that the directors of the East India Company approved the construction of a permanent line, from Calcutta to Diamond Harbour. The work was completed within ten months. An underground section was made of a cable designed by O'Shaughnessy, who was also a pioneer in submarine telegraphy and the single-wire system.

O'Shaughnessy's assistant and companion was Shibchandra Nandi (1824-1903), whom we can surely call the first Indian electrical engineer. As a worker in the refinery of the

34.5 *Chandpal Ghat, showing the chimney of the steam pump. William Wood Jr*

Innovative in a different way was Kalidas Maitra's proposal for telegraph messages in Bengali, with a chart illustrating the Bengali keyboard. It was contained in his Bengali book on the Electric Telegraph (the only comprehensive account in Bengali even today), published in 1855 and giving a state-of-the-art account of the telegraph in India, with O'Shaughnessy's experiments. The year before, Maitra had published the first Bengali work on the steam engine and the Indian railways.

Calcutta by Gaslight

The *Calcutta Gazette* reported in 1822 that 'Nearly two years ago a complete gas light apparatus was brought to Calcutta'. The same year, the *Samachar Darpan* credited one Dr Toulmin of Dharmatala with having devised such an apparatus. It would be thirty-five years before the Oriental Gas Company set up their first plant, of a capacity of 3 lakh cubic feet, near the present Muhammad Ali Park. It was shifted to Wellington (now Subodh Mallik) Square and finally in 1880 to its present site on Canal East Road near Rajabazar, where it ceased production in 1963. The gigantic domes of the gasometers, which at their peak produced 4.5 million cubic feet of gas, still stand to the sky. They urgently need protection as an industrial monument.

Gas was little used as a heating fuel till the end of the nineteenth century, but as a street illuminant it held its own even forty years after the coming of electricity. (There were gas lamps on some Calcutta streets even in the 1960s.) Its inception in July 1857 was not universally welcomed, for a tax was clamped on house-owners to pay fot it. It was also rightly pointed out that drainage, sanitation and water supply were more urgent needs. Yet Raja Shourindramohan Thakur composed a hymn to Queen Victoria in the Bhairavi raga, 'we behold the gas light by thy mercy'; and Radhanath Mitra another song, this time to the religious *Ramprasadi* tune, on the miraculous lamp that needs neither wick nor oil. Meanwhile, Bengali technicians had adapted to the coming of the new fuel. On 6 December 1881, B.L. Ghosh and Co. advertised themselves in *The Statesman* as gas fitters as well as plumbers, obviously ready to compete with European firms in the trade.

Gas found another application in early aero-

Calcutta Mint, he attracted the attention of O'Shaughnessy and soon became his personal assistant. The first Indian in the telegraph department, he was entrusted with the training of other Indians. (Classes began in 1856 at Bengal, Agra, Bombay and Madras.) He was also in charge of lying 900 miles of trunk lines: Barrackpur to Allahabad, Varanasi to Mirzapur, Mirzapur to Seonee and Calcutta to Dhaka. When no steamer company would lend its vessel for laying seven miles of cable below the Padma River, Nandi got the job done with country fishing-boats. There is no doubt that Nandi was no mere technician, but an innovative engineer of a high order. A remarkable letter that he wrote to O'Shaughnessy from Varanasi on 30 September 1855 encloses drawings of his methods, and proposes innovations for telegraph posts.

34.6 Dwarakanath Thakur

nautics. The ascent of one Mr Wintle from the Esplanade on 29 July 1785 is cited as the earliest instance of ballooning in Calcutta. A Mr Robertson made several ascents between 1836 and 1838. After his death, the *Gnananweshan* sadly noted how his three balloons and other equipment, which had cost him Rs 2,400, were sold for a paltry Rs 50.

The first Indian balloonist of Calcutta was Ramchandra Chatterji, a wrestler and circus artiste. With his mentor Percival Spencer, Chatterji made a balloon ascent on 10 April 1889 from the premises of the Oriental Gas Co. A month later, he made a solo ascent in his own balloon, purchased from Spencer and renamed by him the 'City of Calcutta', amid band music and general festivity. He also had an intrepid daughter who went up several times. But alas, Ramchandra died of ballooning injuries.

Calcutta Goes Electric

In the 1830s, O'Shaughnessy lit charcoal lights by battery; but it was only with the advent of the steam-run dynamo that electric lighting became practicable. The first breakthrough in Calcutta was made by another ingenious European from the Telegraph Department: Carl Louis Schwendler (1838-82), Superintendent Electrician of the Government Telegraphs and a founder of the Calcutta Zoo.

In 1877, Schwendler was asked to make a detailed investigation of the possibilities of lighting Indian railway stations by electricity. His remarkable report, based on trial runs, appeared in 1881. With a second-hand 25-horse-power slow-speed steam engine, Schwendler ran four 'dynamo electric machines' at Haora Station, each of which lit a carbon arc lamp for two goods sheds, with zinc reflectors lined with silvered glass. This gave a light of ten candles per 100 square feet.

In 1881, Schwendler achieved another remarkable feat by setting up an electric railway for joyrides in the Zoo. This was just two years after Werner Siemens's first demonstration of an electric railway at the Berlin Exhibition of 1879. The electric tram came to Calcutta only in 1902.

A point which Schwendler emphasized in his report on station lighting was the efficiency and ingenuity of the 'native mistri' in mastering a new technology. He specially mentions the engine-driver who set right the irregular speed of a dynamo, by help of a mercury speedometer. 'The whole trial,' concludes Schwendler, 'has proved that there is no difficulty whatever in the working of the electric light in this country by trained natives.'

This optimism was borne out by the Bengali entrepreneuring firm of Dey, Sheel and Co., 'Electricians, Electrometallurgists and Brass Founders'. Apart from arranging for lights at meetings, parties, wedding processions etc., they manufactured a wide range of apparatus: carriage lamps lit by batteries of their own device, sewing machines and table fans worked by electric motors. These were displayed at important gatherings – including the Second National Congress of 1886 and the 1888 annual conversazione of the Mahomedan Literary Society – and won high praise from eminent scientists as well as the Viceroy himself.

Many attempts were made to replace the hapless punkah-puller with some mechanical device. Scores of European inventors tried their hands; so did Indians like Radhakishore Sinha and Jaminikanta Ray, using clockwork as well as hot-air engines. The only successful attempt was by Heatly and Gresham Ltd. in 1898: using hot-air engines burning paraffin, they erected a machine on the platform at Shealdah Station capable of pulling eight to ten punkahs.

But the 'Heatly punkah' was eclipsed the next year, when the Calcutta Electric Supply Corporation set up its first station at Emambag Lane and popularized the electric fan, which it would hire out at Rs 4 per month. Indeed, it was the electric fan that first brought prosperity to the CESC. Another novelty was the electric lift, introduced at the turn of the century at the Viceroy's House.

On 13 January 1901, *The Statesman* reported how electricity was replacing 'old time-honoured arrangements' in railway workshops, tea warehouses and printing presses. 'It is also used for working sewing machines and will shortly blow the cathedral organ.' Decades later, Tarashankar Banerji was to write his poignant story 'Maydanab', about the anguish of a devoted steam-engine operator robbed by electricity of both his livelihood and his pride.

Bipinbihari Das and the 'Air Carriage'

R.E. Crompton, an outstanding electrical engineer, is named as the man most instrumental in securing for the Indian Electric Company (later the CESC) the licence to supply Calcutta with electricity. But few remember that he also introduced the first self-propelled road vehicles in India, the 'road steamers'. His first steam-driven vehicle, the 'Blue Belle', is now in the London Science Museum. Another, the 'Primer', later used to haul a train of road wagons, arrived in Calcutta in 1870 and was taken to Delhi for trial.

Until a year ago, there lay in the Calcutta Corporation's workshop a number of steam roadrollers, made by Aveling and Porter, Marshall or Fowler, which should have made their way to an industrial museum. (The CIT still possesses two such rollers.) Their immediate precursors were the first 'automobiles' in the streets of Calcutta. William Clark, the first engineer to be employed by the Calcutta Corporation, even designed a new steamroller in 1863, but it proved unsuccessful.

Over two decades were to pass before the first motor car – the *hawagari* or 'air carriage' – appeared in Calcutta. Though the possibilities are remote, it would be the find of the century if the Corporation Workshop still proved to possess the first motor car entirely built in Calcutta. This was the astonishing feat of Bipinbihari Das, a self-taught mechanic with a garage at Baliganj. Except for the tyres, spark

plugs, carburettor and magneto, every part of the 15-horse-power, L-head, 4-cylinder, five-seater car (aptly called 'Swadeshi') was built by Bipinbihari himself. It was bought by the Corporation for the meagre sum of Rs 3,000.

Two years earlier, Das had built another car for the Benares Hindu University. This had been used by Motilal Nehru and Madanmohan Malaviya, and helped Das to get funds from the Corporation for his second venture, in spite of unkind and humiliating opposition from some prominent councillors.

Mechanics and Engineers

Men like Golak Chandra and Bipinbihari Das represent a transitional stage from the traditional wright or craftsman to the modern engineer: the type that founded the Industrial Revolution, akin to such giants as Watt, Trevithick, Maudslay or Stephenson. But in Bengal, this nascent creative talent could not blossom for want of opportunity; and sadly, the inception of formal engineering education did not help.

The Government College of Civil Engineering was opened at Writers' Buildings, Calcutta on 24 November 1856. (The Thomson Engineering College at Roorki had opened already.) One of the three instructors was Mahendralal Som, Professor of Mathmatics. The Lieutenant-Governor indignantly objected 'on principle to give to a Native ... a salary ... sufficient to attract an English candidate.' That obstructionism went deeper and lasted long is shown by the fact that the first mechanical engineers left the college only in 1932, and the first electrical engineers in 1936. (By this time, it had moved to Shibpur as the Bengal Engineering College.)

Indeed, the Engineering College served chiefly to create a new category of 'Babu' for employment in the Public Works Department. It also brought about the yet unbridged gulf between the qualified engineer and the 'uneducated' *mistri* who, verily, was the true inheritor of generations of latent engineering skills. The latter's innovative spirit shows in the Karmakar family of pioneer type-founders: Panchanan (?-1804), Manohar (?-1846) and Krishnachandra (1807-50), from a line of ironsmiths. Rajkrishna Karmakar (1828-?) found high success in Nepal: arriving there in 1869, he set up a gun factory, a mint, and an electricity plant, acquiring the title

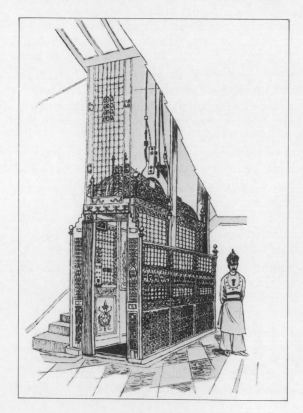

34.7 The lift at Raj Bhavan. Desmond Doig

of Royal Engineer by these achievements.

Nor did Upendrakishore Raychoudhuri (1863–1915), however highly educated and cultured generally, need any formal training to embark upon his investigations in the field of mechanical reproduction. Between 1897 and 1911, he published nine research papers in Penrose's Annual, the 'Printer's Bible' of the times. No later Indian has won comparable international acclaim in the field. Similarly, it is little known that Hemendramohan Basu (H. Bose: 1866–1916), the well-known perfumer, made the first phonographic voice recordings in India from his 'Talking Machine Hall' in 1905.

Jagadishchandra Basu is lauded as a scientist; but we neglect the creative ingenuity with which he designed his own instruments. They were built by local technicians whose names alone survive: Malek, Putiram, Barik, Jamshed and Rajanikanta. It is reported that Jagadishchandra realized the potential skill of the Indian mechanic on seeing Nanak Ram, an unemployed ex-bearer of Presidency College, repair a badly damaged dynamo in the College laboratory.

There were brilliantly innovative engineers from the professional upper classes, needless to say – like Nilmani Mitra (1828–94) and Madhusudan Chatterji (1824–1909), the first two Bengalis to pass out from Roorki, in 1851 and 1852 respectively. (Neither stayed long in the service of the Raj.) The first formally trained Bengali electrical engineer, Girindrachandra Basu (1865–1933) became an assistant to Lord Kelvin. But these were rather

34.8
Hemendramohan Basu

exceptions that proved the rule. When Indian technology, like Indian entrepreneurship, was being confined in the imperial straitjacket by fraud, force and the victims' own acquiescence, it is inspiring to recall those Englishmen who gave freely to India of the legacy of the Industrial Revolution, and the creative-minded Indians who made that legacy their own.

THE VICTORIA MEMORIAL

Hiren Chakrabarti

35.1
Queen Victoria

The idea of erecting the Victoria Memorial as a 'National Valhalla' of British Indian worthies and a period museum of medieval and modern Indian history was conceived by Lord Curzon at the turn of the century, when the British Empire had reached its high noon. On the death of Queen Victoria in January 1901, Curzon proposed the 'great Imperial duty' of setting up a fitting memorial to the 'Great and Good Queen' and a 'standing record of our wonderful history'. Curzon's extended pronouncements on the subject are marked by his characteristic thoroughness of planning as well as his mixture of naiveté and imperialist effrontery. One of his declared motives was to arrest 'the rising tide of national feeling' and to scotch the Indian effort

to find a justification for [nationalism] in the memory of a remote and largely unhistorical past, or in dreams of a still more visionary future. Was there not, I thought, in the history of India itself in the past two centuries sufficient to gratify the sentiments both of pride and of hope?

Little did he dream that in less than half a century, the memorial to the Queen would come to be regarded as a memorial to the Raj itself.

The Indian aristocracy responded liberally to Curzon's appeal for exhibits and funds. The construction of the stately building surrounded by exquisite gardens (covering 64 acres and costing more than ten million rupees) was entirely funded by Indian subscriptions. In designing the building (338 by 228 feet, and soaring to a height of 184 feet), Sir William Emerson, President of the British Institute of Architects, adopted an Italian Renaissance style with an oriental touch in the arrangement of the domes. Indeed, to the layman this marble memorial is a British imitation of the Taj, which too had been built in memory of a queen.

The construction was entrusted to Martin and Company of Calcutta. The marble was quarried at Makrana in the then princely state of Jodhpur, while the statuary on the porches and the central dome was executed in Italy. The Queen's grandson, the Prince of Wales (later King George V) laid the foundation stone on 4 January 1906, but only on 28 December 1921 was the Memorial opened to the public.

An Institution of National Importance since the Act of 1935, the Memorial houses a remarkable collection of paintings, sculptures, weapons, manuscripts, documents, maps, coins, stamps, textiles, artefacts and various other memorabilia of the Raj and of the Indian response to it. Let us take a look at the main exhibits and the galleries that house them.

The Royal Gallery deals directly with the life of Queen Victoria. It has portraits of the Queen and Prince Albert by Winterhalter, as well as copies of a series of paintings in the Royal

Collection in England, illustrating scenes from Victoria's life. The centre of the gallery is occupied by the pianoforte on which she practised as a young girl, and the arm-chair and writing-desk used by her at Windsor Castle. The most impressive exhibit in the Royal Gallery, however, is a masterpiece by the Russian artist Vassili Verestchagin depicting the state entry of the Prince of Wales into Jaipur in 1876. An impressive composition of five richly caparisoned elephants in procession along the Ambar Chaupar, the first of them seating the Prince and Maharaja Ram Singh Jaipur, this is the largest oil painting in India. It measures 274 by 196 inches.

Queen Victoria at different stages of her reign may be seen again in the engravings kept in the annexe to the Royal Gallery and in the Queen's Hall under the central dome. In the annexe, a photograph shows her writing at a table in the garden at Frogmore, Windsor, while an Indian attendant carrying her walking stick stands by. The Queen's Hall is dominated by a life-size statue of the young Queen, sculpted by Sir Thomas Brock. From high above, through the stained glass cover on the central dome, gleams the message 'Heaven's Light Our Guide', a phrase coined by the Prince

Consort. Along the balustraded gallery above, a series of twelve lunette frescoes by Frank Salisbury depicts the main events in the career of the Queen. They also incorporate much symbolism. The sixth lunette presents Britan-

35.2 *The Victoria Memorial*

35.3 *Lord Curzon*

257

nia upon a crystal sphere, flanked by the British lion and the Bengal tiger; while the last, showing the Lying in State, incorporates a full and an empty hour-glass. Extracts from the Queen's Proclamations of 1858 and 1877 are inscribed in marble panels recessed in the walls of this central round hall.

To the left of the Entrance Hall is the Portrait Gallery. Among the persons represented here are empire-builders like Lord Clive. Major-General Stringer Lawrence, J.Z. Holwell of the Black Hole, Major-General William Karkpatrick, Arthur Wellesley the Duke of Wellington, Lord Lake, and Sir David Ochterlony holding the stem of a hookah; a scholar-soldier like Henry Rawlinson, who deciphered the inscription of Darius Hystaspes at Behistan; Bishop Heber, remembered for his memoirs; Alexander Duff, the Scottish missionary and educationist; Charles Metcalfe, who freed the press, and Lord Lytton, who gagged it; Prince Dwarakanath Thakur; Keshabchandra Sen the Brahmo Reformer; and Michael Madhusudan Datta the poet. Also adorning the gallery is R.T. Mackenzie's oil painting of the state entry into Delhi of Lord and Lady Curzon, with the Duke and Duchess of connaught, on the occasion of the Coronation Durbar of 1903. The portrait of Stringer Lawrence was painted by Sir Joshua Reynolds; that of Ochterlony, by Jewan Ram, is one of the earliest oil paintings

by an Indian.

The portrait gallery also contains a valuable collection of manuscripts, some of them illustrated: copies of Abul Fazl's *Ain-i-Akbari* and *Akbarnama; Sirr-i-Akbar* or the Persian translation of the Upanishads; *Majma-ul-Bahrain* or a comparative study of Sufism and the Vedanta by the unfortunate Prince Dara-Shikoh; a volume of letters written by Tipu Sultan; and the *Bhagavat Maha Puran* copied by Ishwarchandra Vidyasagar.

Annexed to the Portrait Gallery is the Arms and Armour Gallery with a fascinating collection of medieval Indian weapons. They are remarkable on account of their design and ornamentation, and some have historical associations as well. The Victoria Memorial has swords once owned by Haidar Ali and Tipu Sultan, and another presented by Maharaja Ranjit Singh to General Van Cortland, Commander of the Sikh forces in the Punjab. A spear with the image of Vishnu on one side of the blade and his carrier Garuda on the other was the prized possession of the Nawab Nazims of Bengal. Also on display here are portraits of various types of Indian army officers belonging to the Imperial Service Troops, and a picture by James Hunter of one of Tipu Sultan's rocketmen. A model of Tipu's fort at Seringapatam can be seen in the Hastings Room upstairs, and another of the battlefield of

35.4 *The Memorial under construction*

Palashi (Plassey) in the main entrance hall. The Hastings Room also contains pictures relating to the Mysore Wars, though as its name indicates, it is chiefly devoted to paintings and prints of Governor-General Warren Hastings and his colleagues and contemporaries.

The Victoria Memorial also has a good collection of antique guns of Indian, Turkish and European make. The Sculpture Gallery at the south entrance contains a fine gun made by an eighteenth-century Bengali blacksmith for Maharaja Krishnachandra Ray of Nadia. It also displays a pair of French guns captured by Clive at the Battle of Palashi.

A life-size marble statue of Clive appropriately presides over the Sculpture Gallery. The work of John Tweed, it is a replica of a bronze statue standing in King Charles Street, Westminster, where the India Office used to be. Among the busts ranged along the gallery's walls are those of Charles James Fox, who so often spoke of Indian affairs in the House of Commons; Major James Rennell, Surveyor-General of Bengal from 1764 to 1777; orientalists like Charles Wilkins and Nathaniel Brassey Halhed; and William Makepeace Thackeray the Calcutta-born novelist. Queen Mary's Room also commemorates 'anyone who was anyone in British Indian history'. Its *pièce de résistance* is a fine portrait of Kipling by Burne-Jones.

The Victoria Memorial is the proud owner of the world's largest collection of the works of Thomas and William Daniell, uncle and nephew, who came out to India in 1786, travelled extensively, and left memorable records of Indian life and scenery in their paintings and engravings. Their contemporaries William Hodges and John Zoffany are also represented: of special note are Hodges's painting of the Allahabad Fort and Zoffany's famous group of the French adventurer Claude Martin and his friends at Lucknow, including the artist himself.

A post-Independence addition is the National Leaders Gallery, with portraits and relics of the men and women who contributed to India's independence and cultural regeneration. Among the painters whose works are featured here are such famous names as Atul Basu and Langhammer.

Of special interest in the present context is the Calcutta Room on the first floor. Engravings, water-colours and oil paintings are displayed here to illustrate the growth of the city from the mid-eighteenth to the mid-nineteenth century, as seen by the Daniells, James Moffat, James Fraser, William Wood, Charles D'Oyly *et al*. They bestow lasting life upon a crowd of images that now seem to belong to another world.

In January 1988, Tata Steel (TISCO) generously endowed the Victoria Memorial with illumination at night. This has brought out new beauties in the structure of the building. A 16-foot, 3-ton yet remarkably elegant, poised Angel of Victory in bronze stands atop the dome. As our eyes follow the outlines of the edifice that it crowns, we realize that the Victoria Memorial is itself a work of art.

LIST OF ILLUSTRATIONS
AND CREDITS

Title page : Procession of the Charak Puja, Charles D'Oyly. Colour lithograph. Victoria Memorial.
End Paper : 'Fort William in Bengal', George Lambert and Samuel Scott, *c* 1732. Oil on canvas.
By permission of India Office Library (British Library)

Note : The works of Mrs Belnos, Emily Eden , Balthazar Solvyns, Charles D'Oyly, and T. & W. Daniell have been used for side-pieces and tail-pieces. The tail-piece on p 23 shows the seal of the East India Company.
The publisher has taken all care to identify and acknowledge all copyright holders of the plates reproduced in this book. However, should any illustration be incorrectly acknowledged, the publisher would be prepared to make suitable changes in future editions of this book.

INDEX